WBI DEVELOPMENT STUDIES

I0093980

Finance at the Frontier

Debt Capacity and the Role of Credit in the Private Economy

J.D. Von Pischke

The World Bank
Washington, D.C.

The World Bank Institute (formerly the Economic Development Institute) was established by the World Bank in 1955 to train officials concerned with development planning, policymaking, investment analysis, and project implementation in member developing countries. At present the substance of WBI's work emphasizes macroeconomic and sectoral policy analysis. Through a variety of courses, seminars, and workshops, most of which are given overseas in cooperation with local institutions, WBI seeks to sharpen analytical skills used in policy analysis and to broaden understanding of the experience of individual countries with economic development. Although WBI's publications are designed to support its training activities, many are of interest to a much broader audience.

J.D. Von Pischke is a senior operations officer for the World Bank's Asia Country Department

Library of Congress Cataloging-in-Publication Data

Von Pischke, J.D.
    Finance at the frontier : debt capacity and the role of credit in
the private economy / J.D. Von Pischke.
    p. cm. — (EDI development studies)
    Includes bibliographical references and index.
    ISBN 0-8213-1818-7
    1. Finance—Developing countries. 2. Economic development.
3. Credit—Developing countries. 4. Economic assistance—Developing
countries. I. Title II. Series.
    HG195.V66   1991
    332'.09172'4—dc20
                                                 91-17956
                                               CIP

WBI Catalog No. 340/051

CONTENTS

PREFACE

*To increase the flow of rural finance permanently and
reliably, `international donors and governments in
developing countries must endeavor to work with, rather
than against, financial-market forces.*
—Edward J. Kane (Adams, Graham, and Von Pischke 1984)

The first purpose of this book is to suggest how good loans can be
made to individuals and firms at the "frontier." This frontier is not
geographic, but market based. On one side are those parts of the
legitimate economy that are not usually considered creditworthy by
formal financial institutions, and on the other are the generally more
prosperous entities that do have access to formal finance. Good loans
are loans that are repaid according to the terms agreed on when they
were issued.

The second purpose of this book is to suggest how lending at the
frontier can be remunerative to commercial banks, development banks
and other development finance agencies that retail credit and assume
credit risk. Remunerative lending is important because most lenders,
regardless of their ownership and institutional form, tend to avoid
activities that are not attractive. Unremunerative lending is
transitory, unstable, and not robust in the face of adversity. Credit
markets function poorly when lenders are not adequately rewarded.
Experience at the frontier clearly indicates that weak financial
institutions do not do a good job serving society in general and firms and
individuals at the frontier in particular.

Making good, remunerative loans is also important because
governments and development assistance agencies try to make more

credit available at the frontier. Their stated intention is to promote development by bringing more people and activities within the frontier of formal finance. One result of their efforts is the accumulation of bad loans, which is often reflected in the poor financial condition of the state-owned banks and other lenders that have been given the task of lending to target groups that would not otherwise obtain credit from these lenders.

The Prospective Reader

This book is intended for readers interested in the relationship between finance and development at the firm and household levels and in the use of credit by individuals in low-income countries. One reason for such interest is the desire to use credit institutions to increase the productivity of groups without effective access, or with greatly limited access, to the financial system.

The sheer volume of development assistance and of government efforts devoted to providing credit at the frontier have led to the involvement of many officials, economists, politicians, and systems specialists who might not otherwise have been inclined to become involved in financial intermediation or in financial policy and who have had little experience with credit markets, accounting, or finance. It is precisely for these technicians, officials, and politicians that this book is intended.

This book will be of particular value to readers who share three characteristics. First, they have direct or indirect responsibility for credit decisions. Direct responsibility is exercised by approving or rejecting loan applications; indirect responsibility is exercised by designing credit projects or shaping policies that influence credit decisions. Second, they lack familiarity with the culture and routines of financial institutions that are subjected to credit risk and guided by commercial principles. For example, they have not worked with balance sheets or income statements or constructed sources and uses of funds statements during their professional careers or have not found these tasks helpful or meaningful. Third, their status as officials of a government or of a development assistance organization shields them from personal financial, career, or professional risks related to the performance of loans for which they have direct or indirect responsibility. Where these characteristics coincide, there is potential to do tremendous damage to financial markets even with the best of intentions, or to create great benefits if intentions can be expressed appropriately in projects and policies.

Others, including bankers, cooperative leaders, trainers, and students of development in general, may also find this book responsive to their concerns.

What Lies Ahead

The book begins with three chapters that explain what finance is about and the context in which it operates. Understanding the raw material helps in fashioning the finished product. Chapters 4 through 7 explore ways in which governments and development assistance agencies often attempt to help people or activities gain access to credit. These chapters discuss the conventional view of what should be done and how to go about it, and why this view leads to bad loans and unremunerative lending.

Chapter 8 discusses informal finance beyond the frontier, which is provided by friends, family members, shopkeepers, landlords, moneylenders, and many others. These sources are often held in disdain by those who do not patronize them and who want to direct credit to people and activities who they think deserve credit. Informal financial arrangements, however, serve individuals and activities not served by the formal financial sector. They appear to perform well in many respects and should generally be regarded as socially useful.

Chapters 9 through 11 present a strategy for making good loans at the frontier. Innovation is emphasized as a means by which financial markets develop, and attempts to create market niches are cited as a sign of dynamism in competitive markets. Cash flow lending is an important feature of innovative developmental finance. It delinks loan size from the value of tangible security, permitting broader distributional impact and facilitating structural change in the economy. Cash flow lending can develop only where levels of confidence are high. Intervention in financial markets can destroy confidence, but to be developmental it should create confidence.

Debt capacity is defined in chapter 12 as sustainable borrowing power. Debt capacity is usually small beyond the frontier, and creating it should be the centerpiece of development assistance and of government efforts designed to use financial markets to assist those at and beyond the frontier. Chapter 13 points out that some of the most effective ways of creating debt capacity do not require intervention in financial markets and that within financial markets debt capacity is created in many ways other than the traditional development assistance format that directly increases the supply of loanable funds. Sustainable borrowing power is impossible without financially successful intermediaries, which are also extremely important for financial market development and for development in general.

Chapter 14 presents a framework for measuring the results of projects and policies that attempt to expand the frontier of formal finance. This framework includes the activities of borrowers at the frontier, the operations of financial intermediaries, the state of financial markets, and the macroeconomic and macrofinancial implications of projects and policies operating in or through financial markets.

Shortcuts and Who Should Take Them

Readers already dissatisfied with the procedures and results of conventional donor-assisted credit projects and receptive to a new formula may wish to read only chapters 1-3, chapter 10, and chapters 11-14. Other readers fall into two groups. The first consists of economists who hold an internally inconsistent position. According to this view, development can occur efficiently if investments can be allocated to activities with high economic rates of return, but the financial performance of credit institutions entrusted with the allocation of donor, government, or even private funds is a trivial matter in this grand process, or possibly something of a nuisance. The second group consists of devotees of the conceptual foundations of conventional credit projects: directed credit through quotas and controls, subsidized interest rates, the importance of meeting credit needs, the inability of ordinary people in poor countries to save, the evils of informal finance, and the imperative to get the aid money out though credit projects to stimulate development. Both groups will find that all the chapters challenge their misconceptions.

Acknowledgments

The book has benefited greatly from comments given on earlier drafts by, among others, Dale W Adams, Ph. K. Heinrich Bechtel, F. J. A. Bouman, Ingrid Buxell, Dennis Casley, Dieter Elz, Hunt Howell, Chita Jarvis, William I. Jones, Peter Kilby, Timothy King, Araceli de Leon, Hans Mittendorf, Paul Murgatroyd, H. B. B. Oliver, Bertrand Renaud, John Rouse, Walter Schaefer-Kehnert, Turto Turtiainen, Jack Upper, Horst von Oppenfeld, and Jacob Yaron. John J. Dean, Peter Bailey, Mateen Thobani, and Zheng Kangbin offered good advice on techncial points. Valuable editorial assistance was received from John Didier and Alice Dowsett, and wordprocessing support was provided by Corazon Centeno, Daphne Glass, Susan Lucinski, Ann Millard, Juliet Nkojo, and, especially, Carmen Alvarado, who prepared later drafts, the final copy and graphics.

This book originated from policy work conducted in the late 1970s and early 1980s in the Economics and Policy Division of the Agriculture Department of the World Bank, under the leadership of Graham Donaldson. It was developed further and more intensively in the Studies Unit of the World Bank's Economic Development Institute, headed by Timothy King. David Davies provided invaluable assistance in facilitating the author's posting to the Studies Unit. This book was substantially completed during the author's assignment to the Industry, Trade and Finance Division of the World Bank's Asia Technical Department, under V. S. Raghavan.

To all those who have provided comments, guidance and other assistance, the author expresses profound thanks. Views, omissions and errors are attributable solely to the author.

This book is dedicated to Dale W Adams, who—in an article in the *American Journal of Agricultural Economics*—without guilt cast the first stone.[1]

---

1. Dale W Adams, "Agricultural Credit in Latin America: A Critical Review of External Funding Policy," *American Journal of Agricultural Economics*. Vol. 53, No. 2, May 1971. pp. 163-172.

Part I

FINANCE AND FINANCIAL MARKETS

Financial markets create value that contributes powerfully to economic growth and development. This book explores creation of value at the frontier of the formal financial system,[1] where official programs offer credit to small farmers and small businesses, and where entrepreneurial lenders offer new services to attract new clients.

Finance Inside the Frontier

Inside the financial frontier, formal intermediaries such as commercial banks, stock markets, credit unions, consumer finance companies, investment banks and insurance companies make up the financial sector. They operate under government charters, are subject to government supervision and reporting requirements, and are restricted by usury laws and by limitations on the types of services they may offer.

These institutions tend to be organized on a formal, structured, hierarchical, impersonal and often centralized basis. Financial markets in which they are active offer a great variety of services, and include primary markets that bring together the parties to financial transactions that create new financial claims, and secondary markets in which existing financial claims are bought and sold.

Most transactions inside the frontier, except for routine consumer purchases, are settled through accounts maintained with financial

---

1. Many months after title of this book was selected, the author found that the concept of the frontier had already been applied to the boundary between formal and informal activities by Hernando de Soto. In *The Other Path: The Invisible Revolution in the Third World* (New York: Harper & Row, 1989) he observes that, "since 61 percent of the hours worked in Peru are informal, there is obviously a long frontier between the informal sector and the state authorities" (p. 154).

intermediaries that make transfers of funds largely by mail or courier or electronically. Savings are deposited with modern financial institutions offering a variety of deposit arrangements with different combinations of maturity and interest rates. These are frequently protected by government insurance. Individuals often devote part of their savings to buying life, old age and other types of insurance. Bonds and stocks also attract the savings of individuals and of institutions, such as pension funds.

Credit is widely available inside the frontier and virtually always carries an interest rate, although these rates do not reach the heights sometimes found outside the frontier. Loans are available in a range of maturities,[2] extending possibly to 30 years for the purchase of land or the construction of buildings. Formal ownership claims, liens and legal infrastructure assist borrowers to obtain relatively large amounts of credit by lowering risk and the transaction costs of credit.

Finance Beyond the Frontier

Beyond the frontier of formal finance, most financial transactions are personalized and conducted directly, without intermediaries. Participants in finance outside the frontier include small-scale farmers and businesses, and members of households of modest means. In terms of numbers, these private entities dominate most economies.

At and beyond the frontier most transactions are small and involve simultaneous exchanges of cash and goods or services. Savings are not deposited with modern financial institutions, but held in cash or converted into assets such as livestock, jewelry and business inventory that are regarded as secure stores of value that may be turned into cash relatively quickly. Savings may also be loaned to kin and friends under terms and conditions that include reciprocal assistance upon demand.

Credit beyond the frontier is often scarce, expensive, or both, or so closely related to social ties that it carries no interest and is readily available, but only in small amounts. Ownership claims are rarely represented by easily transferable registered titles. Loans may be made among friends, family members and others linked by social bonds; by landlords to tenants; by merchants and traders to consumers, farmers, small businesses, and to buyers and tradesmen in their service; and by

---

2. Maturity occurs when a loan or guarantee becomes due for immediate payment.

professional moneylenders. Creditors and debtors deal face-to-face. These transactions, beyond the reach of government control and supervision, are regulated by custom, the negotiating skills of the parties concerned, and by competition among borrowers and lenders.

The Frontier and Development

With development, people and firms at the frontier begin to use deposit, credit and other services provided by modern financial institutions. Their access is facilitated by innovations and economies within the financial system and because their personal and business incomes increase and become less erratic. Development moves the frontier outward to firms, households, and individuals that previously had severely limited or no access.

Much development assistance in the form of credit for small enterprises and farms has attempted to push the frontier outward. This has led to the experience and frustrations upon which this book is based. This book's essential point is that outward movements of the frontier are sustainable only when the characteristics of finance and those of potential customers are related harmoniously. Innovations that create this synthesis are the only means by which institutions offering financial services to the public can independently advance the frontier. Recommendations are provided to stimulate this process, along with tips on how to avoid costly errors.

This book explores the basic building blocks of finance that must be respected if efforts to push the frontier outward are to produce sustainable changes in financial markets. The fundamental elements of finance are *value, risk* and *confidence:* These are discussed in Part I. These fundamentals provide insights into the principal problems of official efforts to advance the frontier of the formal financial system: the extent and stubborn continuation of unremunerative lending and bad loans made to farmers and businesses.

Value, risk, and confidence do not directly address issues such as how credit and the financial environment relate to overall government policies, fiscal and trade regimes, or to the objectives of development assistance agencies. This is not a disqualifying limitation, however. Attention to value, risk and confidence can assist policy formulation and refinement of development objectives that are implemented through financial markets. Use of financial markets to stimulate development becomes more costly financially, economically and socially when actions, policies and objectives destroy value, increase risk and diminish confidence.

Finally, some readers may quibble with the concept of value stated here. An objection may be that it is not consistent with the concept of value in economic theory.[3] In this sense value is a difficult word because its technical meanings vary. In the visual arts value refers to relationships between parts of an art work, to the boldness of a line, for example. In music it is the relative length of time for which a note is held. In religion and philosophy value has other meanings, and even in investment jargon its use varies from that presented here. The term is truly *polyvalent*. Acknowledgement of the diversity of its use blunts criticism that it is improperly applied.

---

3. Whatever that may be. See Joan Robinson, *Economic Philosophy* (Chicago: Aldine Publishing Company, 1962), pp. 26-46, and Robert L. Heilbroner, *Behind the Veil of Economics: Essays in the Worldly Philosophy* (New York and London: W.W. Norton & Company, 1988), pp. 104-133.

1

FINANCIAL MARKETS CREATE VALUE

Value reflects desirable qualities that cause people to create, produce, control, obtain and use things that are considered to have such qualities. This meaning of value conforms to common usage and to the result of "valuation," which is financial terminology for the process by which financial markets price financial contracts. Financial contracts are claims and they consist primarily of written or electronic evidences of debt, shares of stock in corporations, and guarantees. It is only by creating more value that the frontier can be moved outward, so the starting point for examination of the frontier of modern finance is the way in which financial markets create value.

What Financial Markets Do

Active participants in competitive financial markets are preoccupied with the value or price of financial contracts. They relentlessly estimate, calculate and test their value. Transactions arise from this activity when financial contracts are bought and sold in efforts by buyers and sellers to obtain more value reflected in better prices. Transactions enable financial markets to create value.

Promises are Bought and Sold in Financial Markets

Financial transactions monetize promises, exchanging cash in the present for a promise of future reciprocity. *Credit markets create value in the form of loans in the present that are exchanged for promises to pay in the future.* These promises are often supplemented by additional undertakings regarding the rights and behavior of parties to credit transactions. Equity markets create value when a corporation issues shares

5

of stock, promising rights of control and allocations of expected earnings, that are traded for cash in the present. Value is created in markets for guarantees when one party pays another for a promise to assume a financial obligation related to the occurrence of a future event. Thus, value arises when a financial contract or promise is made or traded. The value of a contract equals its price.

Exchange of cash for promises has tremendous social benefits. First, almost everyone can participate in this process. Second, it permits individuals and organizations to transcend the limitations of their present situation. By a spoken or written word, a thumbprint or a signature, or electonic keystrokes, a promise gives access to things that otherwise would be available only after expenditure of further time and effort. Finance brings the future forward telescopically.

Borrowers are originators of promises that help them obtain funds that enable them to demonstrate their abilities, to define their place in the future. Lenders are buyers of promises who support and participate in the activities of those offering promises. Transactions among buyers and sellers of promises spread risks and returns, both actual and expected, over a larger number of economic units, as discussed in chapter 2. They also help to create an expanding network of confidence, as noted in chapter 3. These transactions contribute to economic growth and efficiency when they result in the allocation of land, labor and physical capital to activities that have relatively high economic returns. Because finance and land, labor and capital are scarce, achievement of growth and efficiency requires allocation mechanisms that avoid activities with relatively low returns.

The fundamental valuation question is: *How much is a promise worth?* The procedures used to answer this question determine the amount of value created, which is the primary concern of this book. Elements in valuation include discounting, term structure, transaction costs and the process used to identify value. These basic financial parameters are discussed in this chapter; and risk is dealt with in the following chapter.

Financial Decisionmaking Uses Discounting to Determine Value

Discounting is the basic procedure underlying financial transactions and creation of value by financial markets. Discounting is any technique that compares values at different points in time. Discounting estimates value in the present in return for expected value in the future, and expected value in the future for value in the present. Discounting works both forward and backward in time because value involves a trade-off over time.

Discounting in financial markets is accomplished through a variety of techniques. Some are mathematical, represented by formulas used to calculate compounding and discounting tables.[4] These formulas contain the quantity $(1 + i)^n$, where 1 refers to the principal amount, i is the rate of interest and n is the number of periods for which the calculation is made. Mathematical applications provide precise valuation of a financial claim, and are used where quantitative precision is achievable and important, as in the market for government securities.

At the opposite end of the range discounting procedures are expressed primarily by rules of thumb, tradition or industry practice, and judgment. These predominate where precision is difficult or where precise estimates are not important. In these cases quantification is used to demonstrate that a transaction meets predetermined standards of acceptability, or that a promise is worth at least as much as a specific minimum amount. Standards of acceptability are used to screen propositions and identify those that eventually create transactions following accept/reject decisions. Institutions lending to consumers purchasing household goods and cars, for example, accept or reject loan applications from individuals without estimating precisely the maximum amount of credit each applicant might be able to obtain from all sources. As a general rule, the greater the certainty attached to a promised return, and the fewer the risks and constraints facing purchasers of financial contracts, the simpler the discounting procedure and the standards of acceptability applied.

Between these two extremes are approaches that blend quantitative and nonquantative discounting. In terms of numbers of transactions, nonalgebraic approaches probably predominate. However, a staggering volume of funds is exchanged in highly organized markets where participants' decisions are based primarily on mathematical calculations. Government bond markets are an example: the average *daily* worldwide

---

4. Numerous textbooks discuss the application of mathematics to financial problems. American examples include Steven J. Brown and Mark P. Kritzman, eds., *Quantitative Methods for Financial Analysis* (Homewood, Illinois: Dow Jones-Irwin, 1987); Marcia Stigum, *Money Market Calculations: Yields, Break-Evens and Arbitrage* (Homewood, Illinois: Dow Jones-Irwin, 1981); Robert P. Vichas, *Handbook of Financial Mathematics, Formulas and Tables* (Englewood Cliffs, New Jersey: Prentice-Hall, Inc., 1979)

trading volume in US Treasury securities alone reached $100 billion in 1986.[5]

Discounting requires assumptions about the future. These are distilled into a rate of interest in mathematical approaches. Interest rates form a fundamental part of economic theory and financial practice, which share the view that they reflect expectations. This commonality endures despite the fact that economists view *the* interest rate as a market clearing device and an opportunity cost,[6] while financiers treat interest primarily as a measure of expense and revenue. In economic theory interest rates determine the trade-off between current and future consumption, with future consumption expressed as a function of current investment in goods and services. Financiers consider interest rates as a measure of the return from sacrificing liquidity by committing funds, always at some risk. Common to both is compounding, the proposition that sacrifice is rational only if it seems likely to produce a larger return in the future.

Value Creates an Incentive to Innovate

The quest for larger returns leads financial market participants to seek greater value from their activities. This is seen in the bargaining and bidding processes from which many financial transactions evolve. A more subtle expression of this force is the introduction of new types of financial arrangements, which consist of financial instruments and financial institutions. Innovation provides a dynamic means of creating value where none existed before. Financial innovation, which increases wealth by creating value, is natural in competitive financial markets.

---

5. *The Wall Street Journal.* September 10, 1986. "Endless Dealing: US Treasury Debt Is Increasingly Traded Globally and Nonstop," p. 1. One billion equals 1,000 million.

6. Opportunity cost is an economic concept that refers to the cost of using limited resources for one purpose rather than another. The opportunity cost of an investment equals the return that could have been earned from the best alternative investment. The opportunity cost of the most attractive investment among available alternatives is the return that could be earned from the second most attractive investment. Opportunity cost is sometimes defined as a representative return. In economic planning this might be an estimated rate of return assumed generally to prevail in the economy. In finance, yields on government bonds or on savings accounts are sometimes used as benchmarks for comparing the yields on other investments available to firms and to individuals or households, respectively.

All current financial arrangements—paper money, checking accounts and credit cards, for example—were innovations when they were launched. Their survival demonstrates their sustainability. Innovation occurs because all financial market participants have an incentive to increase value over the long run. In an expanding economy borrowers seek larger loans and lenders have more funds at their disposal. Corporations and their shareholders want a higher price for their stock, and intermediaries seek more funds and transactions.

Term Structure

Discounting incorporates a time horizon. How far into the future do these calculations extend? Term structure is financial terminology that denotes a time horizon and movement toward it by decision makers operating in markets for debt. Term structure is created by exchanges of cash in the present for expected future value. Without term structure there would be no credit and no equity markets because promises would not command any value. Thus, term structure is essential for creation of value.

Term Structure and Loan Size

Term structure has two dimensions: maturities and interest rates. The maturities of financial contracts define the term structure of the markets in which they trade. Markets with short time horizons are dominated by short term contracts, and create relatively few long-term instruments. Long-term housing credit, for example, may be relatively underdeveloped, even though most people may be able to borrow for a few days or weeks against their next paycheck or harvest. The term structure of interest rates is the relationship between maturity and yield on promises differing only in maturity.[7] Interest rates on longer term contracts are normally higher than rates on similar contracts of shorter term. This reflects additional risk that accompanies longer commitments.

As term structures lengthen, the potential for creation of value expands. If a loan is made for a period of a week, the borrower's expected repayment capacity during that week is presumably the major determinant of loan size. By contrast, a loan having a maturity of five years could be

---

7. James C. Van Horne, *Function and Analysis of Capital Market Rates* (Englewood Cliffs, New Jersey: Prentice-Hall, Inc., 1970).

much larger, because five years' cash flow would normally be many times larger than a week's cash flow. This is why term structure is a critical element in the contribution that financial markets make to development.

How Term Structure Is Lengthened

Markets move naturally to extend term structures when long term interest rates exceed short-term rates, which is the relation normally found because risk increases with term structure. By borrowing short-term and lending long-term, intermediaries enjoy an interest spread between short- and long-term rates. However, this mismatch in maturities also subjects them to the risk that their short term obligations may fall due during a period when access to replacement funding (refunding) is limited or achievable only at an unattractive interest rate. Hence, the higher the level of risk, the shorter the term structure, other things remaining equal.

Term structures tend to be longest when the uncertainties of the future are not perceived as threatening financial values. For example, longer term structures develop most easily when inflation remains low. Inflation undermines financial value by reducing the purchasing power of money. High levels of inflation create uncertainty that greatly complicates financial calculation and reduces its usefulness. Because of these characteristics, inflation and expectations of inflation tend to shorten the term structure of credit markets.

Relatively dependable flows of funds over a long period help to lengthen term structures. Because of their power to tax and to create money, stable governments and their state corporations and agencies frequently are able to borrow by selling bonds having longer maturities than those obtainable by private issuers.

Buyers of long term bonds include life insurance companies. Life insurance policies tend to remain in effect for long periods, and policyholders' premiums constitute a steady flow of insurance companies' income. Claims paid when policyholders die are also relatively predictable because mortality risk is highly quantifiable. In countries where mortality data are readily available, actuarial science makes it possible to predict with a high degree of accuracy the rate at which deaths will normally occur in large groups of people, although it is not possible to predict when any individual member of the group will die.

Pools of funds that are not required for daily transactions contribute to long term structures, as illustrated by life insurance. However, long time horizons are not necessarily restricted to low-risk investments. Venture capital provided by entrepreneurial investors in developed economies offers an interesting example. The purpose of venture capital is to assume the high financial risks of starting an enterprise or of rehabilitating a troubled firm, with the expectation that high risks will be rewarded with high returns.

Venture capital normally includes equity contributions, represented by the purchase of stock. Equity has an unlimited life or infinite time horizon because corporations and their stock have no fixed termination date. Venture capitalists expect to sustain several relatively small losses for each large success, but the timing of their losses and gains cannot be accurately predicted. Therefore, venture capitalists commit funds they can afford to lose. Investments that do not work out may become worthless, and those that succeed may be sold to realize capital gains and to free funds for new investments.

Transaction Costs and Value

Transaction costs are admission tickets to financial markets; they govern access to financial services. They must be paid by all parties: depositors, borrowers, intermediaries, guarantors, insurers and others offering or using financial services. Transaction costs are the costs of establishing and conducting financial relationships. They include information-gathering, security arrangements to protect cash, documents and other data, recording systems for transaction processing, and queueing and decision-making.[8] Transaction costs, along with the cost of funds and bad debt losses, are fundamental determinants of which products[9] are generated in financial markets, who provides these products and who uses them. Innovations that reduce transaction costs widen access to financial services, expanding the frontier.

---

8. Transaction cost levels are discussed in chapter 7.

9. Financial markets produce services, which are called products by bankers, brokers and other intermediaries. In their vocabulary, for example, a savings account or a car loan is a product.

Customers' Transaction Costs at the Frontier

The major transaction cost for savers and loan applicants at the frontier is gaining access to the formal market, establishing financial relationships. Savers have to satisfy themselves that institutions willing to accept deposits merit their confidence and treat them respectfully. When they open an account they may have to provide a photograph or document their identity and residence. Personal identity documents, routinely available in many countries, may be difficult and costly to obtain in others.

Modern financial establishments may not have offices in rural centers or in less prosperous urban areas where the frontier economy dominates, and their office hours may be inconvenient. Prospective depositors from these places have to spend time, and possibly money, walking, cycling or riding to banking offices. These trips often have their own challenges, such as temptations to spend, security worries, and possibly long queues for public transport and for service at the banking office.

Would-be borrowers have to obtain information about sources of funds that may be available, and about the terms and conditions attached to each. Would-be lenders have to gather information about prospective clients. Establishing a credit relationship also requires documentation and possibly also a prior deposit account relationship. A loan application is subject to delays in processing, and in certain situations has to be accompanied by a "gift." As with depositors, transport and queueing may consume loan applicants' time, effort and expense. Time spent in these activities has an opportunity cost, consisting of lost opportunities to produce income or enjoy leisure. These costs decrease the attractiveness of borrowing and make it more difficult to obtain value.

Intermediaries' Transaction Costs at the Frontier

The transaction costs of modern financial institutions mount as they approach the frontier; depositors keep smaller and smaller balances while transactions tend also to be small, turnover in accounts may be high relative to average balances held, and related business such as money transfers and use of other fee-based services is limited. Relatively large amounts of noninterest-earning cash have to be held to serve small depositors because they prefer to use cash rather than checks or money orders for transactions. The depository's fixed costs of handling an account or a transaction are not related to the account balance or the transaction amount, making deposit collection at the frontier appear unattractive to many intermediaries.

Borrowers at the frontier may be unaccustomed to making timely payments, difficult to contact and hard to trace, and often lack collateral or credible guarantors. It may be costly for lenders to obtain and verify information from frontier applicants, who may be spread over large geographical areas. Dealings with those who cannot read or who do not speak the business language of the country or of loan department staff take up more time. Loans tend to be small, borrowers' incomes erratic, and sources of repayment not at all clear. Special credit programs for borrowers at the frontier may be imposed on lenders, and these often have other transaction costs, such as organizing these borrowers into groups and extraordinary reporting requirements.

Institutions that penetrate the frontier have to overcome the barriers that make frontier transactions so costly for intermediaries comfortably within the frontier. This is accomplished by innovation in management, by economies of scope and scale, and by devising appropriate financial arrangements; and is not necessarily so difficult as implied by a listing of the characteristics of frontier finance. In fact, the poor themselves have financial institutions beyond the frontier that achieve these ends in order to create value. One of the most common is the rotating savings and credit association, or RoSCA.

RoSCAs Reduce Transaction Costs and Create Value

Saving and lending often involve high transaction costs for poor people. Saving may be difficult, for example, because of pressing uses for funds among the relatively large but intimate social groups into which their society is organized, such as extended families, age groups, and villages. Most members of the group are aware of each others' income and wealth, and asking for and giving assistance are a normal part of daily life. Within the group, at least one person may be sick or need help at any time, there are lots of children to be clothed and educated, and rites of passage require gifts and other expressions of participation. Reciprocity is important, and implies transaction costs.

Borrowing also requires transaction costs. Where no one is particularly wealthy, obtaining funds for a major purchase requires soliciting a number of people. Each loan acquired bears its own terms and conditions, some of which may not be specified in detail but constitute relatively open-ended obligations. These types of obligations involve risks, and soliciting assistance may subject the applicant to gossip and speculation concerning motives and behavior.

THE CLASSIC RoSCA. One of the oldest financial innovations, which survives in most parts of the world and is called by a variety of names, is known generically as the rotating savings and credit association.[10] RoSCAs are a type of informal financial arrangement that reduces transaction costs and creates value by formalizing mutual obligations. The classic RoSCA is *the* financial institution beyond the frontier of formal finance because of its simple yet stunningly elegant design that accounts for its continued popularity and existence in millions of places in developing countries. It consists of members who know each other, usually as a result of social, employment or locational bonds; who have little or no access to formal finance; and who agree to contribute a fixed sum periodically to a pool or "hand" that is assembled and distributed by lot at meetings on agreed dates. One member receives the hand at each meeting. When each member has received a hand the cycle is completed, and the RoSCA disbands or reorganizes.

RoSCAs create pools of funds that are usually difficult for each member to assemble individually, which is one incentive to become a member. RoSCAs permit accumulation because of the contractual nature of membership. Membership is generally taken very seriously—to default on

---

10. There are numerous accounts of RoSCAs in the sociological literature. The most active recent RoSCA researcher and analyst is F.J.A. Bouman. His major papers include "Indigenous Savings and Credit Societies in the Third World: A Message," *Savings and Development*. 1, 4, 1977, excerpted as "Indigenous Savings and Credit Societies in the Developing World," in J.D. Von Pischke, Dale W Adams and Gordon Donald, eds., *Rural Financial Markets in Developing Countries: Their Use and Abuse*. (Baltimore and London: The Johns Hopkins University Press, 1983), pp. 262-268; and "Informal Savings and Credit Arrangements in Developing Countries: Observations from Sri Lanka," in Dale W Adams, Douglas H. Graham and J.D. Von Pischke, eds., *Undermining Rural Development with Cheap Credit* (Boulder, Colorado: Westview Press, 1984), pp. 232-247. Notable books on the topic include C.P.S. Nayar's *Chit Finance*. (Bombay: Vora & Co., 1973), which describes Indian experience, and Carlos G. Velez-Ibanez's *Bonds of Mutual Trust: The Cultural Systems of Rotating Credit Associations Among Urban Mexicans and Chicanos* (New Brunswick, New Jersey: Rutgers University Press, 1983).

a payment is a stigma. Accordingly, accumulating funds to meet RoSCA obligations is recognized as important by the community. This gives the RoSCA a senior claim over the myriad of other purposes that enable kin, friends and neighbors to dip into each others' meager savings. Information about who has how much money when, which otherwise tends to deplete and possibly even discourage individual and communal savings through social pressure, is transformed through RoSCAs into a means to accumulate funds and protect members.

RoSCAs are organized so that transaction costs are minimized—no one except the organizer has to visit a number of people, and terms and conditions are relatively few, straightforward and applied consistently. Everyone's share can be equal, preserving social balance. Each hand is distributed at the meeting at which it is assembled, leaving no group assets requiring management or offering temptations between meetings. Distribution of the hand by lot greatly economizes one of the potentially costly aspects of RoSCA transactions. The frequency of meetings is determined with reference to members' cash flows. Shoeshine boys in Addis Ababa have daily *ekub* meetings because they receive cash every day. Office workers paid monthly have monthly meetings. Market ladies in West Africa have *tontine* or *esusu* meetings when markets are held, often on 4, 7 or 14 day cycles depending on locations and goods traded.

Speculation about motives or behavior can be muted by giving the RoSCA a specific purpose shared by participants. A Society for Iron Sheets, for example, enables members to obtain funds to put roofs on their houses in Kenya; a rice chitty enables each woman member to accumulate a special stock of rice for bad times in Sri Lanka; and a *hui* in Hong Kong or a *paluwagan* in the Philippines enables shopkeepers and stallholders to replenish their inventory periodically.

RoSCAs typically are established by an organizer who takes the first hand. The number of members is identical to the number of hands, and each member receives one hand during the life of the RoSCA. The sequence of distribution of the hand is determined by lot among "nonprized" members, those who have not yet received a hand. At any point before the final hand, members who have not received hands are net savers, while those who have are net borrowers. As the RoSCA moves through its cycle, these savings and borrowing positions rotate. RoSCAs' basic financial value-creating feature is that they accelerate access to funds—all members except the recipient of the final hand receive the cumulative contractual amount of their contributions in the form of a hand before they could have accumulated it by acting alone, by saving the amount of their contribution each period.

This mechanism equates each member's debt capacity and savings capacity, which amounts to the sum of a member's periodic contributions. Value is created by transforming future payments into hands and by accumulating small payments into large pools. Some members typically want early hands and may be called "borrowers," while "savers" seek later hands.

RoSCA INCENTIVES REDUCE RISK. The most interesting aspect of the RoSCA is how it sustains members' incentives to complete the cycle. While debt capacity equals saving capacity, at no point between the first and last hands does any member's net position equal either. A nonprized member's net position is the sum of her contributions, while the amount of the hand minus contributions made equals the net position of a prized member. In the first half of the cycle the majority of members have an incentive to continue contributing so that they can obtain a hand. At this early stage the burden of the obligation to contribute is highest; as periodic payments are made the obligation to make future payments lightens.

In the latter half of the cycle prized members have an incentive to continue contributing because the people who could be hurt by their not doing so, the minority of nonprized members and the organizer, are a diminishing number who are increasingly identifiable. During this phase members' burdens in the form of promised future payments become relatively small; most of their obligations to contribute have already been met, making it easier to contemplate continued participation. Also, the claims of members on each other are by then quite complex, creating a solidarity that fosters continued payment. The juxtaposition of tension and resolution illustrated by RoSCA relationships is common to successful financial contracts.

RoSCAs must incur transaction costs in order to create value for members. The first occurs in organization. Who should belong? How large should each member's contribution be? How many members should the RoSCA contain? These are financial decisions that require information about the character, motives and financial performance of prospective members. Members will be especially interested in the stature and reputation of the organizer. In return for this trust, the organizer has control over who is admitted, and may be expected to make good any defaults arising from the failure of other members to make contributions in full and on time. The major credit risk is that a winner of an early hand may fail to make subsequent contributions. The fixed term of RoSCAs permits exclusion of poor credit risks from future cycles.

Organizational transaction costs are incurred to manage risk. These costs are borne most heavily by the organizer. For this service the organizer usually receives the first hand, which in effect constitutes an interest-free loan repaid over the life of the RoSCA. The value of this position is quite high because of discounting, as demonstrated by auction chit fund data provided by C.P.S. Nayar for India that imply annual interest rates of 20 percent or more.[11]

The member receiving the hand is often responsible for refreshments at the meeting at which the hand is received, especially where RoSCAs meet in restaurants or bars. This transaction cost helps maintain group cohesiveness through eating or drinking together, and impresses on members the importance of continued loyalty to each other. Members can observe each others' health and moods, and gain impressions of each others' current financial status. While many transaction costs are an annoyance to those who pay them, the obligation to provide hospitality to one's friends at RoSCA meetings is usually regarded as an honor or as an opportunity for fun, something to be enjoyed.

Creating Value by Refining Valuation Processes

The transaction costs of financial relationships include the costs of maintaining the valuation process that results in transactions. Closely related to these costs are changes in the valuation process itself. While some changes are driven by efforts to cut costs, others are led primarily by efforts to create value where none existed before.

Refinements in the valuation process give financial claims greater liquidity, which tends to increase their attractiveness and makes intermediaries more willing to provide or process these claims. Refinement

---

11. *Op. cit.* In auction chit funds the order of rotation following the initial distribution to the chairman is established by competitive bidding for each hand by nonprized members.

occurs primarily through the creation of new instruments or types of contracts and of a market that makes them liquid, which in turn provides valuation. It also occurs through more precise valuation of existing instruments.

Innovations in valuation are the most interesting type of refinement because they touch the heart of the fundamental financial question: *How much is a promise worth?* These constitute an especially important class of innovations that permits large entrepreneurial assaults on the frontier. Interesting simple illustrations include recent developments in mortgage markets in the US, the introduction of leasing in Bangladesh, and refinements in pawnbroking when it was a major source of small loans.

The Secondary Mortgage Market in the United States

Deregulation of the United States financial markets since the late 1970s increased competition, producing an explosion of innovation. One that has refined value is securitization of first mortgages on property, especially private homes.[12] Lenders offering first mortgages, primarily banks and savings and loan associations, traditionally held them through maturity, which was normally 30 years, or until borrowers sold their homes.[13] Once on their books, these assets were not subject to intense valuation because they could not be readily sold. Mortgage holders spent their efforts on administration, which was generally not difficult because of the high

---

12. Mortgage is an old French word derived from *mort* or dead and *gage* or pledge, pawn or security. The mortgage was an innovation that eventually replaced the *vifgage* or living pledge. Under a *vifgage* the borrower or a member of his family was given to the creditor until the debt was paid, usually by the labor of the pledge. This type of practice can still occasionally be found in a few developing countries. A first mortgage is the mortgage that is paid off first when payment is made from the proceeds of the sale of the mortgaged property. Securitization refers to the creation of a financial claim that is relatively easily marketable, backed by other financial claims that are not so easily marketable.

13. Over half of all American households own their own homes. Homes are often bought and sold because American society is mobile. Young families want to move into nicer neighborhoods as they grow older and wealthier, old people often move to smaller quarters requiring less upkeep, and lots of families move from one place to another to obtain better employment. These activities result in average mortgage lives of around eight years for many lenders.

quality of this fully-secured paper, on attracting deposits and on the development of new mortgage business.[14]

With increased competition and government encouragement, a secondary or resale market in first mortgages evolved. The market deals in single mortgages or in packages of mortgages, often in multiples of $1 million, with standard terms and conditions. (Nonstandard or "nonconforming" mortgages are traded on slightly less advantageous terms.) Mortgage lenders are now able to choose between holding and selling these assets, and the value of these assets is of great interest because they can be sold at any time for cash. The lender's cost basis may vary from the market price, providing opportunities for profit or loss.

This innovation has had two noteworthy effects. The first is that more of a lender's assets can be tied up in mortgages, and less held in cash reserves and short term investments. This has expanded the size of the mortgage market, advancing the frontier.

The second effect is that more lenders now provide mortgages. Credit unions, for example, traditionally did not offer first mortgages because they were reluctant to make 30-year commitments of members' funds. The large size of a mortgage, compared to the car, consumer and home improvement loans that are traditional credit union business in the US, also posed two problems. One is that the credit union objective of service to members implies relatively open access to funds. Large loans to just a few members could impede open access by exhausting the supply of loanable funds, which could result in loss of membership and withdrawals of deposits. The second problem is that mortgage loans are large in relation to the capital base of many credit unions, concentrating risk.

Credit unions can now offer mortgages by contracting with intermediaries that buy mortgages and assume the credit risk of these loans. By selling its mortgages, a credit union obtains cash that it can recycle into new lending, and the mortages that are sold and the risks that they entail are removed from its books. The buyer of a package creates a security backed by the mortgages and sells it in the capital market, where it can be traded. The credit union benefits from mortgage generation fees and through service to members, which helps to increase member loyalty and

---

14. For an economic critique of US housing finance, see Maxwell J. Fry, *Money, Interest and Banking in Economic Development* (Baltimore and London: The Johns Hopkins University Press, 1988), pp. 414ff.

interest in the credit union. This should increase members' transactions and average balances, making the credit union stronger. In addition, the credit union does not burden its capital with an accumulation of these relatively large loans issued to only a minority of its membership.

Leasing in Bangladesh

Finance leases enable lessees to use equipment belonging to the lessor.[15] The lessor remains the owner of the leased equipment and is responsible for its maintenance. The lessor borrows to purchase equipment selected by the lessee, and the lease charge paid by the lessee covers the lessor's debt service, risk and administrative costs. The advantages of leasing stem primarily from tax treatment; the lessor's interest cost and equipment depreciation expense are operating expenses, as are the lessee's lease payments. Another possible advantage is that lease obligations do not have to be reported as liabilities by the lessee under accounting rules followed in many countries.

In addition to tax and debt reporting considerations, leasing offers an alternative to lending and borrowing that benefits both lessor and lessee. Because the lessor owns the equipment used by the lessee and is responsible for maintaining it under a finance lease, the lessor has more control over the equipment than a lender whose loan is secured by a claim on the equipment. Repossession of equipment pledged to secure a loan that is in default requires judicial approval in many countries, and may be difficult to achieve without incurring relatively high transaction costs. In most countries a lessor can take back equipment relatively easily if lease payments are not made on time.

When leasing gives a lessee access to assets that could not otherwise be obtained, or obtained only at a higher cost, it is a refinement in the valuation process. Lessors can recognize value where lenders cannot when borrowing equipment is more advantageous than borrowing cash.

Modern finance leasing was introduced into Bangladesh in 1985 through formation of a leasing company owned by local interests, foreign leasing companies and a multinational investor. The company brought foreign exchange and expertise to Bangladesh that would probably not

---

15. Jonathan R. Hakim, ed., *Equipment Leasing*. IFC Occasional Papers, Capital Markets Series (Washington, DC: International Finance Corporation and the World Bank, 1985).

have been attracted to other financial activities. The overall loan repayment environment in Bangladesh was not attractive to foreign private lenders, but leasing offers greater security to a financial intermediary by providing lessees an additional incentive to honor their commitments. This combination created more value, giving lessees greater access to productive assets and giving lessors a better mechanism for recovery of funds. The leasing company recorded a profit within a year of starting operations, which would be unusual for conventional term lenders financing fixed assets.

Collating Collateral

The Provident Loan Society[16] was established as a not-for-profit pawnshop in New York City in 1894. At its peak in the late 1930s, before consumer credit, personal bank accounts and lines of credit were widely available in the US, the Provident had more than 750,000 customers. Its success reflects innovative valuation.

Following industry practice, the Provident publicly auctioned unredeemed pledges, which consist of items pawned but not reclaimed by borrowers through loan repayment. The standard loan term was one year; a further grace period of three or four months was given before auction. Reflecting its objectives, the Provident innovated by refunding to the borrower any excess arising from an auction price greater than the amount of loan principle and interest due. This practice was not followed by commercial pawnbrokers, who kept any excess of auction proceeds over the amount owed. But if the auction price were below the amount owing, the Provident absorbed the loss.

The Provident's policy led to conservative valuation. Assigning too high a value could result in a loss if the pledge were unredeemed and auctioned at a price below the amount owed. But too low a pledge value made the Provident uncompetitive with commercial pawnbrokers and defeated the purpose for which it was founded. Innovation was obviously required for the Provident to overcome this self-imposed limitation.

Diamonds were the most frequently pledged high-value item, and subjected the Provident to considerable valuation risk. The great majority of these were "brilliant cut" with the standard round shape and 58 facets.

---

16. Peter Schwed, *God Bless Pawnbrokers* (New York: Dodd, Mead & Co., 1975).

Diamond valuation was largely subjective; to become a skilled appraiser could require 20 years' experience. By the 1930s, partly because of the decline in immigration from Europe, it was difficult for the Provident to hire experienced appraisers from the jewelry and commercial pawnbroking trades in sufficient numbers for its 22 offices. A shortage of experienced appraisers increased the Provident's risk. On one occasion appraisers from six of its branches were assembled and given ten diamonds to value. To the astonishment and dismay of management, the values assigned to individual diamonds by its experts varied by more than 600 percent, and over 100 percent for the lot of ten stones. The Provident responded by innovating.

The vice president in charge of the Appraisal Department, an engineer by training, systematized the valuation process. Studies and experiments, lasting more than two years by Provident staff who had no training in the jewelry trade, included detailed examination of possibly 20,000 diamonds and charting their values realized at auction. This led to the introduction of standard grading scales for brilliant cut stones incorporating cut, color, clarity and carat (weight).

Color was the most difficult variable to standardize: lighting conditions varied from hour to hour and from branch to branch. This problem was addressed by making a series of identical metal rods with six diamonds mounted on them in ascending order of color. These were issued to all branches, permitting valuation of pledges by visual comparison. Cut and clarity grading scales were standardized through the use of charts showing common deviations from the ideal brilliant cut and the most common flaws, and the percentage reduction in value that accompanied them. The vocabulary used by the jewelry trade to describe diamonds was replaced by numerical scales and abbreviations for colors. Determining the weight of mounted stones required no changes in procedures: a caliper device used by jewelers permitted extrapolation from measurements of exposed dimensions.

Grading scales for the four characteristics produced 252 classifications that were collated into tables that were periodically updated to reflect changes in the market value of diamonds. Reference to these collations enabled a relatively inexperienced appraiser to assign a precise loan value that closely approximated the amount the pledge would obtain at auction. This permitted the Provident to give better value to its clients, reduced its risk of loss, made valuation much more consistent across its branches, and reduced staff cost.

By demystifying diamond valuation, making it possible to become a skilled appraiser in 20 hours rather than 20 years, the grading system produced another interesting effect: it improved working conditions. The Provident did not have to recruit appraisers from the jewelry trade, and for the first time lower level staff could become managers by working their way up through the four office ranks: cashier, vaultman, appraiser, and branch manager.

2

VALUE GENERATES RISK

Risk, the possibility of loss, pervades finance as gravity pervades physics. Risk causes the unceasing valuation that animates financial markets. To survive and prosper in financial markets, participants must manage risk in ways that increase their wealth. Risk, not term structure or transaction costs, causes financial executives to lose sleep.

Why risk and finance are inseparable is explained at the outset in this chapter. Exploration of risk as perceived in financial markets follows, begining with a discussion of mismatched or nonsimultaneous flows found in all economies. Liquidity is an important financial concept that governs management of mismatched flows. It is defined in this chapter and its intermediation is dealt with. The discussion then moves to identifying maturity risk, interest rate or pricing risk, and credit risk. The chapter closes with examples of risk pooling, partition and redefinition, and assumption through financial intermediation.

Why Risk Pervades Finance

Risk pervades finance because finance trades the future against the present and the present against the future. Because the future is uncertain, risk is always present.[1] Financial behavior responding to risk is seen even where money is not used. William Allan in *The African Husbandman*[2] describes how clan groups practicing slash and burn agriculture accommodate risk. Their largest risk is that a harvest will be insufficient to sustain the group until the next harvest. If insufficient food is available, the

---

1. Risk and uncertainty are used synonymously here, as is nontechnical English.
2. William Allan, *The African Husbandman* (Edinburgh and London: Oliver & Boyd; New York: Barnes & Noble, 1967).

results are disastrous; clan members are weakened from malnutrition or die from starvation. The spirits of the ancestors may become out of sorts.

The clan invests work in the present for a return in the form of a harvest several months in the future. The work is the tremendously demanding task of clearing bush with simple hand tools and burning it. This provides open space for planting, destroys competing vegetative material and produces ash that will help the crop to grow. One crop exhausts the soil, and the group moves on and clears a new area for the next season. A major strategic question is how much work should be devoted to securing a harvest—how large an area should be cleared?

The response of these farmers, at this extremely low technological level, is to clear and plant a larger space than required to support the group under normal conditions. Based on the food required to sustain the clan and an estimate of soil fertility, the size of the clearing is determined by the expected yield achievable in a *bad year*. In the normal or good year the clan will not have to harvest the entire crop to survive. The difference between the expected normal year and the expected bad year harvest represents a risk expectation, a discount applied to the future to determine the rational level of investment in the present. Allan calls this discount "the normal year surplus."

Finance Harmonizes the Risks of Nonsimultaneous Flows

Where money is used, possibilities for dealing with risk increase greatly. Finance exists because nonsimultaneous cycles of flows arise in the normal course of production and consumption. For example, major dams and canals may require five or more years to build, it may take two years to build a ship, tradesmen can construct a house in several months, and a nail factory produces thousands of nails per day. Farmers work on a seasonal cycle, grocers turn over their stocks every few days, and most people eat several times a day. Each flow has a unique pattern, creating the risk of mismatched flows. *Finance facilitates the management of mismatched flows and diminishes their risk.*

If production and consumption were simultaneous, the economy could function without finance. But workers on the dam, canal, ship and house have to be paid frequently before their projects are completed. Raw materials and other supplies must be ordered long before the finished goods that contain them are sold to users. Because different activities have different financial rhythms, finance in the form of savings and credit arise to permit their coordination. Savings and credit are made more efficient as intermediaries develop to transfer funds from firms and individuals that accumulate funds and are willing to shed liquidity to those that desire to acquire liquidity.

Cash Alone Is Fully Liquid

Risk management in financial markets centers on the sacrifice and preservation of liquidity. The most general definition of liquidity is "nearness to cash," with cash considered fully liquid and relatively riskless.[3] Assets that can be easily sold, or converted to cash, are more liquid than those that are not easily convertible. Assets that can be easily valued in terms of cash are more liquid than those that cannot. Mathematical approaches to discounting are most easily applied to relatively liquid financial claims.

The only way fully to ascertain the liquidity of an asset is to sell it. How long did it take to sell? How large were the transaction costs? Was the expected price realized? Did the price obtained approximate prices for similar assets sold in similar conditions at the same time, or shortly before and after the sale? Answers to these questions describe the liquidity of an asset.

Testing liquidity by sale is obviously inconvenient for those interested in knowing the price of something they would like to keep, or in selling only when a certain price can be obtained. However, markets provide indications of liquidity because market transactions create liquidity. For example, when trades in the stock of a particular corporation occur frequently, and transaction volumes and the range of trading prices are published by sources in which a shareholder has confidence, the shareholder's stock can be valued easily and relatively accurately. In addition, high volumes of transactions enable dealers to offer firm price quotations. Transactions and competition promote the spread of market information, including price, trading volumes and the terms and conditions of sale.

---

3. In economies experiencing high inflation this assumption does not hold. People shed domestic cash for foreign hard currency and stockpile goods that are expected to retain value.

Liquidity Sacrifices: The Dramatic Tension of Finance

Liquidity is the primary means by which value is given and restored in financial transactions. Buyers who pay cash for a promise sacrifice liquidity by reducing their holding of cash. The sacrifice continues until liquidity is restored when the promise is honored or sold to another party. Because modern finance expresses value in terms of cash, sacrifice of liquidity creates a valuation problem—the cash value of noncash assets is always relative and uncertain. Consistency in valuation helps reduce uncertainty and lowers the transaction costs of sacrificing liquidity. Well-functioning markets eliminate inconsistency as buyers shun overvalued assets and compete to obtain undervalued ones.

A more important valuation problem arises because sacrifice of liquidity creates risk. This occurs because the exchange of liquid present value for illiquid future value is completed only in the future, when liquidity is restored. The future is inherently unpredictable, introducing the possibility that liquidity may not be fully restored.

Risk and its impact on value is one of two reasons why financial analysis exists. The other reason arises from the tremendous private and social benefits created by rational markets. Things that belong to people and are traded have to be valued in order for markets to operate rationally. This fact is most easily illustrated by things that do not belong to people or that are not traded. In centrally planned economies, for example, financial analysis is generally not sophisticated because risk is centralized, individual ownership is curtailed and markets are repressed.

Risks Managed in Financial Markets

By intermediating liquidity, financial markets intermediate risk. Risks arise from inability to predict the future and from nonsimultaneous flows. The problems posed by lack of simultaneity are defined primarily as maturity risk and interest rate or pricing risk, which are often interrelated. Credit risk is also a dimension of nonsimultaneity. These three risks are discussed below.

Maturity Risk

Maturity risk arises when financial contracts do not fall due or mature at the same time. This occurs when the maturity structures of a firm or household's assets and liabilities differ. An example is the situation of small farmers on settlement schemes in Kenya in the 1960s. Mismatches in the maturity of settlers' obligations and their ability to produce income, by turning assets in the form of crops into cash, resulted in insufficient liquidity to meet their obligations. Their land purchase loans were initially repayable in twice-yearly installments starting within a year of their moving onto their plots. These loans quickly went into arrears because the first payment became due before settler-borrowers had time to organize their operations. Repayment dates were unrelated to the seasonal schedule of harvests, creating another mismatch that heightened arrears.

Matching of maturities is an important principle of intermediation, exemplified by the perfect matching of RoSCA finance described in the previous chapter. Although matching is a cardinal point of reference in financial planning, many intermediaries actively seek opportunities to mismatch maturities in order to create value. Commercial bankers, for example, usually obtain liquidity through customers' deposits, especially demand deposits (checking accounts) and savings accounts. These are so popular because they are usually withdrawable by account holders on demand, whenever they wish. Bankers often use these deposits to fund loans that are not due on demand but have a fixed term, which creates a mismatch on their books. Borrowers often prefer the certainty created by maturity dates, rather than signing a demand note that the lender can call for repayment at any time.

Interest Rate or Pricing Risk

Interest rate or pricing risk (with pricing used as an adjective) arises from the intervals at which financial claims are repriced. Repricing occurs when an interest rate is fixed for a financial contract. In the most simple case, repricing occurs at the maturity of a financial claim, when the lender recycles funds into new financial contracts, and when the borrower obtains new credit to replace the repaid loan.

Innovations have unbundled or disconnected repricing intervals and maturities, as exemplified by floating rate notes and adjustable rate mortgages. These are assigned a new rate of interest periodically throughout their lives according to formulas incorporating reference rates. A five-year note, for example, may be repriced every six months. The choice of reference rate depends upon the market in which contracts are traded. Government securities rates and commercial bank prime rates often govern adjustable rate mortgages in the United States, for example, while LIBOR (London interbank offered rate) is applied to Eurocurrency floating rate notes.

The pricing risk is that the interest yields on portfolios of assets and portfolios of liabilities may vary. More precisely, variations in the spread between these rates can diminish the intermediary's income. A notorious example was the plight of the U.S. savings and loan (S&L) industry in the 1970s and early 1980s when inflation raised market rates of interest. Virtually all of the S&Ls' liabilities, primarily demand or short-term deposits from individuals, had to be repriced relatively quickly to prevent depositors from taking their funds elsewhere to obtain higher interest. This made the S&Ls' cost of funds tend to fluctuate with the market.

However, the S&Ls' earning assets consisted largely of long-term residential mortages issued at fixed interest rates. Opportunities for repricing occurred only as these assets were slowly paid down, generally in monthly installments over their 30-year lives, or as they were repaid in full when mortgage holders sold their houses. When deposit rates moved sharply upward, the losses that resulted forced many S&Ls out of business. Those S&Ls surviving this crisis, the first in that industry, have innovated around this mismatch by offering adjustable rate mortgages, for example, that reprice periodically, usually every six months or annually.

Credit Risk

Another risk from nonsimultaneous flows is credit risk, the possibility that the borrower may not repay as scheduled at the maturity of a loan. Here the mismatch does not reside initially in the flows of the intermediary, but in the flows of the borrower. But when the borrower's flows do not provide sufficient liquidity to repay a loan, the lender's flows also suffer.

Credit risk is essentially a valuation risk, because credit gives value in the present in exchange for expected future value. There are two contexts for examining credit risk. One is the risk inherent in any relationship with a borrower, which is that the borrower has more information about his activities than the lender does. This means that the lender bears the risk of innocently making poor credit decisions because of inadequate information, and also that the borrower may abuse the lending relationship.

In addition to this common view of credit risk is another that arises from the design of credit arrangements. Credit arrangements generate or diminish credit risk, and this dimension is especially important in attempts to nudge the frontier. Loans too large for borrowers to handle and lending programs too large and complicated for the lender to supervise and account for may result in losses because flows get out of control. For example, lenders may not be able to manage their loan portfolios effectively if their management information systems are overburdened or if they are too aggressive in entering markets in which they have insufficient experience or when they ignore experience. In these cases, lenders overestimate the future value of their activities, which are diminished by bad debt and related losses, as in the case of North American and European commercial bank lending to certain developing countries in the late 1970s and early 1980s.

Credit risk includes problems such as fraudulent and opportunistic behavior, and incomplete documentation of claims through administrative lapses. In well-functioning formal financial markets these rank far behind poor planning and poor management by borrowers and by lenders as sources of bad debt losses. Value creation is extremely sensitive; where a significant proportion of contracts are not honored on time or where fraud is common, value evaporates and financial market development is retarded or reversed. International debt crises are examples of reversals that occur when credit contracts are not honored on time or are regarded as unlikely to be honored on time.

How Financial Markets Manage Risk

Financial markets manage risk by pooling, intermediation and assumption. These processes unbundle risk through partition and redefinition, and repackage risk to make it more attractive. This allows risk transfer to create value because those who seek comfort by shedding risk and those who seek higher returns from assuming risk move toward their objectives. A household or a firm's rational desire for comfort or for risk-taking with an opportunity to gain reflects its financial structure. The examples that follow relate financial structure and risk management, and indicate how risk can be managed through financial markets. While value generates risk, these examples explain why risk management creates value.

Risk Pooling in a Pension Fund

Classic fixed-benefit pension funds offer an example, greatly simplified in this presentation, of risk pooling, of how a financial innovation responds to its users' financial situations, and of how efforts to manage risk shape an innovation. The pension fund product in this example is annuities, or fixed, periodic payments for pensioners. Annuities create value in two ways. They give pension fund members the prospect of stable income after retirement in return for their contributions to the fund before retirement. They also permit this objective to be achieved economically through collective action.

The fixed-benefit pension fund is an attractive innovation because it responds to members' risk. Greatly reduced earning power in retirement following reasonably assured earning power during their working lives is a potentially formidable nonsimultaneity of flows. The task of the pension fund is to collect sufficient cash from workers during an accumulation phase before their retirement, which will yield the target level of annuity payments to these workers during a distribution phase over the rest of their lives.

To manage the risk that insufficient funds are collected, pension funds may classify their members into groups having homogeneous expected retirement dates and life expectancy. The pension fund referred to here is for a homogeneous group of this type. Pooling risk through homogeneous grouping creates value for group members. Barring suicide, individual group members cannot know how long they will live following retirement. Prudent individual planning requires an assumption of long life expectancy to ensure that funds are available even if very old age is attained. For example, if the homogeneous group retired at age 60, prudence might require individual financial planning assuming survival through age 90. If each individual wanted to have an annual income of $10,000 for life, the total annuities would equal $300,000.

However, actuarial predictions suggest that roughly half of the group will not achieve greater than normal life expectancy, which, for example, may be 75. In this case, the average total annuity per individual would be $150,000, or $10,000 per year for 15 years. If each member planned prudently individually and assumed a longer-than-normal life expectancy, the group as a whole would save too much, reducing consumption too drastically during their working years in order to provide for their old age through age 90. By pooling their risks they enjoy greater value because each member's contributions are based on normal life expectancy of 75 years. Pooling enables the fund to intermediate risks: members who die before normal life expectancy receive fewer benefits relative to their contributions, while those who exceed normal life expectancy receive relatively more benefits. ·

This simplified pension fund holds low-risk, long term bonds as assets. These are purchased during the accumulation phase from members' contributions, and from interest earned on bonds already purchased, less fund administration expenses. The fund manager structures the bond portfolio so that maturity dates are "laddered" to coincide with expected annuity funding requirements during the distribution phase. The composition of the fund's assets reflect its operations. As the recipient of a long-term inflow of contributions, eventually balanced by the outflow of annuities, the pension fund is willing to invest in long-term bonds.

Fixed-benefit pensions are funded by variable contributions from members. Members' contributions fluctuate each year. Assuming a target level of benefits, constant life expectancy and projected interest income and pension fund administrative expenses, adjustments in contributions required from a group of members will reflect changes in the interest rate available on bonds. The interest rate determines the extent of compounding, which in turn affects the size of the pool from which annuity payments are made to group members. The higher the interest rate, the greater the compounding, reducing the level of current contributions required to fund annuity payments in the future. Discounting is applied in a straightforward, highly precise manner to determine the level of annual contributions at a given compounding rate that is required to support target pension payments and pension fund administration costs.[4]

Matching maturities avoids pricing or reinvestment risk. If short term bonds or bank deposits were purchased during the accumulation phase, changes in market conditions could make it impossible to reinvest the

---

4. In greatly simplified form and ignoring administrative costs, the compounded amount of cumulative contributions, $(1 + i)^n$ for each year's amount paid in, with i representing the interest or compounding rate and n representing the number of periods remaining before retirement, is equated with the present value at the time of retirement of a constant annuity to be paid out each remaining year of members' lives. The present value of an annuity is $(1 - [1/(1 + i)^n])/i$.

proceeds from their maturity at the rate of interest required to achieve the target level of annuities during the distribution phase. If bonds having maturities exceeding the life expectancy of pensioners were purchased, they would probably have to be sold before maturity to fund annuities. Market conditions at the time of sale could depress their prices below the level required to fund annuities.

Members of this sort of scheme place a premium on certainty, because they expect to be dependent upon annuity income in their old age. Their concern is reflected in the objectives of the fund managers, who follow a conservative investment strategy of minimizing risk by close matching of maturities. The bond portfolio is ideally structured to eliminate maturity and repricing risks in order to ensure that target annuities and all administrative costs can be paid from accumulation phase assets. The efficient fund will exhaust its assets at the same time the last surviving group member passes away.

Risk Intermediation and Diversification by Partition and Redefinition

Virtually all debt, equity and guarantees incorporate risk management and discounting. A fundamental risk management device is division of financing into debt and equity. Equity is the owner's share of an enterprise, represented by shares of stock in a corporation or cooperative, a proprietor's interest in a proprietorship, and the partners' interest in a partnership. Equity holders assume a disproportionate share of the risks of a project or enterprise. This asymmetry attracts creditors who are also willing to provide finance but only at a lower level of risk.

Owners are equity holders. They stand to gain a disproportionate share of the benefits from a successful venture, and to lose all their investment in the event of failure. They bear the risk of variable returns, after all other claims on the project or enterprise are met. Creditors expect a steady return in the form of interest payments and principal repayments, secured by the knowledge that owners stand to lose all before the creditors lose any.[5] Put

---

5. This is the ideal case, based on the classic legal distinction between debt and equity. In many countries and situations debtors have extraordinary rights and institutional factors limit creditors' capacity to pursue debtors or to take over debtors' assets. In these cases, the amount of credit offered is less than would be available if the classic ideal prevailed, other things being equal.

in another way, each of these holders of claims on the project or enterprise operates according to different discounting expectations.

Division of risk creates value: more funds are available for the project or enterprise than if debt or equity finance were relied upon exclusively. Equity finance becomes unattractive as the sole source of funds at some point because the owners may find their risks too highly concentrated in the enterprise. With only limited funds, they may wish to spread their risks over a number of activities. A more common reason for taking on debt is to obtain better returns. Higher returns are realized if the return on the enterprise's activity is greater than the return demanded by creditors in the form of interest. Equity holders benefit from any returns in excess of the cost of debt that are earned on the portion of the investment financed by debt.

Using debt to obtain higher returns on equity is called trading on the equity, or leverage (in the United States) or capital gearing (in the United Kingdom). Greater return to equity than to debt is consistent with the greater risk assumed by equityholders than by creditors, and with the underlying relationship between risk and returns: the greater the risk, the greater the returns from bearing the risk. Greater returns are necessary to attract liquidity to risky investments.

Debt cannot be relied upon exclusively because creditors generally do not want their claims subject to the same risks as the enterprise. Returns to the enterprise are bound to be variable, while creditors expect steady returns. This mismatch makes it difficult to attract debt beyond certain limits that relate closely to the expected variability of returns to the enterprise.

Different types of enterprises attract different levels of debt because of the relationship between risks and returns. For example, the agricultural sector in many highly developed Western countries attracts relatively little debt, generally equal to less than 20 percent of its total assets. In contrast, publicly-owned (in the US sense, which means by large numbers of shareholders, not the government) telephone companies' debts fund more than 50 percent of their total assets. The returns to individual farmers are highly variable, as is their cash flow available to service debt. Phone companies' cash flows, by contrast, are relatively stable.

The further division of equity and debt into different classes, each with its own combination of rights, risks, and returns, extends this basic process of risk partition and redefinition, attracting additional funds and creating additional value. For example, preferred shares offer dividends only after the enterprise satisfies all claims other than those of holders of common stock, who are the owners. Some creditors' interests may be secured by debentures or claims on specific assets such as land or buildings, while other creditors such as those providing short-term trade credit may not have any tangible security for their loans.

Risk Assumption in Financial Markets

Financial institutions assume certain risks they cannot directly match or intermediate. They take these risks under several conditions. One is that they are adequately compensated for their portfolio of such risks. Another is that the risks assumed are not likely to have a significant negative impact on their overall operations.

Forfaiting, which is primarily found in Western Europe, is an example of risk assumption. Forfaiting intermediates payment risks for goods shipped to importers in developing or Eastern bloc countries that have a history of slow or erratic payment for imports. These risks include the possibility of delayed payment or nonpayment due to foreign exchange control problems, default by the importer or on a payment guarantee by the importer's bank, or losses from changes in the rate of exchange between the currency in which the exporter was paid and the currency in which the importer's obligation is expressed.

The Western European exporter issues a promissory note for the amount due from the Eastern European importer. A guarantee for the note is sometimes obtained from the importer's Eastern European bank. The note is sold by the exporter to a Western European bank (or other forfaiting intermediary) at a discount. The exporter receives immediate payment from this sale and is no longer subject to payment risk, which is assumed by the buyer of the note.

The discount reflects the bank's cost of funds, transaction cost, and risk. The foreign exchange risk assumed by the bank through the forfaiting transaction can usually be covered at least partially by instruments traded in foreign exchange markets, but the other risks have to be carried by the buyer of the exporter's note. The discount is usually higher than the cost of a loan for the same amount, but exporters can often pass at least part of this cost to importers through the prices charged for the goods that are exported. Forfaiting creates value for the exporter by relieving him of risk. It also enables the exporter to obtain funds immediately without having to go into debt; in this sense forfaiting substitutes for borrowing.

Forfaiting is conducted primarily by specialized subsidiaries of large banks that can offer this service because they are well informed about international trade, operate in foreign exchange markets, compete for the business of exporters, and because the amount of forfaiting transactions is limited. Forfaiting is a competitive tool because multinational commercial banks want to be able to offer their clients a full range of services, either directly or through subsidiaries. As a condition for taking on high-risk forfaiting, they may request that the exporter route other business through them, such as letters of credit and other money transfers.

Forfaiting transactions are limited by the relatively small volume of trade with countries with doubtful payment histories. Also, some of this trade is covered by guarantees offered to exporters by government-owned export credit agencies or export-import banks. These guarantees are often subsidized, but commonly cover large transactions such as for aircraft or big construction contracts. Transactions covered by forfaiting tend to be smaller, giving the forfaiting house greater opportunity for risk diversification by importer, by guaranteeing bank and by country.

Provident Perpetual Sixes: a Risk Twist

Many types of risk can be accommodated by financial arrangements. Life insurance, credit guarantees and corporate stock represent different vehicles for managing risk. However, financial instruments can also help to determine how an organization conducts its business and establishes its objectives. To its founders, owners and clients these dimensions of commercial behavior are tremendously important. An interesting example is the Provident Loan Society cited in the previous chapter. How did the Provident's founders seek to perpetuate their vision or to define their legacy?

It is late 1893 in New York City. You are a successful businessman who is weathering the Money Panic that broke in May, following a speculative rush in gold and silver that peaked last December. During the depth of the crisis some banks failed, others suspended payment temporarily, and unemployment increased. A number of people of modest means adversely affected by these events approached you and others in your social circle for assistance. You have been a member in the Charity Organization Society (COS) for several years, and are disturbed by the difficulties many people have had getting loans to help tide them over the disruptions of the Panic. Would it be possible to establish an institution that could provide small loans to assist such people?

Some leaders of the COS, including notables such as James Speyer, George F. Baker and Cornelius Vanderbilt, share your concern.[6] A group of them has just returned from Europe, where they reviewed the operations of the Monts de Piété, municipal pawnshops that have existed for several centuries in France, Holland, Germany, Austria, Italy and Spain. At a meeting called to hear their report, you join a committee established to raise funds to establish a similar pawnshop in New York City, to be called the Provident Loan Society. A subcommittee consisting of yourself and two others is given the task of developing a fund-raising strategy. Your target is $40,000, a significant sum when unskilled workers earn less than $1 per day.

Your subcommittee searches for an approach that will ensure that the target can be met in a way that contributes to the objectives set by the organizing committee. Relying only on donations and setting up a board of trustees to administer the pawnshop may pose risks. After a few years the board could turn into just an honorary body, and the business might suffer. The pawnshop management might lack incentives to be efficient because it would not be exposed to much financial discipline. Yet to compete against commercial pawnbrokers management would have to be agile and alert. It would be embarrassing for the COS to have to preside over periodic appeals to replenish capital squandered by inefficient staff and inattentive trustees, and it could also tarnish your reputation as a businessman.

Setting up a corporation to run the pawnshop would, however, pose disadvantages. Shareholders, exercising their voting rights, could try to serve their own interests rather than those of small borrowers. Some stockholders might, over time, try to divert the pawnshop from its charitable objectives in order to obtain dividends or increase the price of the stock. Commercial pawnbrokers might accumulate a sufficient number of

---

6. Herman E. Kroos and Martin R. Blyn, *A History of Financial Intermediaries* (New York: Random House, 1971), p. 123.

shares to gain control of the Provident. Would there be any alternative way of funding that could impose financial discipline on the pawnshop managers without subjecting the Provident to subversion?

Coming back to the present, the record shows that the founders of the Provident Loan Society used an innovative instrument to meet their objectives. Contributors were given "certificates of contribution" with four features. First, they had a face value equal to the amount contributed. Second, they carried a nominal 6 percent interest rate. This gave the Provident an earnings target and a responsibility. It probably attracted additional capital from supporters who wanted some opportunity to enjoy a return. It also created a continuing constituency: if donations were used, contributers might eventually forget their link with the Provident. Periodic interest payments maintained a relationship that could be useful if the Provident ever sought more funds.

Third, the certificates of contribution did not impose on the Provident any legal obligation to pay interest, to allow for the possibility that the commercial and charitable objectives of the business might conflict. Fourth, the Provident could redeem the certificates by refunding the amount of the contribution. These terms allowed the Provident the opportunity to buy its way around the interest burden or to accommodate changed circumstances if its mission turned out to be poorly conceived. These securities were listed on the New York Stock Exchange, where they were well-regarded and known as Provident Perpetual Sixes.

History suggests this instrument served its purpose well.[7] In the first three weeks of the Provident's operation, half of the $40,000 contributed by founders was disbursed in loans averaging about $10 each. Capitalization was soon raised to $100,000 by issuing more certificates of contribution. The Provident was efficient enough to accumulate reserves sufficient to redeem these certificates in the 1930s, when loan demand was again high because of the Great Depression and 6 percent was well above prevailing rates of interest.

---

7. Peter Schwed, *op. cit.* This source does not discuss how the founders decided to use certificates of contribution to fund the Provident. The account given here is a speculative recreation for the purposes of this chapter.

3

CHARACTERISTICS OF FINANCE

What permits finance to create value? The theme of this chapter is that finance has special characteristics that differentiate it from the goods and services produced by the nonfinancial sectors of the economy. The market for finance is basically different from the market for soap or cement.[1] Its characteristics determine how finance contributes to development, and how strategies that attempt to use finance to nudge the frontier outward have to be structured to be sustainable. Characteristics that relate most closely to the role of finance at the frontier are that it is by nature social, intangible, fungible or interchangeable, that a loan produces no return for borrowers, and that finance attracts attention and is easily politicized.

Finance Is Social

Finance often seems to be all numbers, but it is fundamentally social rather than mathematical. Like language, finance is a product of society. Modern finance consists of promises that are accepted. The Latin root of "credit" illustrates this aspect—*credere* is to believe or entrust. In the same way that language facilitates expression and understanding, finance gives promises power in commerce, over the allocation of goods and services to consumers, and over the uses of land, labor and capital in production.

Finance cannot be separated from risk, as explained in the previous chapter.[2] The opposite of risk is confidence; finance harmonizes these

---

1. The special features of financial markets were formally recognized in the modern economic literature only in 1981 with the publication of "Credit Rationing in Markets with Imperfect Information" by Joseph E. Stiglitz and Andrew Weiss in the *American Economic Review*. lxxi, June 1981, pp. 393-410.
2. The social implications of risk are treated by archaelogists in Paul Halstead and John O'Shea, eds., *Bad Year Economics: Cultural Responses to Risk and Uncertainty*

opposites. When risk is sufficiently offset by confidence, transactions occur and value is created. Finance therefore cannot exist without confidence. The relationship between value, risk and confidence is triangular, as shown in Figure 3.1. Value is placed at the top of the triangle because its creation rests on both risk and confidence. Because finance is triangular, a change in any one of these variables cannot occur in isolation. Perceptions of increased risk will reduce value unless offset by increased confidence. Declines in confidence reduce value unless risk also decreases. Risk can never be completely eliminated, nor can confidence be fully retained for extended periods of time without continual renewal. Confidence is emotion and perception. It is ephemeral in a dynamic world and is reevaluated incessantly. Financial markets test confidence with each transaction.[3]

Figure 3.1 The Financial Triangle

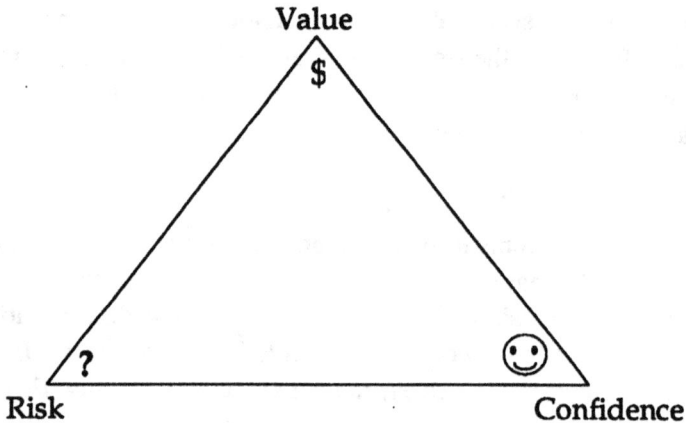

(Cambridge: Cambridge University Press, 1989), which begins with the observation that, "The world about us is in a constant state of flux," (p.1) to which Henry Petroski adds, "Constant change means that there are many more ways in which something can go wrong." *To Engineer is Human: The Role of Failure in Successful Design* (New York: St. Martin's Press 1982), p. 2.

3. "Confidence must grow out of performance." See "The Economic Impact of Trust and Confidence," in The 5th Column, *Far Eastern Economic Review*. 30 May 1985. pp. 78-79.

Confidence is the most challenging requirement for financial market development. Confidence is generated within financial markets by the same tools that are used to manage risk, as discussed in the previous chapter. For example, division of finance into debt and equity creates more confidence. The equity holders already have confidence in the enterprise and use of debt creates additional confidence that is sufficient to attract lenders who may not have sufficient confidence to become equity holders. Confidence is very strongly influenced by factors outside finance, such as society's general view of the future, social structure and the amount of effort or transaction costs required to achieve and maintain consensus or to effect change. These factors also include respect for agreements entered into voluntarily, the legal structure and the costs of gaining access to it, and similar elements that determine social activity.

Confidence Creation through Rural Credit Unions

The efforts of Friedrich W. Raiffeisen[4] to help the poor through voluntary group action illustrate the extreme demands of confidence. Raiffeisen was a civil servant in the Rhine Province of Prussia. He was mayor of Weyerbusch in 1847, which was a very bad agricultural year in that area. To help ensure a supply of bread and potatoes, the staple food of the poor, Raiffeisen and some wealthy citizens formed a cooperative to obtain supplies from distant areas to operate a bakery and to sell good seeds and other farm supplies. Their efforts reduced the price of bread in Weyerbusch by 50 percent within several months, and led Raiffeisen to consider whether similar organizations might help address long-standing rural problems, including the perception of an inadequate supply of credit at reasonable rates of interest.

In 1849 Raiffeisen was appointed mayor of Flammersfeld, an area containing 33 villages. There he launched a second experiment with the support of 60 wealthy citizens. A society of wealthy and of poor citizens was formed to "eliminate the usurious cattle trade."[5] The society bought

---

4. Raiffeisen is pronounced *rai* as in rise, *feis* rhymes with pies, and *sen* as in send. An account of his role in cooperative history is found in J. Carroll Moody and Gilbert C. Fite, *The Credit Union Movement: Origins and Development, 1850-1970.* (Dubuque, Iowa: Kendall/Hunt Publishing Co., 1984).

5. F.W. Raiffeisen, *The Credit Unions.* 8th ed. (1966), Konrad Engelmann, trans. Neuwied on the Rhine, Federal Republic of Germany: The Raiffeisen Printing and Publishing Company, 1970 [1866]. p. 20.

cattle for resale to the poor members, to be paid for in five annual installments. However, this activity was administratively burdensome, imposing high transaction costs. The founders also concluded that supplying cattle to poor farmers did not significantly relieve their poverty. A system of cash loans was instituted, using funds borrowed by the society. Term loans were made available for farmers investing in improved agricultural technology.

To obtain funds for the society, members pledged their entire property, assuming unlimited personal liability to satisfy the society's creditors. This degree of dedication attracted sufficient funds only when the 20 wealthiest members accepted joint liability to borrow a significant amount, equal at the time to about US$1500, from a Rhineland "capitalist." Unlimited liability of members, apparently essential to creating the confidence required to obtain credit at relatively low rates of interest, was an extremely rigorous condition. Many rural people were reluctant to make such a large commitment, risking the loss of their crops, livestock, implements and land, and possibly their reputations. Confidence had to be created among members or prospective members before the confidence of those with funds to lend could be obtained.

As mayor of Heddesdorf in 1854 Raiffeisen helped establish the Heddesdorf Welfare Association to assist the poor financially, to educate neglected children, to provide jobs for the unemployed and for ex-convicts, and to establish a public library. These objectives proved too broad for effective action. In 1864 the group revised its statutes and became the Heddesdorf Credit Union.

From these experiences the early Raiffeisen rural credit union model evolved. It was based on membership of the wealthy as well as of the poor, on the unlimited and joint liability of members, and on voluntary leadership, usually by wealthier members. Their leadership and that of clergymen helped create confidence, which was bolstered by having the accounts kept by a teacher, tax collector, forester or other highly respected citizen. This model proved replicable by others only in 1862, when the second society was established in a nearby village. One can imagine the lengthy discussions required to convince individuals to accept unlimited liability in a new venture over which they would have limited individual control. It had taken Raiffeisen 15 years of tremendous dedication and of trial and error to develop an institutional means of expressing his desire to help the poor in a manner that generated the confidence necessary to ensure financial credibility.

Raiffeisen justified his work in religious terms and stated his objectives in social welfare terms. However, he measured the credit unions' success in a very concrete way, which was that the number of "petty suits, forced auctions, executions [of creditors' rights]...have considerably diminished...where the Unions are active."[6] Numbers of credit unions or members, total loans made or total assets, references to solidarity and the merits of collective action were not the center of Raiffeisen's pragmatic evaluation. Raiffeisen also reported, after 37 years of experience, that no members had incurred losses as a result of assuming unlimited liability.[7]

Rural credit unions had their skeptics, who raised questions of public confidence. In response, the Prussian minister of agriculture appointed a commission of investigation that consisted of two prominent bankers and a professor of economics. In 1875 they visited 26 credit unions and reported very favorably. Relatively rapid formation of rural credit unions followed throughout central Europe.

While Raiffeisen devised his rural credit union model, an urban credit union model was being developed for artisans and shopkeepers by Hermann Schulze-Delitzsch.[8] Schulze-Delitzsch was more flamboyant and less cautious than Raiffeisen, and he concentrated on financial and economic factors as motivators rather than on religious teachings and social ideals. In its initial years his model spread more quickly than the rural model and also suffered some setbacks as societies were dissolved or became moribund due to bad loans and poor performance.

The models developed by Raiffeisen and by Schulze-Delitzsch[9] have been reconciled and operate in modified form on all continents. Innovations within credit unions and in financial markets generally have permitted their evolution as limited liability membership organizations operated democratically under a one-member-one-vote rule, usually

---

6. *Ibid.*, p. 22.

7. *Ibid.*, p. 46.

8. J. Carroll Moody and Gilbert C. Fite, *op. cit.*

9. J.O Müller, "Early Savings and Credit Cooperatives on the Basis of Self-Help to Combat Poverty and Dependence in Germany," in Guy Bédard, Gerd Günter Klöwer and Martin Harder, eds., *The Importance of Savings for Fighting Against Poverty by Self-Help*. Vol. II. Berlin: Deutsche Stiftung für internationale Entwicklung (DSE-German Foundation for International Development), 1987.

financed entirely by members, with voluntary leadership, and having objectives consistent with those of cooperatives generally. Raiffeisen's emphasis on the role of relatively well-to-do members has declined with the adoption of limited liability. The World Council of Credit Unions includes more than 70 national associations, and there are 8.2 million members of more than 15,000 credit unions in developing countries.[10] Members are primarily from low- and middle-income groups.

Collapses of Confidence

The importance of confidence in the operation of financial markets is illustrated by events that occur when confidence declines. Financial history is peppered with failures of intermediaries and collapses of stock and commodity prices following bursts of speculative behavior. These crises have often been associated with wars, efforts to build trade with or infrastructure in less developed areas, international loans, and precious commodities such as gold and silver.

Business cycles and financial crises have inspired a huge literature. Competing theories explain their causes and prevention. Charles P. Kindleberger[11] suggests that the events leading to a crisis begin with an external event that significantly changes profit opportunities in a major economic sector. These events include wars, crop failures, political upheavals, and innovations of the magnitude suggested by the introduction of canals, railroads, and automobiles. If the external shock generates more opportunities than it destroys, businesses respond by increasing production.

To support the boom, finance is created. The creator may be the commercial banking system, the central bank or private sources. The private supply of credit can be very dynamic. Firms at each step in the production and marketing chain can become increasingly willing to accept debt rather than immediate cash in payment from their customers, and

---

10. J. Peter Marion, "Building Successful Financial Systems: The Role of Credit Unions in Financial Sector Development." Madison, Wisconsin: World Council of Credit Unions, September 1987; and *1988 Statistical Report and Directory*. Madison, Wisconsin: World Council of Credit Unions, 1989.

11. An entertaining analysis of financial crises is provided by Charles P. Kindleberger, *Manias, Panics and Crashes: A History of Financial Crises,* (New York: Basic Books, 1978). The pattern outlined here is from Chapter 2, "Anatomy of a Typical Crisis." pp. 14-24.

individuals may invest in or lend to businesses. A modern example of such dynamism is the use of accounts receivable by large corporations in the US as security for commercial paper, which permits using credit outstanding to customers as a base for borrowing.[12]

The boom tends to push production capacity utilization to its limits, raising prices as the demand response is stronger than the supply response. New investment occurs fueling the boom. Up to this point, a normal level of rationality tends to prevail. However, the euphoria of a boom can disconnect investment decisions from the realities of production or sustainable market potential, and certain items become the subject of intense interest by an expanding pool of buyers. Historical examples include precious metals, stock, land, tulip bulbs; recent examples include silver, gold, Australian mining shares, oil, US currency and farmland, works of art and antiques. As suspended rationality becomes widespread, the probability of crisis increases.

At this stage, confidence is pervasive and relatively unquestioning. Feelings of euphoria are reflected in speculation. Speculation is difficult to define and even more so when the economy is booming. The definition given in *Webster's New Collegiate Dictionary* is "to assume a business risk in hope of gain; especially: to buy or sell in expectation of profiting from market fluctuations." But when do vision and entrepreneurship become speculation? At what point can the acceptance of normal business risks be separated from behavior responding to expectations of fluctuations? Another twist is that although speculation in the dictionary's second sense is sometimes popularly regarded as being on the fringes of legitimacy, in fact it can play a stabilizing role by transferring and spreading risk.

Kindleberger suggests that speculation consists of the purchase of commodities for resale rather than for use, and the purchase of equity for resale rather than for income. This definition would presumably be tempered by a presumption of excess or unusual activity. For example, wholesalers, brokers and retailers and other intermediaries buy commodities for resale rather than for use in the normal course of business. Speculation might consist of building up stocks far in excess of

---

12. "Industrial Firms Are Using Receivables to Back Commercial Paper, Preferred," *The Wall Street Journal.* October 7, 1987. p. 41.

normal levels or a surge of new entrants into an industry. Another qualification is seen in the examples of some corporations that limit or pay no dividends on the assumption that their reinvestment in the firm will provide larger returns to shareholders over the long run through increases in the value of the stock. Buyers of these shares seek capital gains, not dividend income. Speculation would have to be driven by expectations of gains greatly exceeding normal yields on equities.

But to return to euphoria. Valuation goes into overdrive as a flood of confidence submerges perceptions of risk and cautious tendencies. Speculation in the object or objects of interest expands as more people engage in it, often supported by credit. Manias or bubbles are created when prices reach great heights.

As speculation continues, the suspended rationality that fuels it is challenged. "Insiders" may feel that present trends cannot much longer continue. They take their profits by selling the object of speculation for cash. As more people withdraw from the market, the influence of new entrants is eventually offset. The market hesitates, and prices fail to continue their steep rise.

At this point some players may have difficulty meeting their obligations because their positions are financed almost entirely by debt, or it appears that they might have difficulty. Speculation attracts opportunism, and frauds or irregularities may be exposed at this stage. Exposure occurs when new debt is no longer easily obtainable. Many types of fraud require an increasing flow of funds to repay existing obligations in order to attract new victims, or to cover bookkeeping manipulations by individuals or small groups working in otherwise respectable financial institutions.

The classic swindle is typified by the operation of Carlo Ponzi in the 1920s. He promised to pay 50 percent interest on 45-day deposits, arbitraging currencies by buying international postal reply coupons in countries where they were cheap and redeeming them in the U.S.[13] By

---

13. International postal reply coupons are sold and redeemed by post offices in the member countries of the Universal Postal Union. Each coupon is redeemable for surface mail postage for a letter of the minimum weight classification (e.g., one ounce in the U.S., 20 grams in certain other countries) being sent abroad. These coupons enable a sender to pay for a reply from a correspondent abroad. This payment innovation overcomes the inconvenience to the sender of sending small coins of his own country to his correspondent abroad (which may be illegal and invites tampering with the post) or of obtaining stamps of the correspondent's country. The

paying 50 percent interest to early depositors, Ponzi attracted an expanding crowd of new depositors. Ponzi used the new deposits to pay off earlier depositors in an ever-broadening spiral. Kindleberger reports that Ponzi took in $7.9 million and had $61 worth of stamps on the day of his arrest in Boston.[14] "Ponzi schemes" that enrich their organizers and obtain increasing amounts of money to repay old loans at high interest rates, rather than to invest in productive activities, take their name from this infamous operator, although they originated long before Ponzi was born.

To return to the cycle of euphoria and crisis: when warning signals occur, confidence erodes and more people try to leave the market and obtain liquidity, driving down prices. As this self-reinforcing movement gathers speed it turns into a stampede. "When the market feels that there may not be enough (liquidity) to go around, the rush to get there first is exacerbated."[15] Bubbles burst and manias become crises as people reject the object of speculation causing its price to collapse. Traders may not be able meet their obligations, creditors may find that they cannot recover their loans, and waves of bankruptcy may slow the economy.

The extent of the crisis depends upon the pace at which liquidation is attempted, and whether there is liquidity to absorb sellers' demands. In this phase too, people may tend to over-react in the same manner, but in the direction opposite to that which occurs with euphoria and speculation. Kindleberger notes that an event that discourages confidence such as a suicide, business failure or an exposure of questionable behavior can begin the collapse.[16] Panic or crash occurs when a crisis reaches major proportions: prices are driven to very low levels greatly disrupting markets and so exhausting liquidity that the settlement of claims breaks down.

Much energy is devoted to finding institutional remedies to contain the effects of disappointed euphoria and reversals of unquestioning confidence. Central banks were established by national governments

---

correspondent is spared the problem of redeeming foreign coins. Post offices are spared the inconvenience of postage-due letters. Ponzi's ruse was possible because the minimum surface mail rate varied from country to country and the cost of a coupon was equivalent to the surface letter rate in the country of purchase. Postal authorities have removed arbitrage possibilities by charging more for the coupons than the cost of mailing a letter abroad. In the US in 1987, for example, a coupon cost 80 cents while the overseas letter rate was 37 cents.

14. *Op. cit.* p. 85.
15. *Ibid.* p. 224.
16. *Ibid.* p. 107.

around the world from 1850 to 1975 for this purpose, among others. International institutions, such as the International Monetary Fund, are relative newcomers to this field. Securities regulation and self-regulation by intermediaries seek to address problems of fraud and opportunism.

Finance Comes in a Tube....

Walter Wriston, former chairman of Citicorp, observed that money comes in a tube.[17] The tube referred to is the cathode ray picture tube in the monitors of the computers and computer stations that portray transactions and constitute the basic medium of trading information for modern financial intermediaries and their clients. The darting symbols on screens illustrate that finance is no more tangible than the promises that create it. Beyond the handshake that affirms a promise in many cultures, the feel of the wind on the face of a child or the warmth of the sunlight on the petals of a rose are more tangible than finance.

Informal finance is often invisible. In illiterate or barely literate societies beyond the frontier there is frequently no formal record, written or electronic, of credit or of the share of the returns from a venture to which each participant is entitled. Paper money may change hands in these transactions, but is one step removed from the creation of credit, which produces no tangible record in these circumstances.

Traditional credit works purely on promise, trust and consent, often before witnesses having intimate knowledge of the consenting parties. Participants clearly recognize that the relationship between borrower and lender is the basis for the transaction, and that their worth in the eyes of others will to some extent depend on their performance under their shared promise. Millions of RoSCAs around the world work very successfully on this basis. Many more millions of viable informal financial relationships also operate invisibly. Their dimensions are understood by participants, but less well documented by researchers; the economy beyond the frontier remains essentially private.

Between paperless finance conducted on the dirt floors of villages at one extreme and through electronic circuits at the other, is the world of documents or paper promises. They include paper money, savings

---

17. Walter Wriston, "In Search of a Money Standard: We Have One: It Comes in a Tube," *The Wall Street Journal.* November 12, 1985. p. 28, see also "A New Kind of Free Speech," *Forbes.* December 14, 1987. p. 264.

passbooks, periodic statements of account for checking account holders, bills of exchange drawn by one merchant on another, letters of credit arranged by banks, loan agreements of all types, stock certificates, insurance policies, warehouse receipts or warrants, and an incredible array of other financial instruments. These attest to the variety of finance, the rigorous demands of confidence, and the complex institutions that attempt to create and maintain confidence. The blizzard of paper that trails finance is a tribute to the tremendous energy that financial markets direct to building confidence.

Paper promises permit finance to venture beyond the face-to-face relationships of informal finance. The passbook holder can initiate transactions with bank tellers who are total strangers. Checks or drafts can be sent to distant places to secure payment through banks or giro systems. Bills of exchange facilitate commercial relationships between parties remote from each other. Letters of credit finance international trade, and stock certificates in bearer form (not inscribed with the name of the owner) can be traded anonymously. These instruments reduce transaction costs greatly because they are generated, processed and enforced in a depersonalized manner within broad institutionalized frameworks of confidence.

Finance is Fungible

Fungibility refers to the interchangeability of things that are identical or uniform. The term is sometimes associated with the grain trade, where each kilogram of a specified type and grade of grain is for all practical purposes identical to every other kilo of the same type and grade. Because of fungibility, a farmer who stores his harvest in a commercial elevator and who withdraws it to ship to a buyer will not be concerned if the grain withdrawn did not come from his farm, as long as the type and grade are the same.

Finance is fungible because one unit of a country's currency is identical to every other unit of its currency. Fungibility underlies the usefulness of money; lack of fungibility creates the inconveniences of barter. The implications of fungibility are illustrated by the fable of Mrs. Kariuki,[18] an

---

18. J.D. Von Pischke and Dale W Adams, "Fungibility and the Design and Evaluation of Agricultural Credit Projects," *American Journal of Agricultural Economics.* 62, 4, November 1980; J.D. Von Pischke, Dale W Adams and Gordon Donald, eds., *op. cit.* pp. 74-83.

African farmer who received a loan from a farm credit agency to purchase three milk cows and other materials for a modern diary operation on her small farm.

The $1,200 loan was allocated in the loan agreement as $800 for three in-calf, improved "grade" cows, $200 for fencing, $100 for a 2,000 liter water tank, and $100 for a milking shed. Mrs. Kariuki went into debt because of the attractive terms offered—80 percent financing, five years to repay, 10 percent interest—and because of the range of attractive investment opportunities in her area. Her neighbors are expanding their dairy and tea-growing operations, and several have started transport businesses. Land prices are increasing and many families are improving their homes.

Mrs. Kariuki is an attractive borrower because her family's four-hectare farm, owned by her husband, is well-maintained. Also, Mrs. Kariuki owns a plot in a nearby village which she used as loan collateral. She obtained the plot several years earlier when she planned to open a restaurant with a friend. The friend died shortly afterward and the plot remains vacant but has increased in value because of the good economic conditions in the area. She also has $600 in her post office savings account, saved from her income from tea production.

Mrs. Kariuki used the borrowed funds to obtain the items specified in the loan agreement. Her loan was disbursed by the farm credit agency against invoices submitted directly by the suppliers from whom Mrs. Kariuki obtained the improved cows and materials. But, the $100 worth of iron sheets and lumber for the milking shed were not used to build a shed, which would be considered extravagant by her neighbors and relatives, but to extend and re-roof the family's house. In addition to the loan proceeds, Mrs. Kariuki invested $300 of her own funds in the dairy project (her 20 percent contribution to complement the 80 percent loan financing). This money was used to pay for transport of loan-financed items to her farm, to hire labor to install the fencing and water tank, and to buy miscellaneous items such as buckets and pipe.

Mrs. Kariuki's first investment priority was to establish an improved dairy enterprise because of its expected profitability, steady labor demands and the family's preference for fresh milk. Before the loan was approved, she sold her entire herd of six inferior dairy animals for $800 in cash. She obtained credit to buy new stock and materials even though she could have financed most of the project from the sale of these cows and the $600 in her savings account.

Her other priorities include planting more tea, which requires hired labor; acquisition of more land; and joining her husband and some of his friends in purchasing a taxi so that their community would be linked more dependably to a market town 20 kilometers away. Mrs. Kariuki spent $250 for tea planting and $300 to purchase a small plot from an elderly neighbor after receiving the dairy loan. She also spent $100 on a new coat for her husband, two new school uniforms for her children, and a visit to relatives. Of her $1,400 in cash and in the post office savings bank, $450 remained after these expenditures. Since she wanted to keep $200 on hand in the event of an emergency or special opportunity, she invested the remaining $250 in a share of the taxi being purchased by her husband and his friends. (These transactions occurred during the time of the year when tea is not harvested. The family's routine income and expenditure were balanced during this time and did not figure in Mrs. Kariuki's planning.)

Table 3.1 Summary of Mrs. Kariuki's Cash Flow

Sources of cash		*Uses of cash*	
Farm credit agency loan	$1,200	Purchase of cattle	$800
Sale of cattle	800	Dairy materials	400
Savings account		Transport, labor, misc.	300
opening balance	600	Tea planting	250
		Land purchase	300
		Clothes, family visit	100
		Taxi share	250
		Savings account	
		closing balance	200
Total sources	$2,600	Total Uses	$2,600

Mrs. Kariuki's behavior is similiar to that of small borrowers generally in developing countries where economic conditions are improving and markets are reasonably competitive. Individuals and households in these circumstances have multiple sources of income. They have a tremendous incentive to diversify their activities because their agricultural incomes are erratic due to natural factors, and relatively low because of market conditions and possibly as a result of government policies.[19] Likewise, their erratic and uncertain incomes give them a great incentive to save.

The tale shows how difficult it is to identify exactly what a loan finances. Did the loan really enable Mrs. Kariuki to establish an improved dairy activity? Exploration of her behavior leads ultimately to the conclusion that the loan gave Mrs. Kariuki liquidity, an increase in her overall purchasing power. For all practical purposes all sources of funds (the loan, the sale of her unimproved cattle, and her savings) contribute to all uses of funds (loan-financed goods, home improvements, clothes, land acquisition, and so on). This is the essence of fungibility, which makes finance different from vegetable seeds, which can only be eaten, crushed for oil, or produce plants; tractors, which can only provide motive power; or nuts and bolts, which can only hold things together. Even here, however, seeds, tractors and nuts and bolts of uniform specifications are fungible.

Fungibility diffuses the impact of finance. A possible exception occurs when a relatively large additional source of funds is matched by a relatively large additional use of funds in situations where alternative investments and alternative sources of finance are severely limited. Except for some large, lumpy industrial projects, this is unusual in developing countries because large injections of funds are not generally available. One reason for this is because the risk of providing such funds tends to be high. It is not so unusual in countries with highly developed financial markets where home buyers can obtain mortgages equal to several years' income for the purchase of a house that is by far their largest asset.

The impact of a loan is also obscured because it is rarely possible to know what would occur in the absence of the loan. What would Mrs. Kariuki have done if she had not received the loan from the farm credit

19. Richard L. Meyer and Adelaida P. Alicbusan, "Farm-Household Heterogeneity and Rural Financial Markets: Insights from Thailand," and Peter Kilby, Carl E. Liedholm and Richard L. Meyer, "Working Capital and Nonfarm Rural Enterprises," in Dale W Adams, Douglas H. Graham and J.D. Von Pischke, eds., *op. cit.* pp. 22-35, 266-283.

agency? Would she have borrowed elsewhere? Would she have scaled back her activities or attempted to accomplish her investment objectives gradually over an extended period of time? Would she have cut back on certain expenditures, and gone ahead with others on the same scale she did with the loan; and if so, which ones? The time dimension of credit and the fact that the future is unknown make the counterfactual or "what if?" case hypothetical or speculative.

Fungibility means that use of finance is often not tightly associated with the purpose for which it is obtained even when borrowers adhere to their loan contracts. This characteristic of finance highlights the role of confidence in financial relationships. Confidence in the project or loan purpose is important, but confidence in the promoter or borrower is even more important. An old banking saying is that the three important elements in lending are knowing the borrower, knowing the project or use of funds, and knowing the collateral, in that order of importance, with collateral running a distant third. Informal markets demonstrate this: friends, kin and others with whom one has dependable relationships are creditworthy; strangers are not.

Credit Earns No Return for Borrowers

Credit enables. It gives borrowers purchasing power that can be used to obtain assets that are expected to yield a return. This is the simple development model that underlies much foreign aid, government intervention in financial markets, and other efforts to promote loans for small businesses, farmers, women or other groups.

The model is valid, but its application is sometimes naive and its progression not fully appreciated. Problems arise when the steps between the promise and the return to the borrower are neglected. In fact, credit is debt; it earns no return for borrowers. A loan is a liability of the borrower, a source of expense in the form of interest and transaction costs. When a borrower receives a loan in the form of cash, the cash also has no earning power until it is invested. If a small businessman who borrows invests in a lathe, the lathe may be used to produce machine parts that can be sold above cost. If a farmer who borrows invests in seeds, they may contribute to a successful harvest that can be sold at a remunerative price.

The intermediate steps between credit access and income generation that are often neglected are receipt of the loan and the purchase and utilization of assets that are capable of yielding a return. Of course, these steps are not entirely ignored in practice. Credit programs and loans from donor agencies, for example, generally have specific purposes often supported by technical assistance designed to make loan use more efficient. Misinterpretation occurs when the returns to the use of funds are attributed to the loan rather than to the activities "financed by the loan" or associated with the borrower's use of funds.

Confusion regarding the source of returns and growth can lead to the unbalanced view that credit is responsible for progress. Credit always has an impact, but because of fungibility, not necessarily the impact expected by lenders or project designers. To attribute a specific impact to a loan requires strong evidence that without the loan there would have been no change in the activities of the borrower. Because this evidence is counterfactual, the assumption of no change without the loan cannot be established unambiguously. In fact, things are usually changing, the poor at the frontier have multiple sources of income and access, and viable alternatives often exist.

False attribution feeds euphoria for credit, creating enthusiasm for lending and for the presumed loan purpose that far exceeds enthusiasm for ensuring repayment. Loans are poorly structured, relationships between borrowers and lenders are not carefully designed or diligently tended, and sources of repayment are regarded too optimistically. This imbalance leads to failures in the credit market when bad debt losses exceed lenders' interest and fee income. Overstatements of the developmental role of credit tend to result in its excessive use, which leads to destruction of confidence in credit markets. An example is the Third World debt crisis of the mid-1980s.

Fungibility and the simple fact that returns result only from uses of funds, not from sources, generally makes it impossible to identify unequivocally the returns to borrowers from credit or from a credit project. This realization challenges widely-held perceptions of the simple development model.

Finance Works to Close Tolerances

Like fine pieces of machinery, finance has very close tolerances. Tolerance is an engineering term for the degree of accuracy between the actual dimensions of a part and its design specifications. Plus or minus one

one-thousandth of an inch or 0.025 mm, for example, is the tolerance permitted certain parts of modern internal combustion engines. This is a very close tolerance, compared to that required, for example, for a shovel or hammer.

In finance, close tolerances are seen in measurements of the performance of commercial banks, where a before-tax profit equal to 1 percent of total assets has traditionally been a measure of good performance. Traders calculate yields on government bonds in terms of "basis points" equal to one one-hundreth of a percent. Close tolerances arise because well-functioning financial markets refine valuation to a high degree. Risk arises from very small changes, especially where large amounts are involved.

Close tolerances pose a problem when credit is used directly as an instrument of development. In agricultural credit project appraisal, for example, consider the tolerances achievable by different members of the project design team. The agriculturalist may be doing an excellent job by predicting within plus or minus 25 percent the average yield that is obtained from a new crop. The rural sociologist may be doing an excellent job by predicting within plus or minus 50 percent the extent of target group adoption of the project–sponsored innovation in any given year. The economist may be doing well by predicting within plus or minus 10 percent the average price that growers of the new crop will receive for their produce in the free market.

The financial analyst faces closer tolerances, which is the reason good analysts have a peculiar point of view that enables them to bring constructive pessimism to bear in any situation. A one or two percentage point change in the bad debt loss rate can make the difference between profit and loss for the farm credit agency lending funds for the project-sponsored innovation. A ten percentage point error in overhead costs may have a huge relative impact on the intermediary's position under the project. Estimates of the projected rate of inflation, where lending rates are not accurately indexed, also have important implications for the ability of the intermediary to enlarge its operations in the direction suggested by the project once project funds are disbursed. Hence, a project can perform relatively well in terms of its agricultural, social and economic specifications, yet be a disaster for the financial institution lending funds to farmers participating in the project. In this respect, credit is a vulnerable and fragile project component, not the robust leading edge so often depicted.

Finance Attracts Attention

While many examples given in this book are based on deals that are or could be concluded, it is also instructive to consider those that are not. Some transactions do not occur simply because finance attracts so much attention. This social aspect of finance is illustrated by anthropologist Parker Shipton's reflections on the role of money beyond the frontier in The Gambia:[20]

> Cash in rural Africa is an odd commodity surrounded by ambivalent attitudes. Nothing in The Gambia is more sought after than money, but nothing is more quickly disposed of. Indeed, money is even seen as something to get rid of, something to convert into longer lasting forms. Several features make money an unstable form of wealth in The Gambia: its nearly universal fungibility, its divisibility, and its portability. These features make money contestable. Everyone needs it for something, particularly in the lean season from June to August; and one with money will usually have an almost infinite number of relatives or neighbors with pressing needs. Inflation, of course, is a further reason not to hold onto money. Though few farmers have the means to measure inflation, nearly all are aware of the process. Rural Gambian saving strategies, then, are largely concerned with removing wealth from the form of readily accessible cash, without appearing antisocial. In communities where one has many relatives, as is usual, this is a delicate balancing act, and beside any ethical issues involved, the "squawk factor," the potential for complaints and accusations, must enter every individual savings decision.

Ways of dealing with these aspects of money include burying it, putting it in strongboxes or containers that to be opened must be destroyed, and placing cash with trusted moneykeepers who return funds only when previously agreed conditions are met. Shipton cites these types of behavior as evidence of illiquidity preference.

But finance also attracts intense attention within readers' more customary points of reference: the valuation process is so powerful and so closely related to economic well-being that it is the subject of public debate and government regulation. Kenneth E. Boulding notes that, "banks and

---

20. Parker Shipton, *"How Gambians Save—and What Their Strategies Imply for International Aid."* Policy, Research, and External Affairs Working Papers: Agricultural Policies. WPS 395. Washington, DC: World Bank, April 1990. pp. 16-17.

other financial institutions occupy a certain nodal position of power in the total structure" of the economy.[21] Inside the frontier, finance is inevitably subject to government scrutiny and attempts at control. Finance is often cited as the most highly regulated industry in many mixed economies. Because of its visibility, formal finance is a relatively attractive target, especially for governments with limited sources of revenue from other parts of the economy.

The two most important prices in many economies are the prices of financial instruments: interest rates and foreign exchange rates. These are important because they affect all other prices. Interest rates, which offer present measures of future values, influence the volume of investment in the production of goods and services. Investment, in turn, is an important determinant of economic growth. Exchange rates are important because they affect the extent to which buyers and sellers can benefit from access to markets in other countries. Access is important because returns can often be increased by buying or selling abroad. Government control of exchange rates can direct these benefits in favor of domestic buyers at the expense of domestic sellers, or the other way around depending on whether government action helps maintain an artificially high or low exchange rate.

Attempts to change access to financial markets affect relationships within a society. Intervention in finance is more than purely economic or financial because it responds to and addresses nonmarket issues of privilege, authority and power. Voters and more active participants in politics may reject financial or economic objectives as too narrow or irrelevant. Issues of privilege, authority and power are fundamentally political, and frequently they are the dominant influence on the role that finance plays in stimulating or retarding development.

Subsidized Credit is a Political Playground

One manifestation of political efforts to control finance is the attempt by governments to push the frontier outward, into areas of the private economy where they have little direct control. The most common means of doing this is by targeting loans or directing credit at below-market rates of interest to borrowers or purposes accorded priority by the government.

21. Kenneth E. Boulding and Thomas Frederick Wilson, eds., *Redistribution through the Financial System: The Grants Economics of Money and Credit* (New York: Praeger Publishers, 1978), p. viii.

Low interest rates are politically attractive. They respond to perceptions that the supply of credit is inadequate and too expensive for a particularly worthy purpose or for deserving classes of borrowers or potential borrowers. Their politically most important feature, however, is that the value created by concessional rates tends to be highly concentrated, while the costs are hidden and widely diffused.

The benefits of subsidized credit are concentrated in a relatively small number of borrowers for three reasons. The first is the finite size of credit programs—governments have only so much money available to lend at subsidized rates. By definition, funds do not move naturally toward government priorities in the volumes and on the terms and conditions that are desired politically. This, of course, motivates intervention to increase flows and reduce rates.

The second reason for concentration is that economies in lending favor large loans. A lender's transaction costs do not greatly vary with the size of the loan. Documentation, recordkeeping and other decision-making and administrative procedures tend to be similar across broad ranges of loan size. Within any given program or budget, the smaller the number of loans, the lower the transaction costs to the lender. Lenders may also believe that large borrowers are less likely to default. Lenders, even if government-owned, generally attempt to avoid losses so that their expansion and institutional continuity are not threatened. If losses are inevitable because of program design or economic crisis, the lender with a constituency of large, politically prominent borrowers may fare better than one with a portfolio consisting only of small loans.

The third reason is that cheap loans tend to attract applicants who have the political status to exploit the windfall they offer. Over time, borrowers under subsidized programs tend to be better off than those for whom the funds were intended according to the initial justifications provided by program promotors. These three forces combine in case after case to concentrate the benefits of cheap credit following Claudio Gonzalez-Vega's "Iron Law of Interest Rate Restrictions."[22]

The costs of subsidized credit are hidden and diffused. If the government borrows abroad to fund the program, repayment in foreign

---

22. Claudio Gonzalez-Vega, "Credit-Rationing Behavior of Agricultural Lenders: The Iron Law of Interest-Rate Restrictions," in Dale W Adams, Douglas H. Graham and J.D. Von Pischke, eds., *op. cit.* pp. 78-95.

exchange will come from the country's reserves at some future date, depriving unseen others of the use of these reserves. If the program's operating and bad debt losses are carried by local financial intermediaries, they can cover their losses, in the long run, only by charging their other customers more, returning less to their shareholders, or by subsidy from the government. Subsidies are a cost to taxpayers or to money holders if the subsidy is financed through inflation.

In the short run an intermediary's bad debt losses can be hidden by artful accounting and nondisclosure. Financial institutions may be able to keep bad loans on their books for long periods without making provisions for losses or charging them off. This behavior by lenders often coincides with politicians' desire to paint a rosy picture. Both have an incentive to underestimate costs so that a credit program can continue without hard scrutiny especially if external assistance is available to support it.

Credit Programs as Tools of Political Power

The appeal of credit programs is illustrated by a real situation in one less-developed country in the mid-1980s. For a number of years the country's system of formal agricultural credit had operated under restrictive interest rate controls, suffered debilitating bad debt losses and was not dynamic. Cooperative credit arrangements languished, beset by poor earnings, organizational and implementational problems, and failed to attract widespread support from farmers, other depositors or from international donors. Donors supported several area-specific rural credit arrangements, but these did not appear to be promising candidates for replicability.

Commercial banks had made loans to large farmers, most of whom were also businessmen, civil servants, military officers or political leaders. The banks had not made many small loans to members of households whose income was derived primarily from agriculture, because they were not enthusiastic about further costly rural lending within the interest rate ceilings specified by the central bank.

To promote rural lending, the central bank imposed agricultural or rural lending quotas on the commercial banks. However, quotas could be met by placing special, noninterest bearing deposits with the central bank in lieu of agricultural lending. (This alternative, or of buying securities issued by a state-owned farm credit institution, is provided in several countries because small banks and foreign banks serving specialized "wholesale" financial markets in major cities cannot reasonably be expected to make rural "retail" loans.) This "penalty" was less costly than the risks of agricultural lending at controlled interest rates as perceived and experienced by the banks, and the banks made large special deposits.

With donor encouragement, foreign specialists were hired to assist the central bank in a review of the country's agricultural finance system. These specialists were experienced agricultural and nationalized commercial bankers from a developing country with a highly regimented farm credit system subject to detailed central bank control. They spent more than a year producing a lengthy report that contained an excellent description of the agricultural situation and of financial instutions and offered several good technical suggestions.

The thrust of the specialists' recommendations was essentially to copy their own country's system. The model was proposed uncritically, without acknowledging the shortcomings that were apparent from its operations in their homeland. The report made a case for agricultural credit at rates of interest similar to those offered borrowers in the commercial and industrial sectors, although experience in both countries had demonstrated that rural lending tends to be more costly than credit for urban trade and industry.

Their report was accepted in the same relatively uncritical manner in which it was proposed. It offered the central bank a system of comprehensive controls over rural finance, which would expand the central bank's authority and staff. At last the central bank would have the teeth to force commercial bankers to make agricultural loans, and it could prescribe exactly how this should be accomplished through quotas, instructions or guidelines, and reporting requirements. Banks that failed to meet their quotas would be deprived of a portion of their access to foreign exchange, a source of lucrative transactions.

The proposals had few attractions for the commercial banks. Commercial banks were considered by some central bankers, government officials, academicians and by many politicians to be at best indifferent to farmers and at worst unpatriotic corporate citizens. The banks, politically isolated, were not brought meaningfully into the process that led to the recommendations of the report. With their exclusion, the financial and administrative transaction costs and risks of the proposals were not well explored.

For large farmers the proposals offered prospects of a revival of the cheap credit machine that had concentrated its benefits in large loans. Wealthier farmers, many of them absentee operators, are likely to get most of the credit. They also face the least pressures for loan repayment because the report did not address in any depth changes that would provide incentives to improve repayment performance. Responding to the relatively low returns in agriculture that reflect government policies, many borrowers will take advantage of fungibility to obtain cheap farm credit for investment in nonagricultural activities. The result will undoubtedly be an accumulation of high-cost bad loans in the financial system.

Small farmers, who constitute a high proportion of the population, were accommodated politically by form supported by little substance. The proposals held out the prospect that some cheap credit might become available to small farmers, which was otherwise unlikely.

For others with easily identifiable interests, the proposals were also largely attractive. For local politicians they offered the promise of new money, more government activity, favors for friends, and opportunities to gain more control over the banks. Office holders could boast that their disappointment with rural lending by the banks and cooperatives resulted in concrete action by the government. For international donors the model provided a framework for assistance for institutional development and for augmenting the supply of loanable funds.

The model will probably perform poorly in the adopting country because corruption is greater than in its country of origin, while administrative capacities are less developed. Nevertheless, the model will probably be adopted because it is so attractive politically to those who stand to gain and is unlikely to be resisted by those who will bear the costs. Commercial banks that will bear these costs directly were isolated politically. The mass of the citizenry to whom the costs will be passed on are not organized to resist or to seek modifications in the model. They have little incentive to do so: the cost is not known, its per capita burden will not be felt in a readily identifiable form, it is unlikely to be inconveniently large, and will be spread over many years. The report's recommendations will probably dominate agricultural credit in the adopting country through the end of the century.

A more stunning and less subtle political use of credit were the loan *melas* held in India during the 1980s. The *melas* were followed with considerable interest by the Indian press, which noted that these meetings were often held in parts of the country that were not firmly in the camp of the party in power nationally (before the 1989 elections).[23] The *melas* were large, festive one-day gatherings staffed by volunteers from the national majority party and presided over by a high government official who disbursed loans to beneficiaries who were brought to the *mela* for that purpose. The funds were provided by nationalized banks, frequently over the objection of these banks' staff and officers who are reported to have had little or no discretion in the allocation of these funds. In one case loans were reportedly issued to 60,000 women at a single *mela*, and in another 10,000 people who actually repaid their loans were reportedly assembled and given small tokens of appreciation by the minister who sponsored the *melas*.

23. A collection of press clippings, official correspondence and other materials relating to these activities is found in "Loan Melas—for whose benefit?" Bangalore: Karnataka State Janata Party, n.d. [1987?].

Part II

The Conventional Assault
on the Frontier

Tremendous efforts have gone into forcing the frontier by providing credit through government programs, often supported by foreign assistance. The World Bank reports [1] that more than US$9.5 billion of its funds have been allocated to agricultural credit projects. The Bank has also provided funds for credit components in other types of agricultural projects. Its cumulative lending for industrial projects through development finance companies was US$19.2 billion. An additional US$4.9 billion has been committed to small-scale enterprise development, much of which is credit. Some of the Bank's urban development projects include credit for housing and for urban entrepreneurs.

The Bank's activities that facilitate the flow of funds to farmers, businesses and home buyers, plus those of the regional development banks and the bilateral aid programs of OECD countries, easily exceeded US$60 billion by 1990, as measured by conversion into U.S. currency at the time loans and grants were made. The volume of operations at the retail level supported by donors' funds over the last 30 years probably exceeds US$200 billion at the very least. This total includes developing country governments' contributions to credit activities assisted by donors and recycled aid funds.[2]

---

1. *The World Bank Annual Report 1989*, Washington, DC: 1989. pp. 176-177. The Bank ceased reporting cumulative sectoral totals in its 1990 Annual Report. One billion equals 1,000 million.

2. Recycling arises when long term development loans to governments or to financial institutions are used to fund shorter term loans to the ultimate beneficiaries of credit projects. A typical agricultural credit project provides "wholesale" funds to a farm credit agency that are repayable to the government or to the donor agency over 15 or more years. They support "retail" loans ("subloans") to farmers that are usually repayable to the farm credit agency in less than ten years. The funds repaid by farmers

This scale of activity invites review and examination. US$200 billion amounts to about 10 years' of World Bank Group lending at levels prevailing in the late 1980s. US$200 billion amounts to about US$55 for each citizen of developing countries. US$55 is about half the annual per capita income of the world's poorest countries.[3] The financial stakes of official credit projects and programs are high: lots of hope and energy are devoted to using credit as a leading strategy for development.

The basic assumptions that underlie these flows are those of development assistance generally, which are beyond the scope of this book. However, there are some crucial factors that determine whether credit projects and programs generate good loans. These issues are specific to the design and evaluation of credit projects, and are the subject of this part of the book.

Part II deals with the progression of problems that afflict conventional efforts to deliver credit at the frontier. These begin with the concepts and assumptions that frequently animate the desire to expand the frontier, and their common expression in terms of allocation criteria, beginning with the bad seed of credit need. Chapter 4 provides this introductory background. Chapter 5 discusses devices such as use of selective credit controls and establishment of specialized lenders that are frequently used to direct credit toward the frontier. The verdict is once again unfavorable: costly means are employed that are unlikely to be sustainable, and that in the long run may even produce results opposite to those originally intended.

Chapter 6 reviews the adverse effects of low interest rates and inattention to results. These are often associated with official efforts to expand the frontier, and they retard financial development. Chapter 7 wraps up this distressing progression by discussing some of the symptoms of the application of misguided concepts, of the use of inappropriate means of implementation, and of harmful policies and practices.

---

that are not immediately repaid to the donor can be used by the farm credit agency to lend to others.

3. Statistics taken from *The World Bank Atlas 1988* (Washington, DC: 1988).

In short, Part II finds that the conceptual framework upon which conventional projects and policies are based is grossly deficient from the perspective of financial development, and thereby tends to produce consistently unsatisfactory results.[4]

---

4. An official policy statement by major development assistance institutions in the Federal Republic of Germany should be consulted by readers who cling to the view that development finance projects generally perform well in rural areas. See R.H. Schmidt and Erhard Kropp, eds., *Rural Finance: Guiding Principles*. Eschborn: Bundesministerium für wirtschaftliche Zusammenarbeit (Federal Ministry for Economic Cooperation), Deutsche Gesellschaft für Technische Zusammenarbeit (GTZ—German Agency for Technical Cooperation), Deutsche Stiftung für internationale Entwicklung (DSE—German Foundation for International Development), 1987. pp. 18 ff, 76 ff.

4

CREDIT NEEDS AND RELATED ALLOCATION CRITERIA

This chapter critically examines the conceptual basis of many credit projects and of related policies. These are a coherent and easy target because a set of common factors motivates virtually all official efforts to provide credit to farmers, businesses, cooperative members, other individuals, and for "priority" sectors of the economy. Common features include meeting credit need and credit demand, and removing credit constraints. Need, demand, and constraints are terms that are often used together or interchangeably. Analytical approaches used to address them are similar.

Meeting credit needs or credit demand, or easing credit constraints of a strategic sector or a target group, are frequently mentioned in documents used to solicit support for projects offering credit. Project identification and preparation, the first stages in the project cycle,[5] often include projections of credit need or credit demand. Credit need, credit demand, and credit constraints combine as a broad criterion for providing funds for credit programs, for credit allocation and for government intervention in finance.

Procedures used to allocate credit critically affect the performance of credit programs. Because of the large volume of assistance devoted to credit, and because of the vast potential for the more effective use of human, financial and other resources in low-income countries, credit allocation strategies and criteria deserve careful examination. Credit need, the most frequently cited member of the set, is the most obvious starting point for inquiry. The development test used in this chapter is simple: Does

---

5. Warren C. Baum, "The Project Cycle," *Finance and Development.* January 1978; expanded and published as "The Project Cycle," Washington D.C.: The World Bank, 1982.

concern for credit need contribute to good loans and the remunerative use of credit?

The following review of credit need begins at the general level, which deals with the rhetoric of development. Subsequent sections discuss efforts to define and quantify credit need, explore related concepts such as credit demand and constraints, and question the relevance of financing gaps.

Basic Weaknesses of the Credit Need Criterion

The fundamental problem with credit need is that need, as the word is commonly used, has so little to do with finance or with a financial view of human activity. Common usage is the appropriate standard for evaluation because credit need has no rigorous technical definition or implication that transcends common meanings of "need." Need implies something absolute, like the necessities for survival. As an absolute, need ignores the subtleties of risk and confidence and denies the possibility that there may be alternative ways to achieve development objectives. When these dimensions are considered, it is clear that equating credit with need easily overstates the role of credit.

Credit Need: The Conman's Pitch

If credit is considered a basic necessity for survival or a critical missing link in processes that ought to produce growth, an attitude is cultivated that does not assist the search for good loans or for efficient measures capable of stimulating development. Those giving "needed" credit may be shielded from hard scrutiny. Project designers may portray their efforts as good works, providing something so clearly valuable that close examination is not helpful or necessary, or as offering something without which other activities expected to have high returns cannot be undertaken.

Emphasis on credit need may also lead to efforts to discredit those who question the concept. At the extreme, skeptics may be portrayed as having no understanding of the problems of the poor, as unsympathetic to their condition, as ignorant of the dynamics of progress, and as generally incompetent to participate in the dialogue of development. Long before the plunge to this level it is useful to refocus the debate on the central issue, which is how to make good loans.

Behind these absolutist defenses, credit need easily becomes a self-serving concept employed by those providing credit, and equally important politically, by those applying for credit. Clearly, not all credit projects, designers and loan applicants seek such protection. However, belief in credit need may increase the possibility of misrepresentation and of efforts to deflect examination. This poses a risk to all parties to credit projects, and should be taken seriously because the problem goes beyond being merely a question of terminology.

The assumption behind credit need is that without credit very little happens: the technology or behavior desired by development planners or project designers would not be adopted by the target group of project beneficiaries. However, evidence from a number of countries suggests that, even without institutional credit, significant advances occur. Examples include expansion of informal credit in the Philippines in response to new investment opportunities in the Green Revolution,[6] the tremendous popularity of savings clubs to facilitate fertilizer purchase by the rural poor in Zimbabwe,[7] and experience with small business development in Colombia.[8] Circumstantial evidence consists of the tremendous progress made in developing country agriculture over the last 25 years, while far fewer than a third of rural households receive official credit. Is it reasonable to assume that these households alone are responsible for all of the progress?

However helpful it may be, credit is not an essential component of development. From the perspective afforded by this realization, the test of a proposed innovation is its rate of adoption under a project promoting its use *without* credit. Very few project designers put their technical

---

6. Orlando J. Sacay, Meliza H. Agabin, and Chita Irene E. Tanchoco, *Small Farmer Credit Dilemma* (Manila: Technical Board for Agricultural Credit, 1985). See especially Chapter 8; Presidential Committee on Agricultural Credit, *A Study on the Informal Rural Financial Markets in Three Selected Provinces of the Philippines* (Manila: 1981).

7. C.J. Howse, "Agricultural Development without Credit," in J.D. Von Pischke, Dale W Adams and Gordon Donald, eds., *op. cit.* pp. 134-137; J.D. Von Pischke and John Rouse, "Selected Successful Experiences with Agricultural Credit and Rural Finance in Africa," *Savings and Development.* VII, 1, 1983. pp. 21-44; Hans Mittendorf, "Savings Mobilization for Agricultural and Rural Development in Africa," in Denis Kessler and Pierre-Antoine Ullmo, eds., *op. cit.* pp. 223-224; Michael Behr, "The Savings Development Movement in Zimbabwe," in Guy Bédard, Gerd Günter Klöwer, and Martin Harder, eds., *op. cit.* Vol. II, pp. 91-112.

8. Jaime Carvajal, "Microenterprise and Urban Development." Speech delivered at the Pan American Economic Leadership Conference, Indianapolis, June 1987. (Bogota): The Carvajal Foundation.

recommendations to this test. This suggests that credit could be used as a response to gaps in project designers' knowledge of the environments they hope to alter or create with new technology. These gaps may be disguised by the assertion that lack of credit is all that hinders progress.

Credit Need Defies Analysis

Credit need fails analytically. Economics, for example, deals with the impact of investment, not need. Financial analysis can justify an investment, identify its optimal size, and find the best means of funding it. Successful financing plans ensure that funds are available at the best trade-off between cost and other terms, and that repayment capacity exists to service the debt incurred. These professional tools cannot adequately address need, which appears to be a much broader or less well defined view of investment that is not directed toward the capacity to service debt. Credit specialists who work with farmers or businesses to select investment opportunities and provide funds for expansion or for adoption of new technologies are not prepared professionally to quantify need. Their task is to quantify what loan applicants can manage and afford.

Credit need is a dangerous concept because it diverts attention to something that is conceptually ambiguous, that defies professional quantification. Government strategies based on satisfying credit needs, if vigorously pursued, destroy the financial institutions upon which the burden of lending is placed. This occurs because credit needs are elastic. Credit needs tend to exceed the quantity of funds that can be prudently loaned to those considered in need of credit. This occurs because political objectives are not necessarily related to financial capacities.

Definitions of Credit Need

What are credit needs and how are they quantified? A comprehensive statement of credit need lending strategy is given in the *All-India Rural Credit Survey*,[9] the results of which were published in the 1950s. This survey was probably the biggest one-shot effort to examine rural credit use. It provided the basis for construction of one of the world's largest

---

9. *All-India Rural Credit Survey.* "Credit Requirements and Creditworthiness," Chapter 16, Vol. I, *The Survey Report, Part 1, (Rural Families).* (Bombay: Reserve Bank of India, 1956). (See pp. 951-957, 974, 1013).

rural credit systems.[10] More than any other event, the survey marks the start of the modern era of government attempts to use credit on a broad scale for purposes regarded as developmental. Along with the European cooperative model and the US Farmers Home Administration model, the Indian rural credit system, at least at one time, inspired credit project designers around the world.

The Survey report defines credit needs variously as:

- The amount of credit a rural family actually obtains.
- The amount of credit a rural family wants to obtain for either
  - proper and legitimate productive purposes that would be economic and enable loans to be self-liquidating, or
  - activities that are not directly productive, such as family consumption. In the latter case, need could be inferred with reference to the maintenance of some accepted or acceptable standard of living and to the ability of the family to repay without sacrificing such a standard of living.
- Funds requested in addition to loans actually obtained that, to be provided, would require changes in prevailing lending terms and conditions (interest, tenor,[11] security, etc.) to permit profitable use by borrowers.
- Arising from "standards of performance and efficiency in production or of living in consumption," related to input requirements for crops and the optimum use of land, or to some minimum acceptable standard of living. This requirement could be demonstrated by differences in husbandry practices and living conditions between strata of society obtaining credit and those not obtaining credit.
- The additional credit that could be supplied by a reorganized or ideal credit system offering terms and conditions different from those presently available, in the form of a demand schedule for credit for productive uses.
- Changes in investment or differences in levels of investment associated with variables other than the size of farming activities; that is, investment used for purposes other than the purchase of land.

---

10. Daniel and Alice Thorner, *Land and Labour in India* (New York: Asia Publishing House, 1962) (see especially chapters XIV and XV).

11. "Tenor" is a technical word meaning the term of a loan, that is, the time between its availability to the borrower and its scheduled repayment to the lender.

- Credit required for the purchase of land.
- Credit use related to actual expenditures by cultivators, or to some fraction or possibly multiple of actual expenditures.
- The reported requirements of cultivators for specific purposes.
- Comparison "between relative importance of an (expenditure) item in the total reported credit requirements and the relative importance of the expenditure on that item in the actual total expenditure incurred on all items under consideration" for a surveyed household and period.
- Indicators of "real efforts that might be made if the reported credit requirements or parts of them could be met on terms that are reasonable, though not necessarily as low as the cultivator reported in reply to the questionnaire used to obtain estimates of credit needs."

These definitions include references to levels of production, administratively-determined standard of living targets, and the amount of credit requested or provided or that might be available under ideal conditions. Concern for repayment is not a prominent feature. The promotors of a credit project can define need as they choose and proceed to meet the need they claim they have identified. False confidence or simplistic approaches based on credit need lead to systems of credit allocation that operate with little meaningful quantification, slight regard for risk and confidence, and lagging loan collections.

The application of definitions of the type presented in the *All-India Rural Credit Survey* is attempted at two levels by government agencies and international assistance organizations. The first derives credit need for a sector of the economy or a specific geographical area where a project or a banking office could be located. The second calculates the credit need of a loan applicant. Each is discussed below.

Quantifying Sector or Area Credit Needs

Quantification of credit needs is generally undertaken in sector or area studies in one of three ways. The first derives credit need from sectoral or area financial flows summarized in input-output tables, the second relates credit need to projected incremental output, and the third infers credit need from a sector's contribution to the economy.

The Input-Output Method

Input-output matrices summarize transactions among all sectors of an economy and have been used to calculate a sector's credit needs. The purchases of a sector from other sectors are aggregated, and that sum or some portion of that sum is defined as the sector's credit need. In one analysis prepared from the most recently available input-output table for a country, agricultural credit need was assumed to equal the amount of agricultural sector purchases from other sectors. These purchases include farm machinery and equipment from the industrial and import (rest of world) sectors, fuel from the energy and import sectors, and haulage from the transport sector, for example.

The credit need calculated in this analysis was larger than the amount of formal credit classified by the central bank as loaned to agriculture. The country did not have a large informal financial market, and the amount of informal credit that was devoted to agriculture was probably small. As the input-output table summarized transactions that had already occurred, it was clear that the "need" identified by this exercise was not critical to achieving the flows that were recorded.

If input-output matrices were projected for future years, would the entire expected increase in purchases by one sector from other sectors, and even from itself (e.g., farmers' purchases of seeds from other growers), have to be financed by credit in order for these transactions to occur? This is a more useful question because it attempts to identify constraints to growth. The question cannot be answered from input-output data, however, because these do not specify how transactions are financed.

Small-farm credit offers the best illustration of problems in identifying credit needs because the access of agriculture to institutional credit is generally limited—self-finance predominates on agriculture's balance sheet in market economies, especially for small farms.[12] Many current transactions are financed from farmers' own funds, and these renewable flows normally continue to be available for transactions that would enable their owners to pursue their livelihoods. As private financial flows, they

---

12. Organisation for Economic Cooperation and Development, *Capital and Finance in Agriculture.* Vol. I, *General Report.* (Paris: OECD, 1970); Doreen Warriner, *Economics of Peasant Farming.* 2nd ed. (London: Frank Cass & Co., 1964); US data are available in *Agricultural Finance Outlook and Situation*, published periodically by the Economic Research Service of the Department of Agriculture.

should generally reproduce themselves with a surplus and continue to respond to attractive investment opportunities. Therefore, only some undefinable fraction of the entire projected annual increase in transactions would presumably be dependent upon an increase in the supply of credit.

The Incremental Output Approach

The key assumption of the incremental output approach is that credit is required to support growth in the same proportion that it is used to fund present levels of activity. Calculation begins with the amount of credit disbursed during a recent period for the sector or area being studied. This amount is multiplied by the quantity one plus a projected percentage increase in the sector's output. The percentage selected depends upon the user. It may be a target growth rate assigned the sector by planners, or a projection of what is considered likely to occur by a forecaster or project designer. Credit need is defined as the difference between the amount of credit disbursed during the recent period and that derived for a future period from the calculation.

The incremental output approach fails to go beyond the mathematical relationship between output and credit. It does not deal with the substance of transactions or of the financial calculation it attempts to influence. It does not provide an indication of the quality of the credit in use or expected to be used. For example, long-run bad debt losses and administrative costs that exceed lenders' spreads suggest that lending cannot be sustained without changes in the credit system. Yet, the incremental output approach would still indicate that more credit should be issued, regardless of the condition of the credit system or of borrowers' incentives to repay loans.

This approach assumes that all credit is homogeneous. Short-term loans and longer term loans, for example, are mixed together as credit disbursed, yet their implications for the growth of output during any given forecasting horizon are greatly different. Short-term loans may assist farmers from one harvest to the next using existing technology, while longer term loans may assist technological transformation and greatly change the relative proportions of land, labor, and capital used by the borrower. Examples include agricultural mechanization and irrigation.

A more serious problem arises when this method is used to identify credit need for sectors that are favored by the government. Credit issued to these sectors tends to be subject to quotas and targets. These controls or guidelines distort reporting by lenders, giving them an incentive to designate as much lending as possible as contributing to the target or quota. Because favored sectors tend to receive loans on soft terms, borrowers also have an incentive to apply for these loans whenever they find a remunerative use for borrowed funds, regardless of whether these uses are those for which the loans are intended. Fungibility destroys the neat compartments that are suggested by quotas and targets.

A creative variant of the incremental output approach found in one project used surveys to quantify borrowing by different types of farmers in the proposed project area. Credit need was defined as the amount of credit that would be used by poor farmers when their incomes rose, under the project, to the level used by representative richer farmers with the same endowments of land and labor at the time of the survey. Capital-output ratios could be misused in a similar manner.

The Proportional Output Approach

The proportional output approach derives credit need from a sector's contribution to the economy. The size of the economy is customarily measured by gross domestic product (GDP). A proportional output ratio is then calculated using GDP as the denominator, while the output of the sector, the value added to the economy by the sector, is used as the numerator. The total amount of credit outstanding is then multiplied by this ratio to quantify the sector's credit need, that is, the amount of credit that ought to be flowing to the sector.[13] Unlike the input-output and incremental output approaches, this measure is generally used to indicate insufficient credit, rather than as a tool for defining an exact amount of credit that ought to be made available. The reason for this conservatism is not clear.

The major shortcoming of the proportional output approach is that it ignores risk. While some industries attract credit relatively easily, others do so with difficulty, as was noted in chapter 2. Those that receive relatively little credit, such as agriculture and small scale industry, are the ones for

---

13. The amount of credit disbursed during a given period may be used instead of the amount of credit outstanding, but the outstanding amount is usually more easily obtainable and more accurate than data on amounts disbursed. This is because commercial lenders measure their risk and project their income from amounts outstanding.

which special credit programs are often designed. Hence, project designers in these sectors can generally use proportional output comparisons to imply that the sector the project is supposed to benefit appears to be tremendously short of credit. This comparison is especially striking, but still irrelevant, in the poorest countries that have relatively large agricultural sectors. Conspiracy theories citing lazy, uncomprehending or unpatriotic lenders, and allegations of "market failure" (an economic term suggesting a sub-optimal market equilibrium) may be offered or inferred.

The reasons why a sector has difficulty attracting credit do not have to be dealt with when this measure is used to advocate credit—the figures speak for themselves. Or, do they? The reasons for different levels of credit use generally revolve around risk. While credit outstanding for agriculture typically equals less than 20 percent of agricultural assets, for example, the liabilities of commercial banks (credit they obtain in the form of deposits and by going into debt in other ways) often exceed 90 percent of their total assets. Agriculture is very risky, while deposits in commercial banks are often insured or backed by government.

Agricultural lenders' bad debt losses may be relatively large even when agriculture has a debt-to-assets ratio of 20 percent, as was the case in the United States in the mid-1980s. However, the proportional output comparison suggests that more lending is in order because agriculture has such a small share of the national credit pie.

Quantifying a Loan Applicant's Credit Need

In projects, identification of an individual loan applicant's credit need typically is based on incremental input or investment. In project design, technical, marketing, and other key variables are examined through feasibility studies, field trials, and review of successful experience elsewhere. These data provide the basis for recommending innovations on the farm or by the firm, or investment to expand operations with familiar technology. A survey of facilities for grinding grain into flour, for example, may suggest that additional rice or posho mills could operate viably in a rural area. This determination would be based on consumption and marketing studies to determine demand, and on the quantity of land devoted to grain production, crop yields, consumption of grain by farm animals, storage losses, location and capacity of existing mills, transport costs, and similar factors to determine supply. From this data a program could be designed to support the development of additional mills through credit and technical assistance.

This sort of data is used to try to ensure that project funds invested could earn a satisfactory return. However, data on technical feasibility, marketing and other non-financial essentials for success are not sufficient for credit project design because they do not indicate whether good loans could be made. The difference between good investments and good loans arises from a number of factors. Some of the more obvious include the following: Do the design data include allowances for risk? Would loan applicants have sufficient equity capital to permit appropriate financing? Would prospective borrowers possess sufficient managerial capacity to obtain the returns envisaged? Would the lender be skillful enough to identify competent borrowers and to obtain timely loan repayment? Could the lender charge a spread high enough to cover costs?

Flows Before and After Financing

Agricultural project analysis uses farm budgets to formalize technical and financial feasibility information and to project the incremental costs and benefits of the proposed innovation.[14] Cost and benefit streams are typically derived "before financing" and "after financing." The before-financing budget shows projected flows from the activity being promoted by the project. The after-financing portion of the budget shows the financing that would be necessary to support the activity initially and the surplus expected from implementation. The financing portion of the budget usually contains relatively large amounts of credit to fund the project-induced investment.

A highly simplified example of a farm budget is contained in Table 4.1. It shows that with the project the farmer's seasonal input purchases jump by $800 from $200 to $1000. This investment in seeds, fertilizers and insecticides doubles the volume of production, from 5 tons to 10 tons, which increases the net benefit before financing from $1,000 to $2,200.

---

14. Farm budgets are described in J. Price Gittinger, *Economic Analysis of Agricultural Projects.* 2nd ed. (Baltimore and London: The Johns Hopkins University Press, 1982); in Maxwell Brown, *Farm Budgets: From Farm Income Analysis to Agricultural Project Analysis* (Baltimore and London: The Johns Hopkins University Press, 1979); and in Walter Schaefer-Kehnert, "Methodology of Farm Investment Analysis." Course Note 030/031 Rev. Dec. 1981. Economic Development Institute of the World Bank, Washington, DC.

This is all made possible, according to the credit need approach, by a loan of $800, which funds all of the incremental input purchases.

Table 4.1 Hypothetical Farm Budget

	Without Project	With Project	Calculation
Produce (tons)	5	10	+
Produce consumed on the farm (tons)	2	2	-
Marketed produce (tons)	3	8	=
Farmgate price per ton ($)	400	400	x
Total farm cash receipts ($)	1,200	3,200	=
Purchased inputs ($)	200	1,000	-
Net benefit before financing[a] ($)	1,000	2,200	=
Loan receipts ($)	–	800	+
Debt service ($)[including a 20% interest charge]	–	960	-
Net benefit after financing[a] ($)	1,000	2,040	=

a "Before financing" refers to the costs and benefits directly related to production. "After financing" includes these costs and benefits and also loan receipts and debt servicing.

The majority of farm credit projects deliver medium- or long-term loans for investments in capital goods. In the more elaborate budgets prepared for these operations a relatively large initial investment cost results in a negative net benefit before financing in the first (or early) years of implementation. This is offset by a term loan, which is repaid from the positive flow of funds in later years.

Basing Loan Sizes on Investment Costs

The design of credit arrangements for project beneficiaries usually starts with the costs of the investment. In the typical case this is measured by the negative funds flow in the initial year or period of the before-financing portion of the budget. Here, project designers usually define credit need arbitrarily as a relatively high percentage of initial costs—hopefully only the cash costs and not the noncash contributions or "sweat equity" of farm family labor unless these would otherwise not be forthcoming. Popular figures used to identify credit need based on cost estimates are 75, 80, 90 and 100 percent of estimated incremental costs. Table 4.1 conforms to this convention, showing a loan of $800 to cover incremental input purchases of $800.

The procedure for determining credit needs of commercial and industrial activities is similar to that used for agricultural projects. Investment cost tables quantify credit need, although more sophisticated analysis uses traditional financial statements (balance sheets, income statements, and sources and uses of funds statements) because these identify flows that are not obvious from cost tables and more effectively communicate financial performance and condition.

Problems of Financing High Proportions of Investment Costs with Debt

Relating credit needs to costs is systematic, but the underlying assumption that most investment costs must be funded by debt bears examination. The conclusion that little equity investment will be forthcoming from the borrower or beneficiary is usually based on the observation that at relatively low levels of economic activity there is little surplus. And, where markets facing small firms are highly competitive, there is also little surplus. However, the surplus produced by an activity and the liquidity that supports the activity are not the same. Although money income not immediately spent is both liquid and "saved," surplus and liquidity are not necessarily closely related.[15]

Low levels of surplus do not necessarily accompany low levels of liquidity. Because of risk and the lack of convenient access to formal financial institutions, large amounts of cash are often held in the countryside. Evidence for this includes the success of efforts to mobilize rural savings, the liquidity of rural bank branches, and the amounts of currency redeemed in rural centers when a currency issue is demonetized and replaced by another.

---

15. J.D. Von Pischke, "Toward an Operational Approach to Savings for Rural Developers," in J.D. Von Pischke, Dale W Adams and Gordon Donald, eds., *op. cit.* pp, 414-420.

The way an investment is financed affects the owner's commitment to ensuring its success.[16] Defining credit needs as a high proportion of investment costs leads to high proportions of debt financing. High debt service burdens result, and debtors may conclude that they are working for their creditor rather than for themselves. This realization weakens the incentive to ensure the success of the investment, and to repay the loan.[17] This is most likely to occur when the borrower encounters difficulties that diminish cash flow—precisely the time that extraordinary efforts are required to overcome problems. As Shakespeare tells us through Polonius, "Borrowing dulls the edge of husbandry." Thanks to legal and financial innovations since the 17th century, recent experience demonstrates that only excessive borrowing does so.

Another faulty assumption is that the most satisfactory method for determining the size of a loan is in relation to investment cost. While there may be no reason for a loan to exceed cost, using cost alone as the major determinant of loan size poses dangers. This is because cost has little to do with the prospects for loan repayment. Future cash flows, not original cost, are the source of loan repayment. Future cash flows are obviously uncertain, and the common flaw in relating loan size to investment cost is that it ignores risk. In agriculture, the most risky of all major industries, this oversight has overwhelmingly important implications. These extend to other rural economic activities that depend on agricultural incomes.

Need is a bankrupt approach to credit allocation because its definition and quantification do not address the core developmental issues of finance. These issues, explored in earlier chapters, are the determinants of value, risk, and confidence. They come together in the basic credit question of how to make good loans that are remunerative to lenders. Similar problems arise when loans are allocated in response to credit constraints, credit demand, and financing gaps.

Credit Constraints Are Ambiguous

Analysis based on credit need deals unsuccessfully with a problem that is also reflected in concern for financial constraints. In a general sense,

---

16. Louis L. Allen, *Starting and Succeeding in Your Own Small Business,* (New York: Grosset and Dunlap, 1968).

17. Stiglitz and Weiss, *op. cit.,* provide an economic analysis of this type of behavior.

finance is a universal constraint. By definition finance is scarce, and scarcity gives it value. The point of interest to developers is that finance may be a binding constraint that discourages the behavior they wish to promote. Finance is a binding constraint when all other ingredients for successful investment are present except finance, and when they can be activated by finance.

Finance is often cited as a missing link or described as a catalyst for development. Portrayal of finance as a missing link is abstract and may represent a special case. While finance is a catalyst for development, it is also a catalyst for poor investment, political patronage, corruption, and other types of opportunism. A more plausible interpretation is that finance is one of a limited and identifiable set of constraints that can be supplied simultaneously through a project expected to create a surplus in a way that is consistent with government priorities, social considerations, and voluntary participation. Shortage of finance, specifically credit, is a virtually universal assumption underlying credit projects and components, and is often cited in documents soliciting support for projects. A publication of the International Fund for Agricultural Development (IFAD), for example, notes that credit is considered an important part of many projects: "...the obvious assumption is that the credit-supported components are important for the success of the project and that credit is vital to implement these components."[18]

In spite of the considerable volume of funds provided to ease financial constraints, no rigorous methodology has evolved to quantify the extent or demonstrate the nature of financial constraints in the economy at the frontier. Estimates of financial constraints are generally derived using the incremental input approach, assuming a low level of equity contribution by the borrower.

Binding financial constraints are not necessarily antidevelopmental. If they stand in the way of bad investment, they are socially beneficial. Some loans do not result in positive returns, some attempts at innovation fail, and some projects have to be reoriented to achieve disbursement targets. Efforts to remove these constraints will result only in losses if they do not contain systems for discriminating against proposals likely to lead to bad

---

18. International Fund for Agricultural Development, *The Role of Rural Credit Projects in Reaching the Poor.* IFAD Special Studies Series, Vol. 1. (Oxford: Tycooly Publishing, 1985). p. 17.

investments and bad loans. For the financial system to make good loans and allocate funds for high-return investments, it must reject poor proposals, unfit applicants, and low-return investments.

Investment Patterns and the Role of Credit

A useful perspective on constraints is provided from observation of how development generally occurs in the frontier economy: progress customarily results from small, incremental actions over time rather than through a "big push." An incremental approach permits the investor's management skills, risk-bearing capacity, and organizational efforts to inch forward along with the investor's financial situation. This process deals with shifting constraints and requires creative responses to keep progress in balance. Success is not the result of a single transaction, but of a continuing activity.

One of the difficulties facing developers is that there is no typology or model that indicates the relative importance of credit in removing constraints. There is little interpretation of experience that identifies the strengths and weaknesses of the incremental and of the "big push" strategies in different situations. The absence of these data or lessons may stem, in part, from the belief that credit is always essential, or that supplying it is so greatly superior to other alternatives that these alternatives hardly merit investigation.

Where could construction of a model or typology of credit constraints begin? For industrial loans, the relative size and indivisibility of proposed investments probably offers a good starting point. Economies of scale may require investments of a certain magnitude that may be considerably beyond the present financing capacity of prospective investors. This would make credit relatively important, while also making investment risk high if the prospective investors lack experience in managing operations of the scale and complexity implied by the size of the investment. In commerce at the frontier, credit constraints may be less important once a size of operation is reached that provides the merchant a reasonable living. Expansion through stocking more lines and a deeper inventory probably can be undertaken incrementally, and facilities may be rented rather than purchased where finance is scarce.

In agriculture it appears that finance could be a serious constraint to farmers with the arrival of major irrigation following the construction of a large dam. Farmers in newly irrigated areas face new, greatly expanded production possibilities almost overnight. Accumulations from their previous activities are probably insufficient to finance the additional inputs required to produce output sufficient to justify the investment made in major irrigation works. While over time farmers would no doubt respond to the new opportunities, enabling capable, trustworthy operators to do so quickly through credit provision would seem to be relatively attractive.

In each of these hypothetical industrial, commercial and agricultural situations, though, attractive prospects for the use of funds do not justify credit programs. Technical feasibility, marketing and other nonfinancial essentials help ensure that funds invested could earn a satisfactory return, but are not sufficient for credit project design because they do not address risk and confidence, and therefore cannot indicate whether good loans could be made.

Many Agricultural Innovations Are Not Capital-Intensive

In contrast to the financial situation created by the arrival of major irrigation, incremental changes in husbandry practices for annual crops have relatively small financial implications. For example, substantial gains in crop yields are often achievable through changes in husbandry practices, such as date of sowing, plant spacing, or soil preparation that require no purchased inputs. Other types of investment, such as fences constructed from local materials available on the farm or from commons near the farm, use family labor during slack periods in the agricultural production cycle and do not require cash.

Adoption of improved seeds and fertilizers also often occurs in small steps. While improved inputs may be the key to production increases, risk tempers the pace of their adoption. Most farmers at the frontier experiment on a modest scale. Their experiments may occur over several seasons, or until a relatively poor crop year provides the information they seek concerning risk, which is reflected in the performance of the innovation in unfavorable circumstances. This strategy gives farmers time to rearrange their affairs, and diminishes the importance of credit to their ability or willingness to innovate. Gains from small changes may finance investment in larger changes, or off-farm activities may be relied upon to provide funds for an investment.

Even for relatively large, indivisible investments such as cattle, lack of finance is not necessarily an important constraint and credit may not be an appropriate means of promoting the adoption of improved breeds. In Kenya, for example, small farmers exhibited great interest in grade cattle in the late 1960s and 1970s. Most farmers buying improved dairy stock used their own savings. However, some farmers obtained loans from official sources under donor-supported projects. About 20 percent of the animals transferred with project loans died from disease and other causes. In many instances animals obtained on credit failed to produce sufficient cash flow to meet loan installments. A number of borrowers abandoned dairying and either failed to repay their loans or repaid from other sources of income.

Other farmers who did not purchase grade cattle also adopted dairying as a cash crop, but over a much longer period using artificial insemination (AI) to upgrade their small, unimproved herds. AI herds are slow to develop because calvings occur once a year, half of the calves are males and have little economic value, and some AI heifers die before breeding.

A typical progression, starting from a one-cow herd owned by a frontier farmer, would start with several inseminations a month or two apart. Several are often required because the farmer may not be able to tell precisely when the cow can be bred, and the inseminator may not be sufficiently skilled to ensure fertilization. Nine months later an improved cross-bred heifer is born, but dies within a few months because the farmer is not experienced in controlling the diseases that affect improved breeds. The unimproved cow continues to produce a little milk for nine months after giving birth. Then insemination is tried again, and about two years after the first AI calving a second AI calf is born. This is a bull calf, and is of little value for herd build-up or for sale. A year later a heifer AI calf is born. Only when that heifer calves, about 30 months after its birth, is there an enhanced supply of milk reflecting the superior characteristics of improved breeding.

This example shows that it may take five years to achieve through AI what can be achieved in a matter of weeks or months with a loan used to buy improved in-calf heifers.[19] However, adoption through AI subjects farmers to relatively small increments of risk and has no massive financial

19. The process may be accelerated by purchase of a second local breed heifer for AI breeding.

implications for farmers or farm credit systems. In addition, AI can be made available to every household with a cow, an old person or child who can take the cow to the insemination center or to a stop along the inseminator's daily route, and a small amount of cash for the insemination. To generate good loans, by contrast, requires a highly selective screening of applicants. Procedures used to encourage applicants also tend to be selective.

The logistics of providing an effective AI delivery system including semen supply and storage, inseminator training, and transport or positioning of staff, are not necessarily simple. But they are eminently susceptible to measurement and management, permitting mastery in less time than that required to construct an effective credit system.

Credit Constraints Summary

To summarize, there is no rigorous means of identifying or quantifying credit constraints on the small farm or in the small firm where the activities of the owner or household are mixed with the commercial aspects of the operation. Farm budgets and investment cost tables fail to quantify liquidity before the loan, and loan applicants may be reluctant to divulge this information. There is also no accurate way to identify the entrepreneurial responses that target groups of beneficiaries might undertake, in the absence of a loan, to gain access to improved technologies. There is not even a typology capable of yielding qualitative indications of the extent to which credit is useful or appropriate for typical investment situations. The widespread existence of binding financial constraints to sustainable innovation remains an intuitively appealing but empirically unverified possibility. When the possibility is invoked to obtain support for a credit scheme, skepticism is the sage and prudent response.

Credit Demand

Credit demand is also a deficient concept for credit project design. In economic theory, credit demand is equated with credit supply at the market-clearing rate of interest. However, credit demand is not homogeneous or transparent, but consists of true demand and false demand.[20] True demand is the sum of loan applications backed by bankable projects. Important characteristics of bankable projects are generally an experienced entrepreneur as a borrower, a liquidity cushion in the form of equity financing that protects the interest of the lender, projected cash flow that will cover reasonably expected claims in a timely manner, a loan purpose related to a technology and an activity, commodity or industry that is likely to perform satisfactorily, and measures to contain the effects of the risks that are most threatening to the success of the project.

False demand is the difference between applications for bankable projects and total loan applications received. False demand consists of proposals for unbankable investments. Unbankable investments may be bad investments that are not remunerative. They may be good investments that are poorly structured financially, so that creditors would profit while suppliers of equity lose, or vice versa. They may also be good investments backed by investors who are inexperienced or not regarded as dependable by lenders.

An important role of development lenders is to separate good proposals from bad. The concept of credit demand is difficult to apply where developmental experimentation at the frontier requires exploration of many doubtful investment proposals. Separating the good from the bad is difficult at the frontier because of risk and other information problems. Areas beyond the frontier are uncharted waters for those within it. Information-gathering requires transaction costs and bad debt losses from experimental lending.

A special problem besets state-owned lenders established to promote investment at the frontier. They find it difficult to be objective in rejecting bad proposals because of the expectations and pressures to lend created by the nature of their ownership.[21] Their objectivity may be further compromised if external funding agencies' enthusiasm for disbursement crowds out prudent credit decisionmaking.

---

20. Sayre P. Schatz, "Government Lending to African Businessmen: Inept Incentive," *Journal of Modern African Studies.* 6, 4, December 1968, pp. 519-529; *Economics, Politics and Administration in Government Lending: The Regional Loans Boards of Nigeria* (Ibadan: Oxford University Press, 1970).

21. Jean Causse, "Necessity of and Constraints on the Use of Savings in the Community in which they are Collected," in Denis Kessler and Pierre-Antoine Ullmo, eds., *op. cit.* pp. 168-169.

Credit demand is distorted by cheap credit policies. Credit demand is theoretically infinite when credit carries a negative real rate of interest. This occurs when the rate of inflation is higher than the interest rate, which is frequently the case for credit issued by official lenders to favored sectors and when rates of inflation are high.[22] The theoretical possibility of infinite demand is not realized because transaction costs are imposed by lenders on loan applicants seeking negatively priced funds. However, the prospect of cheap funds creates an incentive to generate false demand. Applicants who can minimize transaction costs by virtue of the size of their resources or through political influence see a special opportunity in cheap credit. Their applications may not represent the best investment opportunities in a sector or the best structured proposals, and their status may discourage objective decisionmaking by lenders.

Positive real interest rates give borrowers an incentive to be efficient; negative rates do not. Incentive comes in part from risk that is reduced when a portion of the loan is in effect a grant created by a decrease in the value of money used to repay the loan. This effect increases false demand: investments that might be successful when incentives are in place may be unsuccessful in their absence.

Economists' models of loan demand often exclude transaction costs while assuming that markets are perfectly competitive in the economic sense, so that every participant could lend or borrow any amount at the same rate. In this theoretical framework there is no financial constraint, which would be unusual in any financial market. Assuming away transaction costs also assumes away the institutions that facilitate transactions in these markets. Risk is also often assumed away, ignoring the major characteristic of finance. In economic terms, risk (uncertainty) means that financial capital has more than one price and that product differentiation based on information is common and rational. These problems make credit demand difficult to analyze, except possibly in planned economies where "credit demand" is determined and administered centrally through formulas and planning criteria.

---

22. Inter-American Development Bank, "Summary of the Evaluation of Global Agricultural Credit Programs," GN-1493. Washington, DC: February 1984. pp. 8, 11, 21 and 23.

Filling Financing Gaps

Financing gaps are the volume of funds a borrower seeks from sources other than those that are already available. Financing gaps, also called resource gaps, are cousins of credit needs. They are the product of a planning and budgeting approach that is legitimate for those owning or operating an enterprise or activity. Firms require resources for the realization of their objectives. Resources are by definition limited, and a function of management is to push back these limits to improve the firm's performance. Targets are set to focus organizational energy, expressed in budgets or projections of funds required for fulfillment of a plan.

Quantifying and filling resource gaps are part of fund-raising strategies. But they are not adequate for formulating viable lending strategies because debt is only one element of finance, and because the position of the lender is different from the role of the manager or the owners of an enterprise. To the lender, resource gaps are ubiquitous: in the normal course of business all sorts of proposals, applications, and propositions are received. This flow of requests is essential to the successful operation of credit markets.

Lenders in a dynamic credit market are unwilling, and often unable, to satisfy every request for credit. Rationing according to credit standards is necessary to ensure that loans are allocated to borrowers who are most likely to service their debts.[23] Because of risk, rejection of loan applications is a legitimate function of lenders and of credit markets.

A rational lender's motivation for issuing credit is to profit by absorbing unexploited borrowing capacity, not to fill resource gaps. The efforts of a lender striving to fill resource gaps are easily dissipated in unremunerative lending. Resource gaps are never a sufficient condition for issuing credit. They create opportunities for lenders to seek remunerative transactions, but do not generate loan repayments. Resource gaps may offer insights into what would occur in the absence of a loan. But, they tend to be analytically inconclusive because alternative sources of finance

---

23. Rationing in credit markets is different from the nonprice rationing associated with equilibrium analysis in economics because it is a rational response to risk. The lender is not sacrificing or being denied an advantage that would otherwise be attractive or produce greater returns from lending. The supply of loanable funds within the margin may remain interest-elastic even after becoming completely inelastic to those at the margin. The use of nonprice criteria is essential in credit allocation because of the information problem—there is never complete certainty about the outcome of a credit transaction because it extends through time.

are frequently available. Gaps that cannot be filled force loan applicants to alter their expectations, targets, and objectives. This reorientation may be constructive and developmental when it results in selection of better investments and when it contributes to better loan portfolios held by a competitive financial sector.

5

COMMON STRATEGIC FLAWS
IN EFFORTS TO CHANNEL CREDIT
TO THE FRONTIER

Credit need and other deficient concepts used to advocate more credit, which were discussed in chapter 4, are not the only causes of unsuccessful efforts to force the frontier outward. Strategies commonly used by governments and development assistance agencies to achieve their objectives at the frontier are also flawed. This chapter examines direct efforts to move the frontier faster than it would naturally expand through the actions of competitive intermediaries. Direct attempts to hasten credit expansion in selected sectors or regions are found in virtually all countries. They include special credit programs, lending targets and quotas that respond to perceptions of credit need, social equity or financing gaps, and specialized financial institutions established to serve clients or sectors marked for favorable treatment by government and by external donors.

The objectives of special programs, targets and quotas are often regarded as highly laudable, enabling their sponsors to obtain political support for their design and implementation. However, the desirability of objectives is not sufficient justification for implementation—ends do not justify means. Justification for the use of government funds requires examination of costs and benefits, and a search for the best alternative means of achieving the chosen objectives. This requires a broad perspective on government efforts to force the frontier, which is consistent with the political, economic, and financial bases for intervention discussed in chapter 3.

Flaws in traditional strategies to force the frontier discussed in this chapter include overemphasizing credit, use of lending targets and quotas, an emphasis on institutions rather than on instruments, and neglect of transaction costs and incentives. The extent to which these flaws increase costs is a question of degree. Minor strategic flaws diligently imposed may have larger costs than major ones not seriously pursued, for example. But what types of cost do these common flaws entail?

Overemphasizing Credit

Emphasis on loans and on disbursements follows naturally from concern for credit needs and related loan allocation criteria discussed in chapter 4. Because these common allocation criteria fail to identify the potential for good loans, their application through credit programs, targets and quotas is likely to be less than satisfactory.

Emphasizing credit as a development strategy is often based on an argument made by Hugh T. Patrick that "supply-leading" finance stimulates growth by creating financial institutions in advance of the demand for their services.[1] Supply-leading institutions could transfer funds from traditional to modern sectors, create new horizons for entrepreneurs and produce favorable allocation and incentive effects. Patrick hypothesized that financial services that could have a relatively large developmental impact are relatively inexpensive to provide.

While Patrick stated his argument in terms of developing intermediation and financial markets in general, its most notable application has been one-sided, directed at the expansion of loan disbursement. Loan disbursement is easy, and responds to the political definition of the problem beyond the frontier, which is a shortage of credit at low rates of interest. However, there are three weaknesses in a primary emphasis on credit: it does not necessarily produce good loans and therefore is ultimately unsustainable, it ignores savings mobilization and therefore retards intermediation, and it disregards alternative means of stimulating investment and therefore tends to be both inefficient and inequitable.

Disbursement Does Not Necessarily Produce Good Loans

The first problem with emphasis on credit is that disbursement has to be followed by loan repayment for credit operations to be sustainable. In almost all cases an expansion of credit begins with disbursements, as this

1. Hugh T. Patrick, "Financial Development and Economic Growth in Underdeveloped Countries," *Economic Development and Cultural Change.* 14, 2, January 1966. Excerpted in J.D. Von Pischke, Dale W Adams and Gordon Donald, eds., *op. cit.* pp. 50-57.

is the first transaction in a loan.[2] Concentration on the disbursement side of the credit equation ignores the larger issues discussed in chapters 2 and 3. These include creation of confidence between borrower and lender, measurement and management of risk, and accounting and procedural infrastructure for loan administration. When these do not receive the same enthusiasm devoted to disbursement, credit programs tend to self-destruct as arrears mount and bad-debt losses take their toll.

"Savings Mobilization: The Forgotten Half of Rural Finance" [3]

The second flaw in emphasis on credit is that credit is only one financial service: linking credit with saving has many advantages for all parties concerned. Most importantly, the number of deposit accounts normally exceeds the number of loan accounts on the books of the financial sector, especially at the retail level. More people can be served by providing savings facilities than by offering credit.[4]

Robert C. Vogel lists economic arguments for emphasizing savings mobilization.[5] For example, savings mobilization can lead to a more equitable distribution of income by giving the poor access to financial assets with returns that are higher, after considering transaction costs, than those available from savings held in the form of tangible assets such as

---

2. An exception occured in the 1970s when the Agricultural Development Bank of Pakistan assigned mobile officers to groups of villages. Their first task was loan recovery, and access to additional credit was used as an incentive to repay loan arrears. Collections increased markedly, and the arrears recovered that otherwise presumably would have been bad debt losses more than offset the cost of employing the mobile officers. Mobile officers were originally an innovation of the National Bank of Pakistan. See A. Jamil Nishtar, "The Mobile Supervised Agricultural Credit System for Small Farmers." Karachi: National Bank of Pakistan, August 1972.

3. See the article by Robert C. Vogel bearing this title in Dale W Adams, Douglas H. Graham and J.D. Von Pischke, eds., *op. cit.* pp. 248-265.

4. People's Banks in Rwanda, for example, had 107,309 depositors and 7,875 loans outstanding in 1985. See Aloys Rukebesha, "People's Banks in Rwanda" and an accompanying case study by Guy Bédard, in Guy Bédard, Gerd Günter Klöwer, and Martin Harder, eds., *op. cit.* pp. 163-177 and 61-79, respectively. Data cited is from p. 176. In Kenya in the 1970s the number of primary cooperative society members borrowing under the Cooperative Production Credit Scheme rarely exceeded half the active membership, all of whom had Cooperative Savings Scheme accounts. See J.D. Von Pischke amd John Rouse, "Selected Successful Experiences in Agricultural Credit and Rural Finance in Africa," *Savings and Development.* 7, 1, 1983. p. 26; J.D. Von Pischke, "A Penny Saved: Kenya's Cooperative Savings Scheme," in J.D. Von Pischke, Dale W Adams and Gordon Donald, eds., *op.cit.*, p. 305.

5. *Ibid.*

livestock or jewelry or in cash. For this to occur, attractive interest rates and relatively low transaction costs are required.

Savings mobilization improves resource allocation by drawing funds away from less attractive investment opportunities and allocating them to more productive investments. Lending rates are often artificially low under government credit programs, which tends to discourage saving and to favor investments with low returns. Artifically low rates also deter lenders from mobilizing savings, because they cannot lend these funds profitably. Offering attractive rates on savings and basing lending rates on the intermediary's costs promotes efficient investment. Intermediaries will become more perceptive allocators because greater interaction with clients gives them information on investment opportunities and credit risk.

Savings mobilization contributes to good credit and to good financial intermediation. As Vogel notes:[6]

> When financial institutions deal only with clients as borrowers, they forgo useful information about the savings behavior of these clients that could help to refine estimations of their creditworthiness. Furthermore, borrowers are more likely to repay promptly and lenders to take responsibility for loan recovery when they know that resources come from neighbors rather than from some distant government agency or international donor.

A related question is the effectiveness of contracts in general. Where contract enforcement is generally weak, financial intermediation is constrained: the quality of the promises that are the basis of financial value is compromised. Better contract enforcement may occur where existing relationships, such as between neighbors, underlie finance. Where loan contracts cannot be enforced, credit easily converts to grants.

These information and incentive problems are reflected in shortcomings of state-owned institutions that operate only as lenders to farmers or small businesses.[7] They tend to allocate credit by political criteria, to be only superficially in touch with the economies and communities they are supposed to serve, to make loans that are either too large or too small to

---

6. *Ibid.* p. 252
7. J.D. Von Pischke, Peter J. Heffernan and Dale W Adams, "The Political Economy of Specialized Farm Credit Institutions in Low-Income Countries." Staff Working Paper No. 446. Washington, DC: World Bank, 1981. Case studies from nine countries illustrate these effects. Excerpted as "The Pitfalls of Specialized Farm Credit Institutions in Low-income Countries, " in J.D. Von Pischke, Dale W Adams and Gordon Donald, eds., *op. cit.* pp. 175-182.

generate good repayment by borrowers, to become unprofitable because their interest rates are too low and they accumulate bad debt losses, and to use failure as a rationale for continued support and expansion of their activities. These effects tend to arise regardless of the organizational form and location of these specialized lenders.

Savings mobilization is an effective antidote to these problems because it adds value to relationships between intermediaries and clients. The prospect of having access to credit, based on a deposit relationship, is a powerful incentive to depositors. Institutions competing for deposits also have positive incentives to be efficient, to keep their financial housekeeping in good order, and to innovate to retain and attract funds. Depositors constitute a logical market for credit, too, making the interests of intermediaries and clients coincide.

In short, savings mobilization is the half-not of development assistance and of direct intervention in financial markets. If half the effort that has been spent on throwing credit at the frontier had been devoted to stimulating voluntary savings mobilization, the financial landscape in much of the Third World would probably be more attractive today. (And if the other half had been devoted to managing risk in credit relationships, as discussed in chapter 12, this financial landscape would be a lush garden.)

Infrastructure and Policy Improvements Are Often More Developmental Than Credit

There are many barriers to development that cannot be removed by providing loans. For example, rural poverty may be caused by deficient production technologies, low prices received for farm output, and an absence of attractive investment opportunities. The reasons for these problems may include lack of agricultural research, government regulations that restrict the promotion of improved technologies by private firms and traders, corrupt and inefficient cooperatives, high transport costs due to poor roads, and price controls favoring urban consumers or exporters of agricultural products.

Where these problems persist, it is very difficult to use credit effectively as an instrument of development policy except for very narrow purposes. Even if credit is coupled with efforts to build roads, develop improved technologies, or improve cooperative performance, for example, disbursement may not lead to good loans. The reason for this is that credit usually goes out at a faster pace than infrastructure is created, than technologies are adapted and adopted, and than institutions are reformed. In any event, resort to credit as a primary means of attacking the problem of rural poverty means that relatively few farmers or small scale businesses will be involved. This occurs because credit allocation requires standards of creditworthiness, making credit selective.

If underlying problems responsible for rural poverty are attacked directly, a larger number of people benefit than if emphasis is primarily on providing credit. A road, for example, can be used by those who are untrustworthy or who consume too much alcohol, as well as those who are creditworthy. And, even the drunkard and the liar have a potential to contribute to development in their more responsible moments. Improvements in agricultural technology, marketing and input supply arrangements, and movement toward economically rational prices likewise benefit large numbers of producers, not just the minority who receive official credit. Too much faith in credit as a developmental tool can lead to neglect of other opportunities that may take longer to realize but have a broader and more equitable impact. (These possibilities are dealt with more broadly in chapter 13.)

Equity Finance Supports Good Credit Use

Another unfortunate aspect of the overemphasis on credit is that it ignores the importance of equity finance. The role of equity finance was briefly stated in chapter 2, and is touched upon in various places later in this book. But to elaborate a little on the role of equity: First, equity is a commitment, demonstrating the owner's good faith. Second, equity provides an incentive to the owner to make the firm or activity succeed. The positive aspect of this incentive is that profit belongs to the owner, constituting a return on the owner's investment. The negative aspect is that losses consume equity, diminishing the owner's wealth.

Third, equity provides a cushion to creditors. The cash flow dimension of this cushion was explained in chapter 2. And if the lender requires security, equity makes it possible for the value of the security to exceed the amount of the loan. This excess provides a cushion in the event the security has to be realized to repay the debt.

Overemphasis on credit results in underemphasis on equity. This leads to unreaslistic expectations regarding credit and insufficient attention to mobilizing, creating and rewarding ownership capital. More attention to ownership capital would logically include greater government encouragement of profits through favorable tax and other legislation. A related governmental role is definition and protection of property rights to give owners greater clarity and confidence.

Finally, measures to develop stock markets by favorable legislation and by entrepreneurial efforts by brokers and other intermediaries can also have desirable developmental effects.[8] Medium-sized and large firms would have greater access to equity from sources other than their founders and founders' families and friends. Development of equity and of equity markets should improve the quality of corporate finance and of credit markets by providing alternative and mutually reinforcing ways of creating value.

Externally Imposed Lending Targets and Credit Quotas

Governments use lending targets and credit quotas to push lenders through the frontier at a faster pace than they would otherwise undertake. These controls, usually administered by central banks, often require that a certain percentage of commercial banks' loans outstanding must be to politically favored sectors such as agriculture, artisans or rural industry. The specified share is usually less than 20 percent.

Another common quota requires each branch of a bank, or branches in rural areas, to attain a specified loan-to-deposit ratio. Under this control, each branch must have loans outstanding in an amount equal to at least a specified fraction of deposit balances it collects. Requirements usually range from 30 to 50 percent, and presumably promote investment in the local area. Without the quota, many branches would lend less locally and place a larger portion of their deposit balances at the disposal of their head offices for lending to borrowers in other parts of the country, or for investment in financial markets.

Banks not meeting the targeted level of lending may be fined, forced to buy securities issued by an agricultural finance agency, or forced to keep noninterest bearing reserves with the central bank that equal the extent of their deficiency under the quota.

---

8. Antoine W. van Agtmael, *Emerging Securities Markets* (London, Euromoney Publications, 1984); The World Bank, *World Development Report 1985*. (New York: Oxford University Press, 1985).

Quantitative controls in the form of targets and quotas have a number of shortcomings. The most important is that they do not necessarily generate good loans, and they tend to weaken controlled lenders. The following sections point out that lending targets and portfolio quotas do not address the problems that make lenders reluctant to advance the frontier voluntarily, that they are usually designed without reference to the cost of their implementation, that their implementation generally distorts statistics, and that they do not make good economic sense.

Quantitative Controls as a Quick Fix

Controls give governments some allocative power over the funds depositors entrust to banks. Informal explanations given for imposing controls usually cite bank behavior that is regarded as unresponsive to development or governed by outdated colonial traditions. Bankers may be portrayed as lazy, as oligopolists who do not compete, or as an elite or possibly an ethnic minority that is selfish, unpatriotic, or out of touch. Formal explanations may cite a desire to increase production of certain products or to assist specific producer groups. If these perceptions were true, are quotas and targets the best means of changing bankers' behavior?

Insight may be provided by the imposition of quotas and targets in countries where major banks are nationalized and hence presumably already responsive to political priorities and social considerations. Nationalization and controls are sometimes defended as giving government control of the "commanding heights" of the economy. A dimension less often mentioned is referred to in American slang as "deep pockets." Because banks obviously have money, they may be attractive political targets.

Quotas and targets do not address the problems that inhibit lenders from moving the frontier. Designers of quantitative controls apparently regard these as either impossible to change, inconsequential or as something that can be overcome by the experience gained from having to comply with their quotas or targets. A common factor inhibiting exploration of the frontier is interest rate controls, imposed by the same authorities who establish targets and quotas. The maximum rates permitted usually do not enable commercial lenders to obtain spreads sufficient to cover the costs of risk and of administering small loans at the frontier, and quotas and targets simply compound the damage caused by directives or pressures that keep interest rates artificially low.

Other inhibiting factors include the quality of physical, social, and administrative infrastructure beyond the frontier which makes financial intermediation costly. Imposing controls is usually much easier and politically more attractive than correcting the inhibiting factors, and the costs of controls may appear to fall entirely on the banks in the form of diminished profits.

The Costs of Controls Are Rarely Measured

Costs accompany controls, but are rarely measured by those responsible for their design or enforcement. Compliance tends to move banks into areas they purposely avoided as unremunerative. So, it is probably more difficult to make good loans under quotas and targets than it is in the areas where banks have already developed expertise. To the extent this applies, controls and quotas cause banks to lose money or to employ their funds less profitably. Hence, banks' financial positions are generally weakened by compliance.

Another cost is that directing credit to specific borrowers or categories of borrowers tends to deprive others of credit. If those who are deprived are more productive than the favored borrowers obtaining targeted credit, a cost is imposed on the economy. This cost equals the difference between the incremental value of production of favored borrowers and the incremental value of production that could have been realized by those who are deprived of credit if they had credit, plus the incremental transaction costs of designing and implementing the targets and quotas.

Quantitative controls impose transaction costs. Banks must demonstrate the extent to which they comply. This requires reporting systems and the costs of inspection by authorities. Additional recordkeeping must be adopted when quota categories do not match bankers' information systems oriented toward risk and portfolio quality, not toward political or social objectives. For example, farmers may buy light trucks to transport inputs and produce. Banks making loans for light trucks would normally record them as vehicle loans, because the vehicles are pledged as collateral.

Quantitative controls give lenders an incentive to categorize their activities in a way that shows they meet quotas. If an absentee farm landlord or a wealthy businessman with a number of interests including one small business buys a light truck, the lender may be able to report the loan as agricultural or as a small business loan, for example, for purposes of complying with lending targets and quotas. Because of this effect, quantitative controls tend to make liars out of lenders and make compliance statistics useless. What portion of reported "agricultural credit" really has much to do directly with agriculture? These effects are important if transparency, straightforward dealing, and accurate representation contribute to development.

Generating meaningless numbers and enforcing questionable controls requires central bankers to compile statistics and investigate noncompliance and reporting irregularities. Ineffective controls put more people at risk in discharging their duties without engaging in corrupt practices. Collusion and subversion may arise if central bankers understand that money is fungible and that targets and quotas are useful politically but destructive financially and economically. Central and commercial bankers may work together tacitly or openly to devise liberal definitions of loans that qualify as meeting targets and quotas. This type of activity makes central bank relations more complex and confidence more difficult to achieve, and imposes transaction costs on all concerned.

Distortions of data and behavior are exaggerated when quantitative controls are accompanied by concessional loan terms. Prospective borrowers, for example, have an incentive to obtain funds on the most favorable conditions possible, and directed credit is often concessional. Hence, the borrower's stated purpose in borrowing may not correspond to the actual use of funds. Irrigation loans have occasionally financed the construction of swimming pools on ranches, and tractors may be used primarily for road transport rather than for farm work. When borrowers misrepresent their intentions, it is more difficult to develop the confidence on which finance is based.

Edward J. Kane summarizes the effects of these factors in agricultural credit as follows:[9]

> Subterfuge in political purpose tends also to promote subterfuge and corruption in bank operations. No matter how many formal bureaucratic safeguards are established to earmark funds for agricultural purposes or for

---

9. Edward J. Kane, "Political Economy of Subsidizing Agricultural Credit in Developing Countries," in Dale W Adams, Douglas H. Graham and J.D. Von Pischke, eds., *op. cit.* pp. 166-182.

small farmers in particular, career incentives within the bank and opportunities for personal enrichment invariably predispose loan officers toward allowing funds to flow to uses that are only apparently agricultural and to wealthy persons whose connections with farm operations may be tenuous.

An additional casualty of the numbers-fudging game arises from the opportunity cost it imposes. Managerial and clerical energy is consumed by the maintenance of systems of deceit. The time and talent required could be more usefully devoted to the generation of good loans and in loan administration, especially to supervision of client relationships. For example the risks of lending at the frontier imply that borrowers will frequently encounter difficulties. Lenders may be able to help these borrowers by spending more time looking for solutions to their problems. This type of concern and cooperation can improve relationships with these clients as well as contributing to portfolio quality. Development would be better served by confronting these problems rather than by filing fanciful reports to satisfy planners, donors, and compliance supervisors policing targets and quotas.

Quantitative Controls Are Economically Suspect

The economic argument for quantitative controls rests on "market failure." Market failure occurs, for example, when lenders' perceptions of the profitability of certain types of loans are wrong, and when lenders' profitability from certain transactions does not reflect the benefits of these transactions to society. When markets fail, worthwhile transactions are not undertaken because lenders wrongly assume they are not remunerative, or because they would not in fact be remunerative to bankers. Under these conditions, lending is inefficient because opportunities to make good loans are rejected. Economists may advocate quantitative controls to make credit allocation more efficient.

Omotunde E.G. Johnson cites two reasons why lenders' perceptions may be deficient.[10] One is that lenders underestimate creditworthiness because of insufficient information. A lack of competitiveness or high costs of obtaining information may discourage lenders from pushing the

---

10. Omotunde E.G. Johnson, "Credit Controls as Instruments of Development Policy in the Light of Economic Theory," in J.D. Von Pischke, Dale W Adams and Gordon Donald, eds., *op. cit.* pp. 323-329.

frontier. As a result, they overestimate risk and the administrative costs of lending to certain sectors. A second is that certain types of lending may produce "positive externalities," effects such as the reduction of poverty or pollution that are highly beneficial for society but which do not benefit lenders directly. Lenders do not have a monetary incentive to make such loans.

WHY QUANTITATIVE CONTROLS ARE NOT EFFICIENT RESPONSES TO MARKET FAILURE. However, quantitative controls tend to allocate credit inefficiently while failing to achieve their objectives of redistribution of income and wealth. For example, allocation may occur through inflation when the central bank provides rediscounting facilities to support lending to favored sectors. Rediscounting is a form of central bank lending to commercial banks, in this case against commercial banks' loans to favored sectors. It gives commercial banks greater liquidity, which permits them to expand their overall lending. This increases the money supply without necessarily increasing the supply of goods and services. Inflation results. The declining value of money tends to shift purchasing power to net borrowers and away from net lenders throughout the economy. Favored sectors obtain relatively more resources, others obtain relatively less. In this sense, quantitative controls tax nonfavored economic sectors, reducing their efficiency.

Reallocation also occurs through reduction in the net incomes of banks and their nonfavored clients. Banks' income declines because lending under targets and quotas is less profitable than alternative uses of these funds in the absence of controls. Lower returns to intermediaries may reduce the supply of credit and lead to lower interest rates offered to depositors.

Nonfavored clients' income is also decreased because they obtain relatively less credit. This decrease is especially concentrated among relatively less attractive clients outside the sectors favored by targets and controls. Banks react to decreased earnings and greater risk from lending under controls by attempting to increase earnings and reduce risk in other parts of their portfolios. This crowds out the less attractive nonfavored borrowers and provides relatively more credit to nonfavored borrowers who are relatively attractive because of their size or relationships with lenders. More credit to small farmers, for example, could result in relatively less credit to small businesses. These nonfavored clients presumably then seek funds elsewhere, which tends to bid up interest rates. This decreases the incomes of these borrowers and increases the income of nonbank lenders, such as informal moneylenders and suppliers of trade credit.

In certain developing countries with small markets and a narrow range of economic activities, banks may not be able to adjust easily to the decrease in earnings on one part of their portfolios because few alternatives exist or because changes in one direction in one part of the economy directly affect most other parts in the same direction. In this situation banks may choose to lend relatively little, keeping low loan-to-deposit ratios; and may discourage deposit growth through unattractive interest rates and low levels of service to depositors. Controls may be especially damaging in these economies by restricting banks' flexibility even further.

EFFICIENT ALTERNATIVE ACTIONS TO CORRECT ALLEGED MARKET FAILURE. Johnson proposes two theoretically economically efficient alternatives to quantitative controls. Where lenders underestimate the attractiveness of would-be borrowers, he proposes that government establish specialized intermediaries. Specialization would provide a comparative advantage in obtaining information to evaluate the creditworthiness of borrowers favored by government but not attractive to existing lenders. Johnson says these institutions should not need subsidy because their activities would be privately profitable as well as socially beneficial. They should be able to borrow from commercial banks or through bond issues at market rates and re-lend to favored sectors at higher rates. Where prospective borrowers' credit use would benefit society greatly, but have only meager benefits for bankers, Johnson advocates government subsidies to the banks. These subsidies would have to be funded by "society," which is justified economically because "society" benefits from the positive externalities of such lending.

These theoretical solutions suggest just how difficult it is for economic planners and governments to intervene effectively in financial markets. Specialized financial institutions have a poor record, and appear to be much more costly in the long run than imagined by their sponsors. Subsidies, likewise, may be difficult to control or to target. Subsidies are politicized and attract special interest groups that favor their continuation; they are not subject to the adjustments and self-correcting tendencies of competitive markets.

Neglected Transaction Costs

For firms and individuals at the frontier, the transaction costs of obtaining access to formal financial services easily exceed the interest paid on loans or the interest received on deposit balances. Interest rates held artificially low by government policy, presumably intended to benefit those at and beyond the frontier, paradoxically tend to increase loan applicants' and depositors' transaction costs.

Loan Applicants' Transaction Costs

Loan applicants' transaction costs tend to rise because low interest rates generate a false demand for capital. Borrowers inside the frontier will try to lower their costs of borrowing by obtaining concessional credit, and applicants beyond the frontier may be attracted in large numbers by advertised rates greatly below those they pay in the informal market.

Lenders facing an onslaught of questionable applicants attempt to control costs by reducing the number of applicants. In commercial situations, lenders discourage unattractive applicants by raising interest rates or by imposing other conditions, such as minimum loan sizes that exceed the repayment capacity of small farmers or businesses, or by requiring that a deposit account be maintained for a period of time before a loan application is accepted.

In many government-sponsored efforts to advance the frontier, however, these options are not available to lenders. Interest rates are held low, and program design specifies other loan terms and conditions. Standardization is expected to ensure that all target group members receive equal treatment, and that lenders do not subvert program objectives or exploit the target population.

In this situation, the most effective way of discouraging applications is to impose transaction costs. This is accomplished by demanding lots of documentation to support an application; by restricting service, which requires applicants to queue; and by soliciting bribes. The ultimate weapon against a loan applicant is of course "losing" the file containing the application and accompanying documents, which occurs occasionally when lenders find the going extremely rough.

Expanding transaction costs tend to make borrowers' cost of funds roughly equal to the cost of alternative funds that they could obtain elsewhere.[11] This effect is rarely considered in the design of credit projects and other interventions to force the frontier. This omission is especially regrettable when coupled with The Iron Law of Interest Rate Restrictions, which specifies that as government-regulated interest rate ceilings become more restrictive, the share of credit issued to large borrowers increases while that to small borrowers decreases.[12] These effects combine to increase the costs to most borrowers and to exclude a disproportionate share of applicants at the frontier.

Neglecting transaction costs when designing financial market interventions occurs naturally when emphasis is on meeting credit needs or responding to similar perceptions of a shortage of finance, when the importance of credit is overemphasized, and when loan disbursement receives inordinate attention and the other elements required to produce good loans are not seriously addressed.

Depositors' Transaction Costs

When the market for deposits is not competitive and innovative, deposit-takers have little incentive to be sensitive to transaction costs imposed on depositors. Depositors may have little choice of intermediary or there may be little that distinguishes the services of one intermediary from those offered by others. In this case, the depositor may simply bank at the nearest deposit-taking office.

The transaction costs imposed on depositors are similar to those imposed on borrowers by intermediaries not anxious to seek new clients at the frontier. The first consists of queueing, which is often compounded by the use of tellers and cashiers rather than unit tellers. The teller-and-cashier system separates the clerical and the cash–handling functions. For example, the depositor waits in one long line to present a withdrawal request to the teller, or for the teller to prepare the form. While the customer is kept waiting in a second line in front of the cashier's window, this form moves across several desks where it is checked, recorded and

---

11. World Bank, *World Development Report 1987* (New York: Oxford University Press, 1987). p. 76.
12. *Ibid.* p. 118.

eventually forwarded to the cashier, who pays out cash and obtains a receipt of acceptance from the customer.

Unit tellers, by contrast, handle all aspects of routine transactions on a one-stop basis. The teller-and-cashier system permits better control against fraud, while the unit teller system requires greater managerial attention to staff training and integrity in order to serve clients more quickly.

Other transaction costs arise from minimum balance and minimum transaction requirements, which may be relatively high. In certain countries, for example, these may exceed the daily agricultural wage, which discourages small depositors and minimizes the deposit-taker's bookkeeping and other overhead costs. Deposits and transactions may also be subject to fees for deposit of checks drawn on other banks or from other parts of the country, for example, and ledger fees may be levied when a record card is set up or filled in. Money transfers through money orders, cashiers checks or bank drafts may also be relatively expensive.

High transaction costs for depositors are likely when financial institutions do not depend upon deposits as important sources of funds. This may occur when institutions receive funds from the central bank or from development assistance agencies. The cost of processing numerous small deposits, especially in noncompetitive markets, easily exceeds the costs of central bank or donor funds, which are often exceptionally low. There may also be more personal rewards to bankers from dealing with donors, such as travel, training and entertainment, than in serving hordes of noisy, impatient depositors crowded into poorly ventilated banking offices on a hot day.

Overlooked Incentives

Intervention influences incentives.[13] Incentives are important in confidence-building, in obtaining compliance with targets and quotas, and in controlling transaction costs. Overemphasizing credit, imposing binding lending targets and portfolio quotas, and indifference to transaction costs are possible only when incentives that motivate individuals and institutions are disregarded in the design of intervention.

---

13. Edward J. Kane, "Good Intentions and Unintended Evil," in J.D. Von Pischke, Dale W Adams and Gordon Donald, eds., *op. cit.* pp. 316-322.

Disregard for incentives results in failure to address the role of confidence in financial relationships. Confidence is built only when both parties to a transaction or relationship have incentives to consider the interests of the other party or to behave as if they did. Where incentives are disregarded, for example, the merits of linking saving and credit in retail financial institutions are not realized. Specialized institutions are established that do not command confidence, that are perceived as alien and transitory by the local community.

Lack of confidence in a financial institution that provides subsidized credit produces complex effects. The first is that individuals have an incentive to obtain as much of the cheap credit as possible, especially where repayment obligations are likely to be lightly enforced. Heavy use of debt that is casually administered leads to accumulation of arrears.

While it may appear that the community's interest is to keep the cheap credit machine operating well so that it can provide a steady flow of subsidy, this possibility is foreclosed by private decisions by defaulters, whose failure to repay debilitates the institution. By not repaying they obtain a subsidy equal to 100 percent of their loan, while repaying and reapplying for credit involves transaction costs and receipt of a subsidy of much less than 100 percent. In effect, the community as individual borrowers has an incentive to destroy the institution through nonrepayment of loans, rather than to preserve it as an intermediary to which savings can be entrusted and from which future loans are likely to be available if certain rules of conduct are followed.

Incentives are rarely well examined when quotas and targets are established to force lenders to act in ways that are otherwise not in their own best interest. Rediscounting at preferential interest rates for credit issued to favored sectors or borrowers is often offered, but the spread between the retail lending rate and the rediscount rate is often not designed to ensure that the lender will gain from the activities supported by rediscounting. Hence, misreporting of compliance develops into an art form. Retail lenders appear to meet quotas and targets while expanding credit more rapidly to sectors not especially favored by government.

Lenders' incentives to create transaction costs and to pass them to loan applicants and clients stem from the failure to focus competitive forces on the frontier. Lenders shielded from competition may hire superfluous staff because a larger payroll symbolizes greater power. They may shift transaction costs to clients or potential clients to discourage loan applications and would-be depositors.

Competitive lenders and deposit-takers would attempt to cut costs in order to gain customers by offering convenient services at attractive prices. Transaction costs would be reduced. Competitive intermediaries would tend to respond to market-driven incentives by linking credit, saving and money transfer services, reducing documentation requirements, and building their own information systems to facilitate loan decisionmaking.

Emphasis on Institutions Rather Than Instruments

Institutions as referred to in the following discussion are formal organizations registered or chartered according to law. An instrument can be defined as written evidence of a legal claim.[14] A check is a financial instrument in this sense, for example. Instrument is defined more widely here as a financial product or service. In this sense a checking account is an instrument, as are savings accounts, letters of credit, forfaiting arrangements and credit union signature loans.

Emphasis on Institutions

Governments' efforts to force the frontier are often implemented by establishing institutions especially for this purpose. Specialized agricultural credit institutions, cooperative credit societies, small enterprise development funds, special credit programs and similar intermediaries are commonly found in mixed economies. Those that work in one country are often copied in other countries. Those that do not work very well are also often replicated abroad by governments and donors, as discussed in other chapters.

Institutions are important because they can increase efficiency and arbitrate the conflicting claims of different interest groups. "Institution-building" is a task to which much effort is rightly devoted. This term is often used in development assistance to refer to helping a particular government department, state corporation or cooperative to improve its management and operations by developing procedures and information systems, hiring and training qualified staff, obtaining equipment such as

---

14. "Instrument: any written document that gives formal expression to a legal agreement or act." Jerry M. Rosenberg, *The Investor's Dictionary*, (New York: John Wiley & Sons, 1986).

computers and vehicles, and erecting new buildings. These contributions are indeed useful when they are efficient and succeed, even if they do not directly develop society's great institutions, such as markets, property and human rights, systems of justice and education, and the framework for political decisionmaking.

Experience with credit and development finance projects suggests that institutional development is stubbornly difficult, especially when incentives are not carefully analyzed. Efforts to support an institution may be counterproductive if its activities are poorly conceived or if its mission cannot possibly be accomplished. Efforts to build such institutions lead to injections of good money after bad and have a high opportunity cost: the energy they absorb otherwise could have been directed toward tasks that could be successfully undertaken or that could be quickly abandoned if they prove unviable.

Potentially excessive attention to institutions in development projects is the result of several influences. The first is that governments create institutions for political purposes, and they are important sources of patronage in terms of promising services to citizens and providing jobs to the faithful.

Second, development assistance agencies require a certain environment for the use of their funds. Project lending, by definition, sponsors activities that have a separate identity, activities that generally are not just part of the routine functions of the state, or that would not be conducted on the same scale or with the same complexity without external assistance. Assistance agencies often prefer to work with "autonomous" or semi-autonomous state agencies that are perceived as having the flexibility required for creative tasks and that can use budgeting, procurement, and accounting procedures preferred by external assistance agencies.

A third source of potentially excessive attention arises from institutional mystique and outreach. Cooperators want to establish cooperatives because they view cooperatives as a morally superior form of economic organization. University professors believe that instruction in their particular disciplines could be useful in another country. Strong believers in a popular form of government believe that its adoption would benefit the people of other countries. This institution-building context, backed by development assistance funds, produces highly motivated secular missionaries whose objectives go beyond the skills they want to transfer.

Their efforts are tremendously powerful when they are entrepreneurial and adaptive, extending to others the benefits of their expertise. But when they are narrow and imposed, they may be of only limited success, possibly wasteful, or ultimately destructive.

If financial sector institution-building as generally conceived and practiced is a high risk investment for both donor and recipient, what developmental alternative can be offered? One alternative is to focus on transactions undertaken by institutions, which requires attention to financial instruments.

Emphasis on Instruments

Defining instruments as financial products directs attention to transactions, to how these products are sold. Institutions are delivery mechanisms for transactions—through transactions they meet and relate to their clients. Instruments defined as financial services are vehicles for transactions.

Financial markets function through transactions. When transactions fail to attract clients or are structured so that relationships cannot be sustained, institutions will not be viable, become irrelevant, and are unlikely to fulfill a developmental role. The segments of financial markets dealing in these transactions will languish. By contrast, innovative instruments that successfully stimulate and facilitate transactions are developmental.

This perspective suggests that efforts to stimulate financial development and to design credit projects should begin with transactions. The first task is to identify the types of transactions that are or could be useful to the people and for the purpose the project designer expects to serve. When the transaction objective becomes clear and the transaction is fully formulated, institutional form and content follow.

The benefits that could flow from a transactions approach can be illustrated by an example, given below, of failure to comprehend the nature and implications of the transactions required to implement a project. The results were loans that were probably unremunerative to the lender, burdensome to borrowers, and that failed to realize their potential developmental impact.

A YOUNG ANALYST GOES ABROAD. One of the writer's early experiences with development projects was as a member of a team that appraised a small farm credit project. The financial institution that would implement the project was having housekeeping difficulties: tremendously large cash balances were held in a local bank. These balances were large because the institution took about three months to reconcile the numerous bank accounts it kept for its own convenience and to accommodate donors' requirements that separate accounts be maintained for each project, and because disbursement of a loan commitment could take up to six months. Even with this cash cushion, lending was suspended from time to time because it appeared that liquidity might be depleted. Arrears accumulated on loans due for repayment by farmers, and collections of certain large loans were delayed for months or years because the government's loan guarantee program was inefficient.

Suspense accounts were generously used for transactions that were not properly handled. External audits by a multinational firm appeared less than thorough, and the auditor's opinion did not seem to square with the facts. Annual reports were published greatly in arrears because of accounting problems and governmental review procedures. Trends in the financial statements, such as they were, suggested that financial reorganization might be necessary during the expected disbursement period of the project the team was instructed to design.

Two development assistance agencies had provided specialists to review the situation, and their report awaited us. Our team spent considerable time negotiating with the institution's management, the report's authors and ministry of agriculture officials to agree on a plan for institutional development. Objectives were to upgrade accounting performance, to train staff, to obtain more equity capital by persuading the government to convert to equity a loan it had made to the institution, and to expand lending. We left the borrowing country confident that progress would be made.

These discussions occurred after five years of a donor's support for the institution. Fifteen years later, after about 20 years of involvement, an official of the development assistance agency sketched a rehabilitation plan for the institution. The problems enumerated were generally the same as those the author investigated in the early 1970s. They had endured throughout the intervening period, which had been punctuated by suspensions of lending by the institution because of accounting and other internal problems.

Concentration on the institution appeared logical to the author's team and identified problems that inhibited good lending and effective financial management. The author analyzed the institution's finances, which corresponded with his training and the way in which the institution's problems were defined by all involved. Institution dealt with institution.

A TRANSACTION FOCUS: DIFFERENT QUESTIONS, DIFFERENT ANSWERS. A transaction focus might have yielded a useful and sustained contribution to development. A clue that the team might have picked up was that the lender's accounting problems provided an incentive to minimize the number of transactions. This would hopefully permit the backlog of entries to be worked down. However, the institution, the government and the donor wanted to expand lending. The institution's traditions and the interaction of these forces resulted in loan repayment schedules requiring farmers to make annual installments on medium- and long-term loans.

Loan terms: The project provided credit primarily for small-scale dairying. Income from dairying occurs daily as cows are milked and as milk not consumed on the farm is sold. Could small dairy farmers be expected to accumulate enough cash throughout the year to make a single payment? Convenience to 'the borrower favors loans repayable in frequent installments. Could the farm credit institution modify the instrument by offering incentives for the prepayment of annual installments, in small amounts throughout the year? Clearly not, if transactions were to be minimized. Yet, annual installments would probably deter conscientious small farmers from participating in the project, reinforcing the tendency for loans to flow to relatively better-off operators.

A significant proportion of borrowers had incomes from cash crops marketed through cooperatives and parastatal agencies, while others worked for the government as teachers, civil servants, police and members of the armed forces. Loan recoveries from these borrowers might have been made through deductions from cash crop delivery proceeds or from the monthly paychecks of those who worked for the government or for other employers willing to cooperate by splitting wage or salary payments, part to the lender and part to the borrower.

Linking savings with credit: Investigation would have shown that savings account facilities were not readily available in rural areas. Therefore, poor repayment could be expected from those without relatively large incomes from cash crops or off-farm employment, because of the formidable size of the annual installment. Loan collection problems would raise the lender's administrative costs and complicate its cash flow projections.

A transaction focus might have led the team to consider promoting savings facilities as a means of assisting farmers. Savings facilities could be offered by the credit institution (which would have to have good financial housekeeping to sustain confidence) or by banks and rural cooperatives.

Prioritization of assistance efforts: A transaction focus could also have pointed to several other alternatives. One would be no disbursements of donor funds until housekeeping problems were solved, which might have required 18 months. Institutions have to record credit transactions properly to manage portfolios effectively. However, alternatives requiring suspension or reduction in disbursements go against the grain of the "resource transfer" thrust of development assistance. In addition, it is not unusual for a donor that seeks to develop strong intermediaries through project terms and conditions based on high performance standards to be thwarted by another donor in a hurry to move money with fewer and softer terms and conditions.

Cost analysis: Analysis concentrated primarily on the institution's overall revenues and expenses, but not the costs of each transaction. Examining costs per transaction would have permitted calculation of the overall costs and benefits of the project to the institution. This calculation is not usually made, and unremunerative lending may result as a consequence.

Exploration of alternatives: Attention to transactions and their costs might have led to support for alternatives to credit, including artificial insemination for the development of dairying, and leasing or integration arrangements to achieve wider distribution of improved dairy cattle. These alternatives could have contributed to institution-building, but not simply within the credit agency and the ministry of agriculture.

6

POLICY AND PRACTICE THAT REDUCE VALUE AT THE FRONTIER

Intervention based on deficient concepts such as credit need and flawed strategies such as an overemphasis on credit can eventually reach the frontier, but only at high cost as indicated in the previous two chapters. However, the problem of inappropriate actions does not stop here. Further damage to prospects for financial development are imposed by the common policy of keeping interest rates artificially low and the common practice of failure by the sponsors of intervention to keep in touch with the overall performance and implications of the programs they spawn. These traditional features of intervention are the subject of this chapter.

Repressed interest rates tend to keep formal credit entirely away from activities that actually expand the frontier in a sustainable manner. This often reinforces concern for credit needs and recourse to directed credit. Artificially low rates of interest are government-administered rates that fail to compensate lenders for their costs, that are inconsistent with vigorous deposit mobilization, and that are below the relevant opportunity cost of capital. Low interest rates reduce value because they keep term structures short, ignore risk and fail to give incentives for refinement of valuation processes.

The practice of inadequate reporting and accountability of credit programs results in poor information, which reduces value by inhibiting the management and refinement of valuation processes. It also makes the costs of government programs extremely difficult to control, and errors difficult to correct.

This chapter begins by discussing arguments commonly advanced in favor of low interest rates in general and for specific purposes. The second part of the chapter explores information questions and problems, and their relationship with efforts to advance the frontier. Illustrations are cited from the Philippines and from enthusiasm for crop insurance by United Nations agencies and bilateral donors.

Artificially Low Interest Rates

There is a strong and widespread belief that governments should do everything possible to keep interest rates low at the frontier. Its acceptance is demonstrated by credit projects around the world that attempt to expand the frontier by issuing loans carrying interest rates that approximate those commercial banks charge their best customers, who are of course well within the frontier. Dale W Adams cites and refutes eight of the most common arguments for low interest rates that are applied to rural finance, as follows:[1]

- *The usury argument* against high rates of interest is often based on religious and ethical values,[2] which are not open to refutation on their own terms. Other statements of the argument link high rates of interest with exploitation by moneylenders. In fact, *net* returns to moneylending are rarely measured, but the handful of surveys that have been conducted indicate that, although their interest rates are high, moneylenders' earnings are much lower than suggested by the usury argument. (This point is developed in chapter 8.)

- Their defenders argue that *low rates have been used in developed countries,* especially by the US Farm Security Administration and its successor, the Farmers Home Administration. These agencies are often cited because of their visibility and familiarity. They have trained rural credit officials from developing countries, and the United States Agency for International Development (AID) has used technicians from these agencies to work with credit institutions in developing countries.[3] AID has also pushed for higher rates under projects and through research, making American examples especially interesting.

---

1. Dale W Adams, "Are the Arguments for Cheap Agricultural Credit Sound?" in Dale W Adams, Douglas H. Graham and J.D. Von Pischke, eds., *op. cit.* pp. 65-77.

2. Benjamin N. Nelson, *The Idea of Usury: From Tribal Brotherhood to Universal Otherhood.* 2nd ed. (Chicago: University of Chicago Press, 1969).

3. E.B. Rice, *History of AID Programs in Agricultural Credit.* Vol. XVII, AID Spring Review of Small Farmer Credit. (Washington, DC: Agency for International Development, Department of State, June 1973). pp. 12-20.

During the 1930s American farmers paid between 2 and 7 percent on government loans, which appear to be regarded by some as traditional and appropriate rates even though market rates have remained consistently above these levels for the last 30 years. Adams points out that deflation during that period made the real (i.e., inflation/deflation adjusted) rates of interest quite high.[4] U.S. agricultural prices declined by 20 percent or more in 1930, 1931, 1932 and 1938. Nominal interest rates of 2 to 7 percent translated into real rates, measured in terms of the purchasing power of farm incomes, were frequently greater than 20 percent in these years. So, high positive real rates were charged, while in many developing countries rates are negative because low nominal rates are exceeded by relatively high rates of inflation.

- *Development assistance agencies often provide cheap funds* to poor countries. Some argue that these concessions should be passed on to farmers, or that similar concessions should be offered to stimulate on-farm development. Adams notes that this argument ignores the opportunity cost of funds, the foreign exchange risk on many foreign assistance loans, and the costs of lending at the frontier. Cheap credit easily results in losses to the banks or credit agencies offering it.

- *Concern for lender solvency* has led to pressure for continued low interest rates where financial institutions' assets have relatively long maturities and low fixed interest rates. Increases in nominal rates reduce these assets' market value, eroding the capital of these unfortunate intermediaries. However, this is not necessarily reflected in financial statements in many countries, because assets are valued at original cost, not market value. Losses would not occur unless loans were not repaid, or sold for less than the amount outstanding.

Adams notes that this effect is not material for short-term lenders because short maturities limit repricing risk. He also observes that

---

4. The formula for deriving real rates is $r = [(1 + i)/(1 + p)] - 1$, where r is the real rate of interest, i is the nominal rate, and p is the rate of inflation. For an application, see João Sayad, "Rural Credit and Positive Real Rates of Interest: Brazil's Experience with Rapid Inflation," in Dale W Adams, Douglas H. Graham and J.D. Von Pischke, eds., *op. cit.* p. 147.

many medium- and long-term lenders are government owned, and could be subsidized to offset losses; and that raising interest rates on existing contracts by government decree is consistent with accepted practice in many countries.[5] The strongest argument for high lending rates is that they can assist institutional viability by helping to cover the relatively high costs of frontier lending.

• *Low interest rates are often advocated as a means of inducing borrowers to behave in a manner desired by planners,* by adopting new technologies and raising production. However, are low or negative rates essential to promote desirable investments? Experience with fertilizer promotion, for example, shows that new adopters are unlikely to be attracted unless the investment in fertilizer yields a return of at least 100 percent in a normal season. A 300 percent return is often associated with rapid adoption. Given these threshholds for adoption, the difference between an interest rate of 50 percent *per annum* pales beside a return of 200 percent *per season*.

Many small farmers use relatively little debt. Their interest expenses are small relative to their overall financial flows, and not an important element in their investment calculations. Others who do use credit are generally more concerned about cash flow, about availability of and access to credit rather than about interest cost, which amounts to a relatively small fraction of the amount of credit received.

Many remunerative investments are divisible, such as improved seeds and fertilizer, and can be adopted in a series of small steps.

---

5. See, for example, Appendix A, "Farmers' and Fishermen's Usurious Debts Resettlement Order," in David C. Cole and Yung Chul Park, *Financial Development in Korea, 1945-1978,* (Cambridge: Council on East Asian Studies, Harvard University, 1983). *Ex-post* government amendments to private contracts are not unique to developing countries. In 1933 the United States government abrogated the "gold clause" on its own obligations and on private contracts. The gold clause required settlement of an obligation in gold or in currency having a value equal to a specified weight of gold. It was designed to protect lenders against depreciation of a currency relative to gold. The declaration voiding the gold clause was associated with the devaluation of the dollar against gold, from $20.67 per ounce to $35 per ounce. For a description of the action and its implications, see Milton Friedman and Anna Jacobson Schwartz, *A Monetary History of the United States, 1867-1960.* (Princeton, New Jersey: Princeton University Press, 1968). pp. 468 ff in first Princeton paperback edition, 1971.

Their acquisition is not difficult. Also, loans are not effective means of controlling behavior. Fungibility and the Iron Law of Interest Rates intervene when cheap credit is used to attempt to translate planners' objectives into farmers' activities.

- *Cheap credit is often advocated as an income transfer device* to help the poor, who cannot afford expensive credit because the returns they can obtain from investing are low. Returns may be low because government policies reduce their incomes. For example, agricultural price controls keep food cheap or marketing arrangements for export crops permit the government to extract large margins between export and farmgate prices. Credit may be proposed to offset these effects.

  However, it is tremendously difficult to spread cheap credit widely over the poor, and compensation is proportional to loan size: large borrowers get a large subsidy, small borrowers a small subsidy, and nonborrowers no subsidy. This subsidy is regressive, benefiting primarily the relatively better-off who receive the larger loans. Low lending rates also make it difficult for the poor to obtain access to deposit services on attractive terms because deposit rates normally have to be kept below lending rates for intermediation to be sustainable, and lenders may have insufficient income to support aggressive expansion of their operations. In fact, low rates often undermine lender viability.

- *Some observers believe that high interest rates contribute to inflation* by raising costs. Adams points out that this view reverses the causation between inflation and interest rates, and that it confuses the one-time impact of interest rate increases on price indexes with the continuing influence of interest rates on economic behavior.

  High interest rates help to retard or decrease inflation, as demonstrated by experience in Taiwan[6] and in Korea,[7] while rapid expansion of cheap credit to favored sectors is inflationary, as

---

6. Reed J. Irvine and Robert F. Emory, "Interest Rates as an Anti-Inflationary Instrument in Taiwan," in J.D. Von Pischke, Dale W Adams and Gordon Donald, eds., *op. cit.* pp. 393-397.

7. David C. Cole and Yung Chul Park, *op. cit.* See especially chapter 8, "Price-Stabilization Problems and Policies."

demonstrated in Brazil.[8] Higher interest rates enable financial markets to mobilize more savings, permitting government to reduce deficit spending. By making saving more attractive, higher interest rates induce households to spend less on consumption, reducing upward pressure on prices. Also, higher rates should have the largest corrective impact on large borrowers, while opening financial markets to new borrowers at the frontier and stimulating their production.

• *Cheap credit is often regarded as a "second best" alternative.* It is reasonably easy to provide cheap credit, while it may be difficult politically to adjust the structure of the economy to promote equity and stimulate efficiency directly.

The equity argument includes the position that the poor should not have to borrow at high rates while the rich borrow at low rates, as well as concern for the effect that credit access has on the distribution of income and assets in the economy. The second best argument is weak on equity grounds because cheap credit reaches relatively few, who tend to be better-off. It is not generally relevant to donor-supported projects because project design documents normally show that relatively small retail loans are expected to produce relatively large returns. Interest is a small part of borrowers' total costs, and is also small in comparison with projected increases in their incomes.

On efficiency grounds, cheap credit is unlikely to stimulate producers to use more inputs to produce a good that has an artificially low price. Subsidizing input prices is an economically more efficient way of offsetting the effects of low produce price policies. Fungibility also confounds efforts to draw a direct relationship between credit impact and the purpose for which it is disbursed.

---

8. João Sayad, "The Impact of Rural Credit on Production and Income Distribution in Brazil," in J.D. Von Pischke, Dale W Adams and Gordon Donald, eds., *op. cit.* pp. 379-386; Paulo F.C. de Araujo y Richard L. Meyer, "Dos Décadas de Crédito Agrícola Subsidiado en Brasil," in Dale W Adams, Claudio González Vega y J.D. Von Pischke, eds., *Crédito Agrícola y Desarrollo Rural: La Nueva Visión.* (Columbus, Ohio: Ohio State University, 1987). pp. 192-205.

Why Low Interest Rates Reduce Value at the Frontier

Arguments for low rates disregard the fact that the benefits associated with a single cheap loan are unobtainable in financial markets as a whole. Individuals receiving cheap credit reap a benefit but impose a cost on other individuals and on society. These benefits can be stated at two levels. The first is simply the basic observation that economizing, getting more for less, is generally attractive to consumers.

At the second level, discounting formulas show that it is possible to borrow more, presumably producing a greater impact, at lower rates than at higher rates, given certain assumptions: for a single loan, low interest rates create more value than high interest rates. This is most easily demonstrated by an example assuming that debt service capacity is constant, in this case $100, regardless of the interest rate.

The discounting formula, $v = 1/(1 + i)^n$, indicates that the present value v of 1 received at the end of period n diminishes as interest rate i increases. For example, the present value of 1 received at the end of one year (i.e., n = 1) at a 5 percent per annum rate of interest is 0.952 (or 1/1.05). At a 20 percent interest rate, the present value is only 0.833 (or 1/1.2). In other words, an acceptable promise to pay $100 one year in the future could be traded for a loan of $95.20 at an interest rate of 5 percent, but for a loan of only $83.30 at an interest rate of 20 percent. When the calculation is made for a number years, the value-creating impact of low rates is more dramatic: the value of 1 received at the end of the tenth year is 0.614 at a 5 percent rate, but only 0.162 at 20 percent.

This effect can also be demonstrated by compounding: compounding at a low rate produces less future value than compounding at a high rate. Or, given a target value in the future, the amount of money that would have to be committed now in order to compound to the target level varies inversely with the interest rate.

Review of the arguments refuted by Adams indicates the limited relevance of the observation that low interest rates create more value according to the discounting formula. Cheap credit has distributional and incentive effects that overwhelm the application of the formula. The most interesting questions at the frontier are not whether any credit that is obtained is cheap, but who has access to financial services, and what does it cost to provide and obtain these services. Cheap credit retards expansion of the frontier by limiting the number of borrowers, discouraging savers, and inhibiting intermediation.

Low rates limit the number of borrowers, concentrating loans well within the frontier. Because of this tendency, lenders devote less energy to developing business at the frontier, which remains stubbornly fixed. Governments often respond by providing even larger amounts of cheap loanable funds and by imposing more controls, but these measures are unlikely to be sustainable. Funds will eventually become limited, controls will be increasingly subverted over time or their costs of enforcement will rise, and the hoped-for production or welfare results are unlikely to be achieved.

Low rates discourage savers by reducing the attractiveness of intermediated financial assets. Savers are more likely to keep their savings in cash, to invest them in tangible assets or to engage in speculation. These alternatives tend to be less efficient economically; without financial intermediation resources are less easily directed to high return investments. This effect tends to be self-perpetuating: low returns keep saving low.

Low rates inhibit intermediation. They deprive intermediaries of deposits from the community as a source of loanable funds. Intermediaries may have extensive access to other sources of funds, such as from governments or development assistance agencies. However, dependence on these sources deprives intermediaries of information about savings behavior that is valuable for credit decisions and for welding links of confidence. Without such information, lenders have difficulties building strong loan portfolios. Low rates also inhibit intermediation by concentrating loans in relatively few hands, rather than expanding access to financial services that should occur broadly with development.

Low-Interest Rates Accompany Credit Targets

Interest rates on targeted credit are often kept low as part of selective credit controls that attempt to direct credit to "priority" activities. Maxwell J. Fry provides devastating economic arguments against this unholy alliance, listing six internal inconsistencies in selective low interest policies.[9] These combine and summarize the observations of Johnson concerning the preverse effects of credit targets and quotas cited in the

---

9. Maxwell J. Fry, *op.cit.*

previous chapter with several of the points made by Adams about low interest rates.

First, the use of low interest rates to support activities favored by government encourages investments in lower-yielding activities that otherwise have difficulty attracting finance in spite of their alleged high social returns. Fry states that the record of economic planning provides no clear evidence that planners are able to identify investments with high social but low financial returns.

Second, Fry notes that long-term credit is often the target of interest rate controls. As a result, long-term rates are often below short-term rates, which tends to keep term structures short, reducing the supply of credit, and third, unduly encouraging investment in capital-intensive technology. Fourth, low interest rates on targeted credit are often below deposit rates, and flows from cheap credit sources to attractive deposits thwarts the objective of selective credit policies. This leads to the fifth inconsistency, which is that savings are discouraged because low rates on loans tend in the long run to reduce the returns on deposits.

Sixth, Fry notes that low rates on selected loans tend to give the wrong signals to lenders, who have an incentive to lend first at rates they can select, and last at low rates determined for them, which reduces the supply of credit to sectors favored by the government.

Fry concludes that interest rate controls, as part of selective credit policies, seem to be "an ideal recipe for reducing both the quantity and the quality of productive investment."[10]

Political Economy and Interest Rates

The discussion of low interest rates is not complete if it is limited to equity, economic efficiency and creation of value at the frontier. Governments may have less-than-charitable reasons, such as budgetary and patronage considerations for keeping credit cheap. The budgetary dimension arises because governments are major borrowers in their domestic financial markets. Governments want to keep the cost of funds low so that interest payments do not eat into budgets, crowding out more attractive expenditures.

---

10. *Ibid.* pp. 414.

Patronage considerations are more complex. Political use of credit is most attractive to politicians when they can make funds available at rates below or equal to commercial rates prevailing among large formal borrowers and lenders in the economy. Harry W. Blair observes that, "low interest rates just seem to be good for everyone who matters—at least in the short run, and the short run is the time frame that those in positions of power tend to be most worried about. But the long run costs of these policies may be high."[11]

Kane illustrates the dynamics of credit priced low by government regulation:[12]

> The true purpose of real-world systems of economic regulation is seldom to promote greater economic efficiency in the long run. Lobbying activity seeks primarily to employ government power to redistribute current income and wealth from politically weak to politically powerful sectors....Legislative processes help politicians to disguise and legitimize beggar-my-neighbor political activity by special interests....By delegating the detailed operations of regulatory schemes to a semi–autonomous financial agency, elected officials erect still another layer of cosmetic shielding. Regulatory bureaus insulate sponsoring coalitions and their agent politician from being blamed for the unpopular long-run consequences of specific regulatory decisions.

> Although subsidized loan programs may achieve a good portion of their intended distribution effects in the short run, they impose unintended costs that tend to increase the longer the program stays in operation. First, they tend to require a growing diversion of resources to monitoring....Second, they tend to deprive a program's intended beneficiaries from access to program funds. Third, they tend to produce a more corrupt society in general and a more corrupt bureaucracy in particular.

Kane's vividly politicized world illustrates tendencies that appear when nonmarket devices are used to obtain economic power. When subsidized rates are only slightly below market rates, these tendencies develop to a small degree; highly subsidized rates invite rapid and extensive subterfuge. Unlike the case for market rates of interest, arguments for subsidized credit have no built-in limits—the lower the rate, the better the credit program. These effects may not be fully realized because of competition for

---

11. Harry W. Blair, "Agricultural Credit, Political Economy, and Patronage," in Dale W Adams, Douglas H. Graham and J.D. Von Pischke, eds., *op. cit.* p. 186.

12. Edward J. Kane, "Political Economy of Subsidizing Agricultural Credit in Developing Countries," in Dale W Adams, Douglas H. Graham and J.D. Von Pischke, eds., *op. cit.* pp. 172-173, 176.

patronage, but highly subsidized rates can clearly develop, and negative real rates coupled with poor loan recovery can turn a credit scheme into a great give-away.

Blair suggests that governments have three policy choices when considering the removal of rural interest rate subsidies.[13] These concern primarily large farmers, because they receive the bulk of the subsidy. One is to provide another form of benefit to big farmers to maintain their political loyalty. The second is to build an alternative political constituency to compensate for the loss of large farmer support. The third is to suffer the potential loss of their support.

Blair sees no easy choices among these options, and notes that large farmers may already have captured just about all that government is able to offer. He believes that market interest rates, giving broader access to financial services that expand the frontier, might be obtained by using broadly based, participatory local institutions to distribute credit. In the long run, "nondominant" groups such as the poor could presumably be included more easily in the outreach of these types of institutions than in the activities of large, centralized financial intermediaries. Institutions that might satisfy Blair's description could include community credit unions, other cooperatives, village banks and RoSCAs.

Inadequate Reporting and Insufficient Accountability

Careful readers may have wondered why a book on finance contains so few numbers. Surely the billions of development dollars that have assaulted the frontier have left a trail? In fact, data gathering is a formidable challenge for any student of development finance who consults government and aid agency documents and seeks to go beyond reporting disbursements, levels of investment supported by credit, physical counts of wells dug, hectares planted, and loans made, or an individual success or failure here or there. And most of the success stories that do appear are poorly documented from a financial point of view: it is difficult to evaluate portfolio quality and the extent to which lending is remunerative.

The case for good reporting and accountability in development finance is simply that it enables borrowers, lenders and intermediaries to create more value at the frontier. The incessant valuation that occurs in financial

---

13. *Op. cit.*

markets is refined only by experience and information. Without data, valuation is more difficult, errors in valuation—including failed attempts at innovation—are more costly, and sustainability is harder to achieve. Reporting and accountability are especially important because finance works to close tolerances. Small variations spell the difference between success and failure.

Why then, is development finance not brimming with cases, cost studies and widely discussed and carefully reviewed norms and ranges for key variables such as interest spreads, costs per borrower and per depositor, and net returns to lenders? It may be simply that no one likes to report poor performance, but the probable causes are more complex.

Why Is Frontier Financing Data Usually Scarce?

The political use of credit at the frontier leads to biases in the reporting of results. Kane's thesis, that results are disguised to protect those benefiting from patronage, implies that reporting would concentrate on disbursements, which yield immediate political advantage, and reveal less about repayment and subsequent operating results. Blair's perspective, that support-seeking is important to patronage strategies, suggests that results would be reported selectively to attract or maintain the support of beneficiaries and suppliers of funds.

There is little direct evidence that these effects govern reporting of government programs to push the frontier, although it was noted in chapter 5 that the imposition of targets, quotas and controls—the expressions of patronage—is seldom accompanied by detailed analysis. However, circumstantial evidence reported below appears to support conclusions consistent with Kane and Blair's insights.

Financial Reporting by Frontier Institutions

Presentations of financial data by cooperatives and specialized lenders at the frontier often conceal more than they reveal. This reflects financial housekeeping problems, government accounting standards and a low priority accorded to disclosure. Poor presentation is also a feature of many other firms' financial reporting in developing countries, but why would government-owned or -supported institutions that assume a leading role in development, and have access to external assistance, not be in the forefront of disclosure and promptness in financial reporting?

Although governments have auditors and procedures for parliamentary reviews of the accounts and performance of government corporations, financial presentations are often complex, delayed and assembled according to accounting standards and procedures that make interpretation difficult. Prescribed formats may be altered frequently or exhibit excruciating detail to satisfy statutory requirements rather than to provide summaries that communicate results clearly and quickly to parliamentarians, military officers or other citizens not trained in finance. The shares of cooperatives and most government corporations are not traded, and this may result in a relative unconcern for performance and for value as defined in chapter 1.

Use of Financial Data by Development Assistance Agencies

Development assistance agencies also display a selective approach to financial reporting at the frontier. Reporting financial results appears to be less important than disbursing loans to farmers and small businesses, although diligent efforts are made to ensure proper reporting of the purposes for which project funds are disbursed.

Development assistance agencies do not routinely compile quarterly or annual overall summaries of the operations of the frontier financial institutions they support. Definitions, measures of results and reporting standards vary widely. Hence, these agencies' managers and staff are unlikely to have an integrated view of the financial conditions of institutions included in their portfolio of development finance activites. However, their files usually contain voluminous data on each of these institutions. Data in these files are generally treated as confidential government information or confidential bank-to-bank information and are not available to the public.

Lack of an overall view based on detailed financial data reflects official orientations and objectives. Disbursement is important, as reflected in use of the term "resource transfer" to describe development assistance rather than other terms more clearly oriented toward investment performance and risk. Development assistance agencies are seldom exposed to project- or institution-specific risks, and project analysis may not be finely tuned to risk. Development loans are usually made to governments, and donors' risk is general country risk. Accordingly, country economic performance is closely monitored by batteries of economists to evaluate and identify opportunities for further assistance.

Efforts to deal with risk at the farm level in credit projects are generally restricted to mechanical manipulations of cost and benefit flows to test expected economic rates of return. Little sensitivity analysis is done to refine financing plans. Neither economic nor financial analysis is directed toward the substance of risk, the things most likely to go wrong. Most development finance institutions lending to industrial and commercial firms do no financial risk analysis beyond calculating key financial ratios. Projections are rarely adjusted to show the possible impact of adverse events on loan repayment.

In many cases standard assumptions concerning factory capacity utilization rates are employed, e.g., 60 percent in the first year of production, 70 to 80 percent in the second, and 100 percent in the third, with no sacrifices of profitability per unit of output to achieve increased sales. Norms such as these have lives of their own, even though 100 percent of planned output is often not achieved and when it is achieved it generally requires more than three years. (In developed countries, overall industrial capacity utilization rates above 85 percent are usually associated with inflation and are therefore regarded as danger signals.)

However, the best of these development finance institutions in developing countries deal with risk qualitatively. They devote considerable energy to identifying those industries likely to prosper and those likely to decline, to engineering design and other technical questions, and to selecting ventures backed and managed by dependable and promising individuals and groups.

One reason why the debate over so many aspects of development finance strategy, policy, and impact seems difficult and interminable is that development of data is tortuous. Project analysis is oriented toward the impact of these funds on ultimate borrowers. The impact of credit projects on the institutions that disburse project funds at the frontier is often not measured. When measurement occurs, it is usually confined to cost-benefit tables using simplified assumptions concerning bad debt losses and other key impact variables.

Hence, credit project design normally contains no rigorous in-built check to ensure that lending operations at the frontier will be remunerative. During project implementation the usual focus is on the credit institution's·

overall financial condition, which coincides with one aspect of institution-building. But reporting is often patchy and data submitted may not be closely reviewed by development assistance agency officials except at the clerical level.

Deeper investigation and reporting is usually *ad hoc*. An example is policy papers published by donors, such as those compiled on rural credit and development finance companies by the World Bank in the 1970s. Other major efforts were the Spring Review of Small Farmer Credit conducted by AID in the early 1970s and reports from a series of Food and Agriculture Organization (FAO) regional seminars leading up to a world conference on agricultural credit in 1976. Data are also generated by commissions appointed in various countries to review agricultural finance, the performance of financial institutions, or financial policy and policy alternatives. The All-India Rural Credit Survey and similar Indian government enquiries are among the most accessible and well-known examples. Finally, academic economists' research into finance, often for official sponsors, has yielded most of the enlightened insights that have fueled debates on financial policy at the frontier.

Innovation and Efficiency from Information: Two Cases

In spite of the information problem that surrounds official efforts to expand the frontier, there are some examples where accurate, meaningful information has been diligently sought and where this information has changed behavior in developmental ways. The information gathering, analysis and dissemination process helps to refine the definition of issues and provides a basis for designing activities that are likely to have a developmental impact, or that achieve a desired impact at a lower cost than would be possible without information.

Of course, information is also costly, but its costs usually amount to a relatively small fraction of the funds committed to efforts to expand the frontier. An example from the Philippines suggests how information can create an informed body of opinion and facilitate innovative project design. Crop insurance offers another example of how information stopped donor profligacy, but not until damage had been done. These two examples, discussed in detail in the remainder of this chapter, are offered to show the pay-off from good information and to illustrate the costs of unconcern for information or its disregard.

Facts on Finance at the Frontier in the Philippines

A stunning exception to the generally poor data base on finance at the frontier is found in the Philippines. In 1975 a Presidential Commission on Agricultural Credit (PCAC) was established, along with a secretariat called the Technical Board for Agricultural Credit (TBAC). PCAC was a relatively independent interagency body responsible to the president of the Philippines for agricultural credit policy. In 1987 PCAC and TBAC were reconstituted into an Agricultural Credit Policy Council (ACPC) with somewhat expanded functions.

A major impetus to the founding of PCAC/TBAC was the mounting arrears under Masagana-99 (M-99), a national program designed to stimulate rice production that issued seasonal loans to more than a half-million farmers at its peak. The size and objectives of M-99 attracted attention and it was felt that this, and the multiplicity of credit programs and agencies, probably required coordination and impact measurement.

INSTITUTIONALIZING INFORMATION SYSTEMS. The Philippines has several institutional features that are reflected in the formation and role of PCAC/TBAC. One is a lively, decentralized formal institutional structure in rural finance consisting of cooperatives, private development banks, savings and loan associations, and many essentially private rural banks. Active trade associations for each type of intermediary bring issues to the attention of government officials and the press. Another is relatively open administrative processes. The Central Bank, for example, publishes detailed annual summaries of the conditions of rural banks and the other institutions it supervises. A third is an administrative tradition that permits an agency to operate independently.

PCAC, chaired by the governor of the Central Bank, included key ministers, presidents of government-owned banks and the director-general of the National Economic and Development Authority. The functions of PCAC were to advise government-owned financial institutions concerning agricultural credit, to establish priorities in credit allocation, to review credit program proposals and operations, to coordinate credit activities among institutions and at different stages in agricultural production, processing and marketing, and to oversee the use of government funds by nongovernment agricultural lenders.

The TBAC Board, chaired by a Central Bank deputy governor, included key deputy ministers, bank vice presidents and others of similar rank. During most of its existence, TBAC's staff numbered about 35, organized into three sections: planning and research; monitoring, review and coordination; and administrative services. Most of the staff were professionals with master's degrees who designed surveys and analyzed data collected by students and others hired as field enumerators to interview farmers and gather statistics from bankers.

TBAC/PCAC ACHIEVEMENTS. Generating and interpreting data were TBAC's primary purpose, which enabled it to evaluate credit policies and study proposals for new projects, concepts and institutional changes. TBAC staff responded to requests from board members, but many of its tasks were initiated internally by staff to develop interesting lines of inquiry and explore issues arising from their activities. Research on individual banks was confidential, but data on groups of banks were frequently made public.

The TBAC secretariat was flexible and responsive under young, dynamic leadership that was kept in place long enough to obtain and exercise mastery over the work program and issues. Views of the board and the staff did not always coincide, but conflicts were a healthy part of the information and informing process. The staff's primary fora were the quarterly or more frequent meetings of PCAC.

TBAC mounted major studies and undertook minor research tasks, organized seminars, kept in constant contact with government and banking officials having a stake in rural finance, initiated a statistical series on agricultural credit, developed good relations with local academic researchers in prominent universities, and established an international presence by participating in credit conferences abroad. TBAC produced a steady flow of documents, many of which were published as papers, seminar proceedings, and books.

Concrete results claimed by PCAC and TBAC from 1976 through 1980 included design of loan arrears collection campaigns, introduction of restructuring guidelines for distressed borrowers, design of a rural bank rehabilitation scheme, expansion of rediscounting facilities to private development banks, miscellaneous innovations through amendments to the

General Banking Act, simplifications in loan terms and conditions, and lengthening the term structure of agricultural loans.[14]

Its activities contributed importantly to the most innovative rural finance project ever supported by the World Bank through the mid–1980s. A noteworthy feature was pricing project funds to local lenders at adjustable rates consistent with their costs of obtaining retail deposits from the public. This was to ensure that external funds did not displace deposits as sources of funds for participating intermediaries, making the credit program more robust by providing prospects for continuity with or without external support.

Another feature associated with TBAC's activities and those of its successor, ACPC, was noted by many donor agency officials and researchers from abroad. A relatively large number of people in Philippine government, academic, agricultural, policy analysis and financial circles are extremely well informed about the operations and condition of the country's rural financial system. Those having a need to know have a command of the facts. The information base is healthy and walks around on many pairs of legs rather than reclining on dusty shelves.

This brilliant information infrastructure did not save the Philippine rural credit system from tremendous difficulties. Serious problems were associated with Masagana-99 and began before the founding of PCAC/TBAC. Others related to activities initiated during a period when democratic processes were repressed and political patronage through the financial system became rampant. However, opportunities for recovery and institution-building in the broad sense are clearly much greater because of the activities of PCAC/TBAC and its successor agency.[15] This Philippine innovation creates value because it refines the valuation process and facilitates risk management.

---

14. PCAC/TBAC, *The First Five Years: 1976-1980.* (Manila: PCAC, n.d.).

15. For example, ACPC has issued a series of policy briefs of approximately four pages each that receive wide circulation. One dated January 12, 1989, is titled "The ACPC does not favorably endorse Senate Bill No. 743 and views it is unnecessary." The bill it attacks offers "An Omnibus Code to Rationalize and Promote Small Enterprises, Establish a Credit and Guarantees Corporation, Provide Funds Therefore And, for Other Purposes." PCAC holds that the Bill is inconsistent with the Government's policy and privatization and minimum intervention, and notes that the supply of credit is not the most critical constraint to small enteprise development.

Good Information Aborted Premature Promotion
of Agricultural Insurance

Efforts to introduce all-risk agricultural insurance in developing countries during the late 1970s and early 1980s are a striking example of attempts to move the frontier of formal financial markets. The rise and fall of promotion of all-risk agricultural insurance illustrates the danger of acting on insufficient information, and how good information can limit losses from failed innovations.

Agricultural insurance consists primarily of crop insurance, livestock insurance and crop credit insurance. Crop and livestock insurance directly protect a farmer against loss by paying an indemnity when crop failure or accidental animal deaths occur. Crop credit insurance maintains an indebted farmer's access to credit in the event of crop failure by reimbursing the lender the amount due from the farmer. All-risk or multi-peril insurance covers losses from all events other than farmer negligence or purposeful destruction, while specific-risk coverage is restricted to specified causes of loss such as fire, hail, or flooding.

INSTITUTIONAL SUPPORT FOR DEVELOPMENT OF AGRICULTURAL INSURANCE. Specific-risk crop insurance, especially for hail and fire damage to grain, was developed by private insurance companies in Europe and North America in the late 1800s, but the product was not well-established until the 1920s when the risks to insurers were more clearly understood. In the late 1930s the League of Nations commissioned a study on crop insurance,[16] and the United States and Japan established state-owned crop insurance corporations offering all-risk coverage. These served as models for developing country programs in the 1970s.

Several donors and international agencies promoted all-risk coverage, especially to small farmers. The Special Insurance Programme of the United Nations Conference on Trade and Development (UNCTAD) arranged regional crop insurance conferences supported by funds from the United Nations Development Programme (UNDP), prepared promotional materials[17] and advocated subsidies for crop insurance.[18]

---

16. M. Louis Tardy, *Report on Systems of Agricultural Credit and Insurance* (Geneva: League of Nations, 1938).

17. An important example is Jose Ripoll, "Contribution of Agricultural Insurance toward Economic Development," paper delivered at the UNCTAD/UNDP Seminar on

UNCTAD's interest derived from the Programme of Action on the Establishment of a New International Economic Order adopted by the UN General Assembly in 1974. UNCTAD helped establish national insurance markets in developing countries to reduce the use of foreign exchange to purchase coverage from insurers in developed countries. Objectives were "to increase the volume of premiums written [in local markets] and to limit the number of insurance companies sharing these premiums."[19] These goals were promoted by revising insurance legislation, restricting underwriting to locally-owned or -chartered insurers, making coverage compulsory, and nationalizing insurers or reinsurers (which insure insurance companies for a portion of their risks).

The Food and Agriculture Organization of the United Nations was another source of initiative. FAO had an agricultural insurance specialist on its staff for many years, who wrote in 1975 that, "No sustained and steady development of the agricultural economy of the developing countries is possible without some form of crop insurance to underwrite the risks of crop failure."[20] FAO had organized conferences and prepared country studies on agricultural insurance since 1953.[21]

The United States Agency for International Development funded pilot projects in Latin America and related studies with technical input from the US Federal Crop Insurance Corporation. The Japanese government offered technical assistance and access to Japanese experience. Several

Agricultural Insurance, Colombo, Sri Lanka, 1-5 September 1979. Geneva: UNCTAD/INS/33 GE.79-54061.

18. United Nations Conference on Trade and Development, "Invisibles: Insurance—Crop insurance for developing countries." Study by the UNCTAD secretariat for the Trade and Development Board, Committee on Invisibles and Financing related to Trade, Ninth session, second part, Geneva, 29 September 1980, Item 7 on the provisional agenda. TD/B/C.3/163, 5 May 1980.

19. United Nations Conference on Trade and Development, "Third world insurance at the end of the 1970s." TD/B/C.3/169/Add.1/Rev.1. New York: United Nations, 1981.

20. P.K. Ray, "The Role of Crop Insurance in the Agricultural Economy of the Developing Countries," *Monthly Bulletin of Agricultural Economics and Statistics.* May 1975. Repeated in Ray's seminal work, *Agricultural Insurance: Theory and Practice and Application to Developing Countries.* 2nd ed. (Oxford: Pergamon Press, 1981), p. 309.

21. For an historical account see Paul R. Crawford, *Crop Insurance in Developing Countries.* Unpublished masters dissertation, University of Wisconsin-Madison, 1977. Chapter 1.

others, including France, Israel, Sri Lanka, and Sweden, expressed interest as well.

ECONOMIC BENEFITS OF AGRICULTURAL INSURANCE. This institutional thrust was bolstered by economists who believed that all-risk insurance could deliver economic and social benefits. Among the most notable of these was V.M. Dandekar, who maintained that:

> Crop insurance is part of the institutional infrastructure essential for development of agriculture which is basically insecure. Importance of agricultural credit is now universally understood. Without protection from the insecurity of agriculture, the entire structure of agricultural credit is in danger of total collapse, burying under it the cultivator in perpetual indebtedness.[22]

Advocacy grew partly out of the study of risk in agriculture that captivated many development economists in the mid-1970s. The major theoretical argument is that agricultural investment would increase if growers' risks were diminished.[23] This would permit greater specialization in insured crops and stimulate productivity. Insuring priority crops—cash crops, export crops or food crops—could rearrange national cropping patterns, making them more responsive to government objectives. Insured farmers would obtain credit more easily and in greater amounts because insurance provides a cushion to lenders.

Risk management through insurance could be more than merely financial, because insurance makes risks more transparent (by generating data and experience) and by technical assistance to farmers from or in association with insurers. Bumps in the farm economy due to adverse natural events could be smoothed out, benefiting bankers, input suppliers and providers of other services in rural communities where the rhythm of economic life is determined by the fortunes of agriculture.

Insurance was viewed as economically superior to disaster relief because it is easily targeted and the costs of indemnities would be determined in advance according to insurance contracts. Farmers would

---

22. V.M. Dandekar, "Crop Insurance in India," *Economic and Political Weekly*. June 1976. Review of Agriculture, p. A-80.

23. The definitive work on all aspects of agricultural insurance, which arose in conjunction with international interest in promoting it in developing countries, is Peter Hazell, Carlos Pomareda and Alberto Valdés, eds., *Crop Insurance for Agricultural Development: Issues and Experience*. (Baltimore and London: The Johns Hopkins University Press, 1986).

contribute to the cost directly through premium payments, and payments of claims would come from the insurer's reserves rather than from hard-pressed government budgets. Reinsurance could support broad·coverage over the farm population.

DATA PROBLEMS IN DESIGNING AGRICULTURAL INSURANCE PROGRAMS. Development assistance agencies promoted agricultural insurance programs in a number of developing countries in spite of theory and practice that indicated that the conditions required for these programs' success are extremely rigorous. The FAO specialist noted that problems included a lack of basic data, heterogeneous agricultural practices contributing to wide dispersions in yield levels, small and geographically scattered risks that would make administration difficult, poor land tenure and land record systems, the limited ability of some farmers, lack of staff trained in insurance, poor infrastructure inhibiting field administration, and limited financial resources to support introduction of agricultural insurance.[24]

DESIGN WITHOUT DATA. Many writers, including some in the UNCTAD secretariat, expressed caution. But promotors gave little attention at the outset to the question of how insurable agricultural risks could be covered in a financially viable manner. Data from developing countries that had crop insurance were not fully analyzed.[25] Deficiencies were often blamed on characteristics peculiar to the country concerned, rather than to flaws in insurance design, or were said to be readily correctable. Primary problems included difficulties in collecting premiums from reluctant farmers, achieving sufficient volume without making coverage compulsory, and earning the income and obtaining the subsidies to break even financially. The vulnerability of agricultural insurance to politicization was not widely discussed.

Success stories from developing countries were limited to insurance for the highly organized sugar industry on Mauritius, that introduced coverage in 1947, and for European growers of tobacco in Zimbabwe. Coffee

---

24. See P.K. Ray, *op. cit.* pp. 309-330, for a summary of materials that were published earlier as articles.

25. An example is "Crop Insurance," published in Bangkok in 1984 by the Asian Reinsurance Corporation, an intergovernmental organization formed with UNCTAD assistance. It fails to include any information about loss ratios in its country summaries. Loss ratios show the relationship between premium income and claims paid.

insurance in Puerto Rico, available since 1946, was sometimes also cited by advocates. Programs suffering serious problems, such as well-documented experience in Sri Lanka since 1958, and less well-documented operations in Mexico since 1954 and in Kenya since 1942, were not contemplated in depth, nor were unhappy experiences that had been corrected in the United States[26] and France.[27]

How farmers actually manage risks, the magnitude of these risks, and the factors that determine farmers' willingness to pay for insurance were not entirely clear.[28] One option for addressing these problems would have been to inaugurate a battery of studies to build up information bases on variability in yields and on farmers' responses, for example. Studies of this type require data for a number of years to permit statistically sound rate making (i.e., determining the size of the premium required to cover payment of claims). Could development wait for this tedious bean counting (literally) to be completed?

The most creative effort to address these problems was launched by AID in the form of support for pilot schemes in Bolivia, Ecuador, and Panama. Project documents were optimistic, envisaging a Latin American reinsurance pool to spread risks. Insurance technicians and academic researchers were assigned to these efforts, and operations were closely monitored. After two years it was reasonably clear that farmers were generally unwilling to pay and governments were generally unwilling to charge the premiums required to make these programs viable financially. In other words, farmers in the pilot areas had other, more economical ways of managing risk, and politicians viewed insurance as patronage rather than in commercial terms. These pilot results confirmed experience in other developing countries.

26. See Bruce L. Gardner and Randall A. Kramer, "Experience with Crop Insurance Programs in the United States," in Peter Hazell, Carlos Pomareda and Alberto Valdés, eds., *op. cit.* pp. 195-222. Subsequent experience in the US shows that some reforms unravelled. See "Farmers Play Uncle Sam for Uncle Sap: Taxpayers are the big losers in the federal crop-insurance plan that is badly conceived, badly run and made moot by free bailouts," *U.S. News & World Report*, August 8, 1988. pp. 27-28.

27. See *Le Monde*, "Le rapport de la Cour des comptes sur l'indemnisation des calamités agricoles met en evidence de nombreux abus," ["The Controller General's Report on Claims Paid for Agricultural Losses Reveals Numerous Irregularities," trans. ed.] and "La confiance ne paie pas," ["Confidence Doesn't Pay"], 13 juillet 1979. p. 29.

28. R.H. Schmidt and Erhard Kropp, eds., *op. cit.* p. 89.

EFFECTS OF INFORMATION AWARENESS. The activities of AID, UNCTAD, and FAO led to better and more widely spread information. Data were brought together from a number of countries, officials became more widely aware of each other's experiences, and researchers got involved with agricultural insurance issues. The result was a large body of data and theory identifying characteristics of agricultural insurance programs, their costs, and the conditions required for their financial viability. Only a small part of this data was generated directly by promotion of agricultural insurance. Most of the material that was gathered already existed, but was not readily available and had not been synthesized into meaningful summaries with analyses readily adaptable for policy making and project design. These results could, of course have been obtained relatively cheaply through an investigative research project without spending a penny on promotion, pilot programs, or new institutions.

These data indicate that the economic argument for agricultural insurance is not realized in practice. A review of almost 50 years of federal crop insurance in the United States, for example, concluded that, "it is still difficult to find experimental results that will permit inferences about the effects of crop insurance introduced on a permanent basis in an area where it previously did not exist."[29] Furthermore, "with few exceptions, farmers in both developed and developing countries have been unwilling to pay the full cost of all-risk crop insurance,"[30] which explains why less than 15 percent of land under permanent and arable crops in the United Sates is insured.[31] And, the case for subsidy is suspect: "the social benefits of compulsory crop insurance in Mexico are negative, even before the cost of the subsidy is taken into account."[32]

Finally, "there is no existing multi-peril crop insurance system anywhere in the world that could be recommended as a model to other

---

29. Bruce L. Gardner and Randall A. Kramer, *op. cit.* p. 218.

30. Pater Hazell, Carlos, Pomareda and Alberto Valdés, "Introduction," in Peter Hazell, Carlos Pomareda and Alberto Valdés, eds., *op. cit.* p. 7.

31. Coverage of federal crop insurance in recent years has ranged from 9 percent of land planted to major crops and fruits and vegetables in 1983 to 14 percent in 1985. See United States Department of Agriculture, *Agricultural Statistics 1986.* (Washington, DC: United States Government Printing Office, 1986). Tables 559 and 597.

32. This conclusion of a study by analysts of crop insurance in Mexico is reported by Peter Hazell, Carlos Pomareda and Alberto Valdés, "Introduction," in Peter Hazell, Carlos Pomarada and Alberto Valdés, eds., *op. cit.* p. 8.

countries."[33] Although "developed countries are able to afford programs that produce no measurable positive results (and some very negative ones)...severely strained national budgets make these programs doubly questionable for developing countries. They do not productively use state resources and in many cases prove to be counterproductive."[34]

On the design and administrative side, accurate rate making requires a data base that seldom exists in developing countries. Claims adjustment—determining the amount of indemnities to be paid for individual farmers' claims—was more demanding than assumed by promoters. Loss ratios (measuring the relationship between premiums received and indemnities paid) for many existing programs were quite high, requiring substantial subsidies. Government subsidies were cited equal to 25 percent of claims paid in the US, 50 percent in Brazil and 80 percent in Mexico.[35] Promoters simply failed to factor existing data into project design. Initial enthusiasm for insurance was not matched by energetic enquiry into what developing countries could afford.

Realizations from the old and new data that accumulated led to virtual discontinuation of AID support for agricultural insurance. FAO and UNCTAD activities in this area were scaled back simultaneously. Good information resulted in decisions permitting the better use of resources.

While promoters turned their backs on unpromising results, their blind advocacy produced an antidevelopmental impact that is less easily left behind. The surge of international enthusiasm backed by aid left several countries with agricultural insurance programs that continue to absorb government funds. Political attractiveness and bureaucratic inertia keep them alive—it is hard to kill a program that has access to government funds, a constituency, and that claims to be doing good.[36]

33. R.A.J. Roberts, W.M. Gudger and D. Gilboa, *AGS Bulletin on Crop Insurance.* Draft. Rome: FAO, 1987. p. 4.

34. *Ibid.*, p. 1.

35. Pater Hazell, Carlos Pomareda and Alberto Valdés, "Introduction," in Peter Hazell, Carlos Pomareda and Alberto Valdés, eds., *op. cit.* p. 8.

36. William M. Gudger and Luis Avalos, "Planning for the Efficient Operation of Crop Credit Insurance Schemes," in Peter Hazell, Carlos Pomareda and Alberto Valdés, eds., *op. cit.* pp. 278-280.

7

SIGNS OF POOR FITS AT THE FRONTIER

Markets are avenues of self expression and mutual accommodation. They reward harmonization of the interests of buyers and of sellers. Financial market innovations that produce good fits between intermediaries and clients create value and are sustainable. They reduce transaction costs, produce good loans and profitable intermediation, promote mutually beneficial activities voluntarily undertaken, and provide incentives for responsible behavior.

Signs of poor fits deserve attention. They offer scope for corrective action, for refinements in the valuation process that lower costs by reducing behavior that retards financial market development. Common signs of poor fits in development finance are the subject of this chapter. They include irrelevant lending criteria, unnaturally high transaction costs, intensive and extensive credit rationing, substitution and diversion of funds, poor loan collections, unprofitable intermediation, irrelevant reporting, and inappropriate funding.

Irrelevant Lending Criteria

Relevant criteria contribute to remunerative lending and good loans: irrelevant criteria do not. Irrelevant lending criteria indicate a poor fit, that credit is assigned an inappropriate role. Incomplete or poorly applied but relevant criteria are basically consistent with good lending and can be refined with experience and time. Irrelevant criteria tend to have lives of their own in development assistance and government policy, however, and are more insidious in their potentially antidevelopmental impact.

Irrelevant criteria have two unfortunate effects on loan quality. One is that they impose unnecessary *diversionary* transaction costs on decision processes by consuming time, energy and resources that should be devoted to dealing with variables that produce good loans. Diversionary criteria complicate and slow decisionmaking without directly undermining loan portfolio quality. A more serious *destructive* effect occurs when irrelevant criteria bias decisionmaking in ways that increase the incidence of bad loans and unremunerative lending.

Familiar Examples of Irrelevant Lending Criteria

Some examples of irrelevant lending criteria were cited in previous chapters. "Credit needs" and related concepts, explored in chapter 4, impose diversionary effects when they produce meaningless numbers, and destructive effects by focusing on need and related concerns rather than on the source of loan repayment.

Loan targeting can also be irrelevant. If developers want to assist micro-enterprises owned by women, for example, preoccupation with disbursing credit to this target group can divert attention from the fundamental question of whether a credit institution can interact effectively with micro-enterprises. A second question is whether or how micro-enterprises owned by women have characteristics arising from their ownership that are likely to enhance or diminish loan quality. If the fundamental question is not examined, a women's micro-enterprise credit project poses a destructive risk, regardless of the energy devoted to exploring the gender dimensions of credit relationships and entrepreneurship.[1]

Is The Economic Rate of Return a Relevant Lending Criterion?

The best and the brightest red herring in credit projects is the economic rate of return (ERR). The ERR is calculated using actual prices that are adjusted to compensate for factors that distort them from an economic point of view. These factors include monopoly, taxes and subsidies, and quantitative trade restrictions, all of which intervene to make prices unrepresentative of economic or true scarcity values. The ERR is supposed to show the return an investment yields for "the economy." Intermediaries lending project funds for development are often required to include ERR

---

1. Chapter 10 discusses a stunningly successful bank that lends primarily for micro-enterprises operated by women.

estimates in analyses of industrial loan proposals and in farm budgets used for agricultural credit decisionmaking.

The relationship between loans that make good economic sense and those that make good financial sense is unclear. Loan repayment is made possible by cash flows in the currency in which the loan is payable, while ERRs are not based on any currency but on analytical assumptions. Two cases, explained below, reflect the divergence between financial strength and the ERR. One is the combination of a low projected ERR and prospects for good financial performance, while the second is poor financial performance but a high expected ERR.

LOW PROJECTED ERR AND GOOD FINANCIAL PROSPECTS. When importing is cheaper than producing locally, governments sometimes erect tariff and nontariff barriers to reduce imports and encourage local production. Firms that are highly protected by these barriers may be successful financially while imposing high costs economically, and consequently have low ERRs. However, they tend to be attractive loan applicants because they are protected by government from import competition. However, setting up and operating a business is risky, to which is added the risk that protection may someday be removed, while importing involves relatively little risk.

To promote economic efficiency, donors often require intermediaries retailing project funds to calculate ERRs for each investment or borrower financed. However, poor economic analysis results when intermediaries sense that it is irrelevant to making good loans, when it stands in the way of engaging attractive clients, and when donors do not enforce ERR reporting requirements or analytical standards. ERRs frequently impose diversionary costs on intermediaries and fail to deal effectively with risk. (In fact they may even fail to deal fully with economic costs. An Inter-American Development Bank study[2] noted that financial intermediaries' costs of allocating, administering and recovering loans is rarely included in these analyses, which focus exclusively on the activities of subborrowers.)

HIGH PROJECTED ERR BUT POOR FINANCIAL PROSPECTS. A destructive effect occurs when enthusiasm for investments with high projected ERRs diverts attention from their financial characteristics. When the ERR is the major criterion for investment attractiveness, and when credit need is assumed to

---

2. Inter-American Development Bank. *Op. cit.* pp. 18, 28.

equal a high portion of project cost, project design may lock retail intermediaries into unremunerative lending. Borrowers may have difficulty achieving commercial success when elements of success are less carefully studied than ERR calculations in project design. Faltering commercial performance, compounded by relatively high debt service burdens, produces poor loan repayment.

This situation is captured by "Murgatroyd's Inversion," the observation by a World Banker that the greater the sophistication in the economic analyses constructed by industrial development banks in Africa, the greater the probability of serious portfolio problems. Perceiving project performance or returns to a portfolio as a function of average ERR levels is misleading for the reasons suggested above, and also because several large failures can devastate a portfolio confined by the close tolerances of finance.

ERRs ARE IRRELEVANT TO CREDIT ALLOCATION. Properly calculated economic rates of return may be useful guides for economic planning, but they offer no guidance on how investments should be financed. Attempts to clothe credit with favorable ERRs indulge the imagination. Even if projected ERRs for credit-supported investments are carefully calculated and diligently reported, and even if credit is used as specified in the loan contract, fungibility confounds the usefulness of the ERR. The borrower may have other funds that in the absence of the loan would be devoted to activities associated with the project. When the loan is received, these alternative funds can be devoted to activities with low ERRs. Also, the intermediary may use funds for purposes with low ERRs that would have been invested in high ERR activities in the absence of external assistance to such activities.

Under certain circumstances, fungibility may force project funds into the *least* remunerative activities available. This tendency is strongest when project-supported activities are the best available, when projects fail to innovate in ways that would not otherwise have been exploited, and when market fragmentation is low, permitting funds to flow more easily to alternative uses. Market fragmentation is low when households borrow, as they have numerous activities.

Unnaturally High Transaction Costs

Financial intermediation at the frontier is costly, especially for formal institutions. The frontier is often spread over large geographical areas, involves relatively small transactions and balances, and requires relatively large amounts of noninterest-earning cash to serve depositors and borrowers. Obligations to formal institutions may not be accorded high priority at the frontier, especially when institutions are not responsive to clients. These factors create relatively high transaction costs.

The challenge for financial market development is to cover transaction costs and to reduce them. They are diminished by improved management of existing intermediaries and by innovations in intermediation. An advancing frontier reduces transaction costs for people who are brought within it.

While transaction costs at the frontier are naturally high, those associated with credit programs, targets and quotas are probably unnaturally high, demonstrating a poor fit. Intermediaries have little incentive to relate costs to productivity in nonmarket situations, and cost control may be poor. Program design may add costs unnecessarily because credit project operating costs are not always fully estimated in project design.

The problem to be addressed in project design, therefore, is costs that are higher than they would be in a competitive situation and how these costs are distributed among depositors, intermediaries and borrowers. Unfortunately, little data are available to show the extent of unnaturally high costs, and comparisons are difficult because many factors influence these costs. However, transaction costs are material.

Borrowers' Transaction Costs

The first major attempt to quantify small farmer credit transaction costs appears to have been undertaken by Mirza Shahjahan.[3] His pioneering theme was developed in a survey article by Dale W Adams and G.I. Nehman, who identified three types of such costs: noninterest charges by lenders; loan application procedures that require the applicant to deal with agents outside the banking system, such as agricultural extension staff,

---

3. *Agricultural Finance in East Pakistan.* (Dacca: Asiatic Press, 1968).

local officials and cosigners; and travel expenses and time spent promoting and following up the application.[4]

Adams and Nehman noted that new applicants often have to make between five and seven trips to the lending institution before receiving their first formal loan. Based on Shahjahan's data and on the observation that formal lenders reject many applicants who have not borrowed before, they concluded that the overall costs of formal borrowing made informal credit more attractive to many small farmer applicants.

From Shahjahan's data, Adams and Nehman estimated that interest payments amounted to less than half of the borrowing costs of 2,500 sampled borrowers from the Agricultural Development Bank of Pakistan; for a six-month loan, noninterest costs amounted to 91 percent of the amount borrowed, a level that strains plausibility if it is assumed that borrowers know their costs and expect to repay their loans.

A 1981 study of the transaction costs of borrowers from the Bangladesh Krishi Bank, successor to the Agricultural Development Bank of Pakistan, reported material but somewhat lower costs. Zia U. Ahmed surveyed 61 borrowers in 12 villages served by the Raipura branch, and calculated average transaction costs equal to 22 percent of loan size, with a standard error of about 2 percent.[5]

Nehman surveyed 150 farmers in São Paulo State, Brazil, in 1971. He found that, ignoring inflation, noninterest costs on formal loans constituted from 14 to 71 percent of borrowing costs. The smaller the loan and the shorter its term or tenor, the higher the transaction cost relative to the amount borrowed. Adams and Nehman cited data compiled by V.M. Villamil Ortiz for a sample of 63 Colombian farmers, most of whom farmed less than 10 hectares. For formal loans, Villamil found that interest rates averaging 13 percent amounted to only 30 percent of total borrowing costs, which in turn amounted to 42 percent of amounts borrowed.

Lenders' Transaction Costs

The World Bank's 1975 agricultural credit sector policy paper suggests that the annual administrative costs for efficient medium- and long-term

---

4. D.W Adams and G.I. Nehman, "Borrowing Costs and the Demand for Rural Credit," *Journal of Development Studies.* 15, 2, January 1979.
5. Zia U. Ahmed, "Effective Costs of Rural Loans in Bangladesh," *World Development.* 17, 3, 1989. pp. 360-361.

agricultural lenders would amount to between 7 and 10 percent of the size of the loan portfolio. Estimates of administrative costs as a percent of new loans made ranged from 3 percent for a lender in Mexico to 50 percent for a lender in Uganda.[6]

Katrine Anderson Saito and Delano P. Villanueva estimated that lenders' annual administrative costs in the Philippines ranged from 3 to 4 percent of amounts outstanding to small scale agriculture and industry.[7] In a new small farmer credit program in the Yemen Arab Republic in the mid-1970s, Mohammad Rashrash Mustafa reported that administrative costs equalled about 18 percent of amounts loaned for seasonal agricultural inputs.[8] In Malawi, estimated seasonal credit administration costs equalled between 7 and 8 percent of amounts loaned from 1970 through 1973 in the Central Region Lakeshore Development Project, and in the Lilongwe Land Development Project fell from 331 percent to 4 percent of the average loan size between 1968 and 1973 as the number of borrowers expanded from 656 to 21,469 and as average loan size rose from about US$10 equivalent to about US$26 equivalent.[9]

An important and pioneering evaluation of agricultural projects by the Inter-American Development Bank (IDB) reviewed transaction costs and their origins.[10] In one case cited, the costs associated with loan generation and administration amounted to 14 percent of the volume of lending, and 82 percent of this cost was personnel cost. In a second case cited, these percentages were 8.2 percent and 76 percent, respectively. The study found that the level of these costs is directly related to the administrative procedures and staffing practices employed by lenders. Where a credit project involves many lending criteria, terms and conditions, costs tend to be higher than for simpler projects. IDB concluded that on-site visits to

6. *Agricultural Credit*. Washington, DC: World Bank, 1975. pp. 44-45, Annex 13.

7. Katrine Anderson Saito and Delano P. Villanueva, "Transaction Costs of Credit to the Small-Scale Sector in the Philippines," *Economic Development and Cultural Change*. 29, 3, April 1981. pp. 634-635.

8. Mohammad Rashrash Mustafa, "Agricultural Credit Fund Activities in Tihama: April 75 - October 77, Final Report." Yemen Arab Republic, Tihama Development Project, November 1977. pp. 31-32.

9. J.D. Von Pischke, World Bank office memorandum to T.C. Creyke, December 7, 1973, "Malawi—Lilongwe Land Development Project: Smallholder Credit Arrangements and Proposals for the Development of Smallholder Credit."

10. *Op. cit.* pp. 14 ff.

farms and extensive legal reviews of guarantees and other loan documents contributed to high costs, as does overstaffing. In one project, 90 percent of the loan applications required between three and four-and-one-half months to process, while in the most efficient office studied the turn-around time for an application was about three weeks. Processing time did not vary with loan size in one project, while in others it tended to be longer for larger loans. The IDB study indicates that cumbersome procedures create unnecessarily high costs, often without producing good loans, and that the overall costs of lending expressed as a proportion of amounts loaned can easily exceed interest rates charged by agricultural credit institutions.

Carlos E. Cuevas and Douglas H. Graham studied the administrative costs of a private commercial bank and an agricultural development bank in Honduras.[11] Their results suggest that credit program design and institutional organization significantly influence transaction costs. The commercial bank's administrative expenses amounted to about 2.5 percent of amounts loaned, while the agricultural bank's were equal to 8.4 percent. The commercial bank's major costs were associated with deposit mobilization, while the development bank's were related to lending.

The commercial bank was decentralized, and most lending costs were incurred by branches. The development bank was centralized, partly because of reporting requirements associated with loan targeting by donors, and its head office lending costs exceeded those incurred by branches. The commercial bank was more cautious, as reflected in higher proportions of lending costs arising from staff, loan evaluation, and loan recovery costs. About 7 percent of the development bank's lending costs were from loan supervision, against only 4 percent for the commercial bank.

With respect to agricultural lending by the commercial bank, Cuevas and Graham estimated that the average administrative cost of each loan under a donor-supported project was equal to 7.8 percent of the amount of the loan, while for other agricultural loans the figure was 3.1 percent. Also, loans under the donor-supported project averaged more than twice the size of other agricultural loans, which should have reduced transaction

11. Carlos E. Cuevas and Douglas H. Graham, "Agricultural Lending Costs in Honduras," in Dale W Adams, Douglas H. Graham and J.D. Von Pischke, eds., *op. cit.* pp. 96-103.

costs assuming that loan appraisal and administration costs do not vary greatly with loan size.

The Cuevas and Graham study does not compare the clients, credit portfolios, loan terms, and profitability of the commercial and agricultural banks, making it difficult to judge institutional appropriateness or efficiency. However, the data illustrate vividly that costs vary between institutions, and, for agricultural loans, between donor-funded lending and other lending.

Intensive and Extensive Credit Rationing

Well-functioning financial markets value promises efficiently. Loan sizes are appropriate, tailored to borrowers' prospects, adjusted for risk, and finance some portion of the borrowers' costs but not profit. Efficient loan sizes fit borrowers' repayment capacity and stimulate enterprise.

Loan sizes that are inappropriate reflect a poor fit between the objectives of lender and borrower, and tend to result in bad loans and unremunerative lending. Poor loan sizing is illustrated by intensive credit rationing, which allocates too much credit to too few borrowers, and extensive credit rationing, which issues too little credit to too many borrowers. The explanations that follow assume moderate to high degrees of rationing of small farm credit.

Intensive Credit Rationing

Intensive credit rationing occurs when a relatively small target group receives relatively large loans. These loans are issued for purposes that greatly change borrowers' productive activities. Local cows are replaced by exotic breeds; bullocks are discarded for tractors; rainfed land is irrigated; traditional crop varieties and husbandry practices are abandoned to adopt modern varieties or different crops dependent upon purchased inputs.

Intensive credit rationing is often found in agricultural credit projects because it promises great increases in borrowers' incomes as a result of technical innovation. Intensively rationed credit is supply-leading, and responds to the perception that finance is a binding constraint. Borrowers could not reasonably be expected to repay the loan from their pre-loan cash flows, so loan repayment must come from incremental cash flow generated by the loan-supported investment. Credit allocation under these circumstances tends to be quite selective, and elaborate access mechanisms using farm budgets are frequently employed by lenders.

Intensively rationed credit in effect performs the function of equity capital, absorbing the impact of risk. Adversity diminishes borrowers' debt servicing capacity and may be reasonably anticipated in agriculture and in adoption of new technologies. By imposing relatively large debt service burdens and by being designed to change technology significantly, intensive credit rationing can push finance beyond a borrower's managerial and risk-bearing capabilities, especially during the critical initial period of adaptation to change. The new activity may not generate sufficient cash flow to repay the loan that facilitated its adoption. Borrowers may have relatively little of their own resources committed to the loan-supported investment, which tends to reduce their commitment to its successful performance.

Intensively rationed credit may also undermine project objectives. Relatively large loans may tempt poor borrowers to divert a portion for purposes not envisaged by the lender, especially if the borrower is not entirely comfortable with the leap in risk and managerial demands and labor requirements of agreed loan use. Diverted funds not used productively reduce repayment capacity. Lenders have fewer resources to recycle to new borrowers as arrears accumulate, delaying or denying access, and increasing pressures for concentrating loans on well-known large borrowers who already use advanced technology.

Extensive Credit Rationing

Credit is rationed extensively to relatively large numbers of farmers in broad target groups. For example, all members in good standing of a cooperative may have access to seed and fertilizer loans. All commercial growers of wheat having land titles may be eligible for production loans. Extensive credit rationing is most often found in seasonal loan programs for agricultural inputs. It is motivated by considerations of access as well as of production, and access mechanisms are simple.

Broad access to a credit program implies relatively small loans. Loan limits are usually specified as rules of thumb, such as standard amounts per hectare. Small amounts issued to each borrower satisfy the production orientation of planners and inspire broad political appeal.

In promoting broad access to credit through simple procedures, lenders offer credit to some who do not use it wisely, or who have little intention of repaying, or who are so exposed to risk or so close to subsistence that even small cash repayment obligations are formidable. Some who borrowed with the expectation that their agricultural incomes would be increased may be disappointed. Investments, even in seasonal inputs, may have indivisibilities—improved seeds without fertilizers may perform worse than traditional varieties, for example. Borrowers may not use packages of inputs as prescribed because of risk aversion or a desire to convert part of the package to cash for use elsewhere. Lenders find it difficult to supervise large numbers of borrowers, or to ensure that they have adequate information on loan-supported technologies.

Extensively rationed credit does not necessarily stimulate adoption of new technologies, and loans may be too small to produce commitment to their productive use or repayment. As extensively rationed credit operations accumulate arrears, lenders may try to maintain wide access by reducing average loan size, creating even more incentives for default. Inflation may reduce loan size in purchasing power terms, with the same effect.

Repayment Capacity as a Guide to Financial Development

Figure 7.1 portrays intensive and extensive credit rationing as departures from an optimum allocation of a given supply of credit based on repayment capacity. At the intersection, 0, of the axes in figure 7.1, the repayment capacity of individual borrowers and of all borrowers at the point of time portrayed is equal to the debt service payments they have contracted and are expected to be able to make to lenders. Intensive rationing departs from this optimum by lending too much to too few, while extensive rationing lends too little to too many.

The alternative possibilities suggested by the remaining quadrants in figure 7.1 include too much credit issued to too many borrowers, in which case widespread overindebtedness may be a major social problem and a cause of financial market difficulties as massive rescheduling, write-offs and foreclosures may be forthcoming. Too little credit for too few borrowers, on the other hand, provides opportunites for financial intermediation and development by increasing the supply of loanable funds and by innovative changes in the structure of the financial system and in the instruments it trades.

The possibilities suggested by figure 7.1 expand the point that finance works to close tolerances. The initial statement of this fact in chapter 3 used illustrations from a credit project and for a lending institution, while figure 7.1 portrays the situation of individual borrowers and lenders and for the entire financial system. In only one of the four quadrants, that in which too little credit flows to too few borrowers, does departure from the optimum, where debt service equals the ability to service debt, not endanger the strength of the financial system. In three of four directions, being off course can put lenders on the rocks.

Figure 7.1 Credit Rationing and Borrowers' Repayment Capacity

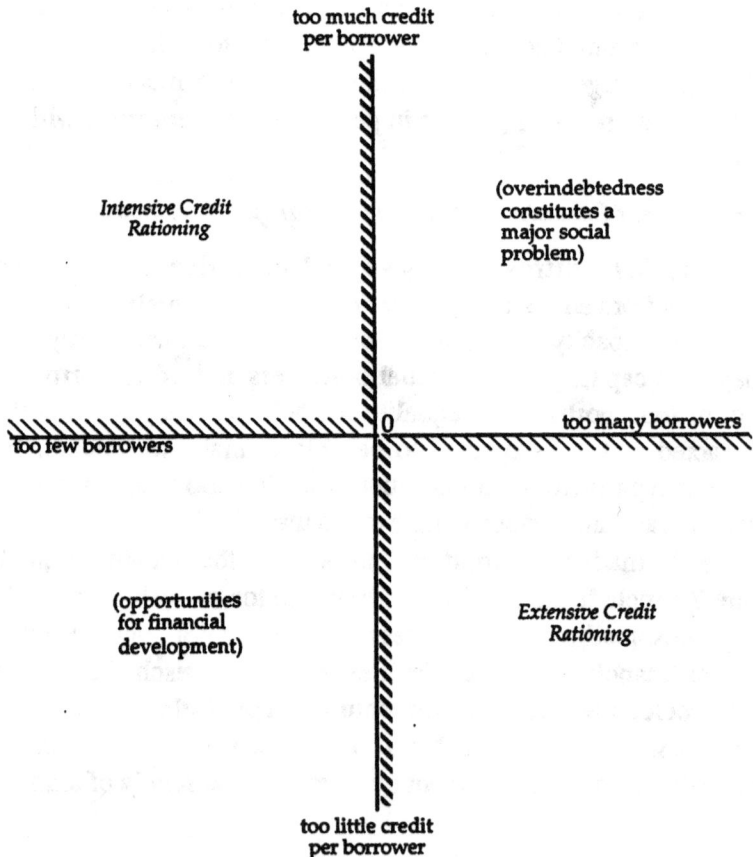

Loan Substitution

Loan substitution occurs when a loan is obtained to fulfill an objective that would be achieved without the loan. The loan substitutes for the borrower's funds, which are devoted to some other purpose, or for another loan.

Substitution is not necessarily a problem or a sympton of a poor fit if the loan is remunerative and if the lender assumes that credit expands overall uses of funds. Lenders with this approach base credit decisions on each loan applicant's overall financial situation and on confidence. Even though a loan may be requested for a specific purpose or activity, the lender is not disturbed if the purpose or activity would have been undertaken without the loan.

Loan substitution becomes a problem when credit is expected to change behavior in a specified way, such as adopting a new crop or technology, for example. If the change would occur in any event, attempts to stimulate it with credit are unnecessary. Credit would be better used in a situation where it makes the difference between a continuation of inferior behavior and adoption of more productive behavior. A larger problem arises when credit is subsidized, as usually occurs in development projects. The economic case for subsidy assumes that without subsidy desired effects would not occur. But if subsidized credit simply substitutes for unsubsidized funds, the subsidy is not required.

When the motive for subsidy is purely political, the economic effects are not regarded as important. Political subsidy attempts to increase the market share of the subsidized program or lender, so that beneficiaries will exhibit behavior consistent with the political objectives of program designers. These objectives may be stated in terms of stimulating social change, displacing usurious moneylenders, or obtaining votes for a certain candidate or party. Substitution does not concern the sponsors, whose objective is met when the subsidy is transferred to target group borrowers.

The greater the subsidy and the greater the emphasis on credit use for specific purposes, the greater the probability of substitution. Subsidy attracts false demand for credit as well as bankable propositions from subsidy seekers. Lenders may have a difficult time discriminating between genuine and opportunistic behavior, and have an incentive, according to the Iron Law of Interest Rates, to use transaction costs as a means of rationing cheap credit. These forces tend to result in capture of the subsidy by those least deserving it.

Loan Diversion

Loan diversion occurs when funds are borrowed for a purpose that is not undertaken. Diversion is more serious than substitution and always points to a poor fit. Substitution is a normal, predictable feature of fungible finance, but diversion demonstrates shortcomings in project implementation or design: the intermediary or others responsible for the selection of borrowers are unable to locate or to serve those whom the project is designed to benefit, or to address the highest priorities of the intended target group, or to ensure that only the intended beneficiaries obtain project credit. Diversion has serious implications for financial development. It compromises confidence and is fraudulent when it violates the loan agreement or other representations made by the borrower.

Diversion indicates disagreement between borrowers and project designers regarding the most attractive use of funds, and the extent to which project activities are relevant. Diversion subverts project design, and reflects rejection of design by implementing agencies or credit recipients. It may arise from unrealistic design. The intermediary may be poorly selected, unable to interact effectively with the target group. Or, the target group may be smaller than expected or have different characteristics than assumed, which makes it difficult to implement the project as planned. Diversion by members of the target group suggests that project designers misunderstood their objectives or that credit does not provide sufficient incentive for target group members to adjust their behavior as project designers desire.

Subsidized and politically motivated credit invites diversion. Subsidy attracts opportunists, and political motivation, except in revolutionary or other turbulent times when loyalties are at stake, tends to result in greater emphasis on "resource transfer" than on monitoring loan use. Many politicized lenders do not call loans for immediate repayment or take punitive action upon discovery of diversion.

Poor Loan Collections

Low collection rates, often less than those required to make project lending self-sustaining, are common in government-sponsored and donor-supported frontier projects. Some relatively well-known cases of poor collections under specific projects include smallholder rubber credit in Liberia, with collections over a ten-year period of less than 1 percent of amounts due, cocoa rehabilitation project credit in Ghana with recovery rates below 10 percent, integrated agricultural development project credit in Kenya with recovery rates of less than 30 percent over a ten-year period, and small scale industry lending in Bangladesh for which lenders collected less than the interest billed. (Under generally accepted accounting principles collections are credited first to interest due and the remainder is used to reduce loan principal balances outstanding.) These horror stories (from a lender's point of view) illuminate the lower bound. None of these projects was strikingly innovative.

Collection Data and Data Collection

The pervasiveness of loan recovery problems, obviously marking a poor fit, could be expected to have stimulated efforts to monitor collection performance closely. However, this has not occurred and collection performance data in projects designed to force the frontier outward are often lacking or difficult to interpret. This reflects low levels of reporting and accountability, as discussed in the previous chapter.

The drafters of the World Bank's *Agricultural Credit Sector Policy Paper* attempted to compile a comprehensive report on loan collection rates for agricultural credit in developing countries in the early 1970s. Their figures were included in the AID Spring Review of Small Farmer Credit and elaborated in Gordon Donald's summary of and commentary on the Spring Review,[12] which is the source cited here. They show collections ranging from 23 percent for the Agricultural Development Bank of Afghanistan in 1970-72, to 98 percent for the Lilongwe Land Development Project in Malawi. Point estimates were given for 26 cases. Of these, collections of between 40 and 60 percent of amounts due were reported for nine cases, between 61 and 80 percent for six cases, and between 81 and 95 percent for 11 cases.

There is no subsequent comprehensive compilation, but data for individual countries confirm the pattern identified in the early 1970s.

---

12. Gordon Donald, *Credit for Small Farmers in Developing Countries.* (Boulder, Colorado: Westview Press, 1976). pp. 140-141. Donald's table records annual arrears rates; collection ratios are 1 minus the arrears rate.

Richard L. Meyer and Aruna Srinivasan reported in 1987 that recovery rates for short-term agricultural loans made by banks in Bangladesh from 1979 through 1984 generally approximated 10 percent on the due date, rising to between 60 and 70 percent five years after the due date, with much less promising trends for loans disbursed in 1983 and 1984.[13] (Their data is shown graphically as Figure 14.1 in chapter 14.) For small enterprise lending, World Bank staff calculated from data collected in Bangladesh that the bad debt risk premium approximated 19 percent per annum.

Orlando J. Sacay, Meliza H. Agabin, and Chita Irene E. Tanchoco report collection ratios for major programs in the Philippines surveyed by the Technical Board for Agricultural Credit.[14] Ratios of loan amounts collected divided by amounts matured, ranged from 49 to 71 percent for supervised credit programs sampled in 1977, and from 58 to 86 percent for others. For another sample of Philippine programs, repayment rates as of 1982 ranged from 67 to 91 percent, with average rates for the period 1977 through 1982 ranging from 72 to 82 percent.

Another important study of repayment rates was compiled by Leila Webster in 1989.[15] She examined the performance of World Bank projects that provided credit to small- and medium-scale industrial and commercial enterprises. The average sizes of loans disbursed to firms receiving project credit ranged from US$5,267 to $325,000. Her data base covered 15 years and included 70 projects. Of these, funds under 33 projects had been fully disbursed. She classified these 33 projects into three groups (high, medium, and low) based on the overall collection rate achieved under each project. Repayment rates classified as high exceeded 90 percent, medium ranged from 90 to 70 percent, and the remainder were classified as low. Her results are presented in Table 7.1.

---

13. Richard L. Meyer and Aruna Srinivasan, "Policy Implications of Financial Intermediation Costs in Bangladesh." Paper presented at the Seminar on Bank Accounting Issues in Bangladesh, Dhaka, October 28, 1987. Economics and Sociology Occasional Paper No. 1389, Agricultural Finance Program, Department of Agricultural Economics, The Ohio State University. Columbus, Ohio: October 18, 1987. p. 30.

14. Orlando J. Sacay, Meliza H. Agabin and Chita Irene E. Tanchoco, *op. cit.* pp. 47, 50.

15. Leila Webster, "World Bank Lending for Small and Medium Enterprises: Fifteen Years of Experience." Industry and Energy Department Working Paper, Industry Series Paper No. 20. Washington, DC: 1989. pp. 18, 72, 73, 76, 78.

Eight projects accounting for 41 percent of the funds disbursed achieved high repayment rates, while 10 projects accounting for 13 percent of the funds had low repayment rates. Overall, almost 60 percent of the funds provided by the World Bank were devoted to projects that failed to achieve a 90 percent collection rate. The weighted average collection rate for the 33 projects slightly exceeded 80 percent.

Interpretation and comparison of repayment data are not possible. In many cases the formula used to calculate the collection rate is not specified, and different institutions use different formulas. The general concept is to divide amounts collected by amounts due. Interpretation and comparison problems arise primarily from differing treatments of amounts in arrears at the start of the period for which the calculation is made. If these are included in the denominator, the ratio is lower than if collections are compared only to amounts becoming due during the period. Some institutions include both principal and interest in the calculation, others may restrict it to principal, and alternative treatments of interest further complicate comparisons.

Orders of magnitude suggested by available information indicate serious nonrepayment problems. A cumulative collection ratio of 50 percent means basically that the lender recovers half of the amount due. When the 50 percent that is recovered is recycled into new loans that also achieve a 50 percent collection ratio, the lender has only one-quarter of the original amount available for lending. And, recycling would cut this to one-eighth, again assuming a 50 percent cumulative collection ratio. Through this cumulative process of decay, institutions decapitalize and programs die.

Collection rates of 75 percent in agricultural credit projects are often cited as relatively "satisfactory" by development assistance agency technicians involved in project design. After five cycles of lending with recovery rates of 75 percent, less than 25 percent of the amount loaned in the first cycle remains available for sixth cycle lending.

Causes of Poor Collections: Borrower-Lender Relations

Low collection rates were for many years attributed to either inability or unwillingness to repay. The literature is filled with examples of each of these situations, and the possibilities of inability to repay out of activities

Table 7.1 World Bank Lending for Small and Medium Enterprises: Distribution of Projects by Repayment Rates

Category	Credit Component Disbursed (US$ million)	No. of Subborrowers	Repayment Rate (percent)	GNP/Capita (1980 US$)	Funds Lost (US$ million)
High Repayment Projects					
Korea # 1	29.95	141	99.0	1,520	0.30
Korea # 2	29.70	266	97.6	1,520	0.71
Ecuador # 1	18.10	651	97.0	1,270	0.54
Ecuador # 2	36.30	3,111	97.0	1,270	1.09
Peru	25.25	1,239	97.0	930	0.76
Mexico # 1	45.30	915	94.6	2,090	2.45
Mexico # 2	87.50	2,120	94.6	2,090	4.73
Jamaica	6.36	158	92.5	1,040	0.48
Subtotal	*278.46*	*8,601*			*11.05*
Average	*34.81*	*1,075*	*96.2*	*1,466*	
Medium Repayment Projects					
Colombia # 2	14.29	696	88.4	1,180	1.66
Colombia # 1	4.93	305	87.2	1,180	0.63
Portugal	33.00	475	87.0	2,370	4.29
Korea # 3	28.20	350	82.0	1,520	5.08
Philippines # 2	24.50	361	81.0	690	4.65
Cameroon	2.78	35	78.0	670	0.61
Colombia # 3	30.10	1,270	77.3	1,180	6.83
Pakistan # 2	48.00	1,273	77.0	300	11.04
Philippines # 1	28.70	801	76.2	690	6.83
Niger	3.25	6	76.0	330	0.78
Pakistan # 1	26.00	654	73.0	300	7.02
Sri Lanka # 2	28.00	1,938	73.0	270	7.56
Tunisia # 2	25.60	170	72.0	1,310	7.17

Category	Credit Component Disbursed (US$ million)	No. of Subborrowers	Repayment Rate (percent)	GNP/Capita (1980 US$)	Funds Lost (US$ million)
Sri Lanka # 1	9.00	1,746	70.0	270	2.70
Mauritania	6.60	9	70.0	440	1.98
Subtotal	*312.95*	*10,089*			*68.83*
Average	*20.86*	*673*	*77.9*	*847*	
Poor Repayment Projects					
Ivory Coast # 1	4.57	84	67.0	1,150	1.51
Nepal	4.50	3,369	66.0	140	1.53
Tunisia # 1	5.26	37	60.0	1,310	2.10
Morocco	17.10	214	55.0	900	7.70
Kenya	4.30	114	53.3	420	2.01
Ivory Coast # 2	11.60	86	50.0	1,150	5.80
Bangladesh # 1	2.90	38	39.0	130	1.77
Bangladesh # 2	4.50	175	36.0	130	2.88
Bangladesh # 3	30.00	678	34.0	130	19.80
Liberia	1.80	85	27.0	530	1.31
Subtotal	*86.53*	*4,880*			*46.41*
Average	*8.65*	*488*	*48.7*	*599*	
Grand Total	**677.94**	**23,570**			**126.29**
Overall Average	**20.54**	**714**	**81.4**		

Note: Repayment rates are not calculated on a uniform basis by the World Bank or by the institutions implementing credit projects. Figures cited should be considered as orders of magnitude. Funds lost are calculated from Webster's data by multiplying the amount disbursed by one minus the repayment rate. Funds lost are probably understated because repayment rates cited are those reported in project completion reports and repayment rates generally deteriorate over time. In addition, conditions have deteriorated in many countries, which could be expected to reduce repayment performance of subloans not fully repaid during the time covered by project completion reports.

Source: Leila Webster, *World Bank Lending for Small and Medium Enterprises: Fifteen Years of Experience.* Industry and Energy Department Working Paper, Industry Series Paper No. 20. Washington, D.C.: World Bank, December 1989 p. 18.

financed by poorly designed projects have been explored in this and earlier chapters.

However, discussion is now most frequently directed toward incentives to repay, largely as a result of arguments posed by Vogel.[16] The incentive argument, simply stated, is that borrowers are more likely to repay when credit and their relationship with the lender are valuable to them. If they perceive the loan as a grant or political handout—an attitude that appears to prevail with regard to government loans in certain countries—or if they view the project or lender as transitory and unlikely to provide additional services in the future, the incentive to repay is diminished. An alternative rendition of the argument is that default is likely if the costs of default are low. There appears to be little in credit project experience to refute Vogel's position. The focus is on finding willing takers for donor funds, there is not much emphasis on building long-term relationships between lenders and farmers or businessmen, and credit is often cloaked in political fanfare and appeals to national goals on the assumption that credit can be targeted and that it will serve as directed.

Regardless of the view taken, credit program design has a major impact on repayment performance. Poor repayment performance is another indication of unrealistic project design that is rejected by project beneficiaries. Inappropriate project design may occur through poor investment recommendations or expected loan use, insufficient attention to credit delivery systems, a naive view of risk and of the requirements for confidence, and inattention to incentives for borrowers and lenders. Projects deficient in these dimensions are unlikely to produce good fits at the frontier.

Causes of Poor Collections: The Economic Environment

An interesting perspective on loan collection and project fit is found in Webster's study.[17] Her results, presented in Table 7.1, indicate a relationship between per capita income and collection performance. Projects achieving high repayment rates were located in five countries having an average GDP per capita of US$1,466 in 1980. Projects in the

---

16. Dale W Adams and Robert C. Vogel, "Rural Financial Markets in Low Income Countries: Recent Controversies and Lessons," *World Development*. 14, 4, April 1986.

17. Leila Webster, *op. cit.* pp. 16-19.

medium range were located in 11 countries with average per capita GDP of US$847, while the worst-performing projects were found in seven countries with an average per capita GDP of US$599.

This pattern was explained by the observation that financial institutions in poorer countries tend to work less well than those in richer countries. These data suggest that the frontier may be more difficult to penetrate in poorer areas because of less favorable conditions overall. Many donors use a standard credit project design model with minor variations that respond to institutional arrangements in borrowing countries. Webster's results imply that a standard model is not likely to produce equally good fits in all environments. It also suggests that credit projects tend to be regressive, in that poorer countries lose more that richer countries when they attempt to use credit to push the frontier.

Unprofitable Intermediation

Profitable intermediation tends to attract competition. Other lenders provide instruments that are clearly expected to be profitable or that have been demonstrated to be profitable by those who pioneered them. New intermediaries may be established to compete in profitable markets. In general, this has not happened in the wake of projects at the frontier, which implies that the intermediation designs embodied in these projects are not profitable. Why is this?

Innovation Is Risky

Imperfect information makes change risky. Entering areas that have not been well explored or in which little relevant experience has accumulated can easily result in disappointment. Therefore, intermediaries' experimentation at the frontier inevitably results in financial losses on some occasions when the innovative service does not sufficiently harmonize the interests of borrowers and lenders.

Management of risk through innovations at the frontier requires identification of risks and quantification of their probable impact, pricing loans and services to minimize probable loss, and flexibility in implementation so that causes of loss can be identified and activities reoriented to overcome or avoid these causes. On these counts, credit projects are often strategically deficient: pursuit of nonfinancial objectives frequently receives more attention than detailed costing and adjustment for risk; interest rates tend to be held low; and reorientation within a project's time horizon is usually difficult, although subsequent projects may respond to earlier problems.

Occasional losses from attempts at innovation are to be expected, but persistent losses reflect systemic project design problems. Persistent losses arise because of uncorrected blind spots: innovation is not well conceived, pricing is inappropriate, or responses to problems are inadequate. Persistent losses are most likely when lenders' and donors' information systems and decisionmaking structures are not efficient. What evidence is there that intermediaries' losses are persistent, showing major uncorrected errors, rather than transitory, resulting from occasional failures of efforts to offer sustainable new services?

Data on Intermediary Profitability

Losses are minimized when experience is used to avoid repetition of mistakes. The frontier has many common characteristics regardless of the country or economy in which a project is based or for which intervention is recommended. These provide scope for international learning from experience and create a large potential demand for information on the activities of intermediaries at the frontier.

Unfortunately, data on profitability of intermediation in credit projects is even more difficult to obtain and interpret than that on loan repayment performance. The profit or loss that projects generate for intermediaries is rarely calculated by development assistance agencies or by state-owned intermediaries undertaking projects. Financial performance data is usually readily obtainable for specific institutions, but are often difficult to interpret because the extent of bad debt losses is not disclosed. Bad loans are carried for years on balance sheets without offsetting provisions for bad debt losses. Hence, intermediaries' profits are often overstated.

Evidence of unprofitable intermediation includes credit quotas and targeting discussed in chapter 5, the IDB study cited in chapter 7, the financial reorganization of credit institutions, and some analysts' assumption that development finance institutions decapitalize themselves in the normal course of events.[18]

---

18. See, for example, William M. Gudger and Luis Avalos, *op. cit.* pp. 271 ff.

Inferences may also be made from intermediaries' interest rate spreads or margins. A spread is the difference between the lender's cost of funds and the lending rate, and is expected to cover the lender's administrative and bad debt expenses. Cuevas found that the Honduran agricultural development bank's administrative cost, estimated at 8.4 percent of the amount of loans outstanding, was more than double the spread of 4 percent permitted it under a donor-supported agricultural credit project.[19] C. D. Datey estimated in 1978 that total costs of formal agricultural lenders in India ranged from 16 to 20 percent of amounts loaned, depending upon the type of institution, while farmers were charged an interest rate approximating 12 percent.[20] Ohene O. Nyanin calculated total annual lending costs ranging from 22 to 48 percent of loans outstanding under a small farm credit program in Jamaica.[21]

In many development projects the spread is set by custom or rule of thumb at 2, 3, or 4 percent. It is clear from these close tolerances that large bad debt losses cannot be sustained out of the lender's income from project activities. A 2 percent bad debt loss per year absorbs a 2 percent spread. Simple comparisons are sometimes misleading, however, because the spread is an annual rate applied to loans outstanding, while bad debt losses may be stated as a percentage of amounts due, funds disbursed or amounts outstanding. However, losses from collection rates of 80 percent, for example, are difficult to cover out of a 2 or 3 percent spread, regardless of the definitions or assumptions used.

Webster estimated, using a simplistic model, that a 90 percent collection rate would permit a term lender to achieve a 15 percent return on equity. This model assumed that loans to ultimate borrowers have a term of seven

---

19. Carlos E. Cuevas, "Costs of Financial Intermediation under Regulations: Commercial Banks and Development Banks." Economics and Sociology Occasional Paper No. 1127, Agricultural Finance Program, Ohio State University, Columbus, September 1984. p. 18; Carlos E. Cuevas and Douglas H. Graham, "Agricultural Lending Costs in Honduras," in Dale W Adams, Douglas H. Graham and J.D. Von Pischke, eds., *op. cit.* pp. 97-98, translated as "Costos de Prestamos Agrícolas en Honduras," in Dale W Adams, Claudio González Vega y J.D. Von Pischke, eds., *op. cit.* pp. 185-186.

20. C.D. Datey, *The Financial Cost of Agricultural Credit: A Case Study of Indian Experience.* Staff Working Paper No. 296. Washington, DC: World Bank, 1978.

21. Ohene Owusu Nyanin, "Lending Costs, Institutional Viability and Agricultural Credit Strategies in Jamaica." *Social and Economic Studies.* 32, 1, 1983. pp. 103-133.

years, including a two-year grace period, that the lender enjoys a 7 percent spread and incurs operating costs of 2.5 percent, that the intermediary contributes 10 percent of amounts loaned, and that profit is taxed at a 40 percent rate.[22] If these conditions apply, almost 76 percent of the fully-disbursed projects she studied would have resulted in returns of less than 15 percent for the intermediaries making loans out of project funds and assuming the credit risk.

Irrelevant Reporting

Relevant reporting gives lenders information that permits them to control costs, manage risk, and develop innovations that generate new business at the frontier. Reporting requirements should be based on objectives and indicate the extent to which they are achieved and the costs of their achievement. Problems arise when unrealistic objectives are assigned to credit, because these signify a poor fit between project designers' expectations and the medium selected to meet the expectation. Reporting requirements designed to show if credit accomplishes what it cannot accomplish are irrelevant.

Familiar Examples of Irrelevant Reporting Requirements

Chapter 6 indicated that comprehensive statistics on rural finance are lacking in spite of the large amount of money poured into rural financial markets. Data that are reported are generally not instructive with respect to the cost of lending, because project objectives are not finely tuned to the production of good loans and remunerative lending. Chapter 5 offered several examples of irrelevant reporting requirements arising from targets and quotas based on loan purpose and borrower characteristics. These included amounts loaned for agricultural purposes, defined to include things not specific to agriculture, like light trucks, and amounts loaned to farmers, defined to include absentee owners and others with a tenuous agricultural connection. Credit impact studies are relatively common attempts to ascertain whether credit meets objectives it cannot fulfill.

---

22. Leila Webster, *op. cit.* pp. 16-19.

Credit Impact Measurement May Be Irrelevant

Considerable attention has been devoted to using credit to encourage specific changes in borrower behavior. This has been followed in some cases by monitoring of borrowers' behavior and attributing changes to access to credit. Survey results may be used to design subsequent projects or justify further credit. Using "credit impact" to refine valuation processes is usually irrelevant because credit impact, while it surely exists, is ambiguous. And credit earns no return for borrowers, as demonstrated in chapter 3.

Cristina C. David and Richard L. Meyer show that methodological problems in measuring farm level credit impact lead to overemphasis on credit, with a potentially destructive impact arising from excessively intensive or extensive credit allocation.[23] Fungibility and interdependence of farm and household decisionmaking confound impact studies. Consumption and nonfarm activities change over time, and some of these changes may be related to receipt of credit. Documenting all changes is a daunting survey task, and even if successfully completed, the problem of attribution remains. As David and Meyer indicate,

> The attribution problem...consists of trying to isolate the effects of loans by observing differences between borrowers and nonborrowers, or by observing borrowers before and after the loans. At least four factors other than credit can explain differences between borrowing and nonborrowing farm households: differences in technology, technical information, irrigation, weather, and other variables not easily quantifed in production models; differences in yield, price uncertainty, and management ability; differences in product and input prices; and differences in household financial constraints or savings.[24]

These authors note that provision of credit with extension or institution-building activities in the usual project format makes it difficult to isolate the effect of credit alone. Artificially low interest rates also intervene. They distort credit allocation, producing systematic differences between borrowers and nonborrowers, so that borrowing is the result rather than the cause of differences in performance.

---

23. Cristina C. David and Richard L. Meyer, "Measuring the Farm Level Impact of Agricultural Loans," in J.D. Von Pischke, Dale W Adams and Gordon Donald, eds., *op. cit.* pp. 84-95.

24. *Ibid.* p. 85.

Studies of borrower behavior and performance can be useful. They can refine credit decisionmaking and valuation and facilitate confidence by making project designers and lenders' expectations more realistic. However, studies that try to measure credit impact are clearly diversionary and probably destructive when causal links are wrongly defined.

Inappropriate Funding

Sustainable innovations in lending require sustainable funding. And, the terms and conditions on which funding is provided have an impact on the performance of the activity financed. Credit projects are often funded externally by donors, rather than with domestic sources of funds. Rarely are frontier projects designed to generate their own resources through target group savings mobilization.

Kenyan and Indonesian Insights

In the early 1970s two major Kenyan institutions designed to expand the frontier had greatly differing levels of dependency on government and external funds.[25] The Agricultural Finance Corporation (AFC) depended on the Kenya Treasury for 97 percent of its capital and long term debt, or 88 percent of its total assets. About one-third of these funds were from external donors, channeled to AFC through the Treasury. The Treasury supplied the Cooperative Bank 58 percent of its capital and long term debt. The Treasury presence amounted to only 2 percent of its total assets, however. The Coop Bank was not at that time supported by donor capital.

Heavy dependence on government and donor funds seemed to be associated with bureaucratic behavior. Lower levels of government funding and an absence of donor capital were more closely associated with dynamic activity, relativly rapid growth, and efforts to engage a clientele at the frontier and to generate deposits.

AFC's expansion was a function of the government budget and donor enthusiasm for agricultural credit, especially small farmer credit. It had a staff of 300, about 20,000 medium- and long-term small farmer loans outstanding and had been in business for eight years. Its organization and decisionmaking were centralized. A significant portion of its managerial

25. J.D. Von Pischke, "Farm Credit in Kenya: The Poor Farmer Paradox." Nairobi: Institute for Development Studies, University of Nairobi, 1973. pp. 51-55.

energy was devoted to cultivating relations with donors; and its business development activities were dominated by donors' expectations. While it appeared at that time that close to 100 percent of principal disbursed was eventually recovered on loans to small farmers, arrears on all its lending programs were substantial.

The Cooperative Bank was the financial apex of a decentralized stucture consisting of district unions and local primary societies, mostly based on coffee processing or other commodities. The cooperative banking system had been in place for about four years. It had 88,000 depositors, about 40,000 borrowers, and was expanding rapidly. It followed conservative credit policies, in effect lending short-term against coffee already delivered by borrowers.

This anecdotal evidence from Kenya should be interpreted cautiously because of differences in the clients, objectives, and operations of the two institutions concerned. However, indirect substantiation of the evidence is given by a World Bank review of rural credit in Indonesia in 1986. The study notes that *the quality of funding determines the life of a credit program:* "An indicator of the adequacy and stability of the resource base of a program is the percentage share of [intermediary] equity and savings deposits to total resources." This realization resulted from comparisons of funding dependency ratios, the extent to which interest collections covered expenses, and repayment rates.

The Indonesian insight implies that the AFC would require repeated injections of government or donor money to remain in operation, because programs dependent primarily on government and donor capital would "die" from exhaustion of funds through administrative costs and bad debt losses. The Cooperative Bank, on the other hand, would be more likely to survive, or would "survive" longer than AFC. Experience since the early 1970s has not refuted this prediction.

Funding Issues for Review

The qualitative impact of the sources of funding of credit schemes is neither rigorously investigated nor well understood. Careful review of experience would permit hypotheses to be formulated for testing. In the meantime, there is no strategic view of optimal funding patterns for different types of credit programs that are intended to be sustainable, or of how emphasis in project design should vary over the life cycle of a donor's relationship with an intermediary.

In spite of these limitations, credit project design has not been static. It has evolved from intense and almost exclusive attention to intended beneficiaries, to more concern for the overall operations of intermediaries, to financial sector issues that influence the environment for intermediation and possibly back again to intense concern for intended beneficiaries who are women or small entrepreneurs. Efforts to disburse more funds have led to support for national institutions, with mechanisms such as rediscounting to transfer project funds from central to local levels. Evolution has occurred through flexible responses to specific situations, rather than from analysis of donors' project portfolios, strategic planning, and detailed statements of objectives. However, the burden of poor fits still appears to be substantial.

Part III

Structural Considerations in Frontier Development

Government planners, policymakers, and project designers may be unable to expand the frontier effectively and cheaply unless their understanding covers two key areas. The first is the current status and organization of financial markets inside and outside the frontier. The second consists of their developmental objectives and the implications of their objectives for the structure and operations of financial markets.

Part III outlines a view of financial markets and their development. It suggests that the market beyond the frontier is more complex and less exploitive than government planners and policymakers generally assume. Insufficient appreciation of the complexity of this market leads to low-quality, high-cost efforts to bring its participants within the frontier. In addition, efforts of this type have some startling implications and humorous dimensions. Some unfortunate cases are cited in chapter 8, along with examples of how better quality efforts to expand the frontier have developed.

Chapter 9 develops the theme that financial innovation is the key to creating value at the frontier. Innovation occurs beyond as well as within the frontier. The connections between financial markets on each side of the frontier are advantageous to competition and may stimulate innovation. Innovation is especially helpful to development when it increases confidence and assists risk management. Cash flow lending, which links credit most closely with expected future performance rather than with current financial status, can develop when risk management is effective and confidence is strong.

Competition is important for financial development because it stimulates innovation. Chapter 10 argues that innovators attempt to create market niches or distinct identities that place them ahead of their competitors and that this behavior should not be discouraged. Market niches must be continually defended with more innovations, or competition will erode them. The market niche concept helps innovators, project designers, and policymakers explore financial market structure by focusing on the strengths and weaknesses of different types of instruments and intermediaries.

Of greatest importance to policymakers and project designers is the realization that a market niche approach to financial market development responds to the concerns that have so often led to credit targeting and quotas. It responds to these concerns in a manner that is conducive to development of markets and efficient institutions that are capable of expanding the services they offer and of enlarging their clientele. By combining these concerns with recipes for good performance, market niche strategies create a grand synthesis, a new vision for an expanding frontier. Grameen Bank in Bangladesh is discussed in chapter 10 as a successful application of market niche development and as an example of this synthesis.

8

Value for the People: Informal Finance

Informal finance and self-finance prevail beyond the frontier of the formal financial system. Informal finance consists of borrowing and lending among individuals and firms that are not registered with the government as financial intermediaries and are not subject to government supervision. Informal finance is tremendously diverse and is generally conducted within broader relationships, starting from kinship and extending outward to friendship and customary social bonds, and beyond to include credit associated with commercial transactions and land tenure arrangements.[1]

The penetration of formal finance is superficial in many countries. Formal agricultural credit, for example, is generally used by far fewer than half of farm households, and in the majority of developing countries probably does not reach more than 20 percent. The formal system in Thailand has served about 50 percent of farm households, while the figure reported for India is approaching 40 percent. In many parts of Africa and Latin America, researchers report much lower levels of formal credit access.[2] Informal arrangements, by contrast, create value for the majority of the population in most countries.

---

1. A comprehensive survey article on informal finance is Jürgen U. Holst. "The Role of Informal Financial Institutions in the Mobilization of Savings." in Denis Kessler and Pierre-Antoine Ullmo, eds., *op. cit.* pp. 121-152.

2. No recent global surveys of formal credit penetration are available and reported data fail to distinguish sustained relationships built on good loans from occasional or one-time transactions. Data for Latin America for the mid-1970s are possibly typical, ranging from 2 percent of farmers receiving institutional credit in Guatemala to 15 percent in Mexico and Brazil. The three highest reported penetrations, which are atypical, were 44 percent in Costa Rica and 62 percent in Peru and Jamaica. Since the 1970s, the proportion has probably declined in several countries as a result of

Efforts to bring more people within the frontier of formal finance are often motivated by adverse reactions to informal financial arrangements. These reactions are commonly articulated by individuals already within the frontier, and by government officials and officeholders. These observers often regard informal finance as inferior, exploitative, and anti-developmental, and the activities of informal financiers, and even the financiers themselves, as evil and immoral.

This chapter explores allegations that informal finance is generally undesirable and presents evidence that this conclusion is unwarranted. Notable efforts to replace moneylenders are reviewed to show how such measures undertaken with taxpayers' funds can lead to unexpected results and costs without directly realizing their stated objectives of driving out moneylenders.

The Malicious Moneylender Myth

The malicious moneylender myth holds that private lenders extract the economic surplus produced by peasant labor, capital and possibly land. According to this view, exploitation occurs through the credit transaction directly in the form of unjustified interest rates, and perhaps indirectly through relationships under which debtor-creditor positions arise, including land tenure arrangements and trading. Trading relationships may be built around inventory supply for small vendors and petty traders, agricultural inputs and produce for farmers, and raw materials and machinery or tools for artisans.

The myth states that exploitation through credit terms is pervasive and highly oppressive. This contention has provided a rationale for government-controlled cooperative credit and for government-owned credit systems and programs in many countries. India is the most notable case, and the Indian press frequently reports sensational cases of abuse by lenders. One economist, Amit Bhaduri, hypothesizes that Indian moneylenders' primary objective is to obtain control over the land of their farmer-borrowers.[3]

---

austerity policies and economic problems. See *Agricultural Credit in Latin America.* Report of the Seminar on Agricultural Credit for Small Farmers in Latin America, Quito, Ecuador, 25-30 November 1974. (Rome: FAO, 1975).

3. Amit Bhaduri, "On the Formation of Usurious Interest Rates in Backward Agriculture," *Cambridge Journal of Economics.* 1, 1977.

How seriously should we take this myth? Is abuse widespread, or an exception? To what extent does it justify massive intervention? Is finance beyond the frontier generally exploitive? In fact, the exploitation hypothesis has rarely been tested. The few credible surveys of informal finance that have been undertaken generally fail to uncover widespread abuse in lending terms.

Factors the Myth Ignores

One flaw in the myth is that extreme cases are often interpreted as common practice. But, the basic flaw in the malicious moneylender myth is that it interprets quoted lending rates of interest, often of stratospheric heights, as evidence of monopolistic practices. High prices do not prove monopoly, however. How many observers would conclude, for example, that because a car costs more than a box of matches that the manufacturer or retailer of the car gouges consumers?

The economic test of monopoly is net return, or good old-fashioned profit. Net returns to lenders may be difficult to identify precisely in credit markets because lending is often conducted in conjunction with other activities on the part of the lender and other relationships between borrower and lender. (The problem of joint costs and interrelated benefits also makes it difficult for bankers to know the exact costs of many services they provide, although overall net returns earned by banks are routinely reported.)

Many commentators on informal finance fail to apply the economic test, which becomes obscured by the attention attracted and the outrage generated by reported high prices for credit. As noted in previous chapters, observers are often not disinterested parties: when government funds are available, attempts to replace informal lending become an avenue to political power.

Refuting the Myth

The attack on the myth of pervasive high levels of abuse by informal, private lenders begins with several theoretical arguments. In the 1950s Martin W. Wilmington suggested that moneylending is not necessarily exploitive, and pointed out the difference between quoted rates of interest and net returns to moneylenders in northern Sudan. He observed that critics of moneylenders give, no thought...to the lack of debtor ethics which makes collection a strenuous and costly affair. Nothing is said about "bad debts" and the annual losses they cause the moneylender in countries where most borrowers are only inches removed from destitution; high residential mobility—particularly between city and country—which produces a high incidence of debt evasion; and low life expectancy....No consideration is given to where the moneylenders themselves obtain funds for business; they, in turn, may have borrowed at exorbitant rates from a tight capital market or abstracted funds from profitable pursuits in other lines.[4]

Critics also appear to overlook many lenders' relatively restricted opportunity to diversify their loan portfolios. First, the number of borrowers they can accommodate is limited by the number of people they know[5] and by the amount of funds they have to lend. A lender with a portfolio of 50 loans of roughly equal size would lose about 2 percent of his funds if one borrower did not repay. To cover this risk, the lender would have to raise the annual rate of interest on the 49 remaining loans by about two percentage points. If ten borrowers failed to repay the capital loss would amount to 20 percent of the portfolio, and the compensating rate increase for the remaining 40 loans would be about 25 percent. Slow repayment, because of a poor harvest, for example, also absorbs funds that the lender would want to recycle into new loans the next season. Inability to continue to lend would jeopardize relationships with established borrowers, diminishing their incentives to repay amounts outstanding and raising the risk exposure on the entire portfolio.

Anthony Bottomley posed the most persistent theoretical challenge to the malicious moneylender myth in a series of articles in the 1960s and 1970s. He argued that rural interest rates are high because of the rural economic environment, not because moneylenders obtain monopolistic returns.[6] Money has a high opportunity cost, loans involve administration costs and lending is risky. Bottomley concluded that moneylenders' profits

---

4. Martin W. Wilmington, "Aspects of Moneylending in Northern Sudan," *Middle East Journal.* Vol. 9, 1955; quotation from J.D. Von Pischke, Dale W Adams and Gordon Donald, eds., *op. cit.* p. 255.

5. Some lenders overcome this limitation by acting as financial wholesalers, using agents to expand their activities beyond people known to them personally.

6. Bottomley's argument is summarized in "Interest Rate Determination in Underdeveloped Rural Areas," *American Journal of Agricultural Economics.* 57, 2, 1975; extracted in J.D. Von Pischke, Dale W Adams and Gordon Donald, eds., *op. cit.* pp. 243-250.

are generally so small that urban commercial banks are unlikely to compete with them.

In 1957, U Tun Wai of the International Monetary Fund published a detailed review of informal interest rates and credit.[7] He defined informal markets as consisting of three segments. The first includes cooperatives, indigenous bankers and other institutions serving traders and medium-sized landlords. The second includes "respectable" moneylenders, traders and landlords serving small farmers at "high but reasonable" rates of interest. The third is composed of "shady marginal lenders" or loan sharks serving high-risk borrowers at "exorbitant rates of interest." U Tun Wai indicated that the third segment did not command a prominent market share.

Both U Tun Wai and Wilmington noted that informal lenders often perform a variety of services for their borrowers. Produce transport, storage and payment of market taxes by traders are examples. Another is commissions to "guarantors" who witness credit transactions between moneylenders and borrowers known to the "guarantor." These third parties have a certain social standing and can persuade the borrower to repay more easily than the moneylender can, but they are not expected to reimburse lenders for bad debt losses caused by clients they have "guaranteed." Landlords also may provide welfare-type assistance to tenants in distress. These links make it difficult to identify the extent to which loan charges reflect only the economic components of interest (that is, cost of funds, administrative expenses, risk, and profit) as opposed to including hidden or not-so-hidden charges for other services.

EMPIRICAL EVIDENCE FROM INDIA: THE ALL-INDIA RURAL CREDIT SURVEY. Lending rates of interest were reported in the All-India Rural Credit Survey, although the treatment and presentations across the various types of lenders surveyed do not appear consistent. This official survey does not support the allegation of widespread use of the exorbitant levels of rates of interest commonly alleged to prevail in India.

---

7. U Tun Wai, "Interest Rates Outside the Organized Money Markets of Underdeveloped Countries," *IMF Staff Papers.* VI, 1957-58.

Rates charged by village moneylenders, for example, were reported to range from zero to more than 50 percent per annum[8] during a long period when rates of inflation had rarely exceeded 6 percent and commercial bank lending rates to customers were 3 to 5 percent. Approximately 8 percent of the amount of village moneylenders' credit was reportedly free of interest, 24 percent of the amount loaned carried rates of less than 9.375 percent, 56 percent was at rates ranging from 9.375 percent to 18.75 percent, and less than 9 percent was at rates exceeding 18.75 percent. (Interest rates were not specified on 4 percent of the volume of lending by these moneylenders.) In terms of numbers of loans, 7 percent were interest-free, 44 percent carried rates of less than 12.5 percent, and fewer than 5 percent were at rates exceeding 25 percent. Summarizing, 88 percent of funds loaned carried rates of 18.75 percent or less. About one-fifth of village moneylenders reported that at least 10 percent of their loans to farmers were of doubtful quality.[9]

Some village moneylenders and traders obtained funds from informal indigenous bankers. For the small number of observations provided, more than 90 percent of these wholesale lenders charged between 3 and 12.5 percent.[10] Although the samples are probably not comparable, the data imply that the spreads between the cost of funds to village moneylenders and their lending rates were relatively modest.

Of the 26 districts for which data is provided on landlord credit, reported rates did not exceed 12.5 percent in ten, while in only seven districts were rates in excess of 35 percent discovered.[11] The survey noted that 35 percent of sampled urban moneylenders reported that more than 10 percent of their loans to farmers were doubtful debts. Apparently virtually all of those sampled reported arrears and resorted to litigation to recover unpaid loans.[12] Data for farmer-moneylenders indicate that 12 percent of their funds were loaned interest free, 13 percent carried rates of less than 10 percent, 40 percent were loaned at rates of 10 to 12.5 percent, 21

· 8. *All-India Rural Credit Survey.* Vol. 1, *The Survey Report, Part 2, (Credit Agencies).* (Bombay: Reserve Bank of India, 1957). pp. 488- 491.

9. *Ibid.* p. 476.

10. *Ibid.* p. 513.

11. *Ibid.* p. 464.

12. *Ibid.* pp. 501 ff.

percent from 12.5 to 25 percent, and only 11 percent at rates exceeding 25 percent.[13]

Data such as these and their interpretation appear to have dislodged few proponents of the myth. The usual progression in their refusal to abandon their strongly-held belief begins with the complaint that interest rates are too high and exploitative. When it is demonstrated that rates are not generally so high as claimed and are not unreasonable by commercial standards, their defense changes. The claim then is that debtor-creditor relationships are much more complex than portrayed by a rate of interest, which cannot capture the nature of the exploitation that they claim prevails in informal credit markets. One wonders why the All-India Rural Credit Survey did not address the presumably broader issue, as it was launched by a newly-independent government with a broad mandate for change and a widely-held view that exploitation prevails. In the meanitme, several individual researchers without official support have examined informal lending in India. Three studies of particular interest merit consideration.

EMPIRICAL EVIDENCE FROM INDIA: STUDIES BY INDIVIDUAL RESEARCHERS. Field studies do not support the myth. Karam Singh surveyed seven lenders in a village in Amritsar District in northern India, and estimated, using linear programming analysis, that monopoly profits approximated 9 percent of amounts loaned, while interest rates paid by borrowers exceeded 140 percent per annum.[14] One lender in his sample suffered a net loss during the period reviewed. More than half of the staggering rate to borrowers reflected the opportunity cost of capital in the village, and about one-quarter was contributed by the risk premium.

Barbara Harriss studied rural markets in North Arcot District in southern India.[15] She found a competitive market with links between formal and informal finance, a general lack of predatory credit relationships, and little opportunity for monopoly profits. She noted the

---

13. *Ibid.* p. 562.

14. Karam Singh, "Structure of Interest Rates on Consumption Loans in an Indian Village," *Asian Economic Review.* 10, 4, 1968; excerpted in J.D. Von Pischke, Dale W Adams and Gordon Donald, eds., *op. cit.* pp. 251-254.

15. Barbara Harriss, "Money and Commodities: Their Interaction in a Rural Indian Setting," in J.D. Von Pischke, Dale W Adams and Gordon Donald, eds., *op.cit.* pp. 233-241; extracted from a paper in John Howell, ed., *Borrowers & Lenders: Rural Financial Market Institutions in Developing Countries.* (London: Overseas Development Institute, 1980).

speed and convenience with which traders deliver informal credit, competition among traders that resulted in zero-interest paddy loans, slow repayment by some borrowers, complete failure to repay traders by about 5 percent of borrowers, and interest rates that increased with the length of time for which credit is outstanding.

Farrukh Iqbal applied econometric techniques to analyze interest rates in formal and informal financial markets in India using data collected from 2,912 farm households between 1968 and 1971 by the National Council of Applied Economic Research.[16] He compared rural interest rates with levels of agricultural technology. His results indicate that improvements in agricultural technology go together with reductions in the moneylender interest rate. He further noted that improvements in technology tend to decrease risk, at least over a period of a few years or more. Iqbal's analysis suggests that moneylenders' costs, especially those associated with risk, are reflected in their lending rates. He found that moneylenders' rates appear to be sensitive to many other variables relating to the status of the borrower, risk and productivity, and to competition from formal lenders. His results provide strong indications that the market is competitive, leaving relatively little space for monopolistic practices such as exploitive interest rates. Iqbal concluded that, "the monopoly surcharge, while not insignificant, is found to be low...."[17]

Thomas A. Timburg and C. V. Aiyar surveyed almost 1,000 persons involved in informal finance in urban markets in India to explore relationships between traders, shopkeepers, restauranteurs, other bussinessmen and the indigenous bankers who were their creditors.[18] They concluded that informal lenders were efficient commercially and that their activities produced "a higher level of intermediation for the economy overall and an increase in savings and productive investment."[19] They

---

16. Farrukh Iqbal, "The Determinants of Moneylender Interest Rates: Evidence from Rural India," *The Journal of Development Studies.* 24, 3, April 1988. pp. 363-375.

17. *Ibid.* p. 375.

18. Thomas A. Timberg and C.V. Aiyer. "Informal Credit Markets India," *Economic Development and Cultural Change.* 33, 1, October 1984. pp. 43-59; and a monograph by the same title, Domestic Finance Studies 62. Washington, DC: World Bank, 1980.

19. *Ibid.* p. 44.

could find no marked negative results, such as monopoly profits, in the informal commercial credit market.

DATA AND ESTIMATES FROM PENINSULAR MALAYSIA. R.J.G. Wells analyzed data collected in 1980 for 331 farms in the Muda River Irrigation Scheme in Malaysia.[20] Of these, 79 percent reported using credit during the study period, 72 percent of the funds borrowed were reportedly obtained to finance agricultural production, and 17 percent were borrowed for family expenses such as food and clothing. Of total borrowings, 91 percent was in cash and 9 percent in kind. Shopkeepers, moneylenders, rice millers, friends and relatives supplied 59 percent of total reported borrowings, or 50 percent of funds borrowed in cash and 92 percent of the value of loans provided in kind. The rate of inflation during the period was 3.6 percent per annum. Weighted average inflation-adjusted interest rates charged by these informal sources ranged from negative 3.6 percent on interest-free loans in kind given by friends and relatives to 24 percent on moneylender credit. The highest rate recorded was 140 percent on a shopkeeper loan.

From survey data and additional material on lending costs, Wells estimated nominal profit margins for informal lenders as follows: shopkeepers, 1.4 percent; moneylenders, 3.7 percent; rice millers, 3.6 percent; relatives, -9.8 percent; and friends, -7.6 percent. Wells assumed an opportunity cost of capital of 7 percent, loan administration costs of 2 percent for relatives and friends and 3 percent for others, and risk premiums from bad debt losses of 2.6 percent for shopkeepers, 11.4 percent for moneylenders, 5.3 percent for rice millers, and 5.4 percent for friends and relatives. The 7 percent opportunity cost of capital is below the 10 to 12 percent usually assumed in development projects, which may mean that Wells overstated profit margins. Wells concluded that there was no evidence of monopolistic exploitation, but noted that certain of his assumptions required verification.

SURVEY RESULTS FROM THE PHILIPPINES. Probably the most thorough investigation and analysis of informal lending was conducted in the Philippines by the Technical Board for Agricultural Credit (TBAC), which

---

20. R.J.G. Wells, "The Informal Rural Credit Market in Malaysia." Working Paper No. 1. Faculty of Economics and Administration, University of Malaya, October 1980.

conducted sample surveys in three rice-producing provinces in 1978.[21] TBAC interest arose in part from the deterioration of the formal rural financial system, accompanied by a revival of informal finance. The study team, headed by Benjamin Quiñones, gathered data from 163 private moneylenders and 915 of their farmer clients. Borrowers' average farm size was 2.1 hectares, and no sampled borrowers had landholdings exceeding 6 hectares; 44 percent were lessees and 15 percent were share tenants. Lenders tended to be older and more educated than their borrowers. Farmer-moneylenders had an average farm size of 6.75 hectares, although about half had farms of 3 hectares or less.

Formal lenders provided about one-third of loans taken by sampled farmers in the three provinces, rice traders about 15 percent, farmer-lenders about 14 percent, landlords about 12 percent, and input dealers about 10 percent. However, 24 percent of households surveyed used no informal credit for production purposes in 1978, and 48 percent used no informal consumption credit. Half of the households taking loans borrowed exclusively from informal sources, while half used both formal and informal credit.

The survey revealed that moneylending was characterized by competitive entry and exit and by flexible and innovative responses to new production opportunities in agriculture associated with the seed and fertilizer revolution. A new class of lenders had arisen with technological change in agriculture: the role of landlords and shopkeepers as lenders had declined, while that of input dealers and farmer-moneylenders had expanded tremendously. Almost half of the lenders surveyed had started their lending operations within the five years preceding the study, and an additional third had six to ten years' experience in the business.

Only 3 percent of lenders reported that lending was their principal source of income; the main source of lenders' income was the sale of merchandise. Sampled lenders reported that borrowings constituted less than 10 percent of their funds, while internal sources of funds from their trading activities provided about 72 percent. Of funds generated by sample lenders, only about 10 percent was loaned out.

Borrowers' motivations also evolved with changes in agriculture and in rural finance. Studies conducted in the 1950s found that farmers borrowed

---

21. Presidential Committee on Agricultural Credit, *op. cit.*

primarily for consumption, while the TBAC team found that farmers obtained credit primarily for production. Fungibility blurs this distinction, but a shift in focus is implied by the growing role of input suppliers as lenders.

TBAC concluded that informal finance helped production of high-yielding varieties of rice. Many farmers who borrowed under government-sponsored programs switched to informal lenders as subsidized funds dried up. Many who adopted new rice varieties after formal funding became unavailable obtained inputs from suppliers who offered informal credit.

Average annual *ex-ante* interest rates on informal loans surveyed, reflecting agreements and expectations at the time loans were made, were 37 percent and yielded a projected profit of 3.6 percent. Lending rates ranged from 0 to 163 percent, depending on loan type. Traditional loans in the Philippines are denominated in cavans of rice, weighing about 50 kilograms. Loan types are identified by the ratio of the amount loaned to the amount to be repaid. A loan with a ratio of 1:1 paid out and repaid in cash carries a zero *ex-ante* interest rate. Adjusting for the period of credit use, TBAC calculated that 1:2 implies an annual rate of 163 percent, 2:3 yields a rate of 105 percent, 3:4 implies a 67 percent rate, and 5:6 equals 47 percent.

One-eighth of the informal loans surveyed had rates of more than 100 percent per year (1:2 and 2:3), and these loans tended to be smaller than those in other categories. One-third had rates equivalent to 47 percent and 67 percent (3:4 and 5:6). One-quarter carried a zero explicit rate, another one-quarter fell outside the traditional classifications with annual rates averaging 36 percent, while the remainder, about 5 percent, carried the "legal" rates charged by formal lenders.

Ex-post rates, reflecting bad debt losses, delayed repayments and prepayments, added administrative costs, differences in the monetary value of rice between loan disbursement and repayment, and lenders' payment for rice at below-spot prices, resulted in an average actual annual rate of about 56 percent and a profit of about 33 percent per annum. Bad debt losses were expected to dwindle to about 3 percent of amounts loaned by the second harvest after that at which loans fell due. The range of imputed monopoly profits varied greatly, however. Input dealers, rice millers, full-time moneylenders and professional practitioners (for example, medical doctors) reportedly lost money, while rice traders and store owners had estimated monopoly profits approximating 45 percent of amounts loaned.

Interest rates and, presumably, opportunities for monopoly profits were lower in better developed areas than in poor areas. This was due in part to the competition provided by formal financial institutions, and in part to the lower transaction costs and risks in favorable economic environments.

Interpreting Informal Interest Rates

Philippine finance raises interesting questions about the meaning of interest rates on informal loans. Five-six terms are very common—five pesos borrowed, six pesos repaid—on commodity-based credit. They illustrate the problems encountered when observers from within the frontier look over the fence into informal financial markets. For example, a street vendor obtains fresh produce each morning from a stallholder in a municipal market. The consignment is valued at P 50, and repayment of P 60 is expected each afternoon. The simple interest rate is 20 percent per day. Compounding at this rate, the original P 50 loaned by the stallholder would equal about P 12,000 after 30 days. If the calculation is continued for one year, the annualized interest rate and compounded amounts are astronomical. Before long the lender's income would exceed the GDP of the Philippines.

Likewise, operators of a dried fish vending cart may obtain P 1,000 worth of dried fish from a wholesaler each Monday morning, and be expected to repay P 200 per day for six days, from Monday through Saturday. After four weekly cycles the original P 1,000 compounds to more than P 2,000. This variety of five-six produces an interest rate of 5.47 percent per day. In one month P 1,000 compounds to about P 5,000 at this daily rate. The annualized rate and compounded amount are ridiculously large.

The produce vendor may clear P 20 per day, while the dried fish vendor may pocket P 300 per week after meeting the creditor's demands. In a similar example, a street vendor may buy a watermelon on credit for P 5, cut it into 20 pieces and sell each piece for P 0.50, clearing P 5. The 100 percent mark-up and the return on assets (assuming free use of a borrowed knife and a fully-depreciated tray on which to place the melon) may also seem excessive, but would probably not generate the same emotional heat and disbelief as a 20 percent daily interest rate. After all, the poor lass earns only P 5 (less than US$ 1) for four hours' work, and who was ever exploited by eating watermelon on a hot day at P 0.50 a slice?

The meaning of these rates is seldom investigated. They must reflect something more than the traditional economic components of interest rates, which are the cost of funds, administrative costs, risk, and profit. Funds are unlikely to cost more than, say, 200 percent annually in any legitimate activity except in a crisis or other highly unusual situation when markets break down.

Administrative costs in informal finance are usually small. They are often largely sunk, because the lender and borrower have known each other for a long time and both are familiar with the environment in which they operate. The incremental costs of gathering information and collecting debts may also be small because the parties concerned may interact frequently in any event commercially and socially. Even where these costs are not small, as in the case of women lenders in Sri Lanka who are "constantly on the move, walking, visiting and talking to their villagers and making housecalls like a family physician,"[22] they are on a scale consistent with the informal economy.

Risk may be high, but the stratospheric levels suggested by daily or weekly five-six transactions implies that the entire principal amount would have to be lost many times a year to justify the annualized rate. Monopoly profits of the sort implied by these examples would surely attract vigorous competition that would severely erode returns. What sort of coercion or other barriers to entry would keep retail dried fish vendors content with incomes of P 300 per week, or P 1,200 per month if the wholesaler can turn P 1,000 into P 2,000 or P 5,000 in a month simply by lending, leaving aside the wholesale mark-up on the fish?

Until further analysis is available, interest rates beyond the frontier cannot be fully interpreted. Tentative approaches to analysis lie in U Tun Wai's observation that these "interest rates" include costs of nonfinancial services, and also in Bottomley's belief that seasonal lending activities linked to agriculture will require high rates if funds cannot be employed in income-generating activities during the periods between agricultural seasons. If the growing season is six months long, and if there is one growing season per year, the lending rate would presumably be based on

---

22. Personal communication from F.J.A. Bouman, 15 June 1989.

twice the average annual cost of capital. However, many developing countries have two growing seasons per year, and informal and formal financial and other markets to which traders have access may provide some scope for off-season uses of funds. Also, many merchants, such as the dried fish dealers, operate throughout the year.

Focusing on the interest charge rather than the rate is also helpful. Most borrowers are concerned primarily with the amount of debt service and whether they can meet payments. These tests of affordability generally overshadow concern for the interest rate. The charge is easily considered because it is a monetary amount, while the rate requires calculations that may be taxing and require mathematical sophistication because of the different ways in which interest is levied and collected. Rates are of great importance in high finance, among bond traders and portfolio managers. But to most participants in informal finance they are probably merely an abstraction and do not provide meaningful guidance as to whether credit is affordable or whether an investment is worthwhile.

One clue regarding interpretation of the cost of money is provided by Parker Shipton, an anthropologist who studied credit in The Gambia.[23] He notes that interest *rates* are used to distinguish fair lending from usury in many industrialized countries, while interest *ratios* are often used for the same purpose in West Africa. The interest ratio is the relationship between the principal amount of a loan and the total amount of interest paid or to be paid on the loan. The time elapsed between loan issue and repayment is regarded as being less important to people using interest ratios as a measure of the cost of money.

Unanswered questions make informal financial market research an exciting dimension of frontier finance. Shipton provides further examples of the insights required to understand informal rural financial markets in a review that deals with definitions and strategies of saving and lending; how interest is charged and paid, including "commodity switches" and nonlinearity in interest computation because of perceptions of time that do not assume all days as being of equal weight; ethnic, age, gender and religious dimensions of borrowing and saving; group financial activities; linkages between "consumption" and "productive" credit; fungibility and "multiple livelihoods;" seasonality; the role of moneykeepers who provide

---

23. Parker Shipton, "How Gambians Save." p. 6.

deposit services; interaction between financial and in-kind saving and borrowing; and preferences and priorities for difference sources of credit.[24]

These dimensions and the questions they raise demonstrate that finance is truly social, as noted in chapter 3. They also suggest the limitations of financial analysis and conventional economic theory in providing a complete picture of informal finance. Consequently, misinterpretation of financial activity in informal markets easily arises when observations are incomplete and when the analytical context is inappropriate. Many of the insights that appear most promising have been developed by anthropologists and sociologists who take a professional interest in issues of risk and confidence. Yet, they are definitely on the sidelines when conventional economic and financial analysis is afoot. Those with an interest in the field can only hope to hear more from them. Who else would be able to offer a simple explanation of the presence of beggar ladies in the streets of Bangladesh who also operate as important informal lenders?

Private Actions by Public-Spirited Citizens: The Credit Union Epic

Regardless of the level of understanding or misunderstanding about informal finance, efforts to force the frontier are a common reaction to information about informal finance. An important example of these efforts is the formation of cooperatives, traditionally advocated by promoters as a means of releasing the poor from the clutches of usurers. Cooperatives have been viewed as especially desirable because of their social objectives, as opposed to informal lenders' presumed preoccupation with profit. Cooperative history is rich in stories of successes that create sustainable value and of failures that destroy value. Examples of cooperative promotion, along with similar efforts to institutionalize moneylending, provide insights into financial innovation.

Private responses to problems often associated with informal finance have produced many financial innovations. The example of F.W. Raiffeisen cited in chapter 3 shows how a religiously motivated

---

24. Parker Shipton, "Time and Money in the Western Sahel: A Clash of Culture in Gambian Local Rural Finance," in Michael Roemer and Christine Jones, eds., *Markets in Developing Countries* (San Francisco: Institute for Contemporary Studies Press, for the International Center for Economic Growth, 1990).

government official, on his personal initiative, devised collective mechanisms to offer farmers an alternative to informal credit. After 15 years of trial and error, the Raiffeisen credit union model was sufficiently developed and enough experience had been accumulated to permit the rapid growth of rural credit unions throughout central Europe. No bad debt losses occured during this experimental period.

Hermann Schulze-Delitzsch, a restless social reformer who like Raiffeisen formed a bakery society during the hard Prussian winter of 1846-47, organized his first urban cooperative credit society of shopkeepers and tradesmen in 1850 after being suspended from the civil service because of his political views. He and some wealthy friends provided the initial capital.[25] He was reinstated and assigned a distant post, but resigned in 1851. He then discovered that his cooperative was in difficulty, and that wealthy members had withdrawn because of bad loans and faulty procedures. He asked municipal authorities for funds, offering them participation in the society's management. The request was refused, which made a major impact on the path of cooperative development. (In fact, these long-forgotten city fathers may deserve high places in the cooperative hall of fame.)

Schulze-Delitzsch then reorganized the society so that members' entrance fees (equal to US$2.50 at the time), share purchases (at $12.00 each, payable in installments), and deposits funded the society, which was operated democratically. As he formed more societies, known as people's banks, he insisted that in each society's initial stages *all* members participate in management, signing passbooks and promissory notes and making bookkeeping entries. By 1859 there were 183 people's banks in Posen and Saxony.[26]

Private efforts by public-spirited individuals led to the further spread of credit unions. Alphonse Desjardins was a parliamentary reporter for Québec Province and later for the Canadian House of Commons, and also worked as a journalist. In his work he heard accounts of suffering by debtors who had borrowed from loan sharks. He responded by forming a

---

25. J. Carroll Moody and Gilbert C. Fite, *op. cit.;* J.O. Müller, *op. cit.* pp. 43-60.
26. The early and subsequent development of financial cooperatives in Germany is described in Gunther Aschhoff and Eckart Henningsen, *The German Cooperative System: Its History, Structure and Strength* (Frankfurt-am-Main: Fritz Knapp Verlag, 1986).

cooperative *caisse populaire*. It opened in 1901 after organizers agreed on by-laws in a series of 18 meetings held during a four-month period. The amount of the first deposit was 10 cents. The banking office was initially in Desjardins's home in Lévis, Québec, open only on Saturday evenings. He and members of his family did the bookkeeping without pay. Within five months, the *caisse* had 840 members. In its first six years, at a time when the daily unskilled wage was less than $3 per day, $200,000 was loaned, with no bad debt losses. By 1914 there were 150 cooperative banks in Canada, and today the movement is an important part of Canada's retail financial system.

Edward A. Filene, a department store owner in Boston, Massachusetts, was a progressive reformer and supporter of many organizations to improve living conditions and uplift local political activities. On a trip to India in 1907 he visited credit cooperatives in Bengal recently established by the British, who had adapted Raiffeisen's model.[27] He was shocked by the poverty he saw, and concluded that credit could help alleviate it. He proposed to President Theodore Roosevelt that a similar system be established in the Philippines, which was then a colony of the United States. Nothing came of his suggestion, but Filene was able to express his concern closer to home as a result of initiatives taken by Pierre Jay, Massachusetts Banking Commissioner.

Jay had learned of the people's banks in Europe through casual reading. Further investigation led him to Desjardins, whom he visited in Ottawa in 1908. Jay had become concerned about workers and tradesmen's use of informal credit at high rates of interest. Jay knew that in certain factories and stores, and at *The Boston Globe* newspaper, employees had established informal savings and loan associations, and he concluded that these "unregulated banks" should be encouraged. He obtained help from Desjardins in drafting legislation and in creating public support for cooperative banks.[28] Commercial bankers did not oppose Jay and the Massachusetts Credit Union Act because the new banks would serve people who did not use commercial banking services.

---

27. B.J. Youngjohns, "Agricultural Cooperatives and Credit," in John Howell, ed., *op. cit.* pp. 179-198.
28. Desjardins had already formed a credit union in New Hampshire, the first in the United States.

Among his many interests, Filene supported Jay's work. Credit unions spread slowly in Massachusetts and neighboring states. Many encountered difficulties and were dissolved. Filene became deeply involved in the 1920s by creating and funding the Credit Union National Extension Bureau, a private body which organized credit unions and worked for the passage of state and federal credit union laws that set the stage for rapid growth of credit unions as savings institutions and sources of consumer finance following World War II. Over his lifetime, Filene may have spent as much as $1 million of his personal fortune supporting credit unions.[29] In response to the deregulation of retail financial services that began in the United States in the late 1970s, credit unions have become providers of a broad range of financial services.

The Quality of Efforts to Replace Usurers

Private efforts to provide financial services to the poor are eventually subjected to the market test. That test is whether a financial institution with strong social objectives can survive financially, outliving its founders and growing beyond the capital they provided. To do so, it must price its services so that it is profitable, and establish sustainable relationships with its clientele. The quality of the promotion of such institutions is an important determinant of their performance; and ultimately, their performance is the measure of the quality of their promotion.

Poor performance and poor quality of promotion tend to occur to the extent that the market test is ignored at the outset in institutional design or set aside at some later stage when other, conflicting objectives are accorded transcending priority. These priorities have historically been social, religious or political, but recently they have also been based on economic theory. Specialized rural credit institutions, for example, have been established, at least in part, to compensate for alleged "market failure," as perceived by economists who often have little interest in accounting or finance, except as borrowers. (Conditions leading to market failure were discussed in chapter 5.)

The Provident Loan Society, which is not a cooperative, was described in earlier chapters. It survives in New York with a reduced branch network, but is no longer significant because it failed to evolve. After 50

---

29. Herman E. Kroos and Martin R. Blyn, *op. cit.* p. 124.

years of exemplary service, the Provident lost its clients to other innovative lenders. Transaction costs to pawnshop customers remain high; other sources of consumer finance have become increasingly convenient. The history of the Provident effectively ends with a soft landing, which cannot be said for many cooperative systems inspired by, but only superficially patterned on, the Raiffeisen, Schulze-Delitzsch and North American models.

Efforts to subject finance to politically-determined social objectives are found in cooperatives in many low-income countries. Comparison of the evolution of government-sponsored cooperatives in India and Malaysia from the first decade of the 20th century shows how two different approaches each failed in its own way, although they shared a common root in the motivations of their promoters. Later, more commercially oriented efforts to institutionalize moneylending in the Philippines encountered some of the same problems. In each case, politically-determined objectives led to politically-dominated financial institutions that ultimately performed poorly.

Raiffeisen and Indian Independence

The Raiffeisen model survived and evolved where credit cooperatives remain essentially private, as in western Europe and North America. It has fared less well where governments have adapted it, as in India. Rural credit cooperatives were launched in India in 1904. By the late 1920s they were highly politicized, with rich farmers in control. Why did rich members of Indian rural society use cooperatives to enrich themselves, often at the expense of the poor, while the larger German yeomen who formed the backbone of Raiffeisen's cooperatives acted unselfishly to help their less-prosperous neighbors?

This question has no simple answer. One difference, however, is the extent of government involvement.[30] Raiffeisen recruited cooperative leaders by appealing to their sense of duty and religious compassion, and asked them to put their land, homes, implements, harvests, and livestock at risk through unlimited liability. He was not implementing a government program, and put himself at risk by acting on his personal initiative. (During his bread society activities he received an official reprimand, and

---

30. B.J. Youngjohns. *op. cit.*

his contemporary, Schulze-Delitzsch, who became a member of the Prussian parliament and of the Reichstag, publicly mocked his piety.) His standing in the civil service no doubt strengthened his appeal, and gave him access that might otherwise have required much more effort to obtain. Rural credit unions, initially the object of popular and official doubt and even hostility, remained essentially independent.

The British launched their version of Raiffeisen's model in India as an instrument of government policy, with special powers and privileges because of the priority attached to the objective of reducing lending and borrowing among farmers and between farmers and moneylenders.[31] The Cooperative Societies Act of 1912 established a government department, headed by a Registrar of Cooperatives, to promote, control and supervise cooperatives.[32]

The results were documented in the Madras Presidency, one of the three divisions of British India, as follows:[33] unlimited liability was not enforced; basing local credit on the mobilization of local savings was abandoned because of the time and effort required to overcome rural suspicion and establish confidence; and apex or cooperative central banks and networks to finance village-level primary societies were formed with government funds. This removed personal responsibility from those most intimately involved. Confidence was not built strongly at the village level, and civil servants implementing government policy are of course immune from the consequences of their actions as long as proper procedures are followed.

The cooperative central banks accepted deposits in urban areas, where savers were largely middle class civil servants and professionals. Interest rates were kept low to assist borrowers, which constrained deposit rates. These institutions were disintermediated as urban depositors transferred their funds to commercial banks offering higher rates during the boom following World War I. Urban depositors' role in cooperative leadership diminished with the departure of their funds. They were not large

---

31. Reserve Bank of India, *All-India Rural Credit Survey.* Vol. 1, *The Survey Report. Part 2 (Credit Agencies).* (Bombay: Reserve Bank of India, 1957). p. 183.

32. B.J. Youngjohns, *op. cit.*

33. Bruce L. Robert, Jr., "Agricultural Credit Cooperatives, Rural Development and Agrarian Politics in Madras, 1893-1937," in J.D. Von Pischke, Dale W Adams and Gordon Donald, eds., *op. cit.* pp. 354-362.

borrowers and had other outlets for their social interests and leadership talents. In response, the government provided more funding while official promotion increased the number of rural societies. Control over cheap funds was a powerful incentive for the politically aspiring, and cooperatives became dominated by rural political figures.

Loan arrears grew with political control and with the depressed economic conditions of the late 1920s. The government did not wish to become a bill collector and reorganized the cooperatives in a gesture of reform. However, cooperatives were viewed by their leaders as vehicles for patronage, and they did not want to lose votes by trying to collect overdue loans. This tendency was reversed in the 1930s when extremely unfavorable economic conditions forced the government's fiscal hand. Unlimited liability was enforced; hopelessly insolvent cooperatives were dissolved. In response to these unpopular measures, cooperative leaders, traditionally members of the collaborationist Justice Party, switched their allegiance to the Congress Party and hastened Indian independence.

Rice, Rubber, and Interpretation of the Koran

The tendency for things to get out of hand when cheap credit from government coffers is on the loose is also illustrated by British efforts to establish Malays as cash crop growers of rice and rubber. Efforts in Perak, documented by Paul Kratoska,[34] began with the colonial administration's concern for the apparently deteriorating economic position of Malays in an economy that was becoming increasingly monetized through mining and cash crop development and that was attracting entrepreneurial Chinese and Indian immigrants.

Development created markets for rice, which was not widely traded in the subsistence economy before colonization, and for land, which had been free for anyone willing to clear it. Land could be registered and pledged as security as a result of innovations introduced by the British. Malays entering the cash economy often borrowed from Chinese shopkeepers, generally in modest amounts related to household purchases. They also borrowed larger amounts from agents of South Indian moneylending firms. Known as Chettiars or Chetties, these aggressive lenders accepted

---

34. Paul H. Kratoska, "The Chettiar and the Yeoman." Occasional Paper No. 32. Singapore: The Institute of Southeast Asian Studies, June 1975.

land as security, took high risks in establishing Malays as rubber growers,[35] charged 24 or 36 percent per annum,[36] and went to court to seize defaulters' land. Planting and tending rubber trees until they could be tapped created collateral of considerable value.

Colonial administrators fervently desired to have Malays adopt cash crops such as rice to make the colony self-sufficient, and rubber to promote development and the fiscal base. But they became alarmed by the extent to which Malays pledged their land to Chettiars and by the amounts of credit obtained, which were sometimes used for feasts, ceremonies or for the *hadj.*

The first official response was to establish an alternative source of credit. A government fund was created in 1908 to lend to smallholders for agricultural purposes at an interest rate of 0.5 percent per month, repayable in installments over not more than three years. While Chettiars provided credit quickly and often in amounts exceeding the value of security, lengthy procedures delayed access to government credit. Loans amounted to only 50 percent of the value of land pledged as security, which was often undervalued by government appraisers, and loan use was restricted. Demand for these funds lagged. Loan sizes were insufficient to permit farmers to pay off their debts to Chettiars. However, the relatively small loan size resulted in no defaults on principal, saving the government the embarrassing task of seizing borrowers' lands pledged as security.

In 1913 legislation was enacted to prohibit transfer of Malay lands to nonMalays, which administrators hoped would end the attractiveness of Chettiar credit. Reservations of Malay land were created, and in these areas the supply of rural credit declined. To reduce hardship, the government permitted the auction of debtors' lands to other Malays, with proceeds payable to Chettiars. Some Malays served as agents and front men for Chettiars, circumventing the law.

Legislation passed in 1919 required that legal remedies under the Land Code be exhausted first when land secured a defaulted loan. This forced

---

35. S.K.D., "Nattukottai Chettiars in Malaya," *The Malaysian Law Journal,* February 1958; Supriya Singh, *Bank Negara Malaysia—the First 25 Years, 1959-1984.* (Kuala Lumpur: Bank Negara Malaysia, 1984).

36. These rates appear to be simple interest equivalent of 2 and 3 percent per month. On a compounded basis, paying interest on interest, these rates approximate 27 and 43 percent annually.

creditors to dispose of pledged land before using civil procedures to seize other assets of debtors in arrears. Lenders and borrowers promptly switched to promissory notes and "equitable mortgages," in which the borrower deposited with the lender the documents establishing the debtor's land ownership, with no official claim entered in the land register. This made it impossible for the debtor to sell the land or to pledge it to others.

Foreclosures on promissory notes under civil procedures involved the sale of assets, including land, to the highest bidder, while under the Land Code a sale could occur only if the highest bid exceeded the indebtedness outstanding against the land. This made matters worse for some distressed debtors. With deterioration of economic conditions, the government in 1930 made foreclosure subject to approval by local rulers and their state councils, and permitted postponements of foreclosures.

In the 1920s, the government began to encourage rural cooperative credit societies as a means of combating indebtedness. To avert public skepticism, the British obtained favorable opinions from the Mufti in Egypt and rulings from Malay sultans that the interest arrangements of cooperative credit did not contravene Islamic law. These societies borrowed from other cooperatives, including thrift and credit societies formed by government employees. Falling agricultural prices in the 1930s effectively put some rural societies out of operation and strained the thrift and credit societies that had loaned them funds. Rural cooperatives failed to expand; having to assume unlimited liability for the existing debts of others discouraged prospective new members. In 1936 the government introduced seasonal credit societies, a new type of cooperative. Their operations were disrupted by World War II.

R.J.G. Wells's research in the 1970s continues the saga.[37] He noted that poor performance by cooperatives led the government to promote multipurpose farmers' associations. Rice farmers "received a relatively elastic supply of loanable funds from noninstitutional sources" at interest rates usually exceeding 30 percent per year—Chettiars or their modern equivalents were still in business.[38] Officials believed there were gaps in the rural finance system and formed an agricultural bank in 1969 to assist

---

37. "An Input Credit Program for Small Farmers in West Malaysia," *Journal of Administration Overseas.* 17, 1, 1978; excerpted in J.D. Von Pischke, Dale W Adams and Gordon Donald, eds., *op. cit.* pp. 218-224.

38. R.J.G. Wells, "The Informal Rural Credit Market in Malaysia," *op. cit.*

smallholders. By this time tenancy was common in rice-growing areas, while the transaction costs of cumbersome procedures and stamp duties discouraged owner-occupiers from offering their land as security.

Institutionalization, Politicization, and Demise with Government Funds

A notable effort to institutionalize informal finance began in the Philippines in the 1950s when the Central Bank encouraged formation of private rural unit banks, allowed to have only one office. They were permitted to accept deposits and to make loans, which would be small because these banks' capital was small and the largest permissible loan could not exceed a small fraction of their capital.

Rural bankers were usually prominent local citizens who were often involved in moneylending. By becoming rural bankers they could obtain some capital from government, represented by preferred stock, to supplement their own. They could expand their moneylending operations by soliciting deposits. The increased volume of lending would offset the somewhat lower interest rates permitted on rural bank loans, compared to those they had charged as informal lenders. In addition, their incomes as shopkeepers, rice millers, transporters, or landlords could increase from growing rural economic activity. The Central Bank provided training and other support for rural banks.

The system worked well through the 1970s. More than 1,000 rural banks were formed, many by citizens whom Raiffeisen and Schulze-Delitzsch would have tried to persuade to form credit cooperatives if they had lived in the Philippines at the time. In 1973 a massive government credit program for rice production, Masagana-99, was implemented.[39] The country was under martial law, and most rural bankers were hardly in a position to challenge a presidential program to promote production of the staple food, which had declined partially as a result of severe hurricanes. The availability of new, Green Revolution rice varieties made the Masagana-99 input credit and supply program all the more incontestable.

Special rediscounting facilities allowed rural bankers to borrow cheaply from the Central Bank in order to fund M-99 loans. The level of financing expanded greatly, and 500,000 farmers, more than one-third of the

---

39. Details of Masagana-99 and its effect on the banking system are summarized in Orlando J. Sacay, Meliza H. Agabin and Chita Irene E. Tanchoco, *op. cit.*

country's rice producers, received M-99 loans at the program's peak in the 1974/75 crop year. M-99 arrears accumulated, causing 145 rural banks to lose their access to Central Bank funds and weakening many others. The number of borrowers fell to fewer than 60,000 by 1983, and some farmers withdrew their deposits from rural banks no longer able to lend. In this condition, many rural banks could not withstand the economic decline of the 1980s. Several hundred suspended their operations by 1986, and only about 135 apeared to be in good financial health, among them a handful that had preserved their capacity to create value by avoiding M-99 participation.

Rural bankers generally fared better than their banks because their other interests cushioned their banking losses. So, as traders, rice millers, transporters, and landlords they were still in a position to lend to their clients and tenants.

9

CREATING VALUE AT THE FRONTIER THROUGH INNOVATION

There are two sources of pressure from inside the frontier that move it outward, creating value directly for more clients. The first is entrepreneurial intermediaries and investors who attempt to leap the frontier and bring formal financial services to those who have not used them before. Competitive financial markets naturally innovate in managing risk, lengthening term structures, reducing transaction costs, and refining valuation, as discussed in chapters 1 and 2. Competition motivates experimentation to devise self-sustaining instruments that survive because they create value for both their buyers and their sellers. Financial deepening, defined by Edward S. Shaw as the growth of financial assets at a rate exceeding the accumulation of nonfinancial assets in the economy,[1] results from these activities.

Government policy is the second source of energy within the frontier that tries to press it outward. Governments seek to control financial markets, as discussed in chapter 3, and they may try to stimulate financial innovation. Government intervention is direct when financial intermediaries are required to lend for certain purposes or to provide services to specified target groups as discussed in chapters 5 and 6. The most common form of direct intervention is control of interest rates.

Intervention may also be indirect, through incentives that cause intermediaries to allocate funds to priorities defined by government. Incentives include tax advantages, credit insurance, and access to government banking business. They may also include changes in laws and

---

1. Edward S. Shaw, *Financial Deepening in Economic Development* (New York: Oxford University Press, 1973), p. vii.

regulations that remove barriers and provide new incentives to facilitate financial intermediation.

Sustainable Innovations Reduce Costs

Traditional intervention using credit to bring larger numbers of people within the frontier of formal finance relatively quickly in developing countries has generally been direct. It has proved neither effective, cheap, nor equitable. Direct intervention often responds to the passivity that characterizes intermediaries in repressed, stagnant financial markets that decline to press the frontier. Intermediaries remain passive because the services they offer within the frontier appear unlikely to be profitable at or beyond it. These intermediaries, lacking competition, wait for potential clients to cross the frontier as a result of development. Higher, regular incomes, urban living, and education create more users of conventional financial services.

In response to intermediary passivity, governments have often forced financial intermediaries to expand branch networks so that access to conventional financial services, offered on conventional terms and conditions, can be made convenient for more people. Forced branch replication has increased the deposit base of many banking systems, but often has not contributed to financial development because intermediaries' rationale for passivity, that conventional services are unlikely to be profitable when offered to frontier clients, is a correct commercial assessment.

In addition to replication, many governments attempt to impose new financial services or instruments on financial markets. These are unlikely to be efficient or sustainable unless they reduce costs. Failure at cost reduction easily occurs because cost and benefits to intermediaries are not a major concern of the designers of these imposed services and instruments as noted in chapter 5.

Replicative efforts, imposition of new services and other coercive measures that attempt to force intermediaries to implement government plans fail when they attempt to work against economic forces, defy financial logic, and give perverse incentives to the individuals who are supposed to make things work and to those who are in theory supposed to benefit. New approaches are needed to expand the frontier dynamically, and these require innovation, which must reduce costs.

To create value, intervention must have the same effects as competitive, market-originated innovation: it must develop an environment and skills that make financial markets function more effectively, reducing costs and creating value for financial intermediaries as well as for their clients.[2] Financial markets easily respond to intervention, but unless responses reduce costs, it is unlikely that intervention makes society better off. Government policies that lead intermediaries to respond in defensive, cost-increasing ways by definition cannot be considered beneficial or innovative.

Joseph A. Schumpeter explored the role of innovation in economic development.[3] He concluded that innovators change the structure of an economy by bidding resources away from established modes of production. Their actions subject them to the risk of failure, but when they succeed they displace established producers and create greater efficiency represented by cheaper goods and services, improved quality, and superior technology.

Successful innovation creates high returns for the innovator, which attracts competition that in time erodes these returns. Innovation and reactions to it constitute "creative destruction" that stimulates additional rounds of innovation and competition that underlie sustained economic development. Schumpeter viewed development primarily as structural change, not simply as greater output per capita. His approach is applicable to the financial sector.

Under what circumstances is an attempt at innovation cost-reducing? Offering new financial services may be more costly than providing existing financial services because rational intermediaries tend to begin with the simple before moving to the complex. However, this comparison is misleading. New services may be innovative and economically and socially worthwhile when they break through the frontier by serving clients who

---

2. V.V. Bhatt raises these points in several of his pioneering papers on financial innovation. See for example, "Financial Innovations and Development," in J.D. Von Pischke, Dale W. Adams and Gordon Donald, eds., *op. cit.* pp. 43-49, and "On Financial Innovations and Credit Market Evolution," EDI Working Papers. Economic Development Institute of the World Bank. Washington, DC, March 1989.

3. Joseph A. Schumpeter, *The Theory of Economic Development: An Enquiry into Profits, Capital, Credit, Interest and the Business Cycle* (Cambridge: Harvard University Press, 1934). [German original published in 1911.]

did not have access to similar services before, or who had access but only at higher costs.

For example, small farmers may not be able to obtain conventional commercial bank credit at interest rates of 12 percent per annum. Beyond the frontier they may borrow from informal sources such as traders. Farmers' cost of borrowing traders' funds may approximate 30 percent per annum, including interest charges and transaction costs. A commercial banker or a cooperative that offers short term loans to these farmers at a comparable cost of 25 percent per annum reduces these borrowers' costs.

For an innovation to be sustainable, overall costs of lending and borrowing must be reduced. Sustainability occurs when the lender earns a profit from the service and when borrowers find the relationship with the lender at least as attractive as alternative relationships with other suppliers of credit. The innovative banker's costs may be increased by a sustainable new service that is relatively expensive to provide, such as loans to small farmers. However, sustainability indicates that the banker's revenues from the service cover its costs. When an innovation holds clients, its costs to users are presumably less than those of dealing with the alternative lender.

Innovation determines the location of the frontier, which is a fault line along which movement occurs in response to innovation. Many examples of successful financial innovation can be cited; several are summarized in previous chapters. This chapter focuses on the frontier, sketching a profile of informal and formal financial markets and their development.

An Overview of Financial Development Processes

Differences and similarities on both sides of the frontier offer clues to the behavior of the frontier. Information on interrelationships of formal and informal financial markets is increasingly available. This permits specification of a model of financial development, summarizing points from previous chapters.

Circles of Intermediaries

Financial markets may be illustrated by two saucers of equal size placed face-to-face, one on top of the other. The lower saucer represents providers of financial services and the upper one represents users of these services.

The lower saucer consists of two concentric circles. The larger, outer circle or edge of the saucer encompasses all providers of financial services, both formal and informal. The smaller, interior circle represents the formal financial sector and defines the frontier. The area between the two circles represents informal finance (Figure 9.1).

Figure 9.1

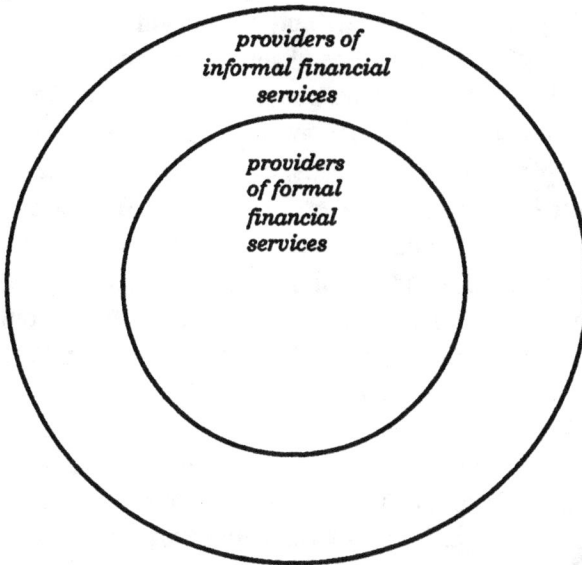

providers of informal financial services

providers of formal financial services

Within the financial sector several factors influence the relative sizes or market shares of the formal and informal subsectors. Growth of the entire market creates a larger saucer and changes market shares in favor of intermediaries leading the expansion. Expansion is most likely to occur in a growing economy with flexible interest rate structures that provide incentives to intermediaries to innovate and grow.[4] With economic development, financial markets deepen; formal finance grows faster than the economy and than the informal market; formal intermediaries reach more customers.

Expansion of formal finance occurs through increased availability of conventional services, as when established intermediaries open new offices. Increased convenience entices potential customers to seek

---

4. Edward S. Shaw, *op. cit.*

relationships with formal financial institutions. More vigorous development is achieved by structural change and innovation. Innovations consist of new services that expand interaction with an existing clientele or cater specifically to a new clientele.

Innovation at the frontier probably occurs most naturally in deposit and money transfer services because many more people can be served through deposit facilities than through credit. The "need" for financial services at the frontier is primarily for a safe and convenient place to keep relatively small amounts of funds. This type of service can be enjoyed continuously, while formal loans at the frontier generally have fixed maturities and are taken in response to special situations and opportunities.

Many people do not want loans, some desire smaller loans than the formal sector is willing to process, and others are not creditworthy in formal financial terms. Those in trade who are not creditworthy may be marginal commercially and not highly skilled at setting prices, obtaining goods competitively or managing their stock. Other people may have "character defects" that disqualify them from formal credit. However, the uncreditworthy can be served by deposit accounts.

Structural changes are most likely when new services that compete with informal finance are not burdened by the practices and government regulations that are applied to mainstream formal finance. (Indeed, some innovations are designed precisely to avoid these regulations.[5]) The first ten years of experience with moneyshops in the Philippines illustrates a partially successful innovation encumbered by certain traditional banking practices.

Moneyshops for Lean and Clean Services

Moneyshops in the Philippines were a striking innovation by formal intermediaries to provide small scale, high turnover deposit services and to compete directly with informal credit. Moneyshops were pioneered by the Philippines Commercial & Industrial Bank (now Philippine Commercial International Bank, or PCI Bank) in 1973.[6] Moneyshops are located close

---

5. Edward J. Kane, "Political Economy of Subsidizing Agricultural Credit in Developing Countries," in Dale W Adams, Douglas H. Graham and J.D. Von Pischke, eds., *op. cit.* pp. 174-177.

6. Data on PCI moneyshops was gathered initially from the author's personal interviews in 1982 with Manuel A. Reyes, PCI Senior Vice President. Subsequent data

to public markets and serve market stallholders and their customers. (Stalls generally measure approximately 3x2 meters. A typical market contains 1,000 stalls.) Moneyshop services to stallholders initially included working capital or inventory financing in multiples of P 1,000 up to a maximum loan size of P 10,000 (US$ 1,500 in 1973) and deposit or "savings" accounts characterized by relatively small daily transactions.

Moneyshop loans are geared to the borrower's inventory turnover cycle, which is often one week. Dry goods merchants having a slow turnover receive "long-term" loans of up to 120 days, the maximum offered. Vegetable wholesalers, with a cycle of only a few days at the longest, have correspondingly shorter loans. Loans enable stallholders to make cash payment for produce and other inventory upon arrival, substituting moneyshop credit for more expensive trade credit. Credit helps stallholders build inventories of nonperishables, yielding economies in purchasing and shipping by replacing small daily orders with weekly orders.

Moneyshop operators devised several formulas to determine loan size or borrower debt capacity. One was that debt service should not consume more than 30 percent of the borrower's mark-up. Another attempted to relate loan size to the income of the borrower's household, less household and business expenses and repayment of other debts. "Gut feel," based on experience in lending, and knowledge of the borrower and the borrower's trade was a third approach.

Moneyshop lending is unsecured. Borrowers do not sign any documents although the moneyshop usually requires a copy of the lease agreement between the stallholder and the market owner before the lending relationship begins. PCI moneyshop loans were made initially to 40 to 45 percent of stallholders. The remainder included traders accommodated by other lenders, those who did not desire loans and those not creditworthy by moneyshop standards. No delinquencies occurred during the first six months of operations. Loan volume exceeded P 500 million during the first year.

Rapid expansion created problems that became obvious after 18 months. These included a lack of urgency in repaying formal loans, loan

is from Romulo Borlaza, "Moneyshops: The Story of One Bank's Social Commitment," *PCI Unibank World*. Manila, January 1984. pp. 4-6.

diversion for social ceremonies, and intimidation of moneyshop staff by thugs and political strongmen on behalf of defaulters. Fires in markets prompted some stallholders to move, leaving behind their debts. After the initial shakeout, 200 to 300 good loan accounts remained on the books of the typical moneyshop, with average outstanding balances of about P 2,500 per account as of 1982. The typical moneyshop had about 5,000 savings accounts, the same quantity found in many PCI Bank branches, with total balances of P 1 to 1.5 million. About 800 savings account owners were stallholders, while the remaining 4,200 were housewives and others who shopped at the market. Most of these deposit accounts were the first opened by customers, rather than business transferred from less convenient locations.

MONEYSHOPS AND THE CONSTRAINTS OF TRADITION AND REGULATION. By early 1982, PCI moneyshop deposit account balances exceeded P 120 million, while loan balances totaled about P 20 million, giving an extremely low loan-to-deposit ratio of about 15 percent. At the end of 1983, moneyshop deposits exceeded P 150 million. PCI Bank continued to apply parts of the format of formal finance to its innovation at the frontier, and moneyshops' loan-to-deposit ratios and interest rates left them unable to cover their costs from interest and fees charged borrowers.

INTEREST RATES. PCI Bank continued to pay interest on moneyshop savings accounts at the same rate offered at its branches, and interest approximated half of the expense of moneyshop operations. It did not introduce transaction fees to recover the costs of servicing these small accounts, which include the bookkeeping arising from large numbers of small transactions. Nor did it boost loan interest rates beyond the levels set initially. In early 1982, moneyshop effective loan interest rates approximated 36 percent per annum, while the commercial bank short-term prime rate was 16 percent. Bad debt losses for banks in the Philippines traditionally approximated 0.5 percent per year on the outstanding loan portfolio. Moneyshop bad debt losses averaged 3 percent per year.

Moneyshop clients would probably have been willing to forego interest on deposits and even to pay fees for the convenience they enjoyed and because the alternative informal lending rates were much higher. Why did PCI Bank not change its deposit pricing policies to adapt to the realities of small scale, rapid turnover, cash transactions? The reasons for failure to adapt remain unclear. Possibilities include the risk of bad publicity that could tarnish PCI Bank's image, competition from other banks eager to open money shops, the possibility of an adverse Central Bank reaction, an unwillingness to compromise on what the Bank viewed as a social service, and attractive uses for moneyshop liquidity elsewhere in PCI Bank operations.

OUTREACH TO CLIENTS. Moneyshops are generally staffed by four persons: two teller-collectors, a supervisor-accountant, and an officer to approve loans and oversee operations. Teller-collectors go through the market once or twice a day to collect loan installments and possibly to accept savings deposits. The daily collection system is critical: it relieves borrowers of the burden of leaving their stalls to make payments, greatly reducing their transaction costs. The discipline of daily collection permits the lender to monitor borrowers' activities and offers a very effective means of packaging formal financial services for those accustomed to informal finance.

Yet, Philippine banks were not generally permitted to compete through "solicitation," which precluded the use of collectors and made it easy for banks to be passive. Structural changes in formal finance often require regulatory reform, and in this case the Central Bank approved the use of collectors by moneyshops.

CONSOLIDATION AND EVOLUTION. PCI Bank closed 30 moneyshops between 1980 and 1982; many that remained were unprofitable. By 1984 it had 63, approximately the number opened in 1973 and 1974. Had banking tradition been applied more flexibly, more might have survived. However, the opposite occurred: the Central Bank permitted moneyshops to become full service banking offices, while PCI Bank's 88 branches were also preparing to provide moneyshop services. By 1984 moneyshop instruments were becoming a new service of conventional banking, losing their separate identity.

Another aspect of moneyshop innovation has a human interest dimension. When PCI Bank was designing the moneyshop concept, it coincidentally was replacing its security guards and janitorial staff with private contractors in an economy move. Management decided that some of those let go could be put to work in the new moneyshops, which were being expanded rapidly to preempt competitive responses by other banks that also began opening moneyshops. Training courses were provided; former guards and sweepers became tellers. For a few, the temptations of handling cash were so great that they ended up in jail. Others eventually became moneyshop managers or moved into other positions in PCI Bank.

Competition and Complementarity of Formal and Informal Finance[7]

Zones of competition between informal and formal finance occur where users explore and compare the advantages of each. Competition is seen in moneyshops' efforts to capture market share, in their ability to replace informal lenders as financiers of stallholders, and in their institutionalization of cash balances in savings accounts. Other things remaining equal, competition in finance should lower interest rates and transaction costs by encouraging efficiency and by mobilizing a larger quantity of resources for lending.

Complementarity is defined here as interaction between formal and informal finance that benefits borrowers and lenders in both. Complementarity arises with intermediation between formal and informal finance, when a borrower from a formal institution lends informally to others, for example, possibly through open account trade credit. This is illustrated by moneyshop credit, which is part of larger market systems. Stallholders in the vegetable trade in the Philippines have long-standing business ties with ambulant vendors and others who do not have stalls but sell small volumes of produce near the market. Parties to these regular trusted client relationships are called *sukis*. The *suki* relationship enables the small vendor to obtain favorable prices, produce in good condition, and credit from the stallholder. As a result the stallholder enjoys greater turnover and risk diversification. Hence moneyshop credit to stallholders facilitates employment and convenience to consumers, and some consumers also obtain credit as part of their *suki* relationships with small vendors.

The coexistence of informal and formal finance is healthy and dynamic, permitting more people to participate in financial markets. Jerry R. Ladman

---

7. Themes of competition and complementarity are developed in Anand G. Chandavarkar, "The Informal Financial Sector in Developing Countries: Analysis, Evidence and Policy Implications." Kuala Lumpur: The South East Asian Central Banks Research and Training Centre, August 1987.

has explained this coexistence. He notes that formal lenders tend to have high fixed costs, high transaction costs, but relatively low interest rates and opportunity costs of capital.[8] The formal lender's break-even loan volume is relatively high, while transaction costs are not very sensitive to loan size. These factors tend to result in relatively large average loan sizes. Competition may make it difficult for formal lenders to pass on their costs to borrowers directly in the form of fees and charges. This may stimulate these lenders to spread the transaction costs of loan generation by offering loans with longer maturities than those available informally.

Informal lenders are in the opposite situation, with low fixed costs and low transaction costs, but charging relatively high interest rates. They have a low break-even point and tend to make relatively few loans, in small amounts and for relatively short periods of time.

Prospective small borrowers are deterred by the transaction costs imposed by formal lenders, primarily in the application and approval stages of the transaction while the outcome remains uncertain, and especially for short term loans. Prospective large borrowers, especially those seeking longer term credit, find the high transaction costs trivial and prefer the lower interest rates of formal finance. Thus, as Ladman argues, the behavior of borrowers and lenders converges to create a market segment in which informal finance is the appropriate form, and another naturally dominated by formal finance. Ladman's model is sometimes misinterpreted by those who assume that informal finance is inherently monopolistic, and who therefore conclude that the model justifies exploitation of small borrowers, which it does not.

Ahmed's work in Bangladesh confirms that transaction costs are lower in informal financial markets than in formal ones.[9] He found that the average transaction costs of 61 sample agricultural borrowers from the Bangladesh Krishi Bank amounted to 22 percent of loan size. These costs increased with loan size, but decreased in proportion to loan size. Average transaction costs equal to about 28 percent of loan size were reported for loans of about US$60 equivalant, while those on loans in excess of about US$200 were 7 percent. Sixty-one sample borrowers from informal

---

8. Jerry R. Ladman, "Loan-Transactions Costs, Credit Rationing, and Market Structure: The Case of Bolivia," in Dale W Adams, Douglas H. Graham and J.D. Von Pischke, eds., *op. cit.* pp. 110-112.

9. Zia U. Ahmed, *op. cit.* p. 360.

sources in the same villages reported average transaction costs equal to 2 percent of loan size. Their average costs ranged from 4 to 1 percent of loan size, declining sharply on loans of more than about US$200.

Users of Financial Services

While the lower saucer in the illustration represents providers of informal and formal financial services (Figure 9.1), the upper saucer represents users of these services. As depositors, users furnish—and as borrowers they ultimately employ—the funds that the formal and informal financial sectors intermediate. Individuals and nonfinancial firms provide deposits in response to attractive financial services, and these funds are in turn allocated to individuals and nonfinancial firms that are borrowers. The lower saucer can rather easily be divided into formal and informal activities, but the frontier in the upper saucer is less clearcut. While each formal financial service has its own frontier, many individuals and firms engage in formal and informal financial activities simultaneously (Figure 9.2), in part because deposits are more accessible than loans are to new users of formal financial services.

The upper and lower saucers expand at the same rate with development. Those initially beyond the outer limits with virtually no contacts with financial intermediation become users of financial services, normally beginning with money. Within the saucer, development creates movement toward formal financial services, although development can also be accompanied by increases in informal financing as suggested by the emergence of new moneylenders in the Philippines along with adoption of high-yielding varieties of rice. As participants in informal financial markets become more involved with the formal economy through employment, markets, education, and the media, they are attractive prospects to formal intermediaries seeking new business. At the same time these sources are increasingly useful to them because of their changed circumstances. Their costs of access decline in relative terms as their incomes increase, and possibly also in absolute terms as intermediaries compete to expand and innovate.

Figure 9.2

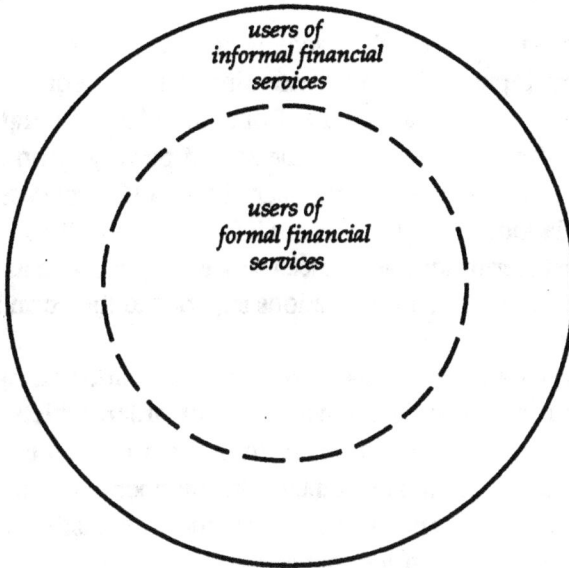

Relative Advantages of Informal and Formal Finance

To users, the advantages of informal financial services include willingness to deal in small amounts, absence of burdensome documentation and bookkeeping requirements, confidence engendered by face-to-face relationships between creditor and debtor, flexibility of terms, rapid lender response to loan requests,[10] and as a result, transaction costs that are generally low. Advantages of formal finance include the confidentiality of institutional finance, ability to deal in relatively large amounts, confidence provided by documentation and legal practice within the formal sector, specialization and related economies of scale and growth of markets, and the convenience of transcending or complementing face-to-face relationships through postal and electronic communication systems that transfer financial claims quickly and cheaply.

---

10. Timberg and Aiyer, *op. cit.* pp. 48-49, point out that some segments of the informal urban commercial credit market in India are not particularly speedy in providing loans.

Is Informal Finance Necessarily Deficient?

Allegations that informal finance is critically deficient, especially in assisting development, deserve examination. A frequent standard of comparison may be called the Four Standard Deviation Spread. Comparisons framed according to the spread portray informal finance as basically evil and inefficient, citing loan sharks and other cases at least two standard deviations below the norm in informal financial markets, and then cite the advantages of formal finance using examples, such as the Grameen Bank, that are two standard deviations superior to the norm in the formal sector.

However, data closer to the norms in each market show that blanket condemnation of informal finance is out of order, which suggests that policies that treat eradication of informal finance as an end in itself are inherently suspect. There are an increasing number of examples that show that informal finance can perform many functions relatively well beyond the frontier, especially in less developed areas where formal finance is repressed and inefficient. These functions include money transfer, realization of economies of scale, information generation and processing, term transformation, and innovation, which are explored below.

MONEY TRANSFER. Informal finance is not necessarily severely limited relative to the advantages of formal finance, as demonstrated by its survival and competitiveness with formal finance. For example, by the mid-1970s informal agents in the Yemen Arab Republic operated elaborate and highly efficient, low cost remittance networks serving Yemeni workers in Saudi Arabia and the Gulf, and their families in relatively remote parts of Yemen, far from commercial bank branches.

Some agents who collected workers' funds bought US dollar drafts issued by commercial banks in Arabia, linking formal and informal systems. Carriers of these drafts, who were often the heads of networks of agents collecting and distributing remittances, flew between Yemen and the oilfields weekly or monthly. They redeemed these drafts in Yemen for local currency, which was distributed to beneficiaries. Others carried cash and journeyed from the oilfields to Yemen by public land transport, reportedly never losing a riyal to thieves. Their immunity was credited to the clearly high social value of their services. A moneychanger in Taiz who handled remittances offered money transfer services to major centers in

Europe and North America on terms competitive with those of commercial banks in Yemen.

ECONOMIES OF SCALE. Planners, officials and others who have easy access to formal financial markets often consider informal finance as deficient for "development." Informal financial markets are generally thought not to provide reliable sources of long-term finance or not to be able to mobilize large amounts of funds that can be concentrated on large scale investments. Yet the following examples show that informal finance is rich and responsive, filling niches not fully catered to by formal intermediaries.

While most informal finance involves relatively small transactions, notable exceptions exist. Rotating savings and credit associations and similar institutions based on craft or ethnic bonds mobilize substantial amounts of liquidity. Associations of this type exist in such sophisticated financial centers as Singapore and Hong Kong. *Tanomoshii* associations of businessmen of Japanese ancestry in Hawaii are reported to put up relatively large sums to finance construction of buildings, financing characterized by relatively high risks from cost overruns and from the thin capitalization of contractors. In less advanced areas informal networks have demonstrated a considerable capacity for mobilizing resources. One outstanding example was the Gurage Road Organization in Ethiopia, which in the 1960s collected subscriptions to finance the construction of an all-weather road from the main town in Gurageland to the nearest national highway.

Elsewhere in Africa RoSCAs are active and some intermediate large sums. For example, *tontines* with a hand equivalent to US$1 million are reported in Cameroon, where these informal groups greatly economize transaction costs for peasants as well as for people active in large scale, modern sector activities.[11] Many have written rules and procedures, and information systems that exclude people who defaulted on earlier and other *tontines*.

Savings mobilization is also a function of moneykeepers who are trusted persons such as a parent, elder or religious leader. In parts of Africa, entrusting funds to moneykeepers removes them from the pool of assets over which others within the kinship system can make claims. Some

---

11. *The New York Times*. Nov. 30, 1987. "Informal Capitalism Grows in Cameroon: Grass-Roots Credit System." p. D8.

depositors make contracts with moneykeepers which permit withdrawal of funds only for specified purposes, giving the moneykeeper the right to refuse the withdrawal demand if the purpose for the request is inconsistent with the deposit-holder's original objective.[12] Shipton also notes that agricultural wage laborers in The Gambia prefer to save by being paid quarterly, in effect keeping claims on others who are more solvent and who have good reputations for honoring their commitments.[13]

Informal finance is usually characterized by small, short-term transactions because these predominate in the informal economy. There is no evidence that these characteristics are antidevelopmental or a serious constraint on development. Large scale and long-term activities are often more efficiently financed in formal markets because the formal economy operates at these levels. Each market segment complements the other, serving separate purposes, like jets and camels as means of transport.

For development, movement between informal and formal financial markets should remain unrestricted by barriers other than those arising from the costs of providing competitive services. V.V. Bhatt points out that informal finance performs an extremely important development role by nurturing enterprises or entrepreneurs before they can obtain formal finance.[14] Credit project experience demonstrates merits, arising from equity considerations and risk diversification, of not having all lenders oriented toward relatively large, capital-intensive projects, especially in agriculture. The tendencies of these lenders to concentrate loans as explained by the Iron Law of Interest Rates violates equity, while also making it difficult to spread lender's risk across a large number of borrowers.

While informal intermediaries naturally tailor their services to individual clients, formal financial intermediation appears to have greater innovative potential to create a diversity of instruments, a wider and expanding array of financial assets. These advantages seem to result from economies in handling risks and in mobilizing and allocating liquidity. Risk-spreading and risk-reducing intermediation requires information. The large scale of formal finance creates opportunities for specialization in information

---

12. Auguste Daubrey, "Mobilization of Savings for Rural Development in Africa," in Denis Kessler and Pierre-Antoine Ullmo, eds., *op. cit.* p. 234.

13 Parker Shipton, "How Gambians Save," p. 26.

14. V.V. Bhatt, *op. cit.* p. 47.

acquisition and processing that are not available in the more limited markets characterized by informal finance.

INFORMATION GENERATION AND PROCESSING. Differences between formal and informal finance in the information generating and processing capacities that arise from economies of scale and scope are not so obvious. One source of information for formal intermediaries is the activities of informal financial markets. Information in informal financial markets is often comprehensive and thorough. Examples are the intimacy with which moneylenders know their clients—often as a result of relationships spanning several generations—and the trust and confidence from familiarity and blood relationships that characterize rotating savings and credit associations and direct borrowing and lending among members of extended families. Informal information generation and processing is probably more resilient because information is vital and private, confined to those with an intimate need to know.

An extensive literature on the role of information in credit markets has blossomed since the seminal 1981 article by Stiglitz and Weiss.[15] An important study by Christopher Udry of informal credit in villages near Zaria, Nigeria, found high levels of information that enabled market participants to use credit as a means of risk sharing consistent with Islamic law.[16] Udry reported that lending and borrowing were often conducted within extended family systems. These loans had no explicit interest rates or maturities and were generally not collateralized.

However, loans to borrowers who suffered shocks or setbacks during the period for which funds were outstanding had lower effective "interest" rates and remained outstanding longer than those to borrowers who had suffered no adversity. At the same time, loans from *lenders* who suffered shocks while their funds were outstanding were repaid sooner and carried higher "interest" rates than loans from lenders who had suffered no shocks. Udry concluded that excellent information enabled this high degree

---

15. Joseph E. Stiglitz and Andrew Weiss, *op. cit.* Examples of this literature are found in *The World Bank Economic Review.* 4, 3, September 1990, which is devoted entirely to imperfect information and rural credit markets and contains articles by Stiglitz and others.

16. Christopher Udry, "Credit Markets in Northern Nigeria: Credit as Insurance in a Rural Economy," *The World Bank Economic Review.* 4, 3, September 1990. pp. 251-269.

of sensitivity to be achieved in an instrument combining credit and insurance. He hypothesized that lower levels of information may prevent direct lending by outsiders, including formal lenders, from penetrating the credit markets in the villages he surveyed.

Thus, information in formal finance is not essentially superior, and formal financial markets can be rendered inefficient by government intervention in the form of projects, controls and lending targets, for example, that distort information processes by providing incentives to mislead, by requiring the reporting of irrelevant data, or by relying on beliefs rather than facts. Intervention may be based on false or insufficient information, and coercive implementation and reporting requirements may weaken or destroy the information processing capabilities of affected lenders, as discussed in chapter 7. This occurs when an emphasis on credit needs, priorities, and targets overwhelms concern for risk and returns, as so often occurs in official programs at the frontier.

The broad scope of formal finance creates economies in information use and enables formal finance to spread risk more effectively than is possible informally in many situations. The pooling and redistribution capacities of financial wholesalers and of diversified intermediaries are superior to those of retailers of financial services and of informal intermediaries doing business in a limited geographical area, highly dependent on agriculture, with limited links with the larger economy.

Formal financial markets are also less fragmented, or more easily integrated, in the sense that similar services will trade at similar prices. This means that information conveyed by prices is more rational in an economic sense and hence more useful for decisionmaking.

TERM TRANSFORMATION. Project designers in development assistance agencies believe that term finance supports development by facilitating investment in long-gestation projects and by spreading investment opportunities beyond the limited number of investors who have large personal or family savings at their disposal. The pooling capacities of integrated formal financial markets contribute to term transformation, or lending at maturities that are longer than those at which an intermediary obtains funding. The law of large numbers permits large scale, diversified intermediaries to lend some of their funds at maturities greatly in excess of the term structure of their liabilities. Large markets also enable formal intermediaries to specialize in instruments designed to attract long-term funds and other liabilities with slow turnover rates that permit lending long. (See table 14.9 and accompanying discussion.)

Even in term transformation informal finance is not necessarily at a disadvantage. Shipton notes, for example, that in The Gambia loans may remain outstanding for several generations.[17] Hans Dieter Seibel and Bishnu P. Shrestha cite research in Nepal that documents RoSCAs with lives of 30 years or more.[18] In other parts of Asia informal arrangements have produced 20-year savings programs combined with 20-year loans in RoSCAs known as chit funds or chitties. These typically consist of 20 members who contribute to the fund at an appointed time each year, when the fund or hand is given to one of the members according to a specified allocation. The annual contribution is often assembled through participation in funds having an annual or shorter life, such as monthly chitties of 12 rounds or weekly chitties running for 50 or 52 rounds.

Interesting footnotes to long-term informal finance in India are that few formal institutions offer 20-year loans, and that the Reserve Bank has outlawed chitties having cycles in excess of seven years. Presumably the Bank did this to protect nonprized members (those not yet receiving a hand) from the effects of inflation (assuming constant money contributions and no interest) and from the risk of failure of the chit fund organizer (who undertakes to keep the chitty in operation) or disputes among members that could disrupt the fund.

The comparative capabilities, strengths and weaknesses of formal and informal finance clearly indicate advantages of the scale of formal finance. However, they also show that definition of formal and informal financial arrangements facilitates stereotypical thinking that is not entirely accurate. Lines between these two subsectors are not so clear; their differences may relate more to scale, costs and integration than to whether they are regulated and chartered by government or deal primarily in written rather than verbal contracts.

17. Parker Shipton, "How Gambians Save." p. 7.
18. Hans Dieter Seibel and Bishnu P. Shrestha. "Dhikuti: The Small Businessman's Informal Self-Help Bank in Nepal," *Savings and Development.* xii, 2, 1988. pp. 183-200.

INNOVATION. Is informal finance a vestigial backwater, unable to create new arrangements to meet new situations and to create new opportunities? Recent evidence from India gives an emphatic "No" to this question. F.J.A. Bouman and his graduate students from the Agricultural University in Wageningen, The Netherlands, conducated a number of studies and observations in semi-arid Sangli District in Maharahstra.[19] As a result of the introduction of new technology and supported by official and cooperative credit, Sangli experienced a sugar boom in the 1950s and a dairy boom in the 1970s.

However, the formal financial sector did not assault the frontier aggressively: priority sectors as defined by the government got most of the rural loans, and default rates were high. Bouman notes that nonpriority activities such as "commerce, transport, distributive trade and consumer finance, could not expect a sympathetic response" from the nationalized banks, which discourage applicants for small loans, and from the primary agricultural credit societies.[20]

In this environment many people began to have higher cash incomes and more opportunities to employ their funds productively. The formal financial sector, bound by regulations and operated with a government service mentality, did not cash in on the new opportunities created for financial intermediation. Bouman and his associates found that infomal intermediaries, in contrast, flowered.

The type of intermediary that expanded most rapidly was the *bishi*, or money club. Bishis are membership organizations in which "members make periodic contributions that are pooled in a fund from which loans are made."[21] There are two types of bishis in Sangli, rotating ones that conform to the RoSCA pattern and nonrotating ones which make loans to members who want to borrow and which distribute the fund to members at the end of the life of the organization, which usually occurs a year after it was formed.

Bouman and his associates found that there were apparently no bishis in Sangli prior to 1960, but that by the mid-1980s many villages in

---

19. F.J.A. Bouman, *Small, Short and Unsecured: Informal Rural Finance in India.* (Delhi: Oxford University Press, 1989).
    20. *Ibid.* p. 115.
    21. *Ibid.* p. 52.

irrigated areas had between five and ten of these informal organizations. Membership size ranged from a dozen to more than 100. Many bishis terminate at or just before the Diwali festival, but as the number of organizations grew so did the variety of starting and termination dates. This accommodated the patterns of members' cash flows. Some people belonged to more than one bishi in order to benefit from participating in different cycles. Multi-year bishis also emerged, partly to diminish cyclicality and also to create a larger fund.

Bishis formed by milk collectors were especially interesting to Bouman because these buyers on bicycles would extend credit to farmers from whom they collected milk. The farmers would often use the funds to buy an additional buffalo. The additional milk from the buffalo would enable the collector to increase his earnings because the volume of his deliveries to the dairy would grow.

Bishi organizers were often merchants. However, bishis were formed by people in all walks of life with regular sources of income from dairying, trading or wages and salaries. Most bishis used cash, but a few received contributions in grain and some completed their cycle with distribution of steel pans to members. Several had ceased to hold periodic meetings because these were no longer needed or convenient (for members who were night shift workers at sugar factories, for example). Members took their funds to the secretary's house at appointed times and loan committees dealt with applications. Another sign of bishi development was adoption of formal sector procedures including passbooks, written rules and procedures, co-signed and collateralized loans, and deposit of funds in a commercial bank.

A less rapidly growing form of intermediary was the UCS or urban credit society, which Bouman classifies as semi-formal.[21] The UCS is a cooperative, but one that, unlike the primary agricultural credit societies, has no official agenda or interference, although it must adhere to Reserve Bank interest rate regulations. UCSs, found in villages as well as in towns, are self-help organizations established by local leaders. The majority of members in several surveyed were farmers. A UCS must have 200 members at formation and Rs 12,000 in share capital, but does not require regular deposits. Bouman reports that there were strong dynamic

21. *Ibid.* pp. 44-51.

UCSs in Sangli District with professional leadership and staff. The remainder were afflicted by arrears, political influence and domination, and other problems. Several had collapsed. Being more formal and rigid and requiring less commitment from members, UCSs did less well than bishis.

NATIONAL ECONOMIC PLANNING AND POLITICS. To economic planners and politicians informal finance, except between kin and friends, may appear undesirable because it is voluntary and private. Its priorities, terms, and conditions are determined by the parties concerned rather than in bureaucracies or through political dealing under the banner of national interest and development. It remains beyond the reach of taxation and is not an important vehicle for monetary policy. From this perspective, formal finance through intermediaries chartered by the state and controlled by the central bank or ministries of agriculture, cooperatives, or housing is more responsible and responsive.

Considerations for Financial Development

What lessons can be drawn from comparisons of formal and informal finance? One is that efforts to develop the frontier should accord considerable attention to informal financial arrangements. Another is that understanding why informal arrangements are attractive to their users is important, as is ensuring that these valuable traits are matched by efforts to expand the frontier. Examples of these traits include trust and confidence, low transaction costs, attention to information, convenient hours and locations for transactions, and continuity of relationships and effective procedures for dealing with defaulters.

Can the formal financial sector be motivated to provide small scale services to compete directly with the services of informal financial intermediaries? Losses are likely to result from retailing small scale financial services in the commercial bank or development bank format with modern offices, national wage scales, and unionized staff. Emphasis on institutional viability makes it counterproductive to force formal financial institutions into activities that are not in their own best financial interest. Hence, structural innovation, the subject of the following chapter, seems essential to any competitive strategy having these objectives. When opportunities for new business are sufficiently attractive for formal financial institutions, they should be encouraged—by the absence of regulation, by exemptions from regulation, or by modified regulations—to respond.

Finance will not flourish where interest rates and loan-related fees do not adequately reflect the costs of lending. These costs include those related to risk. A three dimensional representation of the saucer illustration in the form of a cone reflects the natural levels of commercial interest rates in different market segments in all but the most highly developed financial markets where transaction costs are low and risks are well managed. The heights of the cone represents the cost of funds to borrowers, while the width of the cone represents the number of people served or loans made.

The lowest commercial interest rates and fees are found at the point at the bottom of the cone while the largest circumference of the cone coincides with the highest rates of interest and other loan-related charges (Figure 9.3). In a well-functioning financial market, mainstream formal sector intermediation is located at the bottom of the cone (segment a in Figure 9.3). This is usually conducted primarily by commercial banks.

Above this (in segment b) is intermediation in specialized credit markets such as for housing, consumer finance, venture capital, agriculture, small firms, cooperatives and development finance. Rates and other loan-related income are naturally somewhat higher in this segment than those of commercial banking because of higher risks and fewer economies of scope and scale in these market segments. Beyond these segments lies the informal sector (segment c) with the highest lending rates and loan-related charges, other than those that are interest-free and largely noncommercial between friends and within families.[22]

This representation clearly supports the view that the interest rates and loan-related fees on development finance, including loans to farmers and small businesses for the adoption of new technology, should naturally be higher than those associated with commercial bank lending to established industry and commerce. Low interest rate policies for such activities, as for credit union consumer loans and housing finance offered by parastatals, are unnatural and cause inefficiencies.

---

22. No assumptions or claims concerning the optimal institutional structure for the financial sector are made in this presentation. The primary concern expressed here is that financial development requires an expanding array of instruments, and that these will evolve only when risk/reward ratios are appropriate. The institutional format in which they are offered is not material to this concern.

Figure 9.3

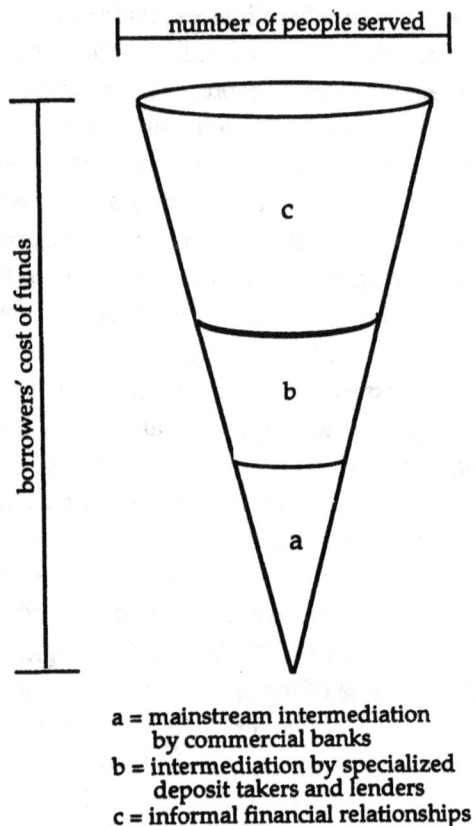

a = mainstream intermediation
    by commercial banks
b = intermediation by specialized
    deposit takers and lenders
c = informal financial relationships

Competition between specialized lenders and informal finance ultimately benefits commercial banks when specialized lenders' operations reduce the risks associated with certain types of lending to such an extent that it becomes attractive to commercial banks. Their operations simultaneously build up borrowers to the point where they are attractive prospective clients for commercial bank services. Activities that were once beyond the frontier move comfortably inside it as a result of this type of competition.

In the natural situation markets could encourage collaboration between specialized lenders and commercial banks for clients in transition between these market segments and as a means of securing economies from the complementarity of different types of financial services. Specialized lenders would have superior capacity to evaluate and respond to the risks around which they create their market niches, while commercial banks would be able to offer relatively cheap short term funds. Borrowers would seek the advantages of each, integrating financial markets.

Figure 9.4 shows two segmented, distorted cones produced by policies that keep lenders' income artificially low for government-defined priority activities such as small farmer credit, housing, and small-scale industry. Case A shows a heavily repressed priority banking sector that offers funds at interest rates and related terms below those commercial banks charge their most favored customers. Case B portrays a less distorted market in which commercial banks and specialized agricultural, consumer and housing lenders charge roughly the same rates. In each case, specialized lenders' regulated, unnatural interest rates restrict the number of people they serve.

Figure 9.4

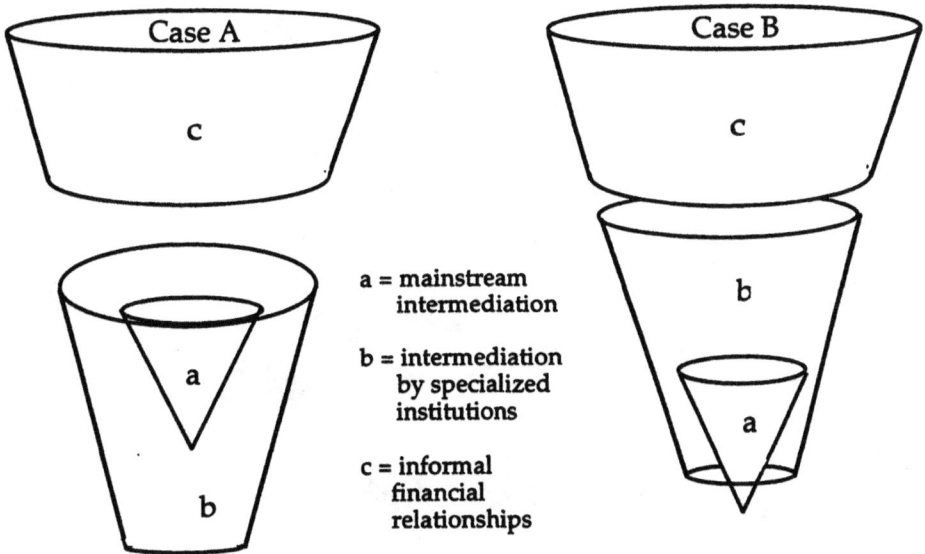

a = mainstream intermediation

b = intermediation by specialized institutions

c = informal financial relationships

In a highly distorted market, commercial bank customers may be attracted by concessional terms offered by specialized lenders if these are not eroded by transaction costs. This possibility makes specialized lenders even less willing to focus on the frontier and concentrates credit in conformity with the Iron Law of Interest Rate Restrictions. Because these lenders are often subsidized, their invasion of commercial bank markets may weaken commercial banks and retard their development into term lending based on innovative measures to attract long term funds.

These fragmented models indicate why lenders to priority sectors sometimes complain that their main competition is from commercial banks. Certain borrowers from specialized low-interest lenders may be attracted to commercial banks because of relatively low transaction costs and because of the wider range of services offered. Specialized lenders view commercial banks as their main competition when their interest rates and orientation prohibit operation at the frontier, which would require them to compete with informal finance. They look inward to the center of the saucer, with their backs to the frontier.

10

CREATING VALUE AT THE FRONTIER IN MARKET NICHES: THE GRAND SYNTHESIS

Innovation provides protection from competition. An innovator is the first to attempt to implement a product, service, or process; no one else is doing precisely the same. By venturing, innovators create a market niche where they stand alone. Successful innovation provides immunity from competition to some degree for some period of time. The protection afforded by the market niche yields a reward for designing a superior product, for serving clients better and for reducing costs.

The quest for market niches is important whenever development is viewed as a product of markets or as a phenomenon expressed through markets. Potential innovators explore the contours of markets, and of the production processes and delivery systems animated by markets. They search for areas that are not well served and for changes that could increase returns. By definition, innovation-based market niches expand the frontier.

The importance of market niches to the general development of financial markets is illustrated by their relation to competition and innovation. Competition and innovation stimulate each other, and they do so through attempts to create market niches. Competition, innovation, and market niches are part of a circular process that works in both directions. In one direction, competition stimulates innovation, which is manifested in market niches which in turn stimulate competition that attempts to penetrate or erode them. In the opposite direction, innovation stimulates competition by creating market niches that attract efforts to destroy them. This process is illustrated in Figure 10.1.

Market niche strategies can expand the developmental role of finance. The concept has attractive dimensions that draw together common concerns embodied in credit projects and in related attempts to develop financial markets at the frontier. These concerns are generally reflected in the soft criteria, fuzzy concepts, and perverse results dealt with so harshly in previous chapters. A market niche focus reorients project design toward operating efficiency, customer service, and innovation.

Figure 10.1 Competition, Innovation, and Market Niches

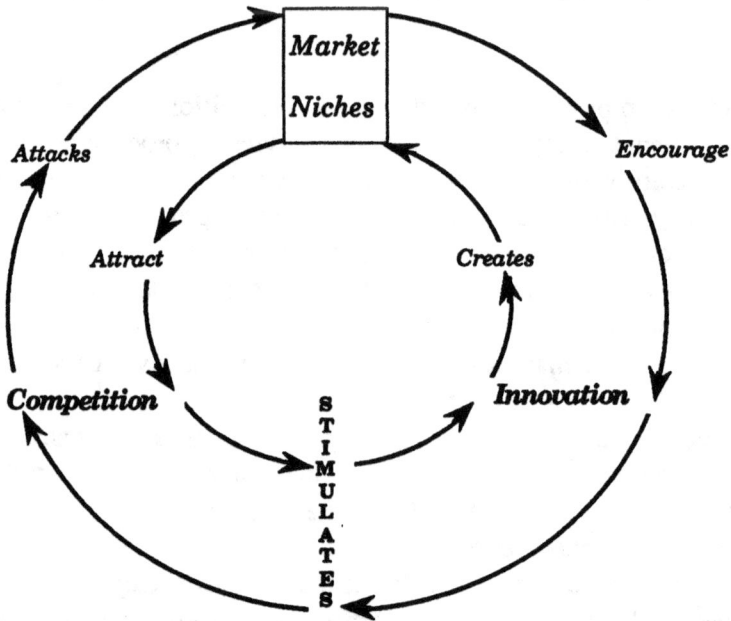

Common Concerns Revisited and Recast

What are these common concerns? One is obtaining powerful and highly specific development leverage, which is attempted through targeted lending that is supposed to be catalytic. Closely related is the concern that credit be "appropriately" priced, which leads to concessional interest rates and inattention to the costs of credit operations. Another is provision of credit as part of a package of services, again to obtain development leverage. Institution-building is a common objective of project designers who promote training and technical assistance and specific organizational forms such as cooperatives. A brief return to traditional expressions of these concerns and their results offers vivid contrasts with the possibilities offered by a strategy of creating market niches through innovation.

Targeting

Targeting is expected to direct credit and related services toward a high priority purpose defined by project designers, or toward a group of individuals or firms deemed particularly worthy of assistance. Targeting is a nonmarket project design response to "credit need." It is reflected in lending quotas and concessional interest rates to borrowers.

Lending targets, quotas, and interest rates imposed on lenders at the frontier fail when they are unrealistic and enforced. These interventions create nonmarket niches that fail to attract competition in the provision of financial services. Administered, nonmarket niches do, however, attract competition among potential users in the form of "rent seeking" or "directly unproductive behavior" based on politics, power, and privilege rather than on commercial performance. The object of this wasteful competition is to obtain goods and services offered at prices below their cost.

Examples of rent seeking or directly unproductive behavior include bribes and other forms of malversation, cronyism, and rent seeking and giving political favors. These responses absorb resources without any clear productivity gain for society, and with arguably high social costs. The Iron Law of Interest Rates explains why they tend ultimately to destroy the programs that attempt to implement nonmarket preferences.

Poverty alleviation rhetoric and political gain underlie traditional targeting, which contrasts sharply with market niche targeting. Traditional targeting responds to deprivation or inability, and on how target group members can be compensated or enfranchised. Targeting as an expression of social concern is usually motivated by nonmarket considerations. One harbored by some project designers and sponsors is a sense of guilt about being relatively wealthy in the midst of so many poor. A more frequently expressed motivation is that "something has to be done" to rectify problems of poverty and slow growth.

Poverty is so depressing, pervasive, complex, and repugnant that coming up with solutions is difficult. A reaction is to fall back on the assumption that almost any attempt to assist can be justified as doing some good. The result is that poverty alleviation targeting is usually based on less relevant analysis than required by an innovator trying to create a profitable market niche.

Creating a market niche requires targeting because the innovator has an incentive to understand potential customers' activities and expectations. By knowing precisely the characteristics of potential users of the new product or service, the innovator decreases the risk of innovation. The innovator will also want to know how the innovation could benefit and attract a clientele. The focus of the innovator's analysis is the capacity and ability of members of the target group. What they can do is of interest because that is the source of the innovator's returns. Market niche strategies target *par excellence*.

Costs and Pricing

To succeed, an innovation has to be priced appropriately. An innovator seeking a market niche has an incentive to ascertain the costs of providing a new service and to control these costs in markets where competition or the threat of competition regulates behavior. In this process in financial markets, interest rates, other fees and transaction costs will be subject to careful analysis. The innovator's targeting effort will normally include attention to pricing the new good or service to obtain positive returns before competition erodes its market niche. An innovation's risks become more apparent with experience following its introduction. Prices that are high relative to costs, including the cost of risk, attract competition. Competition in turn lowers prices to consumers, and cost minimization contributes to productivity and social gain.

Innovation in finance may not lead to rapidly decreasing costs per unit of output with increases in the volume of accounts or transactions because the fixed costs of intermediation are not necessarily large. Although the provision of financial services is often subject to decreasing costs per unit, known as economies of scale, the effect is not necessarily overwhelming. A high proportion of the costs that are reduced by innovation are not the costs incurred by intermediaries, but the transaction costs of users of financial services. This enables a financial innovator to obtain tremendous market leverage by lowering clients' transaction costs significantly through innovations that do not significantly add to the intermediary's costs.

Traditional targeting strategies usually keep prices low to target group members while remaining insensitive to the costs of providing them with goods and services. The emphasis is on getting the credit disbursed or the service in place. This strategy reflects two assumptions and one certainty. One assumption is that target group members cannot afford to pay the costs of those who serve them. The other is that the target group requires an added price inducement to behave as the project designer desires, that the investments promoted by the project are not in themselves attractive enough to achieve the designer's objectives. The certainty is that below-market prices are politically attractive to the target group or the ultimate borrowers, at least in the short run.

These factors result in concessionally priced credit that eventually misses the target while wearing down the lending institution. The problems created by this approach are often very costly and extremely difficult to reverse. A consistently money-losing nonmarket niche will be stubbornly defended by a political faction or government agency that can target its losses for political gain by providing favored supporters with goods and services at concessional prices. In contrast, a market niche that is unlikely to be profitable is unattractive; a persistent money-loser is abandoned by innovators, who by definition seek to reduce costs.

Credit as Part of a Package

Traditional projects often provide credit as part of a package. The package may include technical services for small firms and extension for small farmers, for example. It may consist of membership in a cooperative that sells farm inputs to its members on credit and purchases their produce upon harvest while enriching their community and social life through participation in cooperative management and activities. Emphasis on credit as part of a package is consistent with financial market behavior. Informal credit, for example, is virtually always linked with family, social, or commercial bonds.[1]

Market niche lenders are especially keen to create relationships with their clients based on multiple services such as savings accounts, payment services, and credit. Modern bankers and credit unions, for example, focus on relationships, not simply on transactions. One motive for this focus is confidence creation: the more services a client uses the greater the information available to the intermediary for extending the relationship by

---

1. R. H. Schmidt and Erhard Kropp, eds., *op. cit.* pp. 95-96.

managing risk and reducing transaction costs. Also, the stronger the relationship the greater the transaction cost to the client of switching to a competing intermediary.

In economic terms, financial intermediaries enjoy economies of scope. These arise from providing a larger number of products that can be produced jointly, such as checking accounts and savings accounts and loans. By offering clients a broader array of services they can economize on overhead costs and increase profits. Intermediaries profitably promote "cross-selling."[2] One service that is not very profitable may attract new customers who will also use other services that make money, for example. Use of additional services expands the relationship and reinforces the intermediary's market niche. In sum, relationships are precisely the material from which financial market niches are constructed.

Institution-Building

Efforts to create financial market niches require detailed attention to delivery mechanisms, which results in institution-building. Successful innovation depends on confidence achieved by providing services as promised or as expected by clients. This in turn requires business plans, operating procedures, and staff training. This approach to institution-building helps to form and integrate the strategies and operations of an intermediary.

In the traditional project approach, institution-building is often effectively limited to designing an integrated project package, as suggested in chapter 5, one that offers assistance in a number of dimensions to support the project objective. The difference between an integrated project and an integrated, efficient financial institution rests on the different incentives facing project designers, who may be concerned largely with technical matters and disbursement targets, and the intermediary's managers, who may be more concerned about the political implications of the project within their institution and in the national political context. To the extent project designers' and implementers' expectations differ, an integrated project will not produce integrated results. Funds may be loaned, for example, while systems and skills to ensure good credit

---

2. Dwight S. Ritter, *Cross-Selling Financial Services* (New York: John Wiley & Sons, 1988).

decisions, effective portfolio supervision, and loan recovery are not in place.

The relationship between delivery system costs and benefits is closely examined where an innovation stands or falls on commercial considerations. Costing and market analysis to create and preserve market niches build institutions by enabling them to know more about their activities and markets and the behavior of their clients. Innovative entrepreneurs ask questions such as, "How can costs be reduced without decreasing service?" "What are the costs of exceptions to good performance?" "What is most likely to go wrong that will increase costs or reduce profits?" "Precisely what type of training has the highest pay-off?" and "How much training is sufficient?" These concerns captivate risk takers in their quest to control costs and to create confidence to fortify their market niche.

These questions are not generally examined in detail in traditional institution-building activities. The service format is often inflexible, costs are not closely monitored or contained and risk is not considered in depth. It is apparently assumed by many project designers and managers that more training is always better. In addition, training may not be tailored to the individuals being trained or the tasks to which they are assigned, but rather consist of off-the-shelf courses or study tours abroad. Technical assistance and other institution-building activities are an extremely labor-intensive part of project design, implementation, and supervision. A project sponsor's transaction costs of technical assistance components are usually disproportionate: technical assistance and training may constitute less than 5 percent of credit project cost, (with the other 95 percent going to increase the supply of loanable funds), yet require more than 25 percent of project design, appraisal, implementation, and supervision time. This provides tremendous incentives to minimize these costs and results in less than stellar institution-building inputs.

What are the characteristics of strong, innovative institutions? Their market niches are illustrated by what Warren Buffet, America's best-known, large high-performance portfolio investor, calls "the indestructible franchise."[3] *The Wall Street Journal* is an example of Buffet's concept. He

---

3. "Investing in Equity Markets," special section, *Hermes* (alumni publication of the Columbia University Graduate School of Business, New York), Summer 1985, pp. vii ff.

would ask what the market value of the *Journal's* stock (actually that of its parent company, Dow Jones & Co. Inc.) would be if its entire net worth or capital were suddenly wiped out, as a result of a massive lawsuit, for example. Although the book value of the enterprise would be zero, Buffet maintains that investors would be willing to buy its stock. Their willingness would reflect their confidence that the *Journal* would still be able to produce and sell newspapers and news services because it offers a product that no competitor can fully match, which is why millions of people around the world read *The Wall Street Journal* every business day.

The Grand Synthesis

Market niches in dynamic, competitive markets are built and maintained by superior performance, making continued innovation a necessity. The market niche concept permits expression of nonmarket concerns as roots for innovation to be tested by the market. It offers the strategic grand synthesis for project designers seeking to move the frontier of formal financial markets. It casts the role of government as one of stimulating competition and innovation in finance. The vitality that market niche strategies can produce is exemplified by Grameen Bank in Bangladesh, to which the remainder of this chapter is devoted.

Grameen Bank's Market Niche

The most stunning modern example of a development-oriented attempt to help the poor through credit is the Grameen Bank in Bangladesh.[4] This bank is unusual. It appears to have operated on a financially sound basis

4. Grameen Bank's experience is documented in one of the best reviews of a development credit operation to be found anywhere: Mahabub Hossain's "Credit for Alleviation of Rural Poverty: The Grameen Bank in Bangladesh," published as Research Report 65 in February 1988 by the International Food Policy Research Institute in Washington, DC, in collaboration with the Bangladesh Institute of Development Studies in Dhaka. This study should please economists and financial analysts, while appealing to the general reader as well drafted, concise, balanced, and insightful: an evaluation for all seasons. The account of Grameen Bank activities given in this chapter (excluding parts of the concluding sections that discuss Grameen Bank's franchise) draws heavily on Hossain, on Syed Nuruzzaman, "Grameen Bank in Bangladesh: A Preliminary Assessment," RSI-86-10, Resource Systems Institute, East-West Center, Honolulu, Hawaii, September 1986, and on chapters 3-6 of Andreas Fuglesang and Dale Chandler, *Participation as Process—What We Can Learn from Grameen Bank, Bangladesh* (Oslo: Norwegian Ministry of Development Cooperation-NORAD, 1986). Grameen Bank staff reviewed a draft of this chapter.

for almost ten years. It has linked savings, credit and social progress in a sound and creative manner through a radically innovative instrument, while targeting those far beyond the frontier of formal finance: primarily women in rural households that are virtually landless. In addition, Grameen Bank has demonstrated an exceptional capacity to experiment, to challenge its internal assumptions and procedures, and to evaluate its activities. This capacity has propelled it into innovation after innovation, without the stimulus of competition, but as a result of a tremendous dedication to its corporate sense of mission. However, it has remained market-oriented and requires close consideration by project designers and would-be innovators at the frontier.

The Lending Instrument

The Grameen Bank model continually evolves. As of 1990 its principal lending activities centered on peer groups consisting of five women each from households with less than half an acre of land or with total assets not exceeding the value of one acre of land. Group formation may result from the initiative of one of the five, who has contact with a Grameen Bank worker and who enlists her friends—relations cannot belong to the same group—to form a group in order to obtain credit. Groups may also form spontaneously among those contacted by bank workers. Each group is essentially self-selected.

Because of its new clients' lack of familiarity with institutional credit, Grameen Bank devotes painstaking attention to creating confidence. Confidence is required in the most literal sense: group members are often nervous about taking a loan and striking out on their own in activities funded by their loans. Transaction costs for both the bank and its borrowers are high but absolutely essential. Once a group is formed, it receives seven days of continuous instruction from a bank worker. During this period the group elects a chair and secretary who serve for a year, and becomes well versed in Grameen Bank rules, procedures, and expectations.

Each group attends a weekly meeting of a "center" that typically consists of five groups. The chairs of the groups elect a center chief and deputy who serve for one year only and receive no remuneration. Each center is assigned a Grameen Bank worker who deals with the center chief and the group chairs. The bank worker walks or bicycles to weekly center meetings and typically is responsible for not more than ten centers.

Credit is issued initially to two members selected by the group on the basis of need. The loan application procedure begins with selection of a single-purpose project by a group member. Projects are usually extensions of activities in which the applicant is already engaged. For example, a woman who works as a day laborer husking rice borrows to buy her own rice to husk and market. The group must agree with the member's proposal and is intimately involved in its form, content, and selection through discussion. The bank worker also has to support the proposal which is discussed at a center meeting.

When this level of consensus is reached, the center chief fills in a loan application form. The bank worker endorses the proposal and relays the application to the manager of a Grameen Bank branch, which typically serves 50 or 60 centers within walking distance. After reviewing loan purposes and amounts, each branch submits its loan applications to an area office. Area office approval triggers disbursement at a weekly center meeting by the bank worker assigned to the center. The entire process between group consensus and disbursement typically takes two weeks. All cash transactions at center meetings are conducted openly before all members. Loan sizes are modest, averaging about Tk 3,000 (US$85), with a Tk 5,000 (US$140) limit.

Each borrower is expected to use the loan within seven days. The group chair has to submit a loan utilization form to the center chief, signifying that the loan was used for the purpose intended. The bank worker checks the borrower's progress and submits a written description of the investment to the branch manager. The manager makes a verification, visiting about half of the borrowers for whom bank workers have submitted reports. Loans not used within seven days are returned to the branch to avoid installments and interest charges until borrowers are ready to invest.

The first two members selected by the group typically receive their loans at the same time and begin making weekly repayments at center meetings. Their performance is monitored, primarily by the group chair and the center chief. After a month or two of satisfactory repayment and attendance at group and center meetings, the next two members may receive their loans under the same procedures. When they have performed well for a month or two, the final member is eligible for credit. The group chair and secretary are the last to receive loans. Further loans are available to members who have repaid.

Saving and Loan Repayment

From the time a group receives its initial instruction from a bank worker, each member has to save Tk 1 (US$0.03) weekly, which is accumulated in a group fund. In addition, 5 percent of each loan disbursed is credited to this fund. Each group manages its own fund, which is deposited with Grameen Bank at 8.5 percent interest, the prevailing savings deposit rate in Bangladesh. Members are generally permitted to borrow up to 50 percent of the fund balance in the form of interest-free loans for consumption in times of sickness, for social ceremonies, and for investment. This fund protects loan quality by providing a cushion: group members are less likely to liquidate their capital or resort to informal lenders in times of need. Members who leave their group after fully meeting their obligations can withdraw all their own contributions, while the 5 percent deduction from loans taken is nonrefundable.

Loan repayment is scheduled for 50 weekly installments. An exception is made for loans for seasonal activities, but these are relatively few and a token weekly installment is still required. After the principal is fully repaid, interest and a contribution to an emergency fund, equal to one-quarter of the interest charge, are collected in two weekly installments, which are more than double the size of each of the previous 50. Interest is calculated at 16 percent—the regulated commercial bank agricultural lending rate in Bangladesh—on the outstanding balance. (The effective cost of funds to borrowers exceeds 16 percent because of the 5 percent group fund contribution deducted from the loan amount and the emergency fund assessment. Depending upon assumptions, the effective rate may reach 25 percent or more.) The center manages and maintains the emergency fund, which is drawn on when a member defaults, dies, is disabled, or suffers from a major unforeseen event. Each group, on behalf of its afflicted member, can draw up to Tk 2,500 or 50 percent of the member's contribution, whichever is less. Through 1987, few disbursements were made from this fund.

Groups support repayment performance. At the outset they assist each member's decision on loan use. Members monitor each others' performance and provide mutual help and reassurance. Members who do not conform are subjected to peer pressure, including fines and possibly expulsion. If a member fails to repay before all other members have received loans, credit is denied these other members. Members often help each other in difficulty. If a member leaves a group before fully repaying, the remaining members are responsible for repayment. If an entire group defaults, the center is responsible for repayment.

Repayment performance by Grameen Bank borrowers may exceed that generally obtained by small loan and consumer finance companies in developed countries. It calculates its collection rate on the status of repayments received by the end of the second year following disbursement. By this measure, the reported collection rate exceeds 98 percent. Loan installments are scheduled over a 50-week period, of course, but even by this measure, the Bank reports collections of 97 percent. Women's groups have repayment records slightly superior to those of male groups.

Grameen Bank's reported collection rate is apparently calculated by comparing loans in arrears (by more than one year) with total loans outstanding or possibly with total cumulative loans disbursed since the Bank was founded. The denominator is the rapidly expanding portfolio. The numerator is being fed by that portion of the much smaller cohort of loans issued two years previously which constitute new arrears. These approaches do not compare like with like, such as amounts falling due and collections of these amounts, and they tend to overstate performance. It appears that Grameen Bank may not collect 98 percent of amounts due. But there is no evidence that the bank rolls over arrears or engages in deceptive reporting practices, and Grameen Bank remains an exceptionally good performer.

Repayment discipline deteriorates as groups gain experience. A 1985 survey indicated that 97 percent of groups borrowing for the first time had no installments in arrears, while the percentage fell to 33 percent for groups that had completed four borrowing cycles. Those paying the exact number of installments due slipped from 78 percent of first cycle groups to 25 percent of groups that had borrowed four times. However, this has not been regarded as particularly threatening because loans are generally fully repaid at the conclusion of 50 weeks.

One reason for deterioration may be that members exhaust activities close at hand, venturing into new, riskier enterprises. Also, the marginal return to capital tends to decrease as capital accumulated through previous loans absorbs more labor, up to a point where members cannot or are reluctant to increase their labor. Thus, a larger proportion of loan-induced income is consumed by debt service, which may diminish the incentive to repay.

Market Research for Decentralized Operations

Grameen Bank devotes tremendous effort to market research. Research underlies its operating model that structures its relationships of confidence with its members. Research is also an important part of the six-month training program for recruits who want to become bank workers or branch managers.[5] (In 1986, training consumed one-fifth of Grameen Bank's administrative costs.) Training begins with a two-day orientation in Dhaka that covers reporting forms and procedures, following which each trainee is assigned to a single branch for three eight-week sessions. Branch managers are responsible for training recruits assigned to their branch, and trainees' success enhances the manager's opportunities for promotion.

Training assignments include making two detailed case studies of Grameen Bank members, conducted at each member's house. These studies examine personal and family details, sources and amounts of income and expenditure, uses of time, and expectations and attitudes. Trainees are encouraged to compare the member's situation before and after becoming a member and to report only the facts as conveyed in interviews. Trainees must also make an inventory of the infrastructure in the branch's territory and draw a map. During the training period each trainee visits at least 15 centers and follows up loan use by two or three borrowers at each center, all on foot. (Walking is stressed because the poor seldom have other means of land transport in Bangladesh.)

---

5. Details are given in the sources previously footnoted and in "Training System of Grameen Bank," prepared by Grameen Bank in 1987 and reprinted in Guy Bédard, ed., *Savings and Credit as Instruments of Self-reliant Development of the Poor.* Proceedings of an international workshop held in Feldafing, January 25-28, 1988. (Feldafing: Deutsche Stiftung für internationale Entwicklung [DSE-German Foundation for International Development]). 1988. pp. 79-100.

Trainees are expected to identify deficiencies in Bank operations and to suggest improvements. They present these at short sessions in Dhaka at the conclusion of each eight-week field segment. Suggestions are openly debated and subjected to brainstorming by the cohort of trainees and by trainers. At all times trainees are encouraged to be self-reliant, making their own decisions wherever possible, which is essential to Grameen Bank's decentralized structure. As of mid-1988, 90 percent of its staff were in the field at its 400 branches, area and zonal offices.

This training is rigorous; many trainees drop out. Those who remain have an intimate knowledge of the target group and the self-confidence to proceed. Those training to be branch managers have the capacity to conduct all branch operations including reporting procedures: each branch submits a daily financial report to the area office. Upon completion of training, bank workers are assigned to a center.

Aspiring branch managers may be apprenticed to a manager of a branch that has been open for at least one and preferably two years, or assigned an area in which to open a new branch, which should eventually be profitable. Managers are encouraged to make their branches better than the ones where they were trained. The first task of the manager of a new branch is to take up residence in the area to be served by the branch. Then the manager alone conducts market research, compiling a socioeconomic review of the territory, noting the geography, economy, demographics, infrastructure, and political power structure. Following approval of this report by the Bank's head office, the manager calls a public meeting at which the Bank's operations are explained and its emphasis on the poor and group focus are made clear. Following this meeting, group formation begins. Only after the first groups are formed does the manager receive staff and equipment for the new branch.

The Development of Grameen Bank

Grameen Bank began in 1976 as a research project designed by Professor Muhammad Yunus, who taught economics at Chittagong University and is the Bank's managing director. His hypothesis was that people who had too little land to support themselves as farmers could make productive use of small loans that they would repay. After three years of field experience the experiment became a project of Bangladesh Bank, the country's central bank. The project was designed to replicate results in five districts in collaboration with commercial banks and an agricultural bank. In 1981, the Ford Foundation provided a US$850,000 guarantee to compensate these banks for any losses that might occur. None did: the guarantee fund was never tapped. In 1981, the International Fund for Agricultural Development (IFAD) made a loan that matched central bank contributions to the project.

The project succeeded, but the banks through which it was operated were uncomfortable with it, in part because of the large number of small transactions that had to be processed. This led to the formation of Grameen Bank in 1983 with share capital contributed by the government. As of 1988, the government's stake amounted to 25 percent of total shares outstanding. By 1989 Grameen Bank had 500,000 shareholder-members and disbursed more than US$3 million equivalent in loans monthly.

The first loan was made to a woman in Jobra, a village near Chittagong University. Individual loans became administratively cumbersome, so loans to groups of ten or so persons were introduced. These groups proved too large for solidarity and consensus, and groups of five became the norm.

Groups and centers have always consisted of members of the same sex. Most early borrowers were men who used their loans to go into petty trade, but over time, women borrowers became predominant. Because of their lower economic status, the risk of abandonment by their husbands, and possibily reflecting a longer perspective that men are generally willing to take, women are more willing to bear the high transaction costs of groups and meetings, which they may not regard as costs at all but as valuable opportunities to socialize, learn, and affirm. Turning transaction costs into benefits is the ultimate achievement of voluntary cooperative action. Women apparently also have greater incentive to invest wisely and repay on time. With their ascendency, loan use has been reoriented toward activities conducted primarily at home, such as small scale livestock and poultry ventures and agroprocessing.

Groups typically borrow about three times for activities with which they are familiar, such as rice husking, poultry, and cattle, before its members are willing to take on entirely new activities. In an effort to assist their diversification, the Bank promoted collective enterprises operated by relatively large groups of seasoned borrowers from strong centers who had put up substantial balances in special savings accounts established to fund the formation of collective enterprises. Loans were relatively large, often Tk 50,000 to Tk 100,000 (US$1,500 to US$3,000). Most of these loans were for joint farming, but other purposes included leasing of markets and ferry crossings, trading, storage, livestock, and fisheries development. The rationale for collective enterprises was that they could realize economies of scale, generate employment and increase the labor productivity of the poor.

The performance of collective enterprises has been disappointing, and these loans fell from 8 percent of total disbursements in 1984 to only 1 percent in 1986. One-fifth of these enterprises collapsed; others faltered due to organizational difficulties, poor accounting, distrust, lack of familiarity with the required technology, poor management of working capital, and interference from members of the rural elite who operate similar enterprises. In 1986 Grameen Bank took over management of its members' collective enterprises. The Bank purchased some of the assets of these enterprises and established service centers for equipment owned by others. The Bank hopes to hand surviving enterprises back to members as they gain the competence to operate them.

The evolution of Grameen Bank has produced an array of means by which it relates to its members. For example, members are encouraged to buy one, and only one, share in Grameen Bank for Tk 100 out of their group fund. Their subscriptions constituted 75 percent of the Bank's share capital as of mid-1988. The Bank encourages members to form schools and it sells textbooks, while centers have set up child welfare funds to support schools and other children's activities. Grameen Bank produces construction plans for houses and offers credit to seasoned borrowers for home improvement and construction repayable weekly over 10 years at 5 percent interest; a subsidized rate made possible by central bank refinancing. It has a seed distribution program featuring very small packets to encourage gardening and fruit tree planting in members' small homesteads. Grameen Bank also accepts deposits from the public in the usual retail commercial banking format at some of its branches.

Through democratic procedures the Bank has drawn up "The Sixteen Decisions" that form a pledge taken by members to improve their lives and rural living conditions. The decisions exhort members to grow vegetables, fix up their houses, work hard, plan their families, keep clean, use pit latrines, drink safe water, work together, and refuse to pay or receive dowries. Rejection of dowries is a major assault on tradition, about which women members evidently have strong feelings. Dowries are a major financial transaction for the poor and have a material impact on living standards. One result of credit access could be merely to inflate dowries. Payment often causes households to liquidate capital or to borrow from moneylenders at high rates of interest, thereby reducing their living standard and debt repayment capacity.

Grameen Bank's Franchise

Grameen Bank's franchise[6] has many dimensions or lines of defense against vulnerability. One dimension is that no competing moneylender or institution could entice significant numbers of Grameen Bank members to transfer their savings and loan relationships or hire away large numbers of Grameen Bank's staff. No potential competition can easily preempt Grameen Bank's growth by replicating its model or by introducing a superior model. Grameen Bank enjoys no statutory or administrative protection that creates its franchise, which is based solely on its operations.

Next, Grameen Bank is unlikely to be taken over by another bank despite its huge cash position, because its 500,000 shareholders respect its current management and doubtlessly would regard any offer as hostile. Because it works well, poses no threat, and enjoys widespread grassroots support, the Government of Bangladesh has little incentive to destroy Grameen Bank's character any time soon, even though it is disproportionately represented on Grameen Bank's board. The government is unlikely to nationalize it,[7] subject it to regulatory harassment, burden it with special lending quotas, or interfere in its staffing arrangments or management appointments.

The wealthy and influential in Bangladesh would find it very costly to capture Grameen Bank. Would they pose as loan applicants from the target group, who are normally identifiable by their shabby clothing? Could they conceal their assets and land holdings or bribe Bank staff to admit them to membership? To the wealthy and influential, the transaction and opportunity costs of attending weekly meetings and associating with the

---

6. Inferences of a critical nature in this and the following sections do not reflect the sources cited earlier and are those of the author alone.

7. *The Economist* disagrees. See "A Lender that Gets Repaid," October 18, 1986. p. 26.

very poor are high. In fact, organization of poor borrowers into groups is a means of establishing a franchise by excluding the rich and diminishing the risk of capture through infiltration.[8] The relatively small size of loans issued and the relatively high effective rate of interest also discourage them from seeking Grameen Bank credit.

These defenses and the necessity of weekly loan repayments also discourage village elites, who are generally landowners whose incomes are seasonal, linked to agricultural cycles. They prefer to borrow at planting and repay after harvest. They may also be eligible for cheaper loans from other banks that devote relatively less attention to loan repayment. (Bangladeshi banks have very poor loan recovery records.[9])

Grameen Bank's staff remain highly dedicated. They are well educated. Bank worker recruits must have a secondary school certificate and recruits for positions as branch managers must have a master's degree. So long as the Bank maintains its corporate sense of mission, staff are likely to remain loyal and have little motivation to organize or strike for better wages and conditions, as has occurred in other banks in Bangladesh, or to defect and form competing banks with a greater sense of mission.

Finally, are Grameen Bank's borrowers likely to bring it down? They have so much invested in their relationship in terms of time, physical and emotional energy, socially and as shareholders, that they have an interest in preserving it. Their returns from this investment are so incredibly high in relative terms, possibly transforming their lives, attitudes and futures, that they are unlikely to bite the hand of friendship offered by their bank.

Will Grameen Bank be ruined by the recurrent floods that devastate much of Bangladesh? This is unlikely because the strength of a bank lies ultimately in its relationships of trust and confidence. Grameen Bank has good relationships of this sort with its clients and with external sources of funds. Equally important is Grameen Bank's huge cash position, which was equal to about 50 percent of its total assets when the 1988 floods hit. With these funds Grameen Bank helped clients get back on their feet, which should enable it eventually to overcome the losses that are inevitable

---

8. J. Alister McGregor, "Credit and the Rural Poor: the Changing Policy Environment in Bangladesh," *Public Administration and Development.* 8, 4, October-December 1988. pp. 467-482.

9. "Where the Right Policies Get No Credit," *The Economist.* October 18, 1986. p. 24.

when major natural disasters strike. By helping its clients through the very difficult period following floods, Grameen Bank should emerge with an even stronger franchise! In the mid-21st century the granddaughters of present members will be telling children about the accomplishments of Grameen Bank in the 1980s.

Is Grameen Bank's Franchise Potentially Vulnerable?

No institution is immune from deterioration, and market niches exist to be eroded by competitive innovation, by complacency induced by the comfort of doing well, by reluctance to adjust to changing market conditions, and by the failure of organizations to cope effectively with the departure of key individuals who have helped construct or defend the market niche. However, Grameen Bank has consistently fortified its franchise. Most credit programs aimed at the poor have low interest rates and give little attention to confidence creation, resulting in losses from lending operations and a drift away from their original target in favor of more prosperous clients. Grameen Bank's course, in contrast, has moved toward women and away from men, increasing its concentration on the most highly marginalized major group in Bangladeshi society. It has expanded geographically rather than changing the basic definition of its target group to create more business for existing branches.

Areas in which Grameen Bank's franchise may be negotiable result from its success. By its very prominence it attracts many requests from government officials and proposals from donors who want to use a vibrant institution with demonstrably good management and systems for serving the poor. Government requests for the Bank to undertake development projects quite different from those that constitute its market niche may be difficult to avoid or refuse. For example, some of the Bank's collective enterprises were assumed from government projects that had failed to perform as hoped. Accepting such requests may burden management resources and draw the Bank into political situations where its defenses are relatively weak.

Another area in which Grameen Bank's franchise may be negotiable arises from its reliance on foreign assistance in the form of 2 percent loans. Much of the proceeds of these loans, constituting about 50 percent of its total assets as of 1988, are kept with banks in Bangladesh as time deposits paying 14 percent interest. This interest income permits the Bank to subsidize its lending. It is not likely to lose this source of funding or its concessional terms, and could command an almost limitless amount of long-term funds from donors if it wanted to do so. Grameen Bank insists that it has succeeded in maintaining independent planning and operations despite donor reservations, however.

In one very important typical area of vulnerability, Grameen Bank is protected within its market niche. This area is choice of project and technology: its members select their own investment projects, in effect determining the sizes of their loans and repayment obligations. Many credit programs promote a technology attractive to the government and donor. If the credit-supported technology is not appropriate or successful, the borrower's commitment to repay the loan is diminished. If a Grameen Bank group member's project fails, however, the group is still committed to repay, and additional credit enables the borrower to try again.

Can Grameen Bank's growth continue to be managed effectively? After all, its target group consists of about half the population of Bangladesh and it had not yet reached 10 percent of them by 1990. Does donor enthusiasm for rapid growth diminish management's ability or willingness to experiment, to devise the next innovation? Possibly not, as more management trainees mean more corporate introspection, market research and brainstorming. What of donor reporting requirements and the transaction costs of having to deal with visiting missions?

Is a management able to command a tidal wave of foreign assistance less aggressively profit-oriented than one largely dependent on entirely private, local resources? Will reliance on nonmarket funds transform a superb market niche into a corruptible nonmarket niche? Does the declining profitability of Grameen Bank, from Tk 4.9 million in 1984 to a loss of Tk 750,000 in 1986, pose a threat to its franchise?[10] This decline in earnings results primarily from the heavy expenses of staffing new branches, which generally take four years to become profitable. And between 1984 and 1986, staff salary scales increased by 40 percent as a result of pay hikes imposed by the government throughout Bangladesh, putting pressure on Grameen Bank margins. Grameen Bank's capital-to-assets ratio, which

---

10. These data are from Hossain, *op. cit.* p. 75. Grameen Bank's 1987 *Annual Report* indicates an operating profit of Tk 17,483 for 1986 and an operating loss of Tk 3.0 million in 1987, which was largely covered by a training grant from an undisclosed source.

measures capital adequacy, was 7.1 percent in 1984 but 3.5 percent in 1988. Does this decline make Grameen Bank vulnerable in spite of the accumulation of emergency funds and the nonrefundable portion of group funds and the long terms on which it receives funds from donors?

Conclusions are not possible at this time, but watching Grameen Bank's operations will be instructive.

Part IV

A SUSTAINABLE STRATEGY FOR FRONTIER DEVELOPMENT

Sustainability is an essential feature of financial development because relationships govern financial transactions. A relationship consists of a stream of transactions between a client and an intermediary. This occurs only when services are appropriate and both partners have confidence in each other. Sustainability is also important because people at the frontier can be served better by durable institutions and instruments than by transient ones. Sustainability does not imply a steady state, but signifies that transactions are of mutual benefit to all parties directly concerned. In dynamic markets sustainability requires innovation so that financial intermediaries remain responsive to and participate in opportunities and developments in other parts of the economy. Innovation that extends the frontier in a sustainable manner also helps protect the access to intermediation enjoyed by those inside the frontier.

Sustainability in finance is based on lending strategies that create and protect value. These strategies must include pricing the services of intermediaries so that their efficiency is rewarded with survival. Together, lending and pricing strategies make it possible to extend the frontier without "giving away the bank." Sustainability also obviously requires reliable sources of funding for intermediaries, and the importance of savings mobilization is emphasized throughout this book. But funding is a relatively minor problem compared to the dangers of giving away the bank through traditional approaches to expanding the frontier, and is not explored in detail in the chapters that follow.

The concluding chapters of this book are specifically prescriptive. They begin with an examination of lending strategies used by financial institutions to structure relationships with their borrowers. From this base, guidelines are given for designing credit programs that harmonize the interests of intermediaries with those of their clients. This integration is essential for sustainability. Finally, principles and formats are provided for tracking and evaluating the performance of credit and of credit projects at the frontier. These address attribution and sustainability issues stressed in earlier chapters.

· Chapter 11 outlines different approaches to lending, and contrasts asset-based lending that links loan size to collateral value with cash flow lending strategies that permit credit limits to transcend collateral. It then explores their implications for development and recommends that intervention in financial markets should promote confidence so that the advantages of cash flow lending are increasingly realized.

Chapter 12 is devoted to an explanation of debt capacity. The concept is defined as the amount of debt a borrower can obtain on a sustainable basis. Its usefulness is demonstrated, and some simple examples of its application are offered. Alternative ways of creating debt capacity are presented and compared. Debt capacity is the most important concept presented in this book: *debt capacity defines the limits of the contribution credit is capable of making to sustainable development*. Debt capacity offers a precision not found in alternative concepts such as credit need or absorptive capacity.

Chapter 13 provides principles for designing projects and programs that seek to expand access to credit and other services offered by formal sector intermediaries. These principles are: make good loans and specify project parameters, especially loan terms and conditions, so that lending has a positive impact on the capital of the lender. These tests are currently not routinely applied in credit project design or in financial sector restructuring activities. Their absence contributes to the generally poor financial performance of credit projects.

Chapter 14 specifies how to measure the results of interventions in finance at the frontier. It explores the media for measurement, which include monitoring, evaluation and sector studies. Four important issues should animate measurement. The first is the performance of ultimate borrowers. Are farm credit projects, for example, in fact associated with the changes in on-farm technology that they are designed to promote? Does small scale enterprise promotion credit lead to the development of firms and of commercial behavior as indicated in the documents used to justify and secure approval of such projects?

The second is the financial impact of projects and programs on lenders. This section elaborates on the principles listed in chapter 13 that specify that intervention to expand access to financial services should help lenders build a capital base to assume the risks of innovation.

The third is the financial development impact of projects and policies. Is intervention associated with financial innovation? Does it lead to new instruments as ways of structuring stronger financial relationships between intermediaries and users of financial services?

The fourth issue is macroeconomic and macrofinancial. It includes development of market links; subsidies and their distribution and incidence; fiscal, monetary, trade and external debt effects; interactions between projects and policy evolution or reform; and relationships between credit and value added in sectors to which credit is directed.

11

LENDING STRATEGIES AND DEVELOPMENT LEVERAGE

Participants in credit markets have a concept of what they lend and borrow against. Where lending occurs, some type of valuation process is inevitable. Valuation calculations may be derived from rules of thumb or intricate formulas or even determined by how much cash the prospective lender has available to lend. Each criterion reflects an underlying element or elements of value. In much informal credit, for example, creditworthiness is based primarily on the character of the borrower: character imparts value to the promise. An alternative type of lending is based primarily on land or other transferrable assets as the underlying element of value.

What people believe they borrow and lend against has tremendously important implications for the quality of the contribution finance makes to development. Asset-based lending, as exemplified by traditional commercial bank credit, prevails in the formal financial markets of developing countries and is presented first in the discussion that follows. It also has limitations from a developmental point of view. In contrast, character lending, which prevails in informal finance, and cash flow lending, its formal parallel, are examples of the most developmentally powerful dimension of financial markets.

The second part of the chapter is devoted to cash flow lending and the conditions that make it possible. The third part summarizes common lending strategies of development finance institutions, and points out how certain rigidities can compromise loan quality. The chapter concludes that in order to realize the advantages of cash flow lending, intervention should create confidence.

Asset-Based Lending

Examples of asset-based lending include advances against inventory, accounts receivable, land and buildings; loans secured by floating charges on various types of assets; advances under letters of credit secured by goods in transit to buyers; loans against warehouse receipts for grain or other commodities in storage; and loans secured by guarantees, savings accounts, other deposits or shares of stock.

Asset-Based Lending Strategies

The simplest type of asset-based lending is pawnshop credit. The lender has to know a lot about the item pledged, but does not have to know anything about the borrower. (However, many pawnbrokers do want to know something about the borrower to avoid lending against stolen goods.) Asset-based lending of this type creates value by enabling owners to obtain liquidity by borrowing against assets rather than by liquidating them. By obtaining cash while retaining assets, borrowers enjoy more value than if they merely swapped assets for cash. The risk to the lender is reduced because the borrower's stake in the transaction is the value of the asset pledged as security.

The size of an asset-based loan is determined primarily by the value of the asset pledged as collateral. Risk is reflected in a loan size that is smaller than the estimated value of collateral and in other terms and conditions attached to the loan. For a loan secured by a savings account, a portion of the account balance equal to the amount of the loan is blocked so that it cannot be withdrawn. Other conditions are minimal or nonexistent because the level of certainty is high and because valuation of the security is unambiguous and virtually costless. As a consequence, the banker might not inquire about the use of the loan, and loan size may approach 100 percent of the savings account balance.

In practice, however, bankers may try to restrict borrowing to, say, 90 percent of the deposit balance. This reflects discounting if the banker refuses to lend against the entire balance to protect interest income. The lending rate of interest exceeds the deposit rate, and if the borrower neglects to pay interest the margin between loan and deposit balances gives the lender a cushion from which interest can be recovered. Discounting of a sort may also lead the banker to leave some cushion against which the depositor could draw additional funds in an emergency. The depositor is of course technically free to withdraw the unblocked portion of the savings balance, destroying the cushion, leaving the lender with a relatively small risk equal to the difference between interest paid on the deposit and interest earned on the loan.[1]

Asset-Based Lending and Development

Lending against assets such as jewelry that can be pawned or savings accounts that can be blocked may not seem very developmental. However, it can be, and it may point toward useful instruments for helping the poor. Many rural households, for example, buy things they do not use or that they use only slowly, which is a form of saving. They "hoard" liquidity by converting it into livestock that they intend to sell rather than consume, or devote labor to planting trees that they can harvest in time of need or special opportunity. Small enterprises often carry relatively large inventories to hedge against supply interruptions and because of "illiquidity preference" in response to social norms that make it easy for intimates to ask, and difficult for business owners to refuse, to share cash and other liquid assets with friends, relatives and age-mates. Inventories may provide a basis for short-term asset-based loans when liquidity is tight, as in the period immediately before a harvest.

Asset-based lending is more dynamic when it permits borrowers to acquire new assets directly, and when these assets are productive. A commercial banker, for example, may provide mortgage credit to an industrial firm seeking to buy land and construct factory buildings. The credit is secured by the land that is acquired and the buildings that are constructed with the support of the loan.

In contrast to the simple use of unencumbered assets as security for asset-based loans, lending for the acquisition of assets used as collateral requires more information about the borrower. One response to this information problem is a lender's request that the borrower give

---

1. Reluctance to lend the full amount of the deposit balance may also reflect reserve requirements that reduce the proportion of depositors' funds available for lending. A 10 percent reserve requirement imposed by the central bank would leave only 90 percent of the deposit balance for the commercial banker to lend. Requiring a margin arises in this case from cash management strategies involving matching sources and uses of funds.

undertakings about future behavior. For example, noninterest terms and conditions attached to an industrial mortgage may require that the pledged asset be insured and that the borrower maintain a financial structure defined in terms of working capital and debt-to-equity ratios. Loan covenants may limit the types of business the borrower may undertake, require prior approval by the mortgage holder of other borrowing, restrict increases in dividends or salaries, and specify financial reporting requirements. The lender will often demand a share or all of the borrower's commercial banking business. This reduces risk by increasing the flow of information to the lender, and possibly by controlling access to alternative sources of debt, and also produces income from fees and from interest on other loans.

These conditions are intended to help manage the risk of lending against large, specialized assets that may not be readily saleable if the borrower becomes unable to service debt. This risk includes the difference between the value of the mortgaged assets in use by the borrower, on a going concern basis in accounting terminology, and as idle assets. This difference makes it difficult to value these assets precisely, and gives the lender an incentive to impose conditions that make their valuation more transparent and less costly by reducing the risk attached to the loan. Terms and conditions create value by enabling lenders to make larger advances against these assets than they would otherwise be willing to offer.

Repayment of an asset-based commercial loan is normally expected to occur from a flow of income from the pledged asset or accruing to its owner. Even in the example of a loan secured by a savings account, the lender generally expects that the savings account will not have to be liquidated to repay the loan. In classic commercial banking, loan repayment occurs in the normal course of business. An example is payment for trade goods imported under a letter of credit that the importer sells upon arrival, providing cash to repay the credit. Another is the liquidation of raw materials inventory through its conversion into finished goods and eventual sale. Repayment of an industrial mortgage is usually expected from the income-producing activities of the borrowing firm.

Impediments to Asset-Based Lending

Asset-based lending will always be useful and important where it economizes transaction costs and reduces risk. Measures that can impart more value to tangible collateral by reducing the transaction costs of pledging and of seizing assets can create more value through asset-based credit. For example, clear ownership titles and ability to foreclose on defaulted mortgages are extremely important for the development of housing finance.

Government intervention may limit the value that can be realized through asset-based lending and discourage value-creating innovations. Examples of this type of problem were extensively documented in India by the Talwar Report.[2] This report dispels the view that prior to their nationalization Indian commercial banks were unwilling to lend in rural areas because of urban bias or lack of interest. The fundamental problem they faced was that agricultural land did not constitute good security because of regulations imposed by state governments. A recent small loan from an accommodating cooperative could make it impossible for a commercial bank to collect a larger earlier loan.

A typical situation was that regulations favoring cooperatives worked against commercial banks. Under these regulations a cooperative could establish a first lien or senior claim against a parcel of land regardless of any prior claims registered by other lenders. This right was intended to help cooperatives rid the countryside of moneylenders by compromising their ability to seize their debtors' land. However, it also made it impossible for commercial banks to regard agricultural land as security because their liens could be rendered worthless by subsequent claims made by a cooperative. The possibility that this would occur was more than academic because of the widespread use of cooperative credit as a vehicle for political patronage.

Cultural and social considerations may also weaken the basis for asset-based lending by diminishing the loan applicant's ability to pledge assets, the creditor's ability to enforce the loan contract or by otherwise undermining the creditor's claim. Loan applicants may not be able to offer good collateral because they cannot establish clear title to the land, machinery, vehicles or other assets they want to pledge. Legal systems may be imperfect in this respect and ownership recording procedures may

---

2. *Report of the Expert Group on State Enactments Having a Bearing on Commercial Banks Lending to Agriculture.* (Bombay: Reserve Bank of India, 1971). See also Timberg and Aiyer, *op. cit.* p. 46, who noted that restrictive state moneylending acts also discourage informal urban commercial lenders from funding those with agricultural interests.

be cumbersome and lax. These types of problems also make it difficult for the lender to register a pledge and to be certain that it will be respected. Even where liens are legally perfected, however, delays in repossession imposed by lengthy formalities reduce their value by giving the borrower time for evasive action such as hiding the asset or selling it in an undocumented transaction.

In many cultures, foreclosure on a debtor's property by a lender is morally repugnant, and this general attitude can diminish lenders' willingness to lend. In some countries it may be very difficult for lenders to take possession of borrowers' assets such as land, machinery, or cattle in agriculture or a factory or shop, even though the lender is legally entitled to do so. The feasibility of their use or disposal by the lender may also be problematic. Seized land or other fixed agricultural assets or business premises may not attract buyers because of the solidarity of neighbors or clients and workers against the lender or against anyone who might purchase and work the land or operate the business.

In some countries collateral in the form of pledged assets is routinely required, even though it cannot be realized by the lender as a source of repayment if the loan goes bad. The reasons for this behavior by lenders are not entirely clear. On the one hand it may be that collateral simply provides a false sense of security, and on the other it may be that lenders assume that some collateral, however impaired, is better than none. If all lenders require collateral, then even a pledge that cannot be exercised may restrict a borrower's access to new debt.

Even where creditors' rights are well established, however, and repossession of pledged security is routine, asset-based lending cannot always lower transaction costs and risk. One reason for this is that lenders can never fully control the behavior of borrowers. As borrowers encounter problems, their incentives to mislead creditors increase. Movable assets pledged as security may "disappear." In many cases taking and maintaining control of certain types of tangible collateral may be complex, time consuming, and involve high and uncertain costs. Improvements in confidence, including measures to reduce transaction costs, can improve the value of security in asset-based relationships.

Cash Flow Lending

Cash flow loans are not based on collateral, although they are often secured to prevent the borrower from pledging assets to other creditors and as a test of the borrower's commitment to repayment. *The size of cash flow loans is determined primarily by the projected cash flow of the borrower* available to service the loan, by the length of time for which the lender is willing to have funds committed, and by the interest rate.

Commercial cash flow lending strategies derive loan size by discounting, which includes mathematically incorporating interest in the calculation and also making allowances for risk. In the textbook case the maximum loan size would be an amount for which debt service, consisting of principal repayments and interest payments, equals projected debt service capacity.[3] This capacity is the projected uncommitted cash flow, adjusted for risk, that would be available for servicing the contemplated loan. The discounting period is determined by the most distant maturity the lender is willing to offer.

Estimating projected cash flow is a more difficult valuation exercise than that required to support an asset-based loan. Lenders require detailed background, financial and operational information from the borrower, and usually also from others who know the borrower. This information permits the lender to evaluate the financial prospects of the borrower and of the borrower's industry over the life of the loan or over an economic cycle. Obviously, the projection has to be relatively "hard" for it to be useful, which means that each variable contributing materially to the derivation of cash flow available to service debt must be carefully considered.

Balance Sheet Build-up and Discounting

For corporate borrowers, projections are made by "balance sheet build-up" using historical data and trends, and assumptions regarding the future. This analytical procedure uses the balance sheet, income statement, and sources and uses of funds statement. Projections are constructed through iterative interaction of these financial statements, account by account and

---

3. The classic statement of the debt capacity approach is Gordon Donaldson's "New Framework for Corporate Debt Capacity," which was published in the *Harvard Business Review* in 1962 and reprinted in the September-October 1978 issue, pp. 149-164.

year by year. The funds absorbed or generated by the loan applicant's projected operations ultimately appear in the analysis on the balance sheet as a residual that is either an unfunded liability or debt, or an accumulation of cash.

The build-up in cash on the balance sheet is a stock figure arising from positive "free cash flow" on the sources and uses statement. Free or uncommitted cash flow is the liquidity that would be available to service the loan being contemplated. This liquidity is treated as a residual, after the funds required for the continued operation and normal expansion of the firm are reinvested and after debt service obligations to other creditors are met. The analysis requires many assumptions that reflect confidence.

Risk is often incorporated in the balance sheet build-up through variations that attempt to analyze the impact of specific adverse events or the more general effects of an economic downturn. Impact is traced through projections of each of the related financial statements to quantify implications for the borrower's liquidity and solvency. In the textbook case a decline in sales or in the rate of sales growth in an economic downturn results in lower profits, an accumulation of receivables as buyers encounter difficulties or simply conserve cash by taking longer to pay their bills, a slowing in inventory turnover as sales fall below projections, a decrease in cash that eventually produces a funding gap, and a decline in uncommitted cash flow available for debt service.[4] Old bankers say that knowing how much *more* to lend a customer in difficulty is more important than knowing how much to lend when things are going well. Risk-adjusted projections of cash flow are the basis for their judgments.

Cash Flow Lending for Development

Dynamic formal credit markets tend to move toward cash flow lending because it is flexible. It is a forward-looking refinement in the valuation process and enables lenders to issue more credit than would be possible through strict asset-based lending. This movement occurs first in market

---

4. An uninformed view, too frequently articulated, is that reduced profits or even losses are largely responsible for reductions in repayment capacity. While the fate of earnings clearly contributes, the balance sheet build-up demonstrates that slower payments by creditors and slower inventory turnover tie up cash, and that these effects may greatly outweigh reductions in profits as causes of diminished repayment capacity.

niches as "unsecured" lending on a temporary basis by asset-based lenders to borrowers with whom they have an established relationship: even pawnbrokers are occasionally willing to lend more than the resale value of items pawned by good clients who are frequent pawners. At a later stage rules of thumb and more systematic approaches to cash flow analysis develop as lenders seek to improve cash flow credit decisionmaking.

Another important step occurs as asset-based lenders give credit against assets that produce no cash income for borrowers. Consumer credit that finances private cars and loans on owner-occupied housing fall into this category. In these cases the lender determines loan size based on asset value in conjunction with estimates of borrowers' cash flow and other measures of probable loan quality. Repayment is generally expected to come from the borrower's income rather than from sale of the loan-financed asset.

From a developmental standpoint, valuation processes that promote cash flow lending are clearly preferable when they improve the quality of lending decisions and the lender's ability to bear risk. Asset-based lending too easily reinforces the existing distribution of wealth and may not be oriented toward potential opportunities. Cash flow lending corresponds most closely to Schumpeter's vision of credit as a vehicle of structural change that permits innovators to bid resources away from established patterns of production, which can increase efficiency, improve technology and lower costs, as noted in chapter 9.

Cash flow lending helps to develop financial markets. In simple asset-based loan markets lenders must know a lot about the valuation of assets, but can know relatively little about their clients. In the cash flow loan market lenders have to know about valuation in the broadest sense, including the intangibles of character, integrity, commitment, and competence. They must also deal with fungibility. The asset-based lender may lend against an asset that provides liquidity that the borrower uses for purposes unrelated to the asset that is pledged. The cash flow lender knows, and the balance sheet build-up shows, that the ability to service debt is a function of all sources and all uses of funds and of the hierarchies of claims, risks, and priorities they represent. This view of finance and risk puts a tremendous premium on information and analytical skills.

Access to information through confidential, private relationships between lender and borrower in turn creates market niches based on financing skills, including specialization in risk assessment and management. The result is greater scope for competion in structuring relationships, which yields more creative risk management instruments and strategies. Cash flow lending, when voluntarily undertaken in response to competitive pressures to reduce costs, potentially creates more value than asset-based lending.

Why Is Cash Flow Lending Slow to Evolve?

Formal credit in many countries remains stubbornly asset based. Three major causes seem to underlie this tendency: uncompetitive financial markets, restricted confidence, and information and administrative cost.[5] An absence of competition is to be expected when financial markets are repressed by government policies that severely restrict entry into formal intermediation and tightly control the actions and profits of intermediaries such as banks. In addition, financial institutions may be treated primarily as channels for directed credit, which is antithetical to financial market development. The result of these factors is a lack of incentive to innovate. In these noncompetitive markets lenders tend to offer homogeneous, "plain vanilla" products, and structural change in finance often occurs through emergence of new institutions based on innovative instruments rather than through diversification of existing intermediaries.

In a protected, asset-based credit environment financial information systems that facilitate credit judgments are slow to develop. If lenders do not compete, and if everyone believes that tangible assets are the only real basis of value, why should prospective borrowers inconvenience themselves and bear the transaction costs and risks of disclosing data about their cash flow and profitability? Why should anyone want to develop and apply accounting standards to simplify reporting and interpretation of financial data and to improve its accuracy? Why should lenders bother to maintain credit files documenting the history of their relationships and the performance of their clients? Why would banks want to develop ground rules for the exchange of meaningful credit information on their clients?

A second cause is generally restricted networks of confidence that may be slow to expand to include others because of tradition, corruption, high

5. Roberto Mizrahi, "Credit and Financial Intermediation for the Informal Sector." Sectoral Policies Division, Plans and Programs Department, Inter-American Development Bank. Working Paper No. 4, Washington, DC, August 1988. p. 5.

costs in law enforcement, and poorly developed tort and contract law. However, sufficient confidence exists virtually everywhere to permit relatively active informal financial markets. These include trade credit between nonfinancial firms based on commercial relationships and character. Financial markets can help expand these networks to include formal financial institutions in response to appropriate incentives.

A third cause for reluctance to place more confidence in cash flow approaches includes factors that are more concrete. One is the demand made on staffing and management of financial institutions in terms of skills, integrity, and controls. If financial projections are deficient or "fudged," cash flow lending fails. Another is high rates of failure by borrowers in industry, commerce, and agriculture because of general economic problems, poor infrastructure, and high transaction costs. The result of bad cash flow loans is yet another inhibiting factor: losses can be highly visible when tangible security is not taken or when its value is relatively small.

Administrative costs of cash flow lending may also appear unattractively high to many officers of financial institutions that are not accustomed to vigorous cost cutting. While the informal sector does lots of cash flow lending, it does so at relatively low costs because decisionmaking is decentralized and accountability is strong. Informal lenders generally operate with their own funds, the ultimate in accountability, and face-to-face. Formal institutional arrangements, however, tend to be highly centralized in many developing countries.

Intermediaries owned by governments are especially likely to be centralized because of the requirements of control. Individuals working for such institutions often have strong property rights in their jobs, which limit the amount of quality control managers can exert or the amount and quality of performance data that can be generated on each staff member. Procedures are therefore especially important in the attempt to ensure good performance honestly rendered. These tend to favor centralized and collective decisionmaking, which is costly at formal sector salary levels and government sector staffing levels. Spreading responsibility in this manner is "cool," while efforts to develop relationships with borrowers often have to be "warm." Without the ability to respond clearly and quickly to opportunities to build relationships, these types of formal intermediaries rightly opt for asset-based lending.

Institutional procedures are often seen as sources of comfort by donors providing project funds and promoting formalized approaches to credit information and analysis. An indication of this is found in the discussion in chapter 4 of the technical factors and other variables that would be examined in a feasibility study to justify use of project funds to finance the expansion of posho milling facilities.

If project funds were not being used, several relatively simple observations might result in the same investment. One would be that of an entrepreneur who notices long queues outside existing posho mills and decides to establish a competing mill, or of a mill operator who senses that the potential volume of business justifies expansion. Another possibility is that women from a village without a mill get tired of hauling heavy baskets of grain from their village to a neighboring village to be milled into posho flour, and begin to explore the possibilities of obtaining a mill for their own village and of pooling their savings to finance its establishment.

This case illustrates the potential benefits of informalizing institutional credit by reducing transaction costs. Decentralization and systems of individual responsibility, possibly similar to those of Grameen Bank described in chapter 10, could reduce costs if supported by adequate systems of control.

Do Development Finance Institutions Apply Cash Flow Lending ?

To what degree can the potential advantages of cash flow lending be used to promote development? This important question is difficult to answer directly. Efforts to make development finance more information-based have generally not produced viable credit institutions. A review of the traditional development finance model, which is a form of project lending, suggests the roots of some of its problems.

Project lending by large private credit institutions is essentially cash flow lending. The cash flow generated by the project, such as a hydroelectric dam or port facility, is expected to repay the loans obtained for its construction. The amount of credit provided is determined by risk-adjusted projected cash flow, and the balance of the funding has to be provided in the form of equity, which frequently must be invested first to trigger releases of credit. Lenders' time horizons are an important factor in determining the extent and nature of their commitments.[6]

Project lending on a smaller scale at the frontier through development finance institutions (DFIs) supported by development assistance agencies has many cash flow features but retains asset-based characteristics. These are illustrated in Table 11.1, which compares modern cash flow lending, as conducted by commercial banks in developed countries and in international markets, with the behavior of DFIs in many developing countries. DFIs frequently target the acquisition of certain types of assets only and base loan size on the cost (value) of assets, as explained in chapter 4. Loan size is based on a rule of thumb that results in credit finance for a high and arbitrary portion of investment cost.

DFIs usually base their clients' annual debt service on projected financial flows that are *not* adjusted for risk and that use rules of thumb to estimate an industrial borrower's utilization of capacity created by the investment. For example, it may be assumed that production in the first year following investment would equal 60 percent of capacity, and that this would rise to 80 percent in the second year, and 100 percent thereafter. Debt service derived from this approach may equal a high proportion of projected uncommitted cash flow unadjusted for risk.

The interest rate is generally not negotiable, being fixed by the government or in the agreement governing the provision of funds by the donor to the DFI. The term to maturity is determined in two ways. The first and least creative is to fix a standard term for all subloans, or for all loans for a certain purpose. The second is to make term to maturity the residual parameter, determined by the number of installments required to recover loan principal and interest within the limits of the projected uncommitted cash flow. This twist is permitted by the relatively long terms on which donor funding is provided.

The typical DFI decision process is most easily illustrated by agricultural production credit for seasonal crops. This illustration is simple because financial projections for many types of farm activities can be made

---

6. This is a highly simplified explanation of project finance, which usually includes numerous suppliers and types of debt and a variety of equity claims, each carrying different terms and conditions that are juggled and modified, determining how the project cash flow will be divided up and how risk will be apportioned, as the financial plan is constructed.

Table 11.1 Comparison of Modern Cash Flow Lending and Development Finance Lending

Parameter	Typical Modern Cash Flow Lending Approach	Typical Development Finance Institution (DFI) Lending Approach
Relationship between borrower and lender	On-going, multidimensional	Occasional, when a service is sought or used. Narrow service base. Primary activity is term lending.
Determination of loan amount	Based on borrower's free cash flow adjusted for risk and senior claims, and on lender's capacity to bear cost of delayed payment or bad debt loss.	Agriculture & industry: high and arbitrary portion of investment cost, possibly including permanent working capital. Industry: Foreign exchange (FX) loans or loans to cover FX cost of investment equal direct or direct plus indirect FX cost.
Interest rate and related fees	Negotiated with reference to a base or prime market rate, lender transaction costs, credit risk, and actual or potential associated business to enhance lender's profits.	Standard for all borrowers or for classes of borrowers defined by income level, size of firm, or loan purpose or end use. Standard levels usually negotiated with donor, close to commercial bank prime rate or government-mandated rate. Rule of thumb spreads of 2 to 4% over DFI cost of donor funds often applied.

Parameter	Typical Modern Cash Flow Lending Approach	Typical Development Finance Institution (DFI) Lending Approach
Term to maturity and grace periods	Based on cash flow of project or borrower adjusted for risk and senior claims, and by lender's ability to match maturities or duration of assets and liabilities or to bear risk of mismatch. Maturity usually does not exceed 5 years when the lender is a commercial bank.	Agriculture: usually standard for all borrowers or by purpose. Based on cash flow of the loan-financed enterprise derived from representative farm budgets without risk adjustment but possibly with partial adjustment for senior claims. No generally accepted guidelines exist to determine amount of incremental cash flow that can reasonably be expected to be dedicated to debt service. Industry: often standard for different classes of borrowers, but sometimes tailored to project or borrower, based on cash flows unadjusted for risk. Agriculture & industry: final maturity date rarely exceeds that of donor's loan, typically 7 to 12 years.
Other terms and conditions	Standard loan agreement, plus terms tailored to project or borrower, plus terms negotiated to enhance relationship. Collateralized by liens on assets. Guarantees of owners sought for loans to small enterprises. Inflation adjustment often achieved by shortening maturity.	Agriculture: standard loan agreement. Industry: standard loan agreement sometimes supplemented with terms tailored to project or borrower. Standard debt-to-equity ratio limits often specified for all borrowers. Collateralized by liens on assets. Inflation adjustment often lacking or deficient.

using farm budgets rather than the relatively complex iterative and interacting procedures required for projections using the three basic financial statements of corporate accounting, namely, the balance sheet, income statement, and sources and uses of funds statement.

Farm budgets organize technical and financial information and are used to project incremental costs and benefits of the proposed investment.[7] Future cost and benefit streams are derived with and without the project to show incremental effects, and "before financing" and "after financing" to facilitate the calculation of rates of return to all economic resources used by the project and to the farm operator, respectively. The before financing budget shows projected flows from the activity promoted by the project. The after financing portion of the budget usually contains relatively large amounts of credit to fund the project-induced investment. The net benefit after financing shows the surplus expected from implementation, after payment of debt service.

An elementary example of a farm budget is given in Table 11.2, which shows the activities of a representative farm without the credit project and presents estimates of what would occur with the project. With the project the farmer's seasonal input purchases jump by $800, from $200 to $1,000 (line 6). This investment in seeds, fertilizers and insecticides doubles the volume of production, from 5 tons to 10 tons (line 1), which increases the net benefit before financing from $1,000 to $2,200 (line 7). This is all made possible, according to the credit need approach, by a loan of $800 (line 8) which funds all of the incremental input purchases (the difference between the with and without project cases in line 6). There appears to be ample space for these repayment terms because the incremental net benefit before financing of $1,200 (i.e., $2,200 less $1,000 on line 7) is much greater than the $160 net cost of borrowing (line 9 less line 8).

The major objective of farm budgets is not to design a financing plan, but to permit calculation of an internal rate of return to the incremental investment.[8] In the usual case the investment is a fixed asset and the rate of

---

7. Farm budgets are described in J. Price Gittinger, *op. cit.*

8. Note that Table 11.2 appeared earlier as Table 4.1. Table 11.2 shows only a simplified, single "with project" year during which seasonal production credit is advanced and recovered. The usual analysis incorporates term lending for acquisition of fixed assets and contains annual figures for each year of the investment's useful life, which may be as long as 20 years. An additional modification that is required to use farm budgets correctly for financial and economic calculations consists of stating

Table 11.2 Hypothetical Farm Budget

Item	Without Project	With Project	Calculation
1. Produce (tons)	5	10	+
2. Produce consumed on the farm (tons)	2	2	-
3. *Marketed produce (tons)*	*3*	*8*	=
4. Farmgate price per ton ($)	400	400	x
5. *Total farm cash receipts ($)*	*1200*	*3200*	=
6. Purchased inputs ($)	200	1000	-
7. *Net benefit before financing*[a] *($)*	*1000*	*2200*	=
8. Loan receipts ($)	-0-	800	+
9. Debt service ($) [including 20% interest charge]	-0-	960	-
10. *Net benefit after financing*[a] *($)*	*1000*	*2040*	=

a. "Before financing" refers to the costs and benefits directly related to production. "After financing" includes these costs and benefits and also loan receipts and debt servicing.

return would be calculated from the net benefit before financing over the investment's useful life. Rate of return analysis is used as a primary tool of project analysis and investment justification by large donors, including the international development banks.

The rate of return is calculated using a normal year assumption for the net benefit before financing. The sequence of good, normal, and bad years

---

flows so that they correspond to their actual phasing—discounting used in rate of return analysis treats all transactions as if they occur on the final day of each period. Deferred inflow and time-adjusted phasing are discussed by Walter Schaefer-Kehnert's "Methodology of Farm Investment Analysis," Course Note 030/031 Rev. Dec. 1981, Economic Development Institute of the World Bank, Washington, DC. See also his "Time Adjusted Cash Flow Projections in Farm Investment Analysis," *Zeitschrift für Ausländische Landwirtschaft* (*Quarterly Journal of International Agriculture*). 3/78. p. 233. These modifications are neglected in the farm budgets and related tables used in chapters 4, 11 and 12 solely for purposes of simplicity in communicating concepts, primarily that of risk, without having to explore the finer but essential points of farm investment analysis. Skilled analysts can easily incorporate risk adjustment in farm investment analysis and in financial analysis using balance sheets, income statements, and sources and uses of funds statements.

is impossible to predict, and their distribution is not considered important in calculating a representative rate of return, in part because under a credit project funds are usually committed to ultimate borrowers over a period of two or more years. Some borrowers may invest in a bad year, while others will in normal or good years.

The representative rate of return is used to justify credit support for a specific investment on a relatively large number of farms sharing characteristics with those portrayed in the representative budget. Representative budgets reduce transaction costs by making it unnecessary to construct separate analyses for each small farm loan applicant, although many specialized farm credit institutions still make individual calculations. No allowance is specifically made in conventional farm budgets to accommodate probable variations in prices or yields. (Rate of return sensitivity analysis may be conducted by adjusting costs or benefits by arbitrary amounts, for example, plus or minus 10 percent, and calculating alternative rates of return, or by graphing the slopes of the discounted cost and benefit curves to see how shifts in either would affect the position of their intersection, which determines the rate of return.)

The normal year assumption used in rate of return calculation is not appropriate for credit decisionmaking. Bad years may have relatively little impact on the rate of return for an investment project with a life of 20 years, and good years tend to offset bad years. However, a bad year can have a large impact on ability to repay a loan, and good years may not offset bad years. Borrowers in arrears may devote good year windfalls to priorities that are more important to them than repaying arrears. In effect, the conventional farm budget's usefulness for credit decisions stops with the net benefit before financing,[9] a theme that is developed in chapter 12.

To summarize, DFIs do not completely apply cash flow lending techniques. Incompleteness arises from a failure to address risk, a tragic flaw that of course lowers the quality of lending regardless of the approach employed. But why would these lenders try to sail directly into the financial wind, defying investment logic? This appears to occur because the objectives of many DFIs are not explicitly centered on making good loans, but rather emphasize projected returns to an investment with

---

9. And this is often wrongly calculated. See Walter Schaefer-Kehnert, "Methodology of Farm Investment Analysis."

insufficient attention to how it is financed. Their objectives may also include disbursement of specific volumes of funds to serve political goals or meet donors' targets, which in turn may be motivated by the view that the rate of investment in the economy is insufficient to achieve macroeconomic growth targets. Concern for investment rates without considering investment quality easily produces poor quality lending.

Intervene at the Frontier to Develop Confidence

The design of most frontier assaults by official credit projects is primitive. Problems associated with these projects are subtle, serious, and generally overlooked and misunderstood, as detailed in previous chapters. In view of these problems, tremendous development impact or leverage can be realized by more effective and innovative designs for moving the frontier. Movement toward cash flow lending by formal intermediaries is very important in this respect, and its elements offer insights into useful directions to take. A necessary component of financial development is confidence among borrowers and lenders. Confidence creation is dealt with in the remainder of this chapter.

Confidence is fundamental to finance, as discussed in the explanation in the introductory chapters of how financial markets create value by using confidence to offset risk. Hence, building confidence is the most useful starting point for efforts to enhance finance at the frontier. Without confidence, private credit markets could not operate because loan contracts would have no value.

Finance ultimately depends on trust rather than on calculations. Even if calculations show large debt service capacity, lenders still consider the applicant's character in deciding whether to lend, how much to lend and on which loan terms and conditions. Will the lender actually be able to recover principal and interest out of the borrower's repayment capacity? Absence of confidence increases information costs and other transaction costs. Businesslike behavior engenders confidence, reduces risk, and lowers transaction costs.

Standard practice by private lenders is to reject approaches from people with bad reputations without giving them further consideration. Why incur transaction costs to calculate repayment capacity when the applicant is unlikely to repay? However, some bad payers may have been exploited by "credit need" oriented lenders, for example, that issued loans too large for them to handle. Other bad payers may repent and change their ways. Competitive financial markets may give these potentially good payers a second chance as lenders search for ways to build confidence. (Poor payers may also receive further loans from incompetent lenders in poorly functioning financial markets where credit files and histories are poorly maintained.)

Three Strategic Questions of Confidence

At the early stages of project design, several issues about the integrity of debtor-creditor relationships should be explored. One is: *What services will produce a continuing series of transactions that build mutually beneficial relationships* between borrowers and lenders? Services used frequently offer potential for building relationships and increase the value of a good credit rating. Savings accounts, for example, may remain on intermediaries' books for a considerable time, and transactions may occur several times a year. Money transfer or payment services, likewise, may be extremely important where few people have checking accounts. The volume and frequency of use of these services offer intermediaries opportunities for new business.

Savings and money transfer facilities are also barometers of confidence in financial institutions. Members of the public who use these services do so to reduce their transaction costs and because they have confidence that their deposits are safe and readily accessible and that funds will be available to payees as promised and upon demand. Confidence is tested and hopefully affirmed by each transaction as noted in Part I.

A second question is: *What is the value to the lender of accurate and timely information* about borrowers and potential borrowers? Relevant information is required to provide useful financial services. Deposit accounts and transfer services generate such information: histories of transactions provide a financial record for the lender. The level and rate of accumulation of deposits provide data on the volume of funds that the lender might tap or the borrower might mobilize for loan repayment. The timing of deposits and withdrawals indicates when loan due dates could conveniently be scheduled. Without a sense of history, credit projects fail to build the long-term perspective in both borrower and lender that is essential to confidence.

A third question is: *Should voluntary behavior command a premium over coercion* in development strategy? Regulations and limitations over borrower behavior can weaken confidence, especially when lenders are part of larger control systems—such as those related to land use and husbandry practices—and enforce or implement foreign exchange, tax, and other regulations not of their own making. If development is viewed as a top-down phenomenon, credit constitutes a valuable tool of control and dependence, and regulations are required to direct borrower behavior.

If development is viewed as a voluntary, incentive-driven bottom-up process, the role of savings and of relationships becomes more important, and alternative designs for development programs involving financial intermediation require more attention. Supervised credit, for example, would appear less attractive, and lines of credit more appropriate. Credit unions, with opportunities for member participation in management and decisionmaking, would be preferred to bureaucratic government credit agencies. Savings-led (rather than credit-led) initiatives would become eligible for serious consideration. As Dale W Adams notes, "If a society values expanding individual freedom, mobilization of economic surpluses through voluntary financial savings is preferable to the more commonly used involuntary techniques...through taxes."[10] Jan Rydh, president of the Swedish Savings Banks Association, noted at a presentation in 1990 that, "Savings gives a man a little piece of freedom to himself."

Incentives as Tactical Issues in Confidence Creation Strategies

Incentives can help create confidence. A lender is unlikely to receive voluntary debt repayments unless the borrower has an incentive to repay, as noted in chapter 7. Security and loan documents by themselves do not make a good loan, especially at the frontier, excepting tightly asset-based transactions such as pawnshop credit. The borrower's equity capital does help to make a good loan, by demonstrating a commitment and by creating a cushion for the lender, and provides an incentive to lend and an incentive to repay.

Modern cash flow lenders are unwilling to lend to those who are unlikely to repay unless subjected to threats, recourse to law enforcement

---

10. Dale W Adams, "Do Rural Financial Savings Matter?" in Denis Kessler and Pierre-Antoine Ullmo, eds., *op. cit.* p. 14.

agencies, or by calling loan guarantors or cosigners to repay on behalf of the borrower. Most lenders want to avoid these situations because they can be costly and may create bad feelings in the community. Fortunately, experience demonstrates that if the *lender* has a reputation of serving the community fairly and efficiently, the number of borrowers who wilfully refuse to pay is quite small.

Official credit projects aimed at the frontier generally do not directly address confidence among borrowers and lenders. Project designers apparently assume that components supporting the lender through training, systems development, vehicles and computers, and technical assistance, education and extension services for borrowers will produce confidence or provide a satisfactory substitute. Even if these were capable of creating confidence, they are often implemented poorly. Many projects swamp lenders' thinly stretched management, and technical assistance, education and extension are not always effective, as noted in chapters 5 and 10. Special attention to how credit projects can create or destroy confidence is needed when financial markets are gagged by regulations or force-fed by projects.

Certain arrangements in projects may offer perverse incentives that encourage cheating. High levels of financing that burden debt servicing capacity tempt borrowers not to repay on time. Low interest rates and lax loan administration may tempt them to obtain more credit than they will use for project purposes and to delay loan repayment. Technological bias in project design may force borrowers to accept an entire technical package in order to receive a loan, although they use only a portion of the package. Incomplete adoption may be rational risk management by the borrower but does not help to create confidence, especially in projects founded on optimistic assumptions about adoption rates and productivity.

Political fanfare surrounding a project may also work against good credit relationships. Loan allocation may be based on poverty, loyalty to certain factions, or local political influence. This may lead people to believe that the credit program is transitory, that with political changes it will disappear, that with exhaustion of project funds credit for the project purpose will no longer be available, and that default will not result in denied access to future loans if indeed any are available. This short-run perspective weakens the incentive to establish a good repayment record.

Inflation Can Destroy Confidence

Confidence depends upon a certain level of stability as well as a certain degree of change that creates room for dynamic flexibility and incentives for competition. Many factors that determine stability and change in finance are beyond the control of borrowers and lenders, but depend upon the actions of governments. Intervention to create confidence is made more difficult when inflation rates are high, because high rates of inflation also tend to be more variable than lower rates,[11] and hence reduce stability.

Although the mathematical relationship between 2 and 4 percent is the same as between 20 and 40 percent or 200 and 400 percent, the implications of these pairs of inflation rates for financial contracts as well as for economic performance are vastly different. A change in the rate of inflation from 2 to 4 percent or vice versa is easily accommodated. Changes in either direction between 20 and 40 percent may be accompanied by major dislocations and those between 200 and 400 percent are so massive that they are difficult to comprehend or forecast effectively.

Theoretically it is possible to insulate financial contracts from some of these effects by indexing.[12] Variable interest rates, based on a specified inflation index such as the consumer price index or the government's cost of borrowing, may be used to remove from depositors and bondholders some of the risk of the decline in the purchasing power value of the financial contracts they hold. Variable lending rates may likewise be adjusted in concert with a deposit rate index to lessen lenders' risks. By issuing indexed liabilities and creating indexed assets, intermediaries can minimize interest rate matching problems that accompany maturity mismatches. Maturity mismatches are created by borrowing short and lending long, which is common in retail financial institutions. Indexing on both sides of their balance sheets can increase the supply of loanable funds and contribute to their survival in tumultuous times.

While not indexing or using variable rates can be very dangerous for financial institutions, indexed contracts cannot isolate institutions from the

---

11. Milton Friedman, *Money and Economic Development*. The Horowitz Lectures of 1972 (New York: Praeger Publishers, 1973).

12. A review of indexing is given by Frank Veneroso, "Systems of Indexation and their Impact on Capital Markets," in Nicholas Bruck, ed., *Capital Markets under Inflation*. (Buenos Aires: Stock Exchange of Buenos Aires, 1982, assisted by the Inter-American Development Bank).

underlying problem of high rates of inflation. One reason for this is that governments may intervene to influence the application of an index in economic emergencies. This results in the erosion of lenders' capital.

Failure to charge positive real interest rates—contractual rates that exceed the rate of inflation—reduces the size of a financial institution in terms of the purchasing power of its assets, adding to the reduction in size caused by bad debt losses. For example, in a study of USAID-supported microenterprise credit programs in Brazil, Burkina Faso, Dominican Republic, Honduras, and Peru, Peter Kilby and David D'Zmura estimated this loss of purchasing power at US$35.5 million on US$48.1 million loaned.[13] Of this, US$33.4 million was lost to inflation between 1975 and 1982 on US$42.3 million loaned in Peru, a 79 percent erosion. They conclude, "The lesson is clear:...lending projects should not be located in inflationary economies," unless lenders are willing to charge accordingly.[14]

Another reason why inflation makes intermediaries vulnerable is that high or rising rates of inflation create uncertainty, making risk management much more difficult. Intermediaries' capital may shrink in relation to the growth of their liabilities with inflationary increases in the money supply. This may be partially offset by inflationary increases in the value of their fixed assets, such as buildings in which their offices and branches are located. However, this increase may be difficult to capture under regulatory accounting requirements and may not be regarded as a particularly useful or sufficient cushion against rising bad debt losses from increased risk in the economy.

Economic instability affects borrowers in different ways. Some borrowers may be able to pass inflationary cost increases on to their customers, others may not; and, inflation may reduce their clients' purchasing power, creating another dimension of risk. Calculations of debt service capacity and of other financial variables become subject to increasing skepticism. The basis for cash flow lending, which is the projected risk-adjusted financial performance of the loan applicant, evaporates in the wake of the uncertainty caused by high and rising rates of

---

13. Peter Kilby and David D'Zmura, "Searching for Benefits." AID Special Study No. 28. Washington, DC: U.S. Agency for International Development. pp. 98, 113, 117.

14. *Ibid.* p. 112.

inflation and by the prospect of the economic hard landing that is likely to follow. The risks simply overwhelm confidence.

Inflation can make a mockery of financial calculations. When this occurs confidence becomes more difficult to maintain in financial markets.[15] Intermediaries retreat to conservative efforts to increase the liquidity of their portfolios, or may be tempted to speculate in turbulent markets to obtain windfall gains or to enhance their chances for survival.[16]

---

15. V.V. Bhatt, *op. cit.* p. 47. A comprehensive review of the impact of inflation on securities markets in Latin America is given in Nicholas A. Bruck, ed., *Capital Markets Under Inflation.*

16. Frank Veneroso provides a review of the relationship between economic instability and opportunistic behavior by bankers in "New Patterns of Financial Instability." Washington, DC: World Bank, Industry Department (processed), February 1986.

12

DEFINING THE ROLE OF CREDIT BY DETERMINING DEBT CAPACITY

Lenders are able to recover loans on schedule only when the repayment capacity of the borrower equals or exceeds debt service, which consists of principal and interest due for payment. Borrowers are able to repay their loans on time without suffering hardship only when their repayment capacity equals or exceeds the debt service due according to the loan contract. These simple, self-evident relationships define the role that credit plays in development and influence the fate of efforts to expand the frontier of formal finance.

Debt capacity addresses risk and other important issues in debtor-creditor relationships raised in previous chapters. It does so through a valuation process of inquiry and discovery based on financial projections and their refinement. Projections underlie cash flow lending, and debt capacity calculation facilitates application of cash flow lending strategies.

But projections are also employed in many asset-based credit strategies. Housing lenders, for example, investigate prospective home buyers' incomes and commitments in order to determine the size of monthly payments loan applicants can afford. These monthly payments and the term of the mortgage being offered in effect determine loan size within an upper limit that is related to the market value of the home. In chapter 11 it was noted that DFIs often use financial projections to determine loan maturity. In this case the loan amount and the periodic payment capacity are treated as givens in deriving the term of the loan. Debt capacity approaches permit both loan size and repayment schedules to be determined simultaneously. They also incorporate risk, going deeper than the techniques of asset-based lending.

This chapter explains debt capacity and illustrates the application of debt capacity strategies using simple farm budgets. The debt capacity approach is easily applied to commercial and industrial lending using conventional financial statements.

Debt Capacity Calculation

Credit project design should begin with an analysis of the repayment capacity of prospective borrowers. This is required because repayment is vital to project performance and lender survival. Three steps ascertain repayment capacity: First, quantify the normal year uncommitted cash flow of the loan applicant or investment project. Second, adjust uncommitted cash flow for senior claims on the applicant's or project's liquidity. Third, quantify the impact of reasonably expected adversity on the applicant's or project's cash flow.

Deriving Normal Year Uncommitted Cash Flow

Normal-year[1] uncommitted cash flow is derived in Table 12.1 using highly simplified assumptions and an elementary analytical format. The first two columns of figures in lines A through G incorporate the normal year with- and without-project data previously presented in Table 11.2. They quantify production, on-farm consumption, farmgate prices received for produce, and the costs of inputs used to produce the crop in order to derive net benefit before financing (NBBF). Normal year NBBF is traditionally used to determine loan repayment terms in agricultural credit projects.

Quantify Senior Claims

But, how much of the NBBF will be used to repay the loan? What claims will the borrower consider more important than repaying the loan? These are called senior claims. One of these, subsistence, was already included in the calculation of uncommitted cash flow; consumption of farm produce (line B) was deducted from total output to derive the marketed

---

1. "Year" is used here because the examples are agricultural and because farm budgets are customarily done for project analysis using annual periods. However, shorter periods based on production or sales cycles or on the frequency of loan repayment installments could in many cases be more instructive than 12-month periods.

quantity of produce. Examples of other senior claims on households operating farms and small businesses are purchases of food and fuel, taxes, school fees, and expenditures for emergencies and important social obligations and ceremonies. Additional senior claims on nonfarm enterprises include continuation of the business.

Table 12.1 Hypothetical Risk-Adjusted Farm Budget

		Without Project	With Project	
	Category		Normal Year	Bad Year
A.	Produce (tons)	5	10	5
B.	Produce consumed on the farm (tons)	2	2	2
C.	Marketed produce (tons)	3	8	3
D.	Farmgate price per ton ($)	400	400	550
E.	Total farm cash receipts ($)	1,200	3,200	1,650
F.	Purchased inputs ($)	200	1,000	900
G.	Net Benefit Before Financing ($)	1,000	2,200	750
H.	Senior claims ($)	500	600	600
I.	Repayment capacity = Uncommitted cash flow ($)	500	1,600	150
J.	Loan receipts ($)	0	1,333	125
K.	Debt Service ($) [loan receipts plus 20% interest charge]	0	1,600	150

Behavior the world over confirms that claims by informal lenders at the frontier rank ahead of those of formal credit institutions.[2] A new or prospective lender has to regard older debt supplied by another lender as senior, and where confidence is weak each lender regards every other lender as having a senior claim. To expand the frontier, prospective lenders require financial instruments that change the structure of claims on

2. Shipton notes that "farmers have their own personal hierarchies of creditors and the newest, most distant, and least familiar lenders rank at the bottom." Parker Shipton, "How Gambians Save." p. 7.

prospective loan applicants. Repayment of new frontier lenders can be reasonably expected only when their claims are sufficiently high in the borrowers' hierarchy of claims.

Quantifying senior claims may be easiest where analysis focuses primarily on incremental activities. The without-project situation may include most of the senior claims facing the borrower—at least those that have had priority in the past. However, attention to senior claims is still required with respect to the incremental cash flow created with the project. Because the household's income is higher, its consumption and obligations to the extended family and community may be greater. An increase in liquidity may permit the borrower to make expenditures that have always had high priority but were never realized because of financial constraints. These priorities may compete with loan repayment obligations under the project, and in Table 12.1 senior claims (excluding on-farm consumption) are expected to be greater with the project (line H).

Determining senior claims requires judgment and imposes information costs. But senior claims are essentially no more difficult to estimate than are many other variables contained in farm budgets. However, they do require examination of the borrower's entire cash flow, not simply the net flows related to the crop or activity ("enterprise" in the language of agricultural economics) for which credit is issued. This focus is useful—a lender can lend *for* a crop, but only *to* a borrower. Competent intermediaries with experience in an area are able to give rough estimates for all of the items contained in the agricultural budget in Table 12.1.

The Best Laid Plans....

If credit terms are fixed using normal year assumptions and without allowances for senior claims, borrowers are unlikely to meet debt servicing obligations in situations that may reasonably be expected to occur. This can embarrass the borrower and jeopardize the liquidity of the lender.

Adjusting for adversity begins by calculating a bad year budget as shown by the third column of figures in Table 12.1. In this example production falls by half (line A), on-farm consumption remains constant (line B), and farmgate prices (line D) increase from $400 to $550 per ton, reflecting an overall fall in agricultural output. Input cost (line F) is reduced because a small harvest requires less labor, bags, and transport.

The "bottom line" in Table 12.1 after adjustments for adversity and senior claims shows minimum repayment capacity (line I). In all years—good, normal, or bad—the borrower is expected to have not less than $150 available for loan repayment. Based on this, a loan of $125 could be offered with a 20 percent interest charge. (Twenty percent is used for convenience and also because the costs of formal lending at the frontier are seldom less than 20 percent.) Debt service would absorb all the borrower's $150 adjusted uncommitted cash flow in the bad year. Adjustment for senior claims and adversity severely diminishes loan size from the $800 shown in Table 11.2 to the $125 derived in Table 12.1.

Adjustment for adversity should reflect reasonable expectations about risks. There is no scientific way of identifying the normal expected adverse situation, although an obvious starting point is a distribution of expected results. Some may measure it using standard deviations of yields and prices; others would employ different techniques.

For example, assume smallholder dairy project loans assist small farmers to purchase two improved cows, fencing, and watering facilities. Adjustment for adversity could begin with the question: What if one or both cows die? Once the lender has made 100 of these loans and has several years of experience, the answer will be fairly obvious. Rough probabilities will be known (e.g., one cow in six dies within 12 months of purchase by the borrower), characteristics of farmers suffering accidental stock losses can be identified, and lending terms and conditions redefined.

When the lender has accommodated the probability of accidental mortality, which poses the largest technical threat to loan quality, it can go on to consider the cash flow impact of calving intervals. Once these are factored into lending strategy, feeding regimes, milk prices, or marketing arrangements become interesting to credit decisionmakers, who would then have the information required to tailor dairy credit packages to the performance and characteristics of each borrower rather than issuing a standard package to all successful loan applicants.

Implications of Debt Capacity Strategies

If loan size were limited to $125 rather than the $800 that would cover the incremental purchased input costs, would the borrower undertake the development illustrated in Table 12.1? Where investments are divisible rather than lumpy, a smaller on-farm project may be feasible. Modern inputs could be used on a portion of the farm if the farmer cannot afford the difference between the $125 loan and the $800 incremental input costs. But fewer inputs produce smaller harvests than projected in Table 12.1, requiring a drastically revised farm budget and probably an even smaller loan.

In the end, formal credit in any significant amount may just not be feasible in some situations where senior claims and risks are large. Does this mean that an opportunity for development has been needlessly lost? No, unless it can be demonstrated that development in general and over the long run can be generated by bad loans. By analogy, many technical possibilities, such as mile-high buildings and 100-mile bridges, are not indulged because they are not economic. Likewise, many economic possibilities are not undertaken because they cannot be associated with sufficient debt capacity and hence cannot be financed with debt.

Development of financial markets of course extends the boundaries of financial feasibility by lengthening term structures, reducing transaction costs and refining valuation processes as outlined in chapter 1. Bad loans are essential to the trial and error process required for development and are normal in dynamic markets that test the frontier continuously, as noted in chapter 9. However, as discussed in chapter 3, tolerances in finance are fine, leaving little margin for error. Experience in the United States in the 1980s has shown that bad loans amounting to 3 percent of loan portfolios can give commercial banks and their government regulators major cases of indigestion. Bad loans in excess of relatively low proportions of overall lending stifle financial market development as demonstrated in other chapters. The remainder of this chapter illustrates how debt capacity strategies can create confidence and instruments that promote financial market development

Extending Debt Capacity Quantification

The decisionmaking inputs and assumptions represented in Table 12.1 are simple, yet much more sophisticated than those found in most credit projects and those used by many lenders at the frontier. As such, they offer a reasonable introduction to the problem of risk. They can also be easily extended to embrace a wider range of variables. A more adventurous approach to specifying debt capacity may yield greater opportunities for profitable innovation. Many of these possibilities are closely related to the term structure of credit markets. Selective extensions of lenders' time horizons create debt capacity.

The Lender's Time Horizon: Single Maturity Loans

Minimum repayment capacity for any given bad year differs from long run repayment capacity. The lender may be willing to accept uncertainty arising from loan repayments that exceed the borrower's minimum annual repayment capacity. For example, some lenders may be willing to accept delays in the recovery of principal as long as interest is being paid on balances outstanding. This approach reflects the comfort created for the lender by borrowers' efforts to service debt even while in difficulty, and the fact that payment of interest on arrears protects the lenders' income. Using this strategy, a loan of $750 could be made based on the data in Table 12.1, because interest at 20 percent, amounting to $150, could be paid in the bad year. This approach apparently assumes that the borrower will be able to reestablish operations at the normal level following the bad year without receiving additional credit, which may not be the case. In the example in Table 12.1, however, the borrower could have substantial savings capacity, as uncommitted cash flow leaps from $500 without the project to more than $1,600 with the project (line I), permitting accumulation to cushion the impact of adversity.

An alternative is found in loan contracts that permit conversion of short-term loans into medium-term loans in an adverse year.[3] To enlarge upon the example in Table 12.1, assume that the lender can take a longer point of view and that an area typically experiences one bad year, one good year, and three normal years every five years. Lending decisions responding to the five-year cycle could fix loan size so that sufficient repayment capacity exists in a normal year to permit the full repayment of the amount falling due during a normal year plus full or partial repayment of overdue or converted amounts from a previous, adverse year.

The example in Table 12.2 is based on repayment capacity calculated in Table 12.1, line I. The lender advances $995 in seasonal production credit

---

3. A practice of this type is found in crop production loans issued by primary agricultural credit societies in India. It is not clear, however, whether normal year credit limits are designed to include an allowance for repayment of seasonal loans in normal years as well as additional debt from automatic rescheduling of arrears arising in a bad year.

each year, the interest charge is 20 percent of principal outstanding (which includes interest due but not collected in previous periods), and borrowers can clear arrears in four years after suffering a bad year. Arrears are reduced to zero by the end of the cycle, as shown at the bottom of the right-hand column of figures, by a final payment of $1,585, or approximately $1,600, the normal year repayment capacity.

This calculation assumes that the adverse year is the first in the sequence, will not be repeated until the entire cycle of bad, normal and good years has been completed, and that repayment capacity for the one good year in five is the same as for a normal year.

Table 12.2 Revised Debt Capacity Calculation over a Five-Year Cycle *(U.S. dollars)*

Year	Situa- tion	Repay- ment Capacity	Loan Dis- bursed	Arrears Brought Forward	Principal Amount Due	Interest at 20%	Total Due	Amount Repaid	Arrears Carried Forward
1	Adverse	150	995	0	995	199	1194	150	1044
2	Normal	1,600	995	1,044	2,039	408	2,447	1,600	847
3	Normal	1,600	995	847	1,842	368	2,210	1,600	610
4	Normal	1,600	995	610	1,605	321	1,926	1,600	326
5	Good	1,600	995	326	1,321	264	1,585	1,585	0
Totals			4,975	+		1,560	=	6,535	

Note: For presentational purposes, this example and others that follow employ the simplistic convention of back-to-back periods beginning with loan disbursement and ending with loan repayment.

Managing the Lender's Time Horizon

But, can the lender rely on unutilized repayment capacity during normal years to recover arrears or conversions from a bad year? The answer will depend upon the factors that determine debt capacity, including the flexibility of the lender. Adjustment for adversity has to reflect the lender's willingness to assume the risks of borrowers' inability to repay. The greater the lender's capacity to assume risk, the higher the credit limits the lender can offer.

Financial flexibility is created by sources of liquidity available to a lender. Liquidity, nearness to cash, is absorbed when loans due during the current year are converted to medium-term loans. Unless lenders maintain liquid reserves that can be tapped in adversity, additional liquidity is required to continue to lend in the year following the adverse year assumed in Table 12.2. The liquidity required may be especially large for deposit-based lenders if depositors make withdrawals in response to the adverse event, which decreases their income, prompting them to draw on their savings. Possible sources of new liquidity include new deposits, access to central bank advances against conversions, unutilized debt capacity against which money market instruments could be issued, or a loan portfolio sufficiently diversified by risk.

Diversification shields the lender from those types of adversity that could reasonably be expected to occur with respect to any given type of loan, which could be accommodated by relatively small adjustments in overall lending. Portfolio diversification is often difficult to achieve where agriculture accounts for a major share of the economy, where agriculture is not very diversified and where agriculture is served by specialized rather than diversified lenders.

After calculating the loan that could be issued against the borrower's repayment capacity over the five-year cycle the lender may still feel that debt capacity is in fact smaller than the repayment capacity, that annual loans of $995 involve too much risk. What if interest rates rise? What if two adverse years occur in succession? What if produce prices fall, or the government imposes produce price controls? What if a normal year turns out to be a little worse than normal? What if the supply of inputs is disrupted? What if a member of a borrower's family dies? What if...? For these reasons few lenders regard a five-year time horizon in these circumstances as prudent or practical. Some might be willing to permit rescheduling over two years for very seasoned clients only.

The decision to advance $995 anually means that debt service would absorb all normal year uncommitted cash flow, leaving no cushion. This loan size exceeds the $800 incremental input cost (line F in Table 12.1). Lenders often conclude that developing effective relationships with customers requires unutilized repayment capacity in a normal year. The borrower may encounter adversity greater than that arising from weather-price cycles. Family problems, illness or death might make a claim on cash flow and diminish farm production or increase use of hired labor. An adverse situation or an interesting opportunity might occur that would prompt the customer to seek additional funds. If no unutilized repayment capacity exists, the lender would have to decline the request. If additional funds were sought and the lender did not provide finance, the customer may borrow elsewhere, creating a senior claim and diminishing the client's relevant repayment capacity.

For these and other reasons lenders conclude that unutilized repayment capacity permits sounder relationships with borrowers by providing a cushion for contingencies or new opportunities and the risks they entail. The borrower's unutilized debt capacity obviously has value for the lender. Is it worth anything to the borrower?

The Borrower's Aversion to Debt

Borrowers frequently express risk aversion by not going into debt to the full extent of their debt capacity, a phenomenon known to economists as "internal credit rationing." By conserving their use of debt, borrowers retain flexibility. The borrower's strategy involves balancing the utility of credit in use with the "liquidity value of unused credit," or of unexhausted debt capacity.[4]

The borrower's decisionmaking is portrayed graphically in Figure 12.1. The horizontal axis represents the proportion of the borrower's debt capacity used to obtain credit. The vertical axis represents marginal costs and returns. Curve VL indicates the utility to the borrower of credit employed. VL measures the opportunity cost of debt capacity not used to raise loans, while curve UU is the liquidity value of remaining unused units of debt capacity. Curve VL declines because additional increments of credit yield lower returns than similar quantities previously employed: diminishing marginal returns apply. Curve UU rises because units of unused debt capacity have increasing utility per unit as they decrease in number.

---

4. This material, including Figure 12.1, is based on John A. Hopkin, Peter J. Barry and C.B. Baker, *Financial Management in Agriculture* (Danville, Illinois: Interstate Printers & Publishers, Inc., 1973). pp. 178-180.

The cost of borrowing includes interest, transaction costs plus flexibility sacrificed by borrowing. This sacrifice includes risk and control by the lender. Optimization occurs at C, where the return from using an incremental unit of credit beyond amount A equals the cost of using up an incremental unit of debt capacity. The lender's specification of this point for the borrower usually differs from the borrower's perception, reflecting the different interests, risks and rewards facing each party. When borrowers attempt fully to exhaust their debt capacity they are usually under extreme stress and behaving opportunisticly.

Figure 12.1 The Borrower's Aversion to Debt

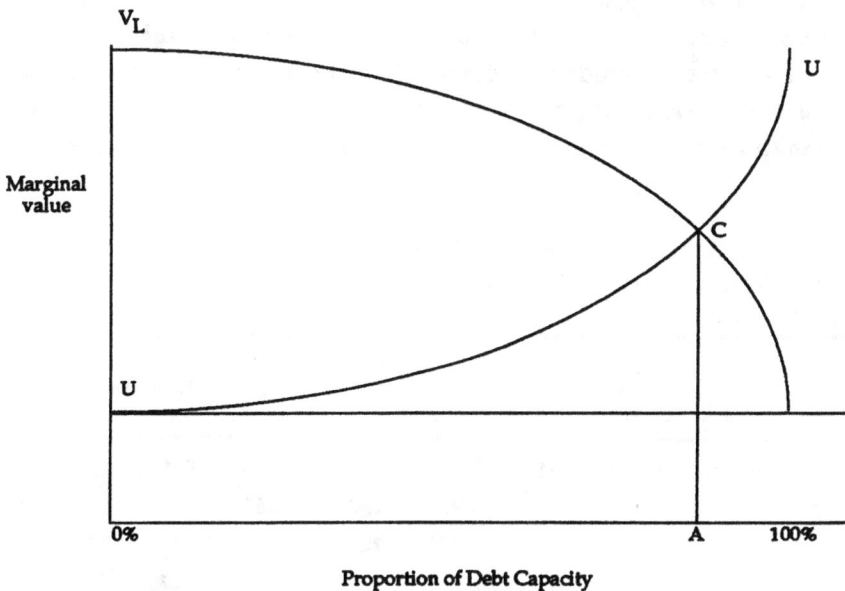

Proportion of Debt Capacity

The Lender's Time Horizon: Two Bad Years in Succession

The financial impact of the weather-price cycle is more complex than the problem of the bad year. Two bad years may occur in succession. The lender estimates that two back-to-back bad years occur once in every 20 years. This unfortunate sequence could jeopardize relations with established customers, impair the portfolio and put an imprudent lender out of business. Farmers would have no access to credit exactly when it is of greatest use to them, in the season following the two bad years when it is especially important that operations be restored to their normal level. Assuming away other contingencies, the lender makes another calculation and derives a loan size of $715, as shown in Table 12.3.

Why recover from two bad years in one five-year cycle when the probability of two adverse years in succession is only once in 20 years? Risk aversion is an adequate answer—it is easier to conduct a relationship with a borrower who is not heavily indebted over a long period. To permit the repayment cycle to go beyond five years increases the probability of encountering another adverse year that would further delay the date when the short-term debt position could be cleaned up. During that period lender and borrower both have less flexibility in accommodating events that may trouble the relationship they desire to maintain with each other. For reasons such as these the prudent lender would probably work out another model which would allow the borrower to be free of debt at the close of the fourth or third year rather than at the close of the five year weather-price cycle.

Table 12.3 Revised Debt Capacity Calculation:
Two Successive Bad Years
(U.S. dollars)

Year	Situation	Repayment Capacity	Loan Disbursed	Arrears Brought Forward	Principal Amount Due	Interest at 20%	Total Due	Amount Repaid	Arrears Carried Forward
1	Adverse	150	715	0	715	143	858	150	708
2	Adverse	150	715	708	1,423	285	1,708	150	1558
3	Normal	1,600	715	1,558	2,273	455	2,728	1,600	1128
4	Normal	1,600	715	1,128	1,843	369	2,212	1,600	612
5	Good	1,600	715	612	1,327	265	1,592	1,592	0
Totals			3,575	+		1,517	=	5,092	

Refining the Guess

Calculations and considerations such as these are novel and virtually never undertaken by project designers and employees of state-owned credit institutions in developing countries. One reason for this may be that confidence is often so low and information systems so poor that embracing a long time horizon or trying to build relationships appears terribly naive.

However, the highly formalized approach used here is not the only way of prudently determining lender exposure. Experienced lenders with a nose for risk would come to similar conclusions, and these should be encouraged. V. S. Raghavan notes that, "Evaluation of risk is...a matter of cautious judgment—perhaps no better than a guess—by an experienced manager. Even then, to make an informed guess it is desirable to institute a procedure for portfolio evaluation," which may include sector studies to determine the status and prospects for industries supported by a lender, analyses of borrowers in arrears, and periodic reviews of each client.[5] Basic valuation calculations tend to be refined in competitive financial markets and eventually become quite elaborate in response to the complexities of risk.

The Lender's Time Horizon: Medium- and Long-Term Credit

Debt capacity analysis for medium-and long-term lending uses the same approach illustrated by the seasonal credit examples in Tables 12.1-12.3. The risk-adjusted uncommitted cash flow (defined in chapter 11) for the life of the borrower's project or for the period for which the lender is willing to have funds outstanding, whichever is shorter, is the basis for the calculation. The period for which the lender is willing to have funds outstanding is a function of the lender's capital and of the lender's term structure of liabilities, which is an important ingredient in liquidity. This period always ranks ahead of the life of the borrower's project in establishing loan tenor (maturity).

For simplicity, the following term lending example uses the data provided in Table 12.1, which shows with-project repayment capacity of $1,600 in a normal year and $150 in a bad year. In this variation, repayment capacity is expected to be created by investment in fixed assets and in incremental working capital, rather than only from seasonal inputs. The question is how large a loan can be repaid over a five year period. The

---

5. V.S. Raghavan, "Some Issues Relating to Financial Policies of Development Banks," in William Diamond and V.S. Raghavan, eds., *Aspects of Development Bank Management.* (Baltimore and London: The Johns Hopkins University Press, 1982). p. 201.

answers could range from a loan size determined conservatively on the basis of the bad year repayment capacity to a larger loan size based on both adverse and normal years.

A lender making a credit decision on the minimum repayment capacity of $150 would calculate the initial advance that could be recovered from equal annual payments of $150 including principal and interest over a five year period.[6] This amount is derived using "the present worth of an annuity factor." At a 20 percent interest rate for five years this factor is 2.991, which multiplied by $150 yields a loan of $448.65, or approximately $445. The schedule of repayments on an annuity or mortgage basis would be derived from "the capital recovery factor," which is the reciprocal of the present worth of an annuity factor, or 0.334, as applied in Table 12.4. In this Table Year 0 denotes the date the loan was issued.[7] The first installment falls due 365 days later, at the end of Year 1.

Table 12.4 Repayment Schedule for a Loan of $445 at 20% Due in Five Installments
(U.S. dollars)

Year	Total Installment	Interest Due at 20%	Repayment of Principal	Principal Not Yet Due
0	-	-	-	445.00
1	148.63	89.00	59.63	385.37
2	148.63	77.07	71.56	313.81
3	148.63	62.76	85.87	227.94
4	148.63	45.59	103.04	124.90
5	149.88[a]	24.98	124.90	0
Total			**445.00**	

a. The final installment is slightly larger than $148.63 because the capital recovery factor was rounded down to three decimal points, making the first four installments smaller than the mathematically correct amount.

6. See World Bank, *Compounding and Discounting Tables for Project Evaluation.* Washington, DC: 1973. pp. 132-133, 143-144.

7. The year 0 convention separates loan receipt from the first installment, which is essential for the correct calculation of a rate of return. It also provides a better understanding of financial flows than can the simple formats used here for illustrative purposes. See Walter Schaefer-Kehnert, "Methodology of Farm Investment Analysis."

An innovative lender could work with the borrower to tailor the repayment schedule to variations in the project's expected cash flow. Considerations might include whether annual installments are appropriate—would more frequent installments be more realistic? In agricultural lending for crops, installments falling due at harvest are usually in order. In small scale industrial and commercial lending, small, frequent payments are usually most convenient because these are most easily accommodated from the borrower's cash flow. In addition, they give the lender greater information about the precise progress of the borrower and the investment, permitting more timely loan supervision.

In some cases in small scale industrial lending to new ventures it may be difficult to fix the installment schedule in advance because the prospects for the firm are so problematic. The original installment schedule should be renegotiated in these cases when experience permits formulation of reasonable debt servicing expectations based on production and sales patterns. Is an initial grace period warranted? New small scale industrial ventures may have little capacity to pay interest during construction, which should probably be capitalized until debt servicing capacity is established. Should installments be of equal size? Some projects generate large uncommitted cash flow in their early years which declines over time; others do the opposite. By considering the pattern of uncommitted cash flow the lender may be able to shape loan repayment terms to increase the borrower's debt capacity.

Dimensions of Adversity

The nature of the project and its vulnerabilities determine the assumptions about adversity to be applied to cash flow projections and the ability to service debt. Expected adversity has four dimensions: type, materiality, probability, and timing. Type refers to what is likely to go wrong. Materiality refers to the seriousness of the adverse event in terms of its impact on uncommitted cash flow and debt servicing.

Probability is the likelihood that an adverse material event will occur. In the example given in Table 12.1 the risk was fairly easily quantified by reference to local experience regarding weather cycles, but the analysis was not refined to specify very precisely how good or how bad the years might in fact turn out. All normal years were assumed to be identical, which is an oversimplification. The effect of the adverse event involved more complex considerations, however, which included yields as well as prices.

Timing refers to when adversity may be expected to occur. In established agricultural activities timing may be random, reflecting circumstances beyond the operator's control. In new ventures in agriculture and especially in small scale industry, adversity tends to appear relatively quickly as the entrepreneur struggles to bring the investment activity on stream and to enter the market.

A related aspect of adversity is whether it is general or specific. The adjustment for adversity in Table 12.1 reflects general factors, i.e., a weather-price cycle that affects many growers in much the same manner. But, adversity is also specific, affecting one farm or enterprise but not others. Examples include fires or localized pests, the death of a cow in a small herd, incapacitation of the borrower, and managerial failure to master the investment activity. The acute lender will be aware of the vulnerability of individual borrowers, of groups of borrowers, and of different types of agricultural, commercial and industrial activities. For example, the risks facing manufacturers using local raw materials and producing for local markets are often quite different from those using imported materials or producing for export. Short-run risks are higher in competitive industries than in less competitive environments, but the latter often face sharp, massive adjustments in the long run.

The importance of examining the impact of adversity is inversely related to the extent of the borrower's unutilized debt capacity. The lender should consider more closely the probability and impact of adversity on the borrower who is relatively heavily indebted than on the borrower who is only lightly in debt with lots of unused debt capacity. Lenders also devote more attention to large borrowers than to small borrowers. The large, heavily indebted borrower will be a greater cause of anxiety to the conscientious loan officer and portfolio manager than will the small, lightly indebted borrower. Loan officers increase their prospects for peace of mind by considering expected adversity in detail before issuing the loan.

Steps in Loan Decisionmaking

Calculations of debt capacity in the tables in this chapter begin with an economic activity and end with loan sizing because projects are traditionally designed in this sequence. For credit decisionmaking, however, it is usually useful to reorder the steps, taking a preliminary broad brush approach to identify possible strengths and problems in the loan application or, at the project level, in examining the feasibility of loan scheme design. In small scale industrial lending and in other cases where investment tends to be "lumpy" because of scale considerations, minimum investment size is fixed, and credit and financing decisions must be taken within this constraint.

Consider first the probability of recovering loans from whatever repayment capacity may be available. Examination of the probability of recovery usually results in an accept/reject type of decision rather than a more/less judgment. If the probability of loan recovery is low because of the applicant's character or past credit behavior, the nature of the recovery channels open to the lender, difficulties in the effective exercise of sanctions against poor payers, and in some cases the absence of a prior relationship (such as a savings account in the case of a bank or membership in the case of a cooperative), etc., the application can be rejected without further analysis. (This is not the same as rejecting the applicant, who may be a future business prospect.)

If the application survives this qualitative test, the next step is evaluating senior claims on uncommitted cash flow. Information may be solicited about other debts, production costs, land tenure arrangements, family obligations and subsistence requirements, and the applicant's assets that could satisfy senior claims in situations of adversity. If the information available indicates that the loan request is out of proportion with the borrower's financial situation, the application may be rejected. Alternatively, the lender may use the opportunity to assist the applicant to adopt a more realistic approach to the projected investment, laying the basis for a relationship based on financial counseling as well as debits and credits.

The next decision step is to ascertain the nature, probability, magnitude, and timing of adverse events that could absorb uncommitted cash flow. The final step is cash flow analysis, which specifies debt capacity by incorporating the information already reviewed in the reordered move through the analytical sequence, with verification and refinement as required.

Debt Capacity and the Lending Environment

Debt capacity is not a disembodied theoretical concept. It is created by people through markets. Debt capacity rests on a social and institutional infrastructure, and management of debt capacity requires sensitivity to the risks and possibilities of the environment in which it is created. Examples of behavior that responds to risks and possibilities include security requirements and other efforts to deal with senior claims, and the inclusiveness of debt capacity analysis.

The Role of Security

The debt capacity approach relegates security to a secondary or residual position, not as something a lender lends against. Repayment is expected to come from repayment capacity, which in personal, agricultural, commercial, and industrial lending is created by future uncommitted cash flow appropriately adjusted. However, security provides a means of recovering amounts outstanding when future repayment capacity proves insufficient because of unexpected adversity or when the relationship between creditor and debtor is beset with disappointment.

In owner-occupied housing finance, for example, loans are generally large relative to owners' cash flows. This poses risks to the relationship, which must be long term. The lender's failure to take the house as security would enable the borrower to use the asset to obtain much more debt. Therefore, clear ownership titles and the lender's ability to foreclose on defaulted mortgages are extremely important for the development of housing finance.

At the tactical level, three aspects of security should be considered in project design and loan decisionmaking: liquidity, feasibility and economy, and risk and uncertainty. Liquidity is simply the ease of conversion of security into cash at a given or expected price. In certain situations quick sale may be possible only by taking a reduced price; in others disposal may be easy and quick at the prevailing price level. Liquidity has a timing or matching dimension, too. For example, partially developed land or an immature crop may be worth only a fraction of the credit advanced based on expectations of full development.

Feasibility refers to the lender's ability to enforce and exercise rights under loan agreements or the degree of control the lender has over the security or which the lender can exert over cosigners or guarantors. Economy considerations include the cost of repossession, and of maintaining the value of security under the lender's control. Risk and uncertainty are another dimension. Does security make the lending institution more vulnerable to political interference? Does it expose the lender to pressures which might not otherwise arise? If so, what are the probable costs or effects?

Financial Links and Cushions Against Senior Claims

Examination of the borrower's situation should encompass resources that might diminish the impact of senior claims, such as savings accounts or credit balances on the lender's books. In fact, many people with relatively low incomes prefer to borrow against their savings accounts. Transaction costs are low because there is no easier loan for a banker to issue and to recover than one secured by a blocked balance in the borrower's account, and because the borrower can obtain the loan quickly. Of course the lender's accounting capabilities must be sufficient to ensure that blocked balances are not drawn.

Agricultural service cooperatives often make short-term loans to their members for seasonal inputs that are repaid by deductions from the crop delivery proceeds when the borrower delivers the crop to the cooperative after harvest. Commercial banks use a similar procedure when they place standing instructions or stop orders with buyers of farm produce such as marketing boards and their agents. The lender ascertains the levels of produce deliveries made by the applicant in the past and likely to be made in the future, estimates future produce prices, and asks the prospective borrower to instruct the buyer to make payments directly to the lender for crediting to the borrower's loan account.

It may appear that the lender who is the beneficiary of standing instructions does not have to consider senior claims on the borrower's uncommitted cash flow or the probability of recovering the loan out of repayment capacity. However, if senior claims are relatively large, borrowers may attempt to circumvent the "irrevocable" instructions they have given. Borrowers in difficulty may resort to subterfuge. One common method is to have a friend or relative deliver the crop or for the borrower to deliver the crop using an alias. Another is to exert pressure on or bribe the management or the staff of the produce buyer so that payments are not made directly to the lender.

The lender that totally disregards senior claims by not knowing borrowers' priorities suffers losses by making credit decisions solely on the size of delivery proceeds (i.e., cash revenue rather than uncommitted cash flow) and on the assumption that standing instructions will not be circumvented. Two other problems frequently occur with standing orders. One is that the produce buyer may not have sufficient accounting capability or managerial control to ensure that instructions are invariably honored. The second is that the produce buyer may delay payment because of accounting bottlenecks or insufficient liquidity. These delays reduce the lender's liquidity through no fault of the borrower.

Workable standing instructions could improve lenders' portfolios. For example, many borrowers from state-owned specialized agricultural or small business lenders in certain developing countries are government employees. Loan repayments could be made by periodic deductions from their salaries. It may be argued that civil servants or other fortunate classes should not have preferential access to credit, but they typically do. A simple response to this fact is to ensure that on loans to these borrowers the costs of loan administration and bad debt losses are kept to an absolute minimum, or that the lender's profits are as great as possible. Economies in administering these easy and relatively safe loans—repaid in monthly installments deducted at source by the government—could free the lending institution to focus its creative efforts on the frontier.

Uncommitted Cash Flow Calculation

Uncommitted cash flow calculations answer two questions: how much cash is used in a production or investment cycle, and how much is generated? Cash is what the lender demands in repayment, normally currency or its equivalent. There are two analytical decisions required to ensure the analysis is relevant: complexity and inclusiveness.

COMPLEXITY. The complexity of debt capacity analysis depends upon the borrower's operation. At the most elementary level in farm lending it can be restricted to items found in the cash budget, as in Table 12.1. However, more complex analyses are often required, as illustrated by the following qualifications. First, seasonal credit is feasible only when farm finances are cyclical. Cash income from an enterpise is not available to service debt if it is naturally absorbed by another having a different cycle. Likewise, working capital lines of credit to small firms can only be "cleaned up" or fully repaid if these borrowers' activities have a seasonal or cyclical pattern.

Second, if production is highly dependent upon physical capital owned by the operator such as machinery, irrigation facilities, processing facilities (tobacco curing sheds, milk coolers, etc.) on farms, or machinery and equipment in industry, or vehicles in transport enterprises, the periodic replacement of these assets is essential. When provisions for asset replacement and for upgrading technology are not made over the life of the asset, the operator or the creditor may suffer if additional credit for this purpose is not available when fixed assets reach the end of their useful lives.

Third, farmers may store harvested crops when the marketing system has limited capacity to absorb large quantities at harvest time, when small quantities are more easily transported, and when seasonal price fluctuations make storage worthwhile. Produce stored does not provide a means of loan repayment unless other, dependable lenders offer credit for commodities in storage. Produce stocks absorb cash, representing costs of production not yet recovered by sale of the produce. If farmers sell their produce for promises to pay in the future, sales do not immediately generate the cash required for loan repayment. Amounts due from the produce buyer absorb the farmer's cash, locking up resources until settled by cash payments. These dynamics also apply to many agroindustrial firms that exhibit seasonal production patterns that contrast with relatively steady sales throughout the year.

Use of simple cash budgets in farm credit decisionmaking is justified only in relatively underdeveloped agriculture and for relatively uncomplicated institutional arrangements. For large, modern commercial agricultural operations, uncommitted cash flow should be computed in the conventional accounting manner from balance sheets, income statements and sources and uses of funds statements. This derivation can be complex and tedious.

INCLUSIVENESS AND COMPREHENSIVENESS OF LENDING MODELS. Debt capacity may be specified for an activity such as a crop (enterprise), for a business such as a farm consisting of several enterprises, and for the borrower or owner. But what determines the appropriate focus for decisionmaking? Under credit need strategies selection of the unit of analysis is simple, corresponding to the unit for which credit need is identified, be it crop, farm, or household. But the debt capacity approach is based on sources of repayment. So that no material factors are overlooked, the debt capacity of the borrower or owner offers the broadest base for analysis. However, analytical economy, the drive to reduce transaction costs, creates incentives for considering alternatives.

The debt capacity of the borrower or of the principals is the most useful analytical base for family farms and other small businesses. Where a personal guarantee is given as security, the guarantor's debt capacity should be examined. Credit analysis for loans to large, commercial farms organized as corporations, partnerships or cooperatives usually focuses on the debt capacity of the business organization. But if the lender and the borrower have an excellent, information-rich relationship and the application is for a small loan or small additional loan, enterprise debt capacity may be sufficient to justify the loan.

Debt capacity should not be calculated in isolation for an enterprise that is part of a chain or complex of enterprises on the farm. For example, cash flow analysis of a commercial dairying operation should include the cash costs of growing fodder crops to support the dairy enterprise. If dairy fodder is a by-product of some other enterprise the cash costs of its production do not have to be included, although the impact on the cost of feed from adversity suffered by the fodder-producing enterprise should be considered. Representative per hectare, per tree or per head of livestock budgets may be useful as benchmarks or comparators for lenders oriented toward debt capacity.

Debt Capacity: A Useful Development Concept

The simple examples and qualifications in this chapter demonstrate that debt capacity is a sound approach—in fact, the only sound approach—to determining loan size once the fundamental aspects of credit use and risk are determined. They also show that there is no purely objective answer to the question of how much to lend. The lender can make good decisions only by considering the factors relevant to each case. This demands judgment. Successful loan officers have a "feel" for customers and their businesses or farms that is built from experience, which always includes learning from mistakes. This feel is to lending what the farmer's feel for land, crops and livestock is to farming. Because of their specialized knowledge, farmers know what to plant, where to plant, when to plant, and how to plant to ensure their survival.

Debt capacity strategy delivers well structured loans. Well structured loans are workable, while poorly structured loans accumulate arrears or require renegotiation or adjustments in terms to remain current. Debt capacity analysis directly addresses the central problem of lending at the frontier. That problem is not simply how to ensure that loans can be recovered. Rather, it is knowing how much credit can safely be provided to a borrower, how the interests of both parties to a credit transaction can be served and protected by appropriate loan terms, and—most importantly—how much more credit can be provided without unacceptable risk when a borrower is in difficulty and unable to repay balances falling due. When these issues are mastered, loan recovery recedes to its proper position as only one of the several problems of debt finance.

Wherever confidence has to be assessed, no decisionmaking tool or model, however inclusive or complex, is a substitute for judgment. Credit decisionmaking remains an art. However, debt capacity analysis identifies factors that all too frequently render official credit ineffective and financially unviable and economically unenviable at the frontier. At the very least, the analytical steps provide a check list of things to be considered by decisionmakers at all levels.

Loan officers should have the authority to use debt capacity analysis to improve decisionmaking and loan portfolio performance and to avoid embarrassing frontier clients by lending them into a hole. Senior managers of a credit institution can use the approach to identify ways to increase the debt capacity of borrowers and to expand the quality and quantity of financial services offered. In this respect, debt capacity analysis permits informed risk taking and innovation by lenders because it quantifies critical factors. It provides decisionmakers with flexibility to weigh alternatives and helps them to refine their own preferences regarding risk and earnings.

Debt capacity analysis can help management to forecast the impact of a bad year or other adverse event on liquidity and on portfolio performance. This should facilitate examination of alternative strategies for maintaining the level of service offered to clients in the period immediately following adversity. If a lender has the flexibility to go beyond the limit specified by minimum repayment capacity, debt capacity analysis provides a tool for estimating the level of arrears that may be reasonably expected to accumulate in the portfolio.

For development planners and project designers debt capacity analysis can ensure that credit is provided on a realistic scale and that the project has a reasonable probability of success. Debt capacity is a development parameter and planners should work to increase it. Debt capacity also provides a common window on both formal and informal finance. It can help to integrate planners' and project designers' views of the roles of each of these financial market components. Understanding how debt capacity is created informally yields insights that could facilitate innovations in formal finance.

Finally, debt capacity assists performance evaluation. The debt capacity perspective says that the accumulation of arrears over the long run which appears to characterize so many government-owned credit institutions in developing countries is not the result of unattractive returns in agriculture, inappropriate technology, inadequate rainfall, illiteracy, natural disasters, poverty, and many other factors often invoked to explain poor portfolio performance. The debt capacity perspective says that the lender and project designer must tailor their innovation or intervention to the conditions that prevail in the markets in which they operate. These conditions include adversity, senior claims on borrowers' uncommitted cash flows, and factors that diminish the chance of recovering cash available for loan repayment. To deal successfully with these variables, designers have to know precisely how their projects may fail: "the failure not anticipated is a clear indication of improper design."[8]

When no attempt or inadequate attempts are made to quantify the impact of events and situations that may reasonably be expected to occur, the lender or project designer gets in the way of development. Portfolio deterioration over the long run indicates that debt capacities have been overestimated. Responsibility rests squarely on the lender and on the project designer.

---

8. Henry Petroski, *op. cit.* p. 209.

13

PRINCIPLES FOR RESPONSIVE INTERVENTION AT THE FRONTIER

Physicians are guided by the ethics of their profession to "do no harm." This instruction was formalized more than 2,000 years ago by the Greeks. Engineers may lose their licenses and their clients when a structure collapses because load factors were incorrectly calculated or design included insufficient provisions for unusual stresses.[1] Engineering standards also have ancient roots.

Designers of development and structural adjustment projects are members of a newer profession that has few clear guidelines or standards relevant to financial development. The internal rate of return serves as a major decision criterion for projects in many sectors. It was traditionally applied to credit projects incorrectly by projecting returns to those receiving loans, as explained in chapters 3 and 7. The effects of fungibility are now better understood and most credit project designers no longer make claims about the rates of return likely to be realized by ultimate borrowers or subprojects. But, effort is seldom made to project the impact of the project on the financial institution lending project funds.

In this void, promoters of credit projects bring boundless enthusiasm to trying to get the poor into debt while generally failing to deal with the ensuing credit risk, which is rarely borne by the international or government agency designing the project. This occurs with the unswerving conviction that credit projects and financial adjustment projects, designed according to no particular financial standards or under ill-defined and unrealistic financial guidelines, promote development. Yet, "the principal objective of the design process is obviating failure."[2]

---

1. Henry Petroski, *op. cit.*
2. *Ibid.* p. 163.

Can standards be devised that would enable financial project designers to meet the socially useful types of tests to which medical practitioners and planners of the built environment are subjected? The answer of course is "Yes," and the solution requires no more than the common sense underlying physicians' objectives and engineering standards. The starting point for the search is a review of conditions at the frontier of formal finance. Two are especially important. One is the small repayment capacity of many prospective borrowers. The second is the inevitable risk of innovation and its implications for the health of frontier financial intermediaries. This chapter offers two specific responses to these problems. These prescriptions follow the general instruction given in chapter 11 that intervention should create confidence.

Responses to Low Repayment Capacity

In many cases adversity and senior claims leave only a very small amount of liquidity for servicing debt, as shown in Table 12.1. Earlier chapters outlined ways of lending around these obstacles for intermediaries possessing creative flexibility. Some intermediaries possess only a small degree of creative flexibility because of unaccommodating cost structures; inappropriate asset, liability and capital structures; traditions of passivity, possibly including government procedures and work rules; and narrow, shallow financial markets in which they make their loans and raise their resources. These intermediaries will often have difficulty responding meaningfully to situations where debt service capacity is very small.

How small is too small? Every intermediary has its own definition or threshold. For a large merchant banking development finance institution, a risk-adjusted repayment capacity equivalent to US$10,000 a year may be small and not regarded as a worthwhile prospect. For intermediaries with lower costs, such as certain commercial or cooperative banks, amounts below US$1,000 may be small and beyond the range of attractive business. Credit unions and agricultural service cooperatives may be able to deal with US$100 per year propositions, while informal arrangements such as RoSCAs, for example, intermediate where risk-adjusted repayment capacity is only US$10 per year.

The Borrower Criterion

All financial intermediaries and all financial market segments have threshold minimum loan sizes. Efforts to push the frontier often attempt to leap these lower boundaries without addressing the factors that determine them. This tendency is dangerous because it compromises the financial viability of intermediaries and hence requires a guideline or rule to govern well-intentioned intervention. This rule may be called the Borrower Criterion:

> Where the risk-adjusted repayment capacity of prospective borrowers is very small, credit from the contemplated source is unlikely to be an appropriate developmental response. In this situation project designers have two alternatives. The first is to locate intermediaries offering different instruments to which the repayment capacity of the prospective borrowers does not seem very small. This will often be impossible because of narrow markets, unwilling intermediaries and donor requirements, in which case other means to increase repayment capacity at the frontier are generally more productive, more equitable, and cheaper than credit. The second alternative consists of locating these other means.

The "need creed" or traditional view leads to precisely the opposite conclusion: the poor especially should be helped with credit, the more the better. Advocates could cite the case of the Grameen Bank, presented in chapter 10, to justify pushing on with the traditional credit-led strategy. Indeed, innovation as radical as the Grameen Bank's lending instrument and its market niche appears to contradict the position that where repayment capacity is very small, provision of credit is probably not the best way of enlarging it.

Contradiction is not refutation. Innovations such as Grameen Bank are extremely unusual. *These innovations are not likely to be originated in government projects or in projects supported by foreign assistance,* whether public or private, as demonstrated by experience since the 1960s. Origination is not likely because the incentives accompanying official or foreign sponsorship are unlikely to be appropriate. Those responsible for project design do not generally bear a full commercial risk or embrace commercial expectations and standards of performance, and they are too removed from the poor to have sufficient information to allow them to innovate successfully. Agencies implementing these projects may not be doing so voluntarily, and may also not apply commercial performance standards to these operations.

Exceptions may occur in a few small privately funded experiments that do little damage when they fail. But, few successful cases of this type exist, as noncommercial motivations frequently drive these efforts. Those that are successful commercially often remain largely outside the replicable mainstream for many years because of the nature of their sponsorship, which may be centered on an exceptional personality or a religious or moral motive expressed to a high, refined degree that is difficult to replicate widely. Both Raiffeisen and Yunus were outsiders working on their own, and both had to circumvent established systems and design unique structures to see their concepts flower. Yet, after almost 15 years, no one has successfully replicated Grameen Bank.

Replication of stunning innovation is something that official or foreign-assisted projects may be able to do, but probably not at an early stage of an innovation's development when flexibility and entrepreneurial management are essential to ensure responsive adaptation and efficient refinement. At the early stages it is unwise to create a bandwagon effect by putting massive assistance behind a relatively untried, immature financial instrument. Also, it is not clear that an innovative model such as Grameen Bank is widely replicable or that even occasional replication could achieve the results the original has achieved in Bangladesh. Each innovative model responds to a specific set of situations which may differ significantly from those on other frontiers. A niche in one market is, unfortunately, often irrelevant in another. Fecundity in imitating the form of one franchise does not ensure fertility in recreating its substance, as cooperative history demonstrates.

The realization that credit is often not an appropriate initial thrust for intervention leads to consideration of alternative means of creating debt capacity. Another point in favor of broadening the alternatives for assistance is that credit typically reaches relatively few members of the target group. It assaults the frontier selectively, usually in favor of those who are relatively attractive because they pose low credit risk, who impose relatively low transaction costs on lenders, and who may have political influence. Broader initiatives, listed below, however, can benefit many members of the community whether or not they are eligible for or obtain credit. These alternatives are presented as extensions of the debt capacity approach, as means of creating debt capacity.

Intervene to Create Sustainable Debt Capacity

Creation of debt capacity is the second objective of developmental intervention in finance, following the creation of confidence. Debt capacity is borrowing power. It is created by a loan applicant's estimated future debt service capacity and is equal to the amount of credit this capacity can command in financial markets. Creation of sustainable debt capacity is a valid objective for intervention. Its validity arises because debt capacity at the frontier is typically small, and because sustainable financial relationships are beneficial to depositors and borrowers, contribute to intermediary capital, and expand financial markets.

Debt capacity is created in many ways, giving project designers a tremendous range of alternatives that include indirect as well as direct measures to increase it. The following paragraphs list a number of areas in which economic planners and project designers could, with skill and luck, intervene to create debt capacity. Effective measures change the environment in such a way that credit becomes available and is attracted to target group activities. These changes can occur in nonfinancial markets as well as in financial markets. Some involve large investment costs, while others can be secured by a stroke of the pen once a policy consensus is reached. In each case, project designers should work to ensure that the benefits justify the costs and that the impact on financial institutions is positive.

HOW NONFINANCIAL INITIATIVES CREATE DEBT CAPACITY. One way of creating debt capacity is through *technological innovation* that increases uncommitted cash flow or diminishes the impact of adversity at the frontier. This is the strategic centerpiece of agricultural development projects and of much DFI lending to industry. *Physical infrastructure* can also increase debt capacity. Roads that expand access to markets, for example, reduce transport costs, which may lower the cost of goods in formerly remote areas and raise the prices paid to producers in these areas. Telephone, telegraph, radio, and postal systems reduce information costs. Improvements in storage techniques and facilities permit increased control over the timing and prices at which produce is sold and inputs are purchased, and greater control over produce quality. Recent information from Bangladesh indicates that infrastructure investment has much greater positive effects that have often been assumed, and that these include social equity.[3]

Likewise, *price policy reforms* may create debt capacity. Price controls may govern the costs of land, labor, and capital. Examples include commodity prices kept low to subsidize consumers, which also keep farm incomes and repayment capacity low. Minimum wage legislation may raise the costs of hiring labor, destroying employers' debt capacity. Decontrol of interest rates should increase access to formal credit for reasons discussed in previous chapters.[4]

Institutional measures outside financial markets affect debt capacity. Nonprice efforts to regulate markets can have an important impact on repayment capacity. For example, monopsony buyers of produce and monopoly input supply systems may offer services that would not otherwise be available, but in other situations they may work against farmers by denying them competitive prices. In addition, contract law and law enforcement are often overlooked in credit project design. Poor loan repayment by borrowers weakens the effectiveness of contract law, raising lending and borrowing costs. Land tenure is closely related to debt capacity. Security of tenure reduces lender's risk, and tenure arrangements influence the operator's incentive to invest. Improvements in lenders' rights in security, enabling them to realize collateral, also increase debt capacity.

Education, extension services, and training for farmers, traders, artisans and other entrepreneurs at the frontier can create debt capacity by reducing risk to the borrower and by reassuring lenders that the technical basis of a borrower's operation is sound. Collective guarantees and aggregation of repayment capacity through farmer or craft organizations may also enhance debt capacity, although efforts in this area have generally proved unviable in developing countries.

An institutional measure that appears to be of great importance for expanding the frontier is a group approach that includes the self-management and close social bonds which characterize RoSCAs. Group

---

3. Raisuddin Ahmed and Mahabub Hossain, "Developmental Impact of Rural Infrastructure in Bangladesh." Research Report 83. Washington, DC: International Food Policy Research Institute, October 1990, in collaboration with the Bangladesh Institute of Development Studies, Dhaka.

4. R.H. Schmidt and Erhard Kropp, eds., *op. cit.* p. 53.

organization was instrumental in giving European farmers access to term credit in the seed and fertilizer revolution of the second half of the 19th century through Raiffeisen credit unions, and later in Japan, Korea, and Taiwan. It has also achieved promising results in Malawi, where group credit for farm inputs has been used in development projects,[5] and by Grameen Bank in Bangladesh as described in chapter 10.

This approach is being promoted elsewhere and is a major emphasis of West German assistance to low income countries, as detailed by R. H. Schmidt and Erhard Kropp in *Rural Finance: Guiding Principles,* the most cogent document on rural finance to emerge from development assistance agencies in recent years.

Credit groups are not, however, a simple solution to the problems of credit programs because confidence, a necessary condition for their success, is not always present and is difficult to build. Kilby and D'Zmura note that successful group lending requires "a well-defined, coherent group; a highly profitable market situation [favoring the group activity] and a technically simple, loan-financed asset that is invulnerable to mismanagement."[6]

Small scale industrial and commercial ventures frequently encounter a range of government-produced obstacles to start up and expansion. Several business and trading licenses may be required to start a business, and all may be difficult to obtain quickly. Importing may require tremendously complex paperwork. Access to electricity, water and telephone lines may involve delays measured in years, in part because state-owned power, water and telecommunications authorities do a poor job of billing and collecting for services rendered those already connected. These problems constrict these utilities' cash flows and their ability to expand. Poorly paid, corrupt officials have a vested interest in restricting service and opposing introduction of streamlined procedures, better power distribution and improved telecommunications technology. Their capacity to command bribes adds to the cost of operating a business. Reforms in the administration of government regulations, enterprises and "services" may

---

5. Walter Schaefer-Kehnert, "Success with Group Lending in Malawi," in J. D. Von Pischke, Dale W Adams and Gordon Donald, eds., *op. cit.* pp. 278-283.
6. Peter Kilby and David D'Zmura, *op. cit.* p. 121. Parenthetical statement added.

reduce costs greatly and produce private responses that yield tremendous financial, economic and social benefits at the frontier.[7]

Institutional measures within financial markets can also increase frontier debt capacity. Staff training and better accounting and controls should increase efficiency in financial institutions, making them more interested in developing new business. Decentralization of decisionmaking accompanied by increased incentives for and accountability of loan officers may expand access to credit and make loan terms and conditions more responsive to local conditions and borrowers' situations, offering a basis for constructing a market niche. In certain instances increased remuneration for employees of government-owned lenders may be necessary to reduce staff turnover and contribute to efficient operations. A more effective alternative may be privatization, possibly in ways that make shareholders out of depositors, borrowers, and staff.

How Financial Initiatives Create Debt Capacity. Financial measures and innovations can increase debt capacity by lengthening term structures of financial markets, by reducing transaction costs from expanding the services of intermediaries, by refining valuation processes through designing more flexible lending and repayment terms, and by increasing the supply of loanable funds by mobilizing local resources, and external assistance. These effects often overlap, as the following examples suggest.

Lengthening the term structure of financial markets should be especially beneficial to agriculture and small scale industry. But many countries are beset by great uncertainty, high and variable rates of inflation, low interest rate policies, and deficiencies that increase the cost of access to legal systems and enforcement practices that discourage long-term financial contracts. This works against investments that have long gestation periods. Land reclamation, drainage, irrigation, pasture development, tree crops, terracing, and other capital improvements in agriculture frequently have long asset conversion cycles, with slow cash flows that cannot quickly reproduce the initial investment. In industry, financial markets' short term structures can retard investment in relatively large, lumpy assets. Lengthening term structures, which increases the supply of term credit, can

---

7. Hernando de Soto, *op. cit.*

greatly expand debt capacity because cumulative cash flow normally increases as the repayment period lengthens.

Term structures lengthen primarily through the voluntary responses of financial market participants. These responses can be encouraged when government faces the very difficult task of creating the confidence that is the fundamental requirement for long time horizons. Government stimulation for the development of secondary markets for long-term instruments and of money markets can lengthen time horizons because these markets mobilize resources and create liquidity for term lenders. Secondary markets give intermediaries more flexibility in asset/liability management, diminishing the mismatching risks of term lending.

Expanding the lending services of intermediaries may also increase debt capacity. For example, the lender that provides only medium- or long-term loans is in an unfavorable situation, as suggested in chapter 5. Contacts with borrowers begin with intensive start-up periods while loan applications are processed and funds are disbursed, but then decline markedly as interactions are limited to periodic repayments by borrowers. In some cases the borrower is expected to visit the lenders' office once a year to make an annual loan payment. This relationship is too limited to build a good understanding of the borrower's business on the part of the lender or of the lender's expectations on the part of the borrower. Monthly or other installment schedules may be helpful to borrowers whose cash flows are relatively uniform throughout the year, while also enabling the lender to supervise loans more effectively. Such a lender may increase service to clients by offering short-term loans. Experience accumulated through lending on different terms provides information that makes it possible for the lender to have greater confidence in borrowers and more information about their use of finances.

Flexible lending and repayment terms increase the debt capacity of borrowers. Tables 12.2 and 12.3 demonstrated how flexible terms refine valuation processes and enable lenders to exceed limits based on minimum repayment capacity for clients in whom they have great confidence. This frequently occurs in competitive financial markets, with implicit or explicit arrangements for rescheduling debt servicing obligations in response to adversity. The amount of money that the lender is prepared to tie up in arrears or rescheduled loans determines how much credit the lender can offer above the limit of minimum repayment capacity.

While flexible lending terms increase debt capacity, farm credit is often rationed on a per hectare, a per tree, or a per animal basis. These rules of thumb minimize lenders' costs of dealing with large numbers of farmers. Such cost-saving efforts are especially attractive to lenders when interest rates are low, because they reduce the lender's transactions costs. They may also shield lenders to some extent from excesses by incompetent or corrupt loan officers. This form of lending, however, may not be optimal for development. Farmers with great potential are given the same per unit credit limits as others, while the limits may in fact be too high for some borrowers to handle adequately.

Obtaining flexibility is often difficult without decentralized credit decisionmaking based on loan officers' knowledge of their borrowers' operations. Inflexible systems limit borrowers' and branch officers' participation in credit decisions, consistent with top-down strategies. Flexibility could give officers a greater incentive to develop their skills, but could require greater accountability and controls over their activities.

Flexibility may also be difficult in lending agencies that are limited by budget allocations rather than by their ability to mobilize deposits. This is because the scope for negotiation and competition in attracting clients is greater than in dealing with a central bank, national treasury, or aid agency.

Whither Savings Mobilization?

Deposit mobilization can be a powerful means of creating debt capacity, and is a major area for service expansion at the frontier. Deposit-taking may be especially useful in efforts to improve the performance of specialized lenders. The institution providing only credit, for example, may increase service by offering deposit account facilities. Deposit takers frequently find it relatively simple to expand into money transfer operations, further broadening their business.

Deposit services help establish a basis for long-term relationships, require performance by the deposit-taking intermediary to earn the confidence of the depositor, and give intermediaries information about the activities of their depositors. Local resource mobilization in the form of deposits increases frontier debt capacity by generating valuable information about financial behavior, which offers a basis for confidence creation. This permits responsive lending and creates incentives for businesslike behavior by both the lender and the borrower. Funds mobilized also increase debt capacity by providing a borrowing base for the depositor and a supply of loanable funds for the lender. Deposit-taking also serves more people than credit services, moving the frontier with less effort.

In spite of all these very positive features, savings mobilization should not be viewed as an easy addition to credit projects or a natural area of expansion for specialized lenders. In fact, it may not be an appropriate immediate or general objective of development projects or of development assistance agencies. The performance of credit projects and of the financial institutions that implement them in poor countries should give pause for consideration: can they effectively intervene in financial markets and can they design sustainable financial instruments? Does their inability to perform well in these respects reflect deeper problems that would lead to costly miscalculations or omissions in savings mobilization? Can those who have failed the lending test be expected to earn passing marks as deposit-takers?

The damage done by failed deposit takers can be large and politically awkward, with disastrous social consequences. It would be especially unfortunate for small savers to find that their savings had disappeared as a result of bad bookkeeping, fraud, or poor lending decisions leading to bad loans and ultimately to the failure of the institution accepting deposits. One response to this possibility is deposit insurance by governments. Yet, the risk of failure may be enhanced by government deposit insurance.

Lenders using well-insured deposits in the United States, for example, ran up an estimated US$500 billion in losses in the 1980s. These losses, roughly equal to US$2,000 per American citizen, or to the combined GDPs of Canada and Mexico, will ultimately be paid by American taxpayers. Lenders concluded that their risks of business failure were reduced by deposit insurance. Depositors had little reason to care about the financial health of the institutions that held their savings. This combination created perverse incentives which helped attract incompetent and unscrupulous individuals to the savings and loan industry, where these losses were most heavily concentrated. Insider transactions compounded unsound lending. Directors of some savings and loan associations paid for and obtained political favors, and the savings and loan industry had political influence. Their losses outran their capital, and the government deposit insurance funds were saddled with a large part of the loss. A number of people had gone to jail and many cases were pending as of 1991.

All this happened in a rich democracy with a highly developed legal system, easy access to the courts, a literate and numerate population, a well-respected accounting profession, and government supervision of financial institutions. In many countries there is no formal deposit insurance system, and deposit insurance is hardly needed where deposit-takers are owned by the government. Where deposit-taking is conducted by private, domestic institutions that do not have government insurance, there is usually an expectation or assumption that sooner or later the government will make good any losses of depositors' funds. So whether or not there is deposit insurance, it seems reasonable to assume that in many countries a dollar, riyal, pound, peso, or rupee mobilized in a savings account could someday result in a charge to the government treasury and ultimately to taxpayers equal to some fraction of a dollar, riyal, pound, peso, or rupee. This will occur where deposit-takers make bad loans that produce losses that exceed their capital.

The conclusion to be drawn from recent experience with failed deposit-takers is that institutional sustainability requires a high quality of lending and capital adequate to bear the risks of intermediation. Thus, deposit-taking is not a panacea for poorly-performing lenders. The first order of business in improving their performance should be reform of their lending operations, not the addition of deposit-taking. Before deposit-taking is introduced, capital should be sufficient to protect the interests of depositors. It is also important to realize that international standards of capital adequacy, such as capital equal to 8 percent of risk-adjusted assets, are not necessarily adequate at the frontier or in financial environments that are generally harsh. High risk loan portfolios require a larger capital base than low risk ones. Separate evaluations of risk should be made and separate capital adequacy standards determined for each financial institution at the frontier.

Safeguarding Lenders

Do projects create sustainable value for the participating financial intermediaries (PFIs) that make loans to project beneficiaries and assume the credit risk of project activities? This is an important question because, as a general rule, an institution lending project funds will not be developed by project activities that weaken its financial position. To ensure that project activities contribute to growth and soundness, the impact of a project on PFIs should be quantified in project design and monitored throughout implementation.

Measuring project impact on PFIs is important because the costs and risks of lending at the frontier under the typical project format are substantial. Interest rates are usually close to those charged by commercial banks on loans to their best customers, average administrative overheads frequently amount to 20 percent of amounts loaned, while repayment rates in the 70 and 80 percent range tie up significant amounts of lender liquidity in arrears. Bad debt loss experience has not been systematically monitored, but analyses show that these often exceed 2 percent of principal disbursed and interest earned by the PFI, and may reach more than 90 percent.[8]

These characteristics require close attention to loan pricing. Appropriately priced loans should be remunerative to the lender. This requires fees and interest charges that cover the cost of funds, administrative expenses related to the lending operation, risk represented primarily by bad debt losses, and that generate a profit that permits and motivates the lender to expand operations.

Impact Measures

Two measures quantify project impact on a PFI's financial position, as explained in detail in chapter 14. The first is the residual net worth (RNW) or retained earnings the project produces for the intermediary. The RNW criterion is met when the final project balance sheet shows that (a) the intermediary's outstanding contribution to the project is nil, having been fully recovered, and (b) the sum of retained earnings plus any project grants received is positive. A project that contributes to the intermediary's net worth leaves the intermediary financially stronger for having participated in the project. Residual net worth is a distant, undiscounted figure, but estimates of RNW can of course be made at any time.

The second criterion of project acceptability is that the project have an inflation-adjusted positive net present value (NPV) to the PFI at the cost of all funds used in project implementation. This analysis answers the

---

8. See, for example, Leila Webster, *op. cit.*, and Table 7.1. The sector dealt with in this paper reportedly has a better repayment performance than all others in the World Bank's portfolio (e.g., large scale industry, agriculture, housing, etc.).

question whether the project is worthwhile to the intermediary. NPV is used rather than the rate of return primarily because of typical patterns of flows in credit projects. Many credit projects involve annual net flows to the intermediary which are negative in the project disbursement period when disbursements to subborrowers occur prior to reimbursement to the PFI from project funds, then positive in the middle years of the intermediary's project loan as disbursements for project activities wind down and subloan collections exceed debt service on the project loan, and finally again negative in the latter part of the project life as subloan bad debt losses accumulate and as debt service on the project loan erodes the float accumulated during the middle years. This juxtaposition of negative and positive flows yields multiple rates of return, all of which are mathematically valid. NPV calculations are preferable because they are not subject to the possibility of an indeterminant result.

Use of both indicators, RNW and NPV, is important because neither fully demonstrates financial performance. Each measures a separate dimension of impact, and the results achieved in each are not necessarily consistent. A project with a high NPV, for example, could ultimately bankrupt an intermediary because distant but catastrophic losses are deeply discounted in NPV analysis. These could be overwhelmed mathematically by early, positive flows that are far less discounted. Projects that create a large residual net worth could likewise theoretically exhibit a pattern of flows having a negative net present value, which indicates they constitute an unremunerative use of funds relative to others yielding a return equal or superior to the discount rate used in the NPV calculation. In view of this problem, satisfactory performance obviously requires both a positive NPV and RNW.

Use of Impact Measures Over the Project Cycle

These two impact quantification criteria apply to all stages of the project cycle. Institutional impact is a major, if largely unrecognized, project design variable. Projected impact measurement should begin at the initial or identification stage of the project cycle, and refinement of project design and quantification of estimated impact should be interactive steps in planning. Important variables for which estimates are required include the cost of funds, rates of credit flows including loan and subloan issue and repayment, and associated administrative costs.

As design is refined through project preparation and appraisal, impact quantification has to be revised accordingly. During project implementation, actual data replace future performance estimates and provide a basis for new projections. During implementation NPV and RNW yield insights for modifying lending strategies, correcting subloan pricing, and guiding subloan administration. When the project is completed, in the sense that all project credit and associated cost flows have occurred, impact measurement is ideally based entirely on actual data. "Ideally" because record keeping may be deficient and because administrative costs may be difficult to allocate, requiring assumptions by the analyst.

If either the residual net worth or the net present value of the project is negative, project participation is not financially worthwhile for the PFI. Negative *ex ante* results warrant redesign. RNW and NPV analyses assist redesign by facilitating the testing of alternative values for key variables that determine impact.

In those cases where the project does not appear likely to remunerate the credit agency adequately for its participation, project design should be modified to protect the intermediary's net worth and to provide an activity with a positive NPV. Options include revised interest rates, search for lower cost intermediaries, greater and better technical assistance and supervision, a grant for project implementation, and contractual arrangements for reimbursement by the government for losses incurred by the intermediary for its participation in the project. If the enthusiasm for lending is greater than the enthusiasm for the original target group, redefining the target group may also benefit the intermediary by decreasing lending overheads and risks. But often these alternatives are not feasible and developmental energies should be channeled away from credit and finance to activities outside the financial sector.

The second rule for responsive intervention is the Intermediary Criterion:

> Where a credit project or intervention is unlikely to produce a positive residual net worth and positive net present value for intermediaries making subloans from project funds and assuming credit risk, project designers have two alternatives. The first is to locate more effective intermediaries offering different instruments. This will often be impossible because of narrow markets, unwilling intermediaries and donor requirements, in which case credit should be discarded as a development tool and other means should be

explored to achieve broad developmental objectives. The second alternative consists of locating these other means.

The Debt Capacity Perspective

Misplaced concern for credit need and other bankrupt approaches listed in Part II leads to excessive emphasis on increasing the supply of loanable funds. In contrast, the debt capacity perspective emphasizes improvement in the operations of financial markets. First, it views credit as one of many means of stimulating investment, not as a tool for working against basic economic signals perceived by farmers, small businesses and private lenders. For example, credit would not be used to promote technologies with attractive normal year returns but with risks beyond the capacity of borrowers to manage effectively.

Second, the viability of financial intermediaries is important because nonviable institutions serve the community poorly and do not respond meaningfully to risk. Viability in the financial sector is measured in financial terms; the financial health of intermediaries should be of paramount concern. The debt capacity approach requires measurement at all stages in the project cycle of the extent to which financial institutions are, or could be, strengthened financially.

Third, financial intermediation is a process consisting of value, risk, and relationships. The developmental objective is to improve the process in order to mobilize and allocate resources more effectively. Under the debt capacity approach the primary importance now accorded the amount of credit delivered is replaced by attention to indicators of the vitality of financial intermediation. These variables include access to and delivery costs of financial services, risk premia, real interest rates, the service mix of institutions, and the return to investments in the financial sector. The function of financial markets is to develop and exploit debt capacity: debt capacity created is a proxy for development. Those whose debt capacity increases enjoy more value.

14

MEASURING THE RESULTS
OF EFFORTS TO EXPAND THE FRONTIER

"Credit is self-evaluating. It either comes back or it doesn't." This observation by Hank Jackelen of the United Nations Capital Development Fund illustrates the reality underlying credit projects and markets. While this basic fact can be simply stated, the issues involved are complex. They are particularly so when promoters assign to credit a weighty agenda that goes beyond financial market considerations and possibly even leaves them behind.

This concluding chapter provides a framework for determining the effectiveness of policies and projects that attempt to create value at the frontier. It begins with a review and elaboration of the concept of the frontier and a discussion of the importance of good loans. It goes on to explain how performance information is gathered. Then the discussion turns to determining impacts of credit projects and policies on borrowers of project funds and on their activities, on financial institutions, on financial markets, and on the economy.

The Frontier Revisited

The concept of the frontier provides a framework for measuring the impact of projects and policies implemented in or through the financial sector. The frontier is defined as the limit of the activities of formal financial institutions. Preceding chapters present simple illustrations of the limitations of the formal sector in creating value for poor people, small farmers, and small businesses.

Projects and policies in the financial sector influence transactions, instruments and institutions. Financial markets are created by transactions including credit, equity or risk capital, and guarantees or insurance, all of which are promises. These promises are bought and sold in financial markets, creating value for their issuers. Expansion of the frontier occurs when participants' transactions costs are reduced and when new instruments and services are offered. Transactions are conducted by buying and selling financial instruments, which define the content of transactions. Financial institutions such as banks, credit unions, insurance companies, and those who sell goods on credit process transactions and support the delivery of formalized financial instruments.

Instruments and institutions that assault the frontier must be innovative and sustainable to be successful. Sustainability does not require an infinite life or constantly increasing market share, but rather that innovation be remunerative to the intermediary and the client.

Innovation is more intricate. It carries a risk of failure, and may even *require* failure: "No one *wants* to learn by mistakes, but we cannot learn enough from successes to go beyond the state of the art."[1] But in credit markets the capacity to endure failure is small. On a technical level, limited capacity occurs because of the relatively small amount of risk capital supporting transactions in competitive markets and the fine margins that make it difficult for intermediaries in these markets to accumulate risk capital. Where markets are not competitive, innovation, which is cost-reducing, is likely to be slow. Capital to support the extraordinary risk-taking required for innovation is also unlikely to be generated rapidly in noncompetitive markets. Inefficiency in intermediation inflates costs without necessarily creating profits retained by intermediaries.

However, these technical inhibitors are less important than the social dimension of unsustainable transactions and institutions: failure destroys confidence, and as confidence diminishes, risk erodes value. The indestructible links between value, risk and confidence make good loans an essential objective of frontier projects and policies. This often neglected point is clarified by examining the impact of bad loans, using three categories of failure, explained below, to identify results.

First is a very small margin of creative, useful failure that has no significant adverse impact on confidence. This degree of failure is part of the cost of innovation and is financed essentially by the innovator's equity,

---

1. Henry Petroski, *op. cit.* p. 62. Petroski defends exploration of the dark side of behavior by noting that, "The rational analysis of failures...is of incalculable value" to innovative design. p. 186.

which is risk capital. It is quickly and easily corrected. Valuable experience is gained by the would-be innovator and by potential competitors from bad loans arising from innovations that fail. Losses of risk capital help redirect competitive energy in positive directions.

Second is a larger degree of failure that credit institutions and financial markets can accommodate in unusual circumstances without collapse. Bad loans that accompany this type of failure bring no more than temporary disruptions to these markets. While the failure destroys some value, a level of confidence is confirmed by the market's continued operation and eventual recovery.

Finally, a higher level of failure causes long-term damage to the ability of credit markets or institutions to grow and to perform efficiently. This type of failure overwhelms normal operations and risk management. In private financial markets, it is often accompanied by sharp and drastic changes in interest rates and in the demand for and supply of financial instruments, from which recovery is sluggish. In markets dominated by government-owned financial institutions, the impact of unsustainable failure tends to be less sharp, in part because it may be infrequently or less well measured, or not so visible. However, value is often destroyed over a longer period as services evaporate while government funds, and possibly donor support, underwrite continued inefficiencies and low levels of service that perpetuate bad loans and inadequate lending policies and procedures.

Lenders that incur no bad debt losses are obviously well inside the frontier and are unlikely to be competitive. But even the most innovative lenders should avoid bad loans that exceed the margin of creative, useful failure because these destroy value and impose other net losses on society. Even within the margin of creative failure, innovators seek to avoid bad loans: efforts to minimize them should characterize all attempts to expand the frontier. Loans that turn sour because they fund unremunerative investments in real assets misallocate resources. Loans that are bad because of deceitful behavior by borrowers raise the cost of intermediation, which taxes other users of financial services and the owners of financial institutions.

Institutions that continually and progressively issue bad loans beyond the small creative margin do not serve society well. Their behavior is antisocial because they fail to contribute to *risk management which is the most important qualitative function of financial markets*. Risk management is important to society because risk is pervasive and because it lowers the rate of investment. Purveyors of failure reduce confidence, and ultimately they are unsustainable. Can institutions that continuously issue bad loans be expected to perform well by central economic tests of performance, such as efficient resource allocation and least-cost production? Can they reasonably be expected to have decisionmaking procedures and capacities that contribute to development? Should they be entrusted with key developmental responsibilities and large volumes of funds?

These concerns demonstrate that the concept of the frontier is applicable to the development of financial markets in general. A second definition of the frontier is that it is a limit that is pierced by any financial innovation. All efforts to design new instruments and to create new roles for finance in market economies have the same requirements for success. The frontier is expanded not only where the poor and other small economic operators have their first direct, sustainable interactions with the formal financial system, but also when additional capacity for syndicating large loans is created, when new risk sharing mechanisms become available, when securitization creates liquidity and expands markets, and when new share trading procedures make stock ownership more attractive in the long run. The frontier also moves outward when new financial arrangements offer attractive opportunities to sophisticated savers, intermediaries and borrowers. And, the frontier of formal finance is not watertight—informal transactions occur among families, friends and investors who are well within this frontier, for example, and some individuals generally outside it, having no deposits with or loans from formal intermediaries, may occasionally use money orders as a form of payment or money transfer.

From this perspective, this chapter develops a framework for assessing and measuring the performance of credit projects and policies in the financial sector of less-developed economies.

Monitoring, Evaluation, and Sector Work

Efforts to promote sustainable formal finance at the frontier require a rich flow of information to facilitate responses to changing conditions and opportunities and to produce the raw material for innovation. This information is generated by monitoring and evaluation (M+E), which measures project performance, and by sector work which consists of studies of the financial sector or of its subsectors, such as the commercial banking industry, small enterprise finance or rural financial markets.

In this chapter the noun "review" is used to denote all three types of fact finding: monitoring, evaluation, and sector work. This usage is consistent with the description of management functions as planning, execution, and review. Review assists planning, and the management cycle is continuously repeated.

Monitoring is a routine function essential for good management. It is the continuous generation of performance data by management information systems (MIS) within an institution or by a project implementing agency and the use of this data to guide decisions. Monitoring may also include diagnostic studies of problem areas, but is not usually research oriented. In contrast, "evaluation is a periodic assessment of the relevance, performance, efficiency and impact of project activities" and may be conducted by parties other than those responsible for project management.[2] Evaluation uses MIS data and frequently supplements these by undertaking and interpreting research studies of special problems and opportunities.

Monitoring and evaluation of credit projects are based fundamentally on the records of the participating financial intermediaries that disburse subloans and assume credit risk. Sector studies are broader and are normally undertaken prior to intervention to help design projects or policies. The cycle of intervention and impact repeats itself, which is why sector work usually has to explore the impact of previous or existing policies and projects.

Sector studies normally contain much descriptive detail and analysis, and are issue- and policy-oriented. They are a basis for credit project design because they identify activities that projects could introduce or

---

2. Dennis J. Casley and Krishna Kumar, *Project Monitoring and Evaluation in Agriculture* (Baltimore and London: The Johns Hopkins University Press, 1987), pp. 2 ff. This book is a standard work in the field and deals with management information systems and data gathering and analysis techniques that are widely applicable. The principal modification required for their application to finance is recognition that transactions with credit project target groups include promises to pay in the future, and therefore involve a risk of loss that is qualitatively different than those that accompany, say, distribution of fertilizer to a project target group. Monitoring and evaluation are often treated as one function, a practice deplored by Casley and Kumar, who "disapprove of the use of the universal acronym 'M&E'" (p. 8). In deference to their view, this chapter uses M+E to denote these two related but separate activities.

assist. They are even more important for policy-based intervention, which includes financial sector loans and financial adjustment loans. Financial sector loans are made primarily to support government policy changes designed to increase competition in financial markets and to improve intermediaries' financial condition. These loans frequently include traditional credit project elements such as technical assistance and subloans for industrial, agricultural, or commercial purposes.

Financial adjustment loans are intended to support major policy and institutional reforms that will quickly alter the structure of financial markets. These loans are usually given following deterioration of financial markets and intermediaries' performance associated with wider macroeconomic problems and declines in a country's foreign exchange reserves.

Four Review Issues at Two Levels

This chapter offers a broad perspective on review. But why is a broad review perspective appropriate when projects by definition have highly specific, limited objectives? The principal justification is that the impact of finance is complex because of its fungibility and because of the role of money in the economy. But project-related reasons also dictate a broad search for project impact. First, projects attempt to develop and apply financial instruments to create value at the frontier. Accordingly, project M+E is essentially instrument- or transaction-based, offering a window on innovation. Second, projects are important vehicles for intervention, which has policy implications and creates institutional impact. Third, projects generate data and experience that should influence financial sector policy.

Because of its frontier and project focus, the discussion that follows outlines a central element of sector studies but does not offer a comprehensive formula for financial sector work, which often includes more attention to macroeconomic factors than could easily be linked to project concerns. Nor does it discuss M+E delivery systems that collect, process and present data, which Casley and other contributors to the MIS and M+E literature cover, and which are familiar to the informed development assistance agencies, research institutes, consulting firms, and academic researchers that undertake sector studies.

PROJECT IMPACTS. Four major issues confront M+E and sector work. The first is investment performance by people and firms receiving credit. These ultimate borrowers in the chain that starts with project funds provided by a development assistance agency to a government of a developing country and then to a financial institution are called subborrowers. Subborrowers' activities for which subloans are made are called subprojects. The second concerns the impact of credit policies and projects on financial intermediaries, which is given considerable attention in this chapter because it has been largely ignored in the project analysis literature. The third addresses the relationship of credit and financial adjustment projects and policies to the development of the financial sector, and the fourth briefly examines macroeconomic and macrofinancial implications of credit projects and policies.

Each issue can be explored on two levels. The first level is relative. It compares performance with the designers' expectations: did the project do, or is it doing, what its designers said it would do? Reviewers should examine deviations from design objectives and the project designers' perceptions of risks. Their perceptions may be found in project or policy documents, or where they are not clearly stated, inferred from project design. Focus on risk at an early stage of review is required because risk is the central problem of finance.

Good evaluation searches for broad impact, and all financial transactions provide fodder for sector studies. Good sector work meticulously reviews lessons from policy implementation and project performance. This necessitates the second level, which measures project performance against broader development objectives. What is or was the impact of the project beyond that envisaged by designers? Is the project consistent with financial market development, macrofinancial and macroeconomic growth, and the integrity of society's great institutions such as markets, property and human rights, and contract law or justice? Was design realistic and appropriate within the broader context in which the project operated? Who lost and who gained as a result of the project, and by how much?

Table 14.1 outlines these two review levels in project impact analysis and identifies the review activities—monitoring, evaluation, and sector work—that are generally appropriate for each of the four review issues. Because project design is often narrower than the M+E frame outlined here, many M+E systems will contain fewer than the eight dimensions (arising from four issues at two levels each) indicated in Table 14.1. For example, where project design expresses no expectation concerning one or more of the four stages, monitoring of such stages at the first level is not necessary.

Table 14.1 Application of Financial Project Review Activities

The Two Levels of Review	*Subproject & Subborrower Performance*	*Participating Financial Intermediary Performance*	*Financial Market Development Impact*	*Macroeconomic & Macrofinancial Impact*
		The Four Issues for Review		
Did or does project performance match the designers' expectations? Was risk correctly perceived?	Monitoring Evaluation Sector work	Monitoring Evaluation Sector work	Evaluation Sector work	Sector work
What are or were the broader effects of the project?	Evaluation Sector work	Evaluation Sector work	Evaluation Sector work	Evaluation Sector work

Simple credit projects usually have no financial market development objective beyond those associated directly with the performance of participating financial institutions (PFIs) that make subloans. Consequently, it is not feasible to monitor extended project impact. Evaluation and sector work should explore this dimension, however. Likewise, macro impacts are usually even more remote from the design expectations underlying typical credit projects, and macro impact monitoring is not generally warranted.

Policy Impacts

More complex credit projects include a policy element or component. A common example is interest rate conditionality, which is designed to make national interest rate structures more rational economically. A government borrowing under such conditionality undertakes, in conjunction with a project, to raise interest rates not only on subloans but also on transactions other than project subloans. Policy elements contained in projects should be analyzed separately as policies, and questions applied to project impact, such as those posed here, are equally applicable to policy review. All eight dimensions, depending on the nature and importance of the policy, can be included in policy review.

Issue 1: Subproject and Subborrower Performance

Examining subproject and subborrower performance is justified in three cases.[3] First, credit use increases or decreases the size of the economy and influences resource allocation, and savings and investment behavior by households and firms are extremely important development variables. Thus, review is a useful building block for sector studies that are undertaken to guide future projects and policies. Second, when credit is targeted, project objectives are stated in terms of subborrower and subproject selection and performance. These should be monitored and evaluated to explore what project designers expected to happen and deviations from these expectations that occur in implementation, so that design can be improved. For example, if credit to small traders is expected to increase their inventory, turnover and profits, these variables should be measured.

The third case that justifies review of subproject and subborrower performance occurs when PFIs conduct market research, such as assembling farm budgets, lending models for commercial and industrial firms or price projections for credit decisionmaking. In well-run lending institutions this activity is routine, although it may not be highly formalized. (Lack of formalization is not necessarily a deficiency in small institutions where lenders know their clients intimately.[4]) The review task is to judge the quality of market research and its application. Were the data credible? Did they facilitate good lending decisions? Did lenders know their borrowers? Was the system for generating and processing information responsive to problems arising during implementation?

---

3. Sector surveys may review the characteristics and activities of people and firms using credit from sources other than project funds disbursed by PFIs. The procedures described here largely apply to this type of inquiry as well, although the terms subborrower and subproject have to be amended to read borrower and investment projects.

4. Timberg and Aiyer, *op. cit.*, describe an informal system that is rich in information using simple procedures and little paper.

Review of subprojects' and subborrowers' performance has three major purposes. The first is to ascertain the extent to which the activities for which subloans were issued are undertaken. The second is to quantify subborrowers' returns: did they reach projected levels, were they sufficient to fund debt service, and were they remunerative to subborrowers? The third is to identify and contrast the characteristics of good payers and of defaulters, and of good subloans and of bad subloans. This information permits an assessment of the thoroughness and quality of project and subproject appraisal, including its effectiveness in dealing with risk. It also facilitates refinement of lending criteria and project design. Together, these dimensions of performance permit review of the quality of the lender's credit decisionmaking.

Review should identify changes in subborrowers' sales and profits. It may also be helpful to examine changes in subborrowers' output and in their assets. Changes involving assets include their production capacity, their value and their composition. Output and assets related to a loan can be compared to the total output and assets of the firm or household. This comparison is especially useful where sales and profit are difficult to measure. Attention to the continued use of key inputs or raw materials, to changes in cropping patterns or industrial and commercial product lines and to credit use also helps review. An important question is whether loan-financed assets are still in place and being used for project purposes. Have assets been replaced, expanded or enlarged, or upgraded? If so, did this occur in response to enhanced investment opportunities, to mastery of new skills by the subborrower, or to a poor choice of scale or technology under the project? How has savings behavior changed? Has the investment facilitated the more productive use of labor and has it increased employment?

Earlier chapters have expressed reservations about subloan targeting, especially by subloan purpose, that is not market-niche oriented. In the absence of targeting, a project reflecting these reservations would have the refreshing objective of simply making good subloans. Review for a project of this type would focus on differences among subborrowers' behavior, assets, and other characteristics suspected or demonstrated to be related to their repayment and savings performance. Purposes for which loans are taken would be important only when things purchased with subloan proceeds serve as collateral or if the subloan were expected to create debt capacity by increasing the subborrower's income.

Keeping Informed

Well-run financial institutions are well informed about their clients, their clients' activities, and about the markets in which their clients operate. In addition to surveillance of transactions on deposit and loan accounts, and periodic visits to clients' places of business, lenders within the frontier normally obtain annual audited and more frequent unaudited financial information from their commercial borrowers. These data are routinely analyzed for loan administration and credit decisionmaking. At the frontier these procedures are more difficult to apply because borrowers may keep few records and their operations are too small to justify the costs of external audits. Lenders at the frontier have to use alternative techniques. Projects focusing on the frontier can usefully include sample surveys conducted according to standard social science procedures.

Desk and field surveys are research activities that are often part of evaluation. They are formalized ways of generating information on subborrowers, on subproject performance, and on the relationship between the lender and subborrowers. Surveys use samples selected according to procedures that ensure randomness, usually interpreted to mean that each subloan has a known, nonzero equal probability of being included in the sample. Often a simple random sample is drawn, meaning that each subloan has an equal probability of being selected.

However, where subloan size distribution is greatly skewed, researchers may use stratified samples composed of subsamples selected from different groups of subloans with different sampling fractions for the various strata or groups. This ensures adequate representation in the sample of groups which, although small in size, are of importance in understanding the relationships being studied. When subloan sizes are skewed and where portfolio risk is of special interest to reviewers, currency units rather than subloans are used as the unit of selection, so that each peso of credit issued rather than each subborrower has an equal chance of being sampled.

Researchers should normally select the sample from the files of the PFI. They can ascertain the before-project situation and characteristics of the subborrower from information used in the credit decision. Next, they should compare the sample with target group specifications listed in the project appraisal report or related legal documents to ascertain whether funds were distributed as envisaged. Researchers should examine lenders' records to determine the thoroughness and consistency with which farm budgets or lending models were compiled, and their contribution to credit decisions. Specialists with financial or accounting skills but no research experience can help with this activity. To obtain an indication of the project designer's and lender's approach to risk, models reviewed should be categorized according to whether they are partial, dealing only with the flows of an activity, or complete, covering the farm or firm or the subborrower's household.

DESK ALONE, OR DESK AND FIELD SURVEYS? Desk surveys are a required and relatively inexpensive first step in research. They can yield valuable insights when lenders systematically record accurate data. Where data in files are deficient or where the survey objective goes beyond their contents, the additional expense of field surveys may be justified. Field visits and interviews can supplement desk studies to confirm the status and characteristics of the subborrower and identify changes in product lines, cropping patterns, technologies, labor input, yields or productivity, investment and asset value, income and expenses, and whether the purposes for which subloans were issued yielded sufficient income to repay them as scheduled. Changes in sources of credit and in patterns of credit use, such as a trend toward borrowing for productive purposes rather than for consumption, should also be identified in order to obtain indications of credit risk, including senior claims.

At the least, field surveys should reveal differences between the subborrower's operations at the time of the credit decision or just prior to loan approval, and the present or just before the survey. This "then and now" focus compares two points in time. A more comprehensive approach, requiring much more data and making greater demands on its quality, is to gather information for each year during the period under review, generating a time series of data. Researchers should attempt this "expanded approach" where they can obtain reasonably reliable statistics, possibly through crop delivery or product sales records or other indicators of output, yields and incomes. Few records are kept at the frontier, and relying on subborrower recall for detailed statistics for several years past does not produce high quality data.

Chapter 7 indicates that calculation of the economic rate of return (ERR) is superfluous to good loans and may even contribute to bad lending by distracting attention from more important considerations. The financial rate of return (FRR) is more useful because it is more closely related to subborrower behavior. Its calculation at any stage in the project cycle can be highly instructive. Where economic rates of return are not calculated at appraisal, there is generally no reason to include them as a review variable. If, however, project designers calculate an ERR and use it as a justification for the project, project review should test it.

Issues to be addressed in ERR and FRR recalculation include transparency or disclosure, methodological integrity and realism, which reveal the quality of project design. Recalculation of the ERR or FRR is feasible only if two conditions are met. The first is that project appraisal documents or files are intelligible sources of technical communication: they must provide sufficient disclosure to permit recalculation. But it is sometimes impossible to reconstruct the original calculations because the assumptions used were not clearly stated. The second condition is that subproject data quality is sufficient to support use of the expanded approach. Reconstruction of intervening year results between subloan appraisal and the present under the then and now approach produces data that are usually too vague or inaccurate to be useful.

Review should include ERR recalculation using the prices and conversion factors employed in appraisal to test actual volumes of inputs, raw material and labor, for example, that create costs, and the volume of sales that create revenue. This recalculation tests the validity of input-output relationships assumed at appraisal. A second ERR recalculation should be made using current prices and conversion factors to test actual economic performance.

SURVEY BREADTH. Where project focus is narrow, field survey objectives often appear to dictate a relatively narrow focus. But in many cases enlargement of the scope of the survey may not greatly increase the cost of data collection, although it greatly complicates data processing. A survey that examines the entire operations of the subborrower can yield results many times more powerful than a survey of only the activity for which credit was issued. These greater insights from survey results are possible because credit is usually only one of the stimulants of subborrowers' behavior. The complexity of their activities generally invalidates the narrow view that changes in the operations financed by a subloan are directly attributable to the subloan, as explained in chapter 3.

Even if attribution were possible, provision of credit with technical assistance, membership in a cooperative or other promotional activities blurs the impact of credit alone. Where nonfarm activities or activities outside the business are important or have changed significantly, reviewers should document them and ascertain their effect on the farm or the business. Again, surveys are incomplete if they provide no insights into changes in savings behavior that accompany subborrower gains or losses associated with credit use. Field surveys should check whether partial budgets or lending models lead to problems that reliance on complete budgets or models might avoid. If model specification is deficient, reviewers should explore the cost of its correction.

FUNDS DRAWN AND REPAYMENT PERFORMANCE. At the frontier it is not unusual to find that significant proportions of individual subloan commitments made under official projects are never drawn, and that entire subloans are canceled without being drawn by subborrowers. Investigation of why subborrowers leave this money on the shelf may reveal gaps between the expectations of project designers, lenders and the target group, or serious constraints facing subborrowers that the appraisal did not uncover. These may also reflect rapidly changing conditions in markets in which subborrowers operate, poorly conceived investment proposals or incompetent subborrowers. Greatly underdrawn loans usually reveal large gaps between plans and performance, and they tend to perform poorly.

The performance of each sample subloan is reviewed in the desk study. Variables to be examined include how quickly funds were drawn, whether the full amount approved was disbursed, and whether repayments were made as scheduled. Repayment performance may be measured by the Repayment Index, described in Annex A, which permits cross-tabulation, correlation analysis and other statistical comparisons with subproject, subborrower, and other survey variables.

Field enumerators should be informed of the repayment performance of the subborrowers they survey to help them discover characteristics of good payers and poor payers and of good loans and bad loans. Dimensions to be explored include the content and quality of loan supervision, how loans may be linked with other services as parts of larger relationships, and the quality of these relationships. However, survey staff generally should not reveal to sample subborrowers that they are aware of their repayment performance. Nor should they ask subborrowers directly about repayment, thereby avoiding a sensitive area prone to evasive or deceitful answers.

Gathering good data is a survey objective, and the overall results of a well-designed survey will distinguish the traits of good and bad payers. Loan officers are the ones who should explore causes of poor repayment directly with defaulters because they are in a position to take remedial action. For example, some arrears reflect poor scheduling of installments, which can be solved by rescheduling. Enumerators may inquire generally about repayment problems facing subborrowers, and honest subborrowers having difficulties will often reveal them with candor, whereas others will present facts selectively, if at all.

Control Groups and Other Populations

Credit surveys should not include control groups that have not received credit, because of the difficulties and costs of locating a meaningful control. This would consist of individuals, households, or firms that could have obtained project credit but chose not to. The usefulness of a subborrowing control group is also reduced by the realization that fungibility makes it difficult to attribute specific borrower behavior to receipt of a loan. Valid review procedures recognize that credit involves a systematic bias in borrower selection, based on project design specifications that determine creditworthiness.

Surveys of nonborrowers may be useful for other purposes, such as business development, including design of marketing strategies. And, where sector work is policy oriented or directed at creating market niches beyond the frontier, there may be no projects that provide a precedent and hence no population of subborrowers that could offer insights. In this situation studies of households or firms in the prospective target group may be helpful. The issues and questions explored in this chapter concerning subborrowers and subprojects can also be applied to the financial behavior of the proposed target group.

Case Studies

Full-blown field surveys can be expensive, and obtaining and processing the data required to generate interesting and useful results is very demanding. Where good data are not obtainable at costs that are reasonable in relation to the usefulness of the desired information, spending large sums on analysis is not worthwhile. In these instances and when large research budgets are not available, impressions can be quickly gained from case studies of small numbers of subborrowers, farms or businesses.

These impressions are not scientific but can usually be meaningfully organized to identify qualitative and quantitative dimensions of finance at the frontier, especially when surveyed operations are relatively small and simple. However, construction of case studies requires greater skills than those used to complete data collection forms in large surveys. Researchers with an understanding of finance and of subborrowers and their activities are needed, rather than survey enumerators, which raises the per unit cost of gathering data.

Issue 2: Intermediary Performance

The second review issue is the impact of project participation on financial intermediaries disbursing project subloans. Where wholesale secondary or apex institutions pass project funds to retail lenders, investigators should also calculate project impact on these secondary institutions.

Chapter 13 discussed intermediary performance, measured in financial terms, as a fundamental indicator of the appropriateness of interventions in financial markets. This emphasis is based on the realization that financial performance is the most critical element in the long-run survival and effectiveness of financial institutions. It is also normally the fundamental determinant of the contribution a lending institution and a project make to financial sector development. Money-losing credit projects shrink the size of the financial sector, constraining efforts to penetrate the frontier.

This stage of review is independent in timing and organization from review of subproject and subborrower performance. It yields a separate report assembled by persons with financial skills that the specialists responsible for review of subprojects and subborrowers do not necessarily possess.

The focus for analysis is the first analytical question in review of the performance of a participating financial institution (PFI). Two alternatives exist: analysis of project subloan operations or portfolio performance, and analysis of the participating financial institution. Selection depends on the type of funding provided under the project. Where a project finances readily identifiable activities that can be meaningfully defined separately from other operations of the PFI, project subloan operations are the appropriate focus. In other cases project funds may support the overall operations of a PFI, and the impact of the project is not identifiable or separable from overall PFI performance. In these cases the PFI is the focus of analysis. Each alternative is dealt with in the following discussion.

Focus of Analysis: Project Subloan Operations or Portfolio Segment

The classic project targets subloans to achieve specific production or political objectives. Donors' funds support a clearly defined PFI activity or portfolio segment, such as term lending or lending to small firms. Targeting permits identification of the project's financial impact on the institution. Most donors require that transactions involving project funds be recorded in separate accounts on the PFI's books, and these subloan accounts are the raw material for review.

Chapter 13 introduced the use of net present value (NPV) and residual net worth (RNW) to measure a project's impact on a PFI. Both indicators are positive in a successful project. The discussion that follows explains how subloan portfolio data and other relevant statistics may be organized to calculate NPV and RNW. The formats used for illustrative purposes are applicable to term lending, which is the usual project instrument, but they could be simplified for short-term lending.

Subloan portfolio analysis uses financial worksheets or tables constructed for the project lending operation from the PFI's records. The minimum level of data available may quantify PFI disbursements to subborrowers, donors' or government's reimbursements to PFIs from project funds, debt service received by PFIs from subborrowers, and PFIs' debt service payments to donors or government on project funds.

Analytical convenience favors dividing the quantification of project impact on a PFI into two major components. The first consists of portfolio analysis that traces the impact of loan and subloan flows alone. The second completes the analysis by adding overhead costs and other project operating costs and revenues. The results of these components are summarized in project balance sheets, income statements, and sources and uses of funds statements for project activities as they appear on the books of PFIs. These statements may occasionally be available, but in most cases analysts have to construct them for review purposes. In effect, the analysis treats the project activity as a profit center in accounting and managerial terms, or as a shell subsidiary.

Portfolio Analysis

Portfolio analysis shows the flows generated by project loan and subloan terms and performance. It permits evaluation of PFI gain or loss from the purely financial aspects of its project role, which consists of borrowing project funds and lending them, before considering operating expenses and expenses of or revenues from any other project activities the intermediary undertakes. Portfolio analysis is conducted in two steps. The first quantifies the flows between the PFI and subborrowers, and the second quantifies transactions between the PFI and the government, donor or other source of project funds.

Transactions between the PFI and subborrowers consist of disbursement of project subloans by the PFI and collection of subloan principal and interest from subborrowers. The following Tables 14.2 to 14.5 summarize these flows and show the behavior of subloans over the life of the project. Table 14.2 shows subloan commitments and disbursements. Table 14.3 presents subloan principal flows for each year of a hypothetical credit project's life. Its bottom line shows principal collections. Table 14.4 shows subloan principal amounts outstanding based on the flows quantified in the previous table. Table 14.5 lists subloan interest flows. These tables are analytical building blocks. They show extremely important variables in project design and performance: disbursements and the volume of collections of subloan principal and interest. They are worksheets that relate collections, the situation at the opening of each accounting period, and summaries of transactions for each period.

Table 14.2 Project Subloan Commitments and Disbursements

ABC Frontier Credit Project

	19X1 [ ]	19X2 [ ]	19X3 [ ]	20ZZ [ ]	Cumulative
Subloan commitments	—	—	—	—	—
Subloan disbursements of 19X1 commitments	—	—	—	—	—
19X2 commitments		—	—	—	—
19X3 commitments			—	—	—
....					
Disbursements for the period	—	—	—	—	—
Undisbursed amounts committed in 19X1	—	—	—	—	—
19X2		—	—	—	—
19X3			—	—	—
....					
Total undisbursed commitments	—	—	—	—	—

a. Use this footnote to explain the relationship between subloan commitments and subloan disbursements. How long is the disbursement lag?

335

Table 14.3 Project Subloan Principal Flows

ABC Frontier Credit Project

Principal Flows	19X1 [ ]	19X2 [ ]	19X3 [ ]	20ZZ [ ]	Cumulative
Subloan disbursements of					
19X1 commitments [T14.2]	—	—	—	—	—
19X2 commitments [T14.2]		—	—	—	—
19X3 commitments [T14.2]			—	—	—
....					
Disbursements for the period	—	—	—	—	—
Interest capitalized on subloans committed					
in 19X1	—	—	—	—	—
19X2		—	—	—	—
19X3			—	—	—
....					
Principal falling due from subborrowers a/					
on 19X1 commitments not rescheduled	—	—	—	—	—
on 19X2 commitments not rescheduled		—	—	—	—
on 19X3 commitments not rescheduled			—	—	—
....					
on rescheduled subloans committed					
in 19X1	—	—	—	—	—
in 19X2		—	—	—	—
in 19X3			—	—	—
....					

336

ABC Frontier Credit Project

Principal Flows	19X1 [ ]	19X2 [ ]	19X3 [ ]	20ZZ [ ]	Cumulative
Principal falling due during the period	—	—	—	—	—
less: principal falling due during the period but not collected b/					
on 19X1 commitments not rescheduled	—	—	—	—	—
on 19X2 commitments not rescheduled		—	—	—	—
on 19X3 commitments not rescheduled			—	—	—
....					
on rescheduled loans committed					
in 19X1	—	—	—	—	—
in 19X2			—	—	—
in 19X3			—	—	—
....					
Principal falling due but not collected	—	—	—	—	—
Collections of principal falling due during the period	—	—	—	—	—
Collections of principal falling due in previous periods b/ 19X1			—		—
19X2			—		—
19X3					—
....					
Prepayments of future years' installments received	—	—	—	—	—
Principal collected during the period	—	—	—	—	—

a. Use this footnote to explain loan repayment schedules.
b. Use this footnote to list assumptions about future collection rates.

Presentational Conventions

The financial tables that follow contain several features requiring explanation. First, the tables contain only five data columns to simplify presentation. The extent of the actual exercise required is suggested by a project with a five-year disbursement period and a ten-year maximum loan term. These would require 15 columns to accommodate ten-year loans made in project year five and several more to record the recovery of arrears after project year 15. Omitting columns for presentational simplicity also has to be reflected in rows, and is noted by the use of .... in the sequence of row labels.

The tables are arranged so that the performance of each year's cohort of subloans is separately identified by row. This assists in making projections because trends in the performance of the oldest subloans, made in project years 1 and 2, for example, offer a basis for making assumptions about newer subloans made in years 4 and 5.

The usefulness of tracing each period's lending activity is shown graphically by Richard L. Meyer and Aruna Srinivasan in their study of agricultural lending by nationalized commercial banks in Bangladesh.[5] Their results are shown in Figure 14.1, and they confirm the tendency of credit projects to deteriorate over time. The stubborn tendency of the recovery curves to become flat implies how extremely difficult it is to reverse their trend and get them pointing upward once again, especially as arrears age. However, the curves do show that it was possible for a time to obtain faster recoveries, as the curves rose more steeply through the third year following the due date for each of the tranches between 1979 and 1982.

The column for cumulative or aggregate figures is used to check the mathematical accuracy of totals of columns with totals of rows, and assists the construction of summary statements for a project's life. Project life as defined here ends at the close of the final period, during which all subloan collections that can be recovered have been recovered, all bad loans will have been written off, and the project loan has been fully repaid. Accordingly, no loan principal remains outstanding in the bottom line of

---

5. Richard L. Meyer and Aruna Srinivasan, *op.cit.* p. 30.

Table 14.4 Project Subloan Principal Portfolio

ABC Frontier Credit Project

Subloan Principal Outstanding	19X1 [ ]	19X2 [ ]	19X3 [ ]	20ZZ [ ]	Cumulative
Subloan principal outstanding - opening a/	-0-				
Disbursements for the period [T14.2]	—	—	—	—	—
plus: capitalized interest added to principal during the period	—	—	—	—	—
less: principal falling due from subborrowers [T14.3]	—	—	—	—	—
plus: principal falling due rescheduled to future periods	—	—	—	—	—
less: prepayments [T14.3]	—	—	—	—	—
less: loans not yet due written off	—	—	—	—	—
Subloan balances not yet due	—	—	—	—	—
Total falling due but not collected [T14.3] = principal going into arrears	—	—	—	—	—
less: arrears written off	—	—	—	—	—
Subloan principal outstanding - closing a/	—	—	—	-0-	

a. The subloan principal outstanding at the close of a period is the same as the subloan principal outstanding at the opening of the following period.

Table 14.5 Subloan Interest Flows

	ABC Frontier Credit Project				
	19X1 [ ]	19X2 [ ]	19X3 [ ]	20ZZ [ ]	Cumulative
Interest falling due from subborrowers on:					
subloan balances not yet due [T14.4] $a/$					
principal falling due during the period [T14.3] $b/$	—	—	—	—	—
principal in arrears [T14.4] $c/$	—	—	—	—	—
interest in arrears (see below) $d/$	—	—	—	—	—
Interest falling due during the period before rescheduling	—	—	—	—	—
less: interest falling due rescheduled to future periods (capitalized)	—	—	—	—	—
Interest falling due after rescheduling	—	—	—	—	—
less: interest falling due during the period but not collected on:					
subloan balances not yet due $e/$	—	—	—	—	—
principal falling due during the period $f/$	—	—	—	—	—
principal in arrears $g/$	—	—	—	—	—
interest in arrears $h/$	—	—	—	—	—
Interest falling due after rescheduling but not collected = interest in arrears (see above)	—	—	—	—	—

ABC Frontier Credit Project

	19X1 [ ]	19X2 [ ]	19X3 [ ]	20ZZ [ ]	Cumulative
Collection of interest falling due in previous periods: i/ 19X1				___	___
19X2		___	___	___	___
19X3			___	___	___
....					
Collection of interest falling due during the period	___	___	___	___	___
Interest collected during the period	___	___	___	___	___

Note: Use footnotes to explain interest calculations on:

a. balances not yet due.
b. principal falling due during the period.
c. principal in arrears.
d. interest in arrears.

and to explain interest collection rates:

e.
f.
g.
h.
i.

Table 14.4 for year 20ZZ, which represents the final year of project life. When annual data measure flows, the cumulative figure is the sum of the annual figures, as for subloan commitments in Table 14.2. When annual data portrays stocks, as for total undisbursed commitments in Table 14.2, the cumulative figure is identical to the figure for the final year of the analysis, 20ZZ.

Figure 14.1 Loan Recovery Profile for Short-Term Agricultural Loans Made in 1979-84 in Bangladesh: All Banks

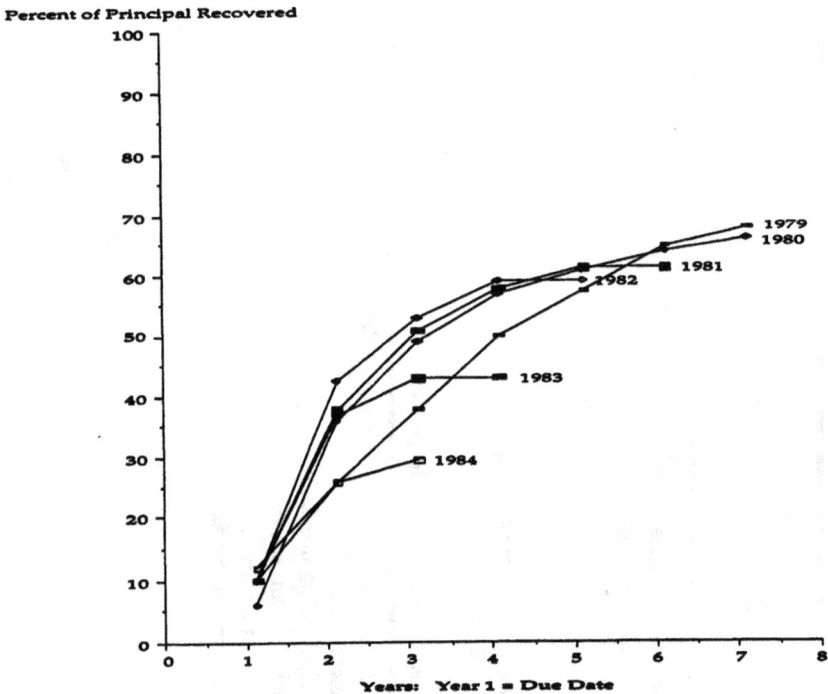

Source: Richard L. Meyer and Aruna Srinivasan, *op.cit.* p. 30; Aruna Srinivasan, *A Multiproduct Cost Study of Rural Bank Branches in Bangladesh.* PhD Dissertation. Department of Agricultural Economics and Rural Sociology, Ohio State University. 1988. p. 96.

Under the data column heads, the tables have brackets [ ] in which to record indicators of data quality: audited, unaudited, provisional, or projected. Audited data is from accounts that have been examined by external auditors who have provided an opinion on their quality. If the auditor's opinion is qualified (to the effect that generally accepted accounting principles have not been consistently applied), the nature of the qualification should be footnoted. Unaudited data has been fully reviewed by the PFI's internal auditors and management but not yet adjusted, if adjustment is required, by external auditors. Preliminary data has not been fully reviewed within the PFI. Projected data are estimates of future performance.

Data found in one table are often also used in others. References to their original location are shown in brackets: [T14.2] refers the reader to Table 14.2. Later tables frequently use data derived from earlier tables, and references to the original figures include an asterisk, for example, [T14.2*]. The most common derivatives are calculations of the change in balances during a period, defined as the difference between the balance at the close of the year and at the close of the prior year.

The tables' formats are comprehensive and often would be simplified. Many analysts would rearrange them for their own purposes or to suit more conveniently the form in which their data are provided. Prepayments and rescheduling could be excluded for analytical economy in projections of new programs that have no relevant history on which to build assumptions, for example. For review purposes, however, the actual record is required in a form comprehensive enough to show how the lender and subborrowers operate, including attention to prepayments and rescheduling. Provisions for bad debt losses and write-offs do not have to be dealt with at this stage as the effects of uncollected amounts due are fully recognized by the repayment record. Accordingly, all stocks and flows may be shown before provisions and write-offs, but interest falling due can be shown for performing loans only, omitting that calculated on nonperforming loans, without disturbing the thrust of the analysis. However, Table 14.4 includes write-offs and rescheduling to assist refined analysis.

Table 14.6 External Funding Flows

	ABC Frontier Credit Project				
	19X1	19X2	19X3	20ZZ	Cumulative
	[ ]	[ ]	[ ]	[ ]	
Generation of External Project Funds					
Subloan disbursements [T14.2] (memo item) [a]	_____	_____	_____	_____	_____
Project funds received [b]	_____	_____	_____	_____	_____
External Project Funds Debt Service					
Principal falling due to external source	_____	_____	_____	_____	_____
Interest falling due to external source	_____	_____	_____	_____	_____
Project Funds Debt Service	_____	_____	_____	_____	_____
Project Funds received less Project Funds					
Debt Service = Net External Funding Flow	_____	_____	_____	_____	_____

a. Disbursements are shown only for purposes of comparison with project funds received. They are not mathematically related to other flows in this table.

b. In this footnote state assumptions or procedures regarding access to project funds. These would frequently be provided in response to subloan disbursement rates, which is why subloan disbursements are included in this table, although they make no mathematical contribution to the table.

External Funding Flows and Float

The second step in portfolio analysis quantifies the flows between the PFI and sources of project funds that are external to the intermediary, such as a development assistance agency, government or central bank. These flows consist of the receipt of project funds by the intermediary for on-lending, and repayment of project funds and payment of interest by the PFI. They are summarized in Table 14.6. Arrears on these payments are highly unusual because the creditor is the central bank or government treasury. Tables 14.3 and 14.5 provide formats that could be adapted to show arrears in debt service by a PFI in Table 14.6.

Table 14.7 builds upon previous tables to identify differences in phasing between intermediary borrowing and lending under the project, and the impact of arrears. The treatment of principal flows is intended to highlight the liquidity generated or absorbed by arrears and by differences in the term structures of the intermediary's borrowing and lending under the project. The interest analysis shows the results of the spreads between the interest rate paid on project funds and the interest rate charged on subloans, different interest rate term structures including grace periods, and interest arrears. The bottom line in Table 14.7 is the net impact of the disbursement-reimbursement-collection cycle. Project Portfolio Sources (Uses) of PFI Funds shows the net liquidity position of the intermediary as a result of financing flows associated with the project.

The amount of reimbursement from the project loan is normally different from subloan disbursements during an accounting period because reimbursement may be only partial, less than 100 percent of advances made, with the unreimbursed balance coming from the lender's own funds. Also, a lag between subloan disbursement and project reimbursement is normal because of the time taken by the PFI to aggregate subloan disbursements and prepare a reimbursement claim, and for the donor to process the claim and to transfer funds to the PFI. These differences in amount and timing absorb liquidity, as indicated by "Net disbursements funded by PFI," the third row in Table 14.7

Some projects are supported from the outset with a revolving fund, sometimes known as a "special account," established by the donor to reduce the net disbursements funded by the intermediary. Reduction occurs because the special account is maintained in the country in which the

Table 14.7 Project Portfolio Funds Flow--Project Basis

Project Flows--Project Basis	ABC Frontier Credit Project				
	19X1 [ ]	19X2 [ ]	19X3 [ ]	20ZZ [ ]	Cumulative
Project Principle Flows-- Project Basis					
Subloan disbursements [T14.2]	___	___	___	___	___
less: Project funds received [T14.6]	___	___	___	___	___
Net disbursements funded by PFI	___	___	___	___	___
Principal falling due from subborrowers [T14.3]	___	___	___	___	___
less: Principal falling due to external source [T14.6]	___	___	___	___	___
Contractual sources of funds from term structures	___	___	___	___	___
less: funds absorbed (released) by:					
rescheduling subloan principal [T14.4]					
other changes in subborrowers' principal in arrears [T14.4*] a/	___	___	___	___	___
prepayment of future years' principal installments [T14.3]	___	___	___	___	___
Actual sources (uses) of funds from principal accounts	___	___	___	___	___

ABC Frontier Credit Project

Project Flows--Project Basis	19X1 [ ]	19X2 [ ]	19X3 [ ]	20ZZ [ ]	Cumulative
Project Interest Flows--Project Basis					
Interest falling due from subborrowers [T14.5]	—	—	—	—	—
less: Loan interest falling due [T14.6]	—	—	—	—	—
Contractual sources of funds					
from interest accounts	—	—	—	—	—
less: Funds absorbed (released) by:					
rescheduling subloan interest in arrears	—	—	—	—	—
other changes in subborrowers'					
interest in arrears [T14.5*] a/	—	—	—	—	—
Actual sources (uses) of funds					
from interest accounts	—	—	—	—	—
Total Project Portfolio Flows =					
Project Portfolio Sources (Uses)					
of PFI Funds -- Project Basis	—	—	—		—

a. Before write-offs.

347

project is located and can be tapped frequently and quickly, without the time lag required for submission and processing of reimbursement requests. When revolving funds are used, and if the interest earned on them is for the benefit of the PFI, the analysis should be modified accordingly.

Subloan disbursements usually run ahead of reimbursements received from the project loan in the early years of the project. These disbursements are seldom offset by net interest flows, especially when subloan terms include an initial grace period on debt service. This creates negative "project portfolio float" that the PFI funds from additional outside sources or diverts from other uses. In later years the project may be a net supplier of funds if subloans are collected more rapidly than the project loan has to be repaid to the donor or government. (Use of the accounting year-end data in the tables in this chapter injects an arbitrary element into these calculations because project portfolio float can vary greatly within an accounting year.)

Accounting for Recycled Funds

Project lending through PFIs uses two types of loan repayment terms. One, often used for industrial credit projects, is to determine repayment by the PFI by the maturities of its subloans, within a maximum period such as seven to 12 years. The loan repayment schedule is the aggregate of subloan repayment schedules. The principal repayment schedules for subloans and for the loan that funds them are simultaneous, or in banking jargon, back-to-back. (There may be a short grace period between the scheduled receipt of subloan repayments and loan repayments to permit the PFI to aggregate small amounts into a single quarterly or semiannual payment, reducing transaction costs.) The PFI is responsible for choosing the appropriate maturities on subloans within the maximum specified under the project, and these often range from three to eight years. Subloan rescheduling reschedules the loan, but late payments do not: the PFI has to repay the project loan according to schedule, even if subborrowers are late in repaying or completely fail to repay their subloans.

The second type of loan term is frequently found in agricultural credit projects, where loans are repaid over 10 to 15 years according to a schedule established in advance and entirely independent of subloan repayment terms—except that final maturities of subloans would almost always fall due before the final maturity of the loan. Some donors require that all subloans using project funds conform to project specifications such as targets by loan purpose and size, subborrower characteristics, and interest rates. Others specify that only the initial subloans, those that trigger disbursement of the project loan, conform to project specifications. These may be termed "project round" subloans. Their maturities are typically considerably shorter than the maturity of the project loan that funds them, which requires special analytical treatment.

In these cases, where donors do not control the recycling of project round subloans, subloans repaid to the PFI faster than the PFI repays the project loan generate funds that the PFI can use essentially as it wishes. These funds are positive project portfolio float. Positive project portfolio float arises when the cumulative total of debt service collected from subborrowers and any other sources of funds exceed the PFI's cumulative commitment of its own funds to the project plus cumulative debt service paid on the project loan.

CALCULATING THE INTEREST BURDEN ON PROJECT ROUND SUBLOANS. Positive float creates an analytical problem because the total interest received on subloans outstanding for a few years is usually much less than interest paid on the project loan outstanding for many years. For this reason, the net interest flows calculated on the project basis in Table 14.7 would often be negative when back-to-back repayment is not required. Clearly this treatment violates the banking principle of matching the cost of funds with income from their uses. This analytical problem is resolved by adjusting the interest calculation on the loan. Adjustment is made by assuming that loan principal is repaid simultaneously with subloan principal repayments, as in Table 14.7A. On a matching basis, loan interest is calculated only on subloan balances outstanding to obtain the interest cost of funds used for project purposes.

DISREGARD RETURN ON THE FLOAT. Positive float is recycled outside the project, which has implications for the PFI that extend beyond the round of subloans issued under the project: positive float creates an opportunity for the PFI to earn additional benefits from recycling these funds, at the usual risk of additional losses. But adjustment to exclude the cost of the float from the cost of project funds supporting subloans is preferable to

Table 14.7A Project Portfolio Funds Flow—Matching Basis

Project Flows--Matching Basis	ABC Frontier Credit Project					Cumulative
	19X1 [ ]	19X2 [ ]	19X3 [ ]	20ZZ [ ]		

Project Principle Flows--Matching Basis

	19X1	19X2	19X3	20ZZ	Cumulative
Subloan disbursements [T14.2]	—	—	—	—	—
less: Project funds received [T14.6]	—	—	—	—	—
Net disbursements funded by PFI	—	—	—	—	—
Principal falling due from subborrowers [T14.3]	—	—	—	—	—
less: Principal falling due to external source [T14.6]	—	—	—	—	—
Contractual sources of funds from term structures	—	—	—	—	—
less: funds absorbed (released) by:					
rescheduling subloan principal [T14.4]	—	—	—	—	—
other changes in subborrowers' principal in arrears [T14.4*] a/	—	—	—	—	—
prepayment of future years' principal installments [T14.3]	—	—	—	—	—
Actual sources (uses) of funds from principal accounts	—	—	—	—	—

ABC Frontier Credit Project

	19X1	19X2	19X3	20ZZ	Cumulative
	[ ]	[ ]	[ ]	[ ]	
Project Flows--Matching Basis					
Project Interest Flows--Matching Basis					
Interest falling due from subborrowers [T14.5]	—	—	—	—	—
less: Adjusted loan interest falling due [T14.6]	—	—	—	—	—
Contractual sources of funds from interest accounts	—	—	—	—	—
less: Funds absorbed (released) by:					
rescheduling subloan interest in arrears [T14.5]	—	—	—	—	—
other changes in subborrowers' interest in arrears [T14.5*] a/	—	—	—	—	—
Adjusted actual sources (uses) of funds from interest accounts	—	—	—	—	—
Total Project Portfolio Flows = Project Portfolio Sources (Uses) of PFI Funds -- Matching Basis	—	—	—	—	—

a. Before write-offs.

351

imputing income on the float, for several reasons. First, the focus of the analysis is the impact of project activities, which consist of project round loans. Subproject activity is defined in project design and is expected to create developmental impacts greater than, or of a different quality from, those that could be achieved if the PFI simply borrowed local or foreign currency commercially.

Second, these benefits or losses are difficult to predict because positive float normally is not generated in a project's early years. The float is a residual and the quantity can vary greatly as a result of relatively small changes in subborrower repayment performance. Hence, estimates are inevitably soft. Finally, the float provides project promoters an opportunity to inflate project benefits using spurious assumptions regarding returns. Many development assistance agencies do not have quality control procedures sufficient to spot this type of deception.

While interest accounts should be adjusted for the float, the principal accounts used to calculate the PFI's Project Portfolio Sources (Uses) of Project Funds do not have to be adjusted in Table 14.7A. Any mismatches are actual project sources or uses of funds for which no interest costs or returns are calculated. The repayment of the project loan is a "project activity" and is a determinant of the impact of the project on the intermediary.

Portfolio Flows: Their Residual Net Worth and Net Present Value

Table 14.7 (or 14.7A if back-to-back repayment is not required) summarizes the financing flows under the project that include loan and subloan contractual repayment terms and the modifications to them caused by arrears. These data are used to calculate the NPV and RNW for these flows. The RNW from the financing flows is the cumulative Project Portfolio Sources (Uses) of PFI Funds on the matching basis.

The NPV to the PFI from project participation is determined by the cash absorbed or released during each accounting year by project activities. The NPV of financing flows can be obtained by discounting the annual Project Portfolio Sources (Uses) of PFI Funds from Table 14.7 or 14.7A, as appropriate, at the blended cost of capital for the project activity. This cost is approximated by the weighted average of the rate of interest charged on the project loan to the PFI and the PFI's marginal cost of the funds it subscribes to the project according to the project financing formula. If a donor finances 80 percent of subloan disbursements, for example, the PFI's portion would be 20 percent. (Calculation of the project's costs of capital is refined below.) Where funds are interest-free but subject to an annual service charge, the service charge may be treated as the cost of donor funds.

Discounting portfolio flows by the actual cost of funds permits evaluation of the lending activity on its own terms. However, the results can be misleading if inflation is not taken into account. A program that appears worthwhile may not be attractive in the long run if it fails to enable the PFI to earn a return at least equal to the rate of inflation. Inflation rates exceeding rates of return earned by a lender reduce the value of the lender's business, measured in terms of the purchasing power of money. Therefore, the discount rate used for NPV calculations should equal the cost of funds plus a projected rate of inflation.

Because the project's major impact on a PFI is through the financing flows, these calculations yield a major preliminary analytical result. They are an initial indication whether loan and subloan terms are appropriate. They also permit "what if?" calculations to determine trade-offs between the subloan collection rate and the subloan interest rate, for example, that would yield a positive NPV and RNW, as discussed in chapter 13.

Chapter 13 advocated repeated calculation of these measures of project worth throughout the project cycle. Usually, project life will not have ended at the time calculations are made. Actual information should be presented and evaluated, and projections should be made to cover the remaining years. If either of these projected portfolio measures is negative during project identification, preparation or appraisal, design modifications are required to increase interest spreads or collections or both. If projected indicators turn negative during implementation, remedial action is called for, usually directed first at subloan recovery and second at lending decision criteria and subloan terms and conditions. In extreme cases project lending should be aborted to stem a swelling tide of projected losses.

Completing the Analysis

Portfolio analysis does not fully portray the impact of the project on the PFI, and the NPV and RNW calculated for financing flows are only partial indicators. Calculation of the overall project impact requires analysis of the costs to the PFI of delivering and recovering subloans and obtaining and administering a project loan. Also, the loan may include a small portion for technical assistance, and projects may generate noninterest income from project activities or from related (collateral) business from subborrowers. The refinements required to capture all project-related lending revenues and expenses and other flows tend to decrease the partial NPV and RNW of project activities calculated from the financing flows. This is because overhead expenses are likely to be significant. Therefore, the credit terms derived from partial indicators based only on portfolio flows should produce a generous margin to cover overheads.

If, however, the partial NPV and RNW are massively negative, further analysis is usually not necessary, especially for ex-post evaluation. The project is clearly inappropriate; no additional calculations are required to support this conclusion. Completion of the analysis is helpful in other cases, as outlined in this section.

When portfolio analysis is completed, the second major component in measuring a project's impact on a PFI can be addressed by incorporating data from Tables 14.2 through 14.7A. These tables are henceforth referred to as Set 1 tables. Unless the PFI keeps detailed records and treats the project as a cost or profit center or as a shell subsidiary with its own financial statements, further worksheets and financial statements must be constructed to complete the analysis. These are called Set 2 tables. No examples of their formats are given because several of these are impressionistic, with more fluid formats than Set 1 tables, and because they can be constructed by any financial analyst worthy of the title. (The mechanics of financial statement construction are covered in basic accounting and corporate finance textbooks.)

INCORPORATING OTHER PROJECT EXPENSES AND REVENUES. Variables quantified in Set 2 worksheets include: (a) additional financing costs of project funds such as commitment fees and front-end charges where these are applied; (b) noninterest income from charges such as loan application and ledger fees levied on subborrowers, and letters of credit issued; (c) cash and the cost of cash required to support lending operations and project overheads; (d) operation, maintenance and sale of repossessed assets; (e) the cost of project supplies; (f) capital and operating costs of project fixed assets; (g) incremental staff costs associated with project implementation; (h) other loan-financed technical assistance expenses; and (i) foreign exchange gains or losses where the lender is subject to foreign exchange risk by borrowing in one currency and lending in another; and (j) travel and representation costs the PFI incurs in dealing with suppliers of project funds and others involved in project activities other than as subborrowers.

Separate tables are required to derive each of these variables. The data for some of these tables can be taken directly from project records, while others require analytical assumptions and estimates. In all cases, the assumptions or bases for the estimates required should be fully explained and disclosed. Assumptions are most commonly required where joint costs are attributable in part to project activities and in part to other PFI activities. Two types of joint costs are usually especially important in project impact analysis: staff costs and noninterest costs of project funds.

With respect to staff costs, for example, a branch office may process project subloans, other loans, money transfers and deposit transactions. What proportion of the branch manager's, the credit manager's and the branch accountant's time, if any, should be treated as a project overhead? With respect to noninterest costs of project funds, for example, what portion of loan commitment fees should be allocated to subloans and what proportion to positive project float?

OVERHEAD COST ALLOCATION. Cost accounting is usually difficult in financial institutions because of the complexity of joint costs, and their costing systems are not so highly refined as in modern industrial firms. This tests analysts' skills. Reflecting their training and sense of professional standards, many financial analysts prefer not to participate in highly speculative cost allocations, but quite often the PFI's chief accountant can offer guidance about reasonable ranges of allocations of overheads.

Several natural categories may help organize the analysis of cost data. At the very crudest level, the PFI's overhead costs could be allocated according to the relative size of project operations as determined by the percentage of total assets represented by project assets. More refined approaches would examine the sources of cost in more detail. For example, certain project activities are undertaken at the PFI's head office, while others may be conducted at branches, and their related costs may be estimated accordingly. Staff hours devoted to project activities by employees at different salary grades provide a basis for allocation.

Numbers of loans processed may be used to weigh costs by organizational unit, as does the time taken to process different types of loans, including project subloans. Focusing the analysis on the incremental costs associated with the project is generally useful. These overheads would not be incurred in the absence of the project, and hence are clearly allocable to it.

ADDITIONAL FINANCING COSTS OF PROJECT FUNDS. The cost of funds from many sources is not limited to interest, but also includes commitment fees on loan funds that are available but not yet drawn and front-end charges such as loan processing fees and "points" equal to one percent of loan principal that are deducted as fees by the lender at the time a loan is issued. In projects where positive float is expected to occur, the noninterest financial charges paid by the PFI on the project loan and special account interest income should be prorated over the subloans and the positive project float because they are related to the use of project funds, not just for subprojects.

Prorating noninterest costs of funds and special account interest is not routinely done by a PCI's accounting system, but can be accomplished by several simple analytical steps.[6] The first allocates these items according to loan balances outstanding each year, and the second allocates these to subloan balances outstanding each year:

Step 1: (a) calculate the sum of total noninterest charges over the life of the loan; (b) calculate the average outstanding loan balance each year; (c) aggregate these average balances; (d) divide each annual average loan balance by the aggregate to establish the relative weight of each year's average outstanding balance; and (e) multiply each year's relative weight by the total net charges calculated in step 1:a to determine the net charges allocable to each year of project life.

Step 2: (a) calculate the average subloan principal portfolio each year; (b) determine the portion of each year's subloan principal portfolio that is funded by the loan (as opposed to the PFI's own resources); (c) for each year, multiply this proportion by the net charges allocable to that year, as determined in step 1: (e) above to derive the prorated net charge.

---

6. More complex procedures using discounting could also be used instead of the simple accounting treatment listed here.

The Final Analysis

Set 1 and Set 2 tables permit construction of project financial statements, consisting of annual balance sheets, income statements and sources and uses of funds statements. These financial statements can be analyzed using the customary tools of financial reporting and management. Although their contents are noted below, the formats for this analysis require no detailed elaboration here because they follow general practice in the trade. They should contain the fullest possible disclosure through account headings, footnotes and other notes and text, especially with regard to arrears and bad debt losses. Where project life has not yet ended, the analyst should present and evaluate actual data and make projections to cover the remaining years.

Traditional project analysis often omits the balance sheet, income statement, and sources and uses of funds statement, and instead relies on "cash flow" tables to derive the net benefit stream for rate of return analysis. The project NPV and RNW could of course be quantified using the "cash flow" statement, and this technique was used in Set 1 tables to derive the partial NPV and RNW from the financing flows. However, the temptation to use the "cash flow" approach should be resisted in the final analysis for three reasons:

1. Inclusiveness: The balance sheet, income statement and sources and uses methodology that is most conducive to identifying all relevant financial stocks and flows in a credit project. The "cash flow" approach easily omits the impact of changes in certain balance sheet accounts.

2. Conceptual accuracy: The relationship among the balance sheet, income statement and sources and uses statement ensures that all items must be treated consistently. Debits and credits cannot be confused, so the direction of all flows is accurately shown.

3. Mathematical accuracy: The balance sheet, income statement and sources and uses statement must reconcile. The "cash flow" methodology has no internal check.

PROJECT ASSETS. The assets on the project balance sheet would normally consist primarily of the following accounts:

1. Cash and near cash held to support project activities. The size of these balances would generally be related to the volume of subloans

committed but not yet drawn by subborrowers, and of funds to service the project loan, pay staff and cover incidentals. Assumptions used to forecast the cash requirement should be disclosed.

2. Loans outstanding to project subborrowers. This is normally the major asset during most of the life of a credit project. Subloans outstanding should be disaggregated as principal not yet due and principal in arrears, interest accrued and interest in arrears. Term loan balances are customarily broken down into a current portion consisting of amounts falling due within 12 months, and a long-term portion falling due after 12 months.

3. Bad debt allowance (a contra-asset account) for project subloans, with a footnote or other explanation of how its size is determined and of the basis on which this valuation reserve is credited and debited.

4. Miscellaneous project assets including vehicles, data processing equipment and other fixed assets funded under the project for which accumulated depreciation should be shown as a contra-asset account. Other assets arising from or required for project implementation may include minor receivables, inventories of supplies, and repossessed assets.

PROJECT LIABILITIES. The project balance sheet normally contains the following liability accounts:

1. Administrative and staff expenses accrued, representing project overhead.

2. Miscellaneous liabilities, such as deposits placed by subloan applicants in fulfillment of down payment requirements, for example.

3. Accrued interest expense on the project loan, with any overdue portion broken out.

4. The balance outstanding on the project loan, broken down to show the current portion due within the next 12 months, the noncurrent portion due beyond the next 12 months, and overdues, if any, of project loan principal.

PROJECT NET WORTH. The net worth accounts of the project normally consist of equity contributed by the intermediary out of its own resources, retained earnings or losses, gains or losses from changes in the PFI's foreign exchange exposure, if any, on the project loan, and possibly equity invested by the government in the form of grants. The equity contributed by the intermediary is an important variable, arising from start-up expenses incurred before project funds become available and from the reimbursement method of financing subloan disbursements. This contribution is risk capital, representing the PFI's commitment to bear losses from bad debts and operations, if these occur.

Risk capital committed by the PFI is not necessarily contributed in the same manner as a capital subscription in one big block. Rather, it arises simply through project operations. For example, cash is required to fund the negative float when subloan disbursement begins. In double entry accounting this transaction is represented by a debit to project cash and a credit to project equity. Likewise, the PFI incurs expenses generating loans before interest income is earned. In other words, the PFI's equity contribution to the project funds the negative float in the early years of many credit projects.

Negative float should disappear as projects age. They ideally become net generators of cash as collections from subborrowers exceed operating expenses and debt service on the project loan. The assumption applied to project net worth accounts for this analysis is that the intermediary taps any net positive funds flows to recoup and retire its own equity investment in the project and then to build up cash and retained earnings on the project balance sheet. Positive project float is the source of the positive net worth that should be on the project's final balance sheet to satisfy the RNW criterion. The final project balance sheet ideally consists of one asset (cash), no liabilities, and net worth consisting of retained earnings equivalent to cash.

PROJECT INCOME AND EXPENSE. The income statement for the project activity should show interest earned on project subloans; other income such as subloan application fees and legal fees; interest expenses; commitment fees earned on subloans or incurred on the loan; the bad debt provision, preferably disaggregated into accounts arising from disbursements of principal and from interest earned; and staff costs and administrative expenses. The income statement should not stop with net profit, but permit transparent derivation of the funds flow statement by showing "below the line" items that change project net worth. These include capital contributions or withdrawals by the intermediary as well as net project profit after tax and any other changes in project net worth.

The first income statement should record expenses before project funds are available to fund loans that generate revenue. These include development expenses incurred to obtain the loan from the donor or government. Likewise, the opening balance sheet should show these expenses contributed by the PFI as a charge to net worth, offset by equity.

CONSTRUCTING THE SOURCES AND USES OF FUNDS STATEMENT. The format for the sources and uses of funds statement is flexible, giving the analyst an opportunity to tell the story of the PFI's participation in the most expressive way possible. Some sources and uses statements simply show total sources, total uses, and the difference, which is the change in cash. This presentation demonstrates only that the analyst has succeeded in getting the statements to balance. A more instructive format would follow the pattern of Table 14.7 or 14.7A, but adding all other sources and uses to show overall project float.

The bottom line of the sources and uses statement shows changes in cash, which are discounted to obtain the net present value of the project to the PFI. The discount factor is determined by the cost of project funds to the PFI. The cost of funds in the final analysis is the weighted average of the yield equivalent of commitment fees, up-front charges and interest paid by the PFI on the project loan, and of the PFI's marginal cost of funds from sources other than the project loan. This is a more refined measure than the simple cost of funds applied to the portfolio flows which gave a useful first approximation. The yield equivalent is a discount rate that provides the same NPV over the life of the loan as the combination of fees, charges and interest due as specified in the loan agreement, discounted at the rate of interest charged on the loan.

SUPPLEMENTARY ANALYSIS. Once the NPV and RNW are quantified, the analysis of project subloans and related overheads may be supplemented by comparative analysis of other portfolio segments or the PFI's overall term lending, for example. It can also be placed in context by an analysis of the general situation of the PFI. This can show how the project performs relative to the PFI's overall activities. Of particular interest is the relative importance of the project in the institution's overall operations. The overall operations of the PFI are also the proper focus of analysis when it is not possible to calculate the project's NPV and RNW, as detailed in the section that follows.

Focus of Analysis: The Lending Institution

Project funding strategies determine the appropriate focus of project review, as noted earlier. When the strategy consists of making a line of credit available to a PFI to support its overall activities, M+E emphasis must be on the PFI's overall operations and policies. In these cases the project's contribution to the PFI's overall activities is often either relatively minor, as when the PFI is large because it operates nationally in a large country, or relatively large when the institution is small. Using this approach, the donor "buys a time slice" of a PFI's lending program, and the impact of the donor's funds cannot usually be meaningfully identified or distinguished from the PFI's other sources and uses of funds. The institution is the focus of the project, and project appraisal documents often make representations about the operations of the institution and outline measures, agreed under the project, to improve its performance.

The Content of the Analysis

A standard analysis of a credit institution determines the intermediary's quality from its financial statements and related statistics. The analytical objectives are to judge financial performance and financial condition. Performance is measured primarily by earnings after adequate provisions are made for bad debt losses. Analysis of the PFI's condition requires detailed review of the loan portfolio to determine its value, which ultimately is reflected in liquidity and its capital adequacy. Financial ratios identify major elements and trends in costs, earnings, and spreads, and indicate important balance sheet relationships and their development over time. Sources and uses of funds statements are constructed to show changes in financial, income and cost structures, and in liquidity. From these data the quality of the PFI's lending decisions may be determined, and additional investigation into specific subloans is usually undertaken to identify problem areas.

The period covered by the analysis ideally begins with a base year immediately or several years prior to the PFI's access to project funds, extends through the present or the close of the most recent accounting year completed, and may go on to make projections by extrapolating from recent performance. Loan and investment portfolio quality is the most important variable because it determines the quality of earnings: interest earned in accounting terms but not ultimately collected on bad loans clearly does not strengthen the PFI, for example. Portfolio quality and earnings quality in turn determine the capital adequacy or solvency of a financial institution because capital is created by earnings and destroyed by losses from bad debts and inefficient operations.

PFI analysis should include measures of overhead costs and relate them to the volume of loans the PFI commits and disburses, to loan portfolio size, and to other measures of activity. Loan volume can be related to the number of staff, and to staff and other noninterest costs, to obtain insights into productivity. Performance, not their paper qualifications or time in service, should underlie evaluation of staff quality.

The degree of dependence on project resources should be calculated as a proportion of total commitments, disbursements, the loan portfolio and total assets. The analyst should examine comparative costs of funds from different sources, and of changes in the composition and volume of lending, to look for clues whether project resources were used as substitutes for other foreign or domestic resources that the PFI could have mobilized.

The analyst should quantify subsidies for PFIs, use of central bank advances or rediscounting, equity injections by government, and recourse to credit guarantee funds. These nonmarket sources of funds may be important determinants of institutional viability and of PFIs' incentives to be associated with projects that include them.

The CAMEL Rating System

The most well-documented analytical approach to retail financial institutions that accept deposits and make loans is known as CAMEL, an acronym for capital adequacy, asset quality, management, earnings and liquidity.[7] U.S. regulatory authorities developed CAMEL for application

7. See for example, Board of Governors of the Federal Reserve System, *Commercial Bank Examination Manual.* Available in looseleaf form from Publication Services, Board of Governors of the Federal Reserve System, Washington, DC 20051, USA. Section 900.503.1 "Overall Conclusions Regarding Condition of the Bank" summarizes the CAMEL rating system. The CAMEL rating system for credit unions is described in NCUA Letter No. 111, September 29, 1989. National Credit Union Administration, 1776 G Street, NW, Suite 800, Washington, DC 20006, USA.

to commercial banks, savings and loan associations, and credit unions. It can be adapted to many other types of project lenders. Adaptation requires the development of ratios relevant to the type of institution being reviewed. CAMEL places great emphasis on comparing an intermediary with its peer group of similar institutions. These comparisons may be impossible where the country contains no similar institutions, or meaningless where most of the peer group are poor performers and cannot offer a useful standard for comparison. In these situations peer group comparison should not be attempted.

Data Quality Problems

Data on PFI financial performance and condition are often grossly deficient because of poor financial housekeeping or because other goals are more important than financial goals. This can be a serious complicating factor because analysis is not very useful if portfolio value cannot be accurately and consistently determined.[8] In this situation the analyst should begin with an examination of debt service payments collected and then examine other flows. These will often provide insights into the quality of the stocks to which they are related, such as the loan portfolio and capital.

Further analysis of poor quality data may be limited to calculating probable performance ranges or thresholds that permit conclusions such as, "if the target quantity A is to be achieved, then variable B would have to equal or exceed (or not exceed) value C." If the data base is massively deficient, the futility of analysis should be noted and the exercise terminated in the interest of economy. Energy should be redirected to improving the quality of information, although that may not be a feasible short-run objective. But the concern that poor data not be deeply analyzed is broader: extensive analysis of bad data conveys that the data are worth something. Why else would a reasonable person devote so much effort to their interpretation? Then the conclusions drawn from the analysis may take on a life of their own, far from reality, and lay the ground for further costly mistakes in the form of additional irrelevant or unresponsive projects. Analysis of fiction is properly a literary pursuit, not a task for which accountants or financial analysts are trained.

---

8. See Morris C. Mould, "Financial Information for Management of a Development Finance Institution: Some Guidelines." World Bank Technical Paper Number 63, Industry and Finance Series. Washington, DC: 1987.

Review can identify MIS problems for projects to address through technical assistance (TA). Projects that are closely tied with a discrete set of activities usually offer opportunities to make a fresh start in recordkeeping with the implementation of a new activity or a new phase of an established activity. However, this opportunity is often not developed because the overriding objective is disbursement to meet lending targets, not reinforcement for the PFI. Serious attention to financial housekeeping might require temporary suspensions of lending operations to reduce the flow of paperwork and to redeploy staff to work on back office problems. Where project design fails to include adequate TA or to create incentives for better accounting, attempts to start afresh are often contaminated sooner or later by the financial housekeeping problems endemic to the PFI.

Summary of the Analytical Framework

The analytical framework used to determine project impact on a PFI encompasses two types of analysis. Table 14.8 lists these types and their characteristics. Review of the project activity alone is appropriate where the project activity is clearly identifiable because the PFI maintains separate accounting records for it. This analysis focuses on the subloan portfolio and related overheads. The tests of the net present value of project activities to the institution and the residual net worth generated for the institution by these activities measure the loss or benefit to the PFI from participating in the project. Analytical problems most frequently encountered include limited data availability, poor data quality, inadequate provision for bad debt losses, and lack of transparency in project design.

Where the institution's overall activities are the focus of the project and the PFI does not maintain separate files on project-supported subloans, the PFI's overall performance should be analyzed to determine its financial performance and condition. This analytical task is a standard one, and analytical packages such as CAMEL can be adapted for this purpose. Major problems likely to be encountered include limited data availability, poor data quality, and inadequate provision for bad debt losses (which overstates the value of the PFI's portfolio and its net worth).

Issue 3: Financial Development Impact

Profitable financial institutions and projects that have positive NPVs and RNWs are important for development, but good financial performance

Table 14.8 Analytical Paths to Determining Project Impact on a Participating Financial Intermediary (PFI)

Project Funding Method	Focus of Analysis	Measurement Criteria	Analytical Method	Most Serious Problems Likely To Be Encountered
Funds for specific project activities	Project subloan portfolio and related overheads	Net present value (NPV) and residual net worth (RNW) created by project activities	Subloan portfolio analysis followed by project overhead analysis	Data inaccessability. Poor data quality. Inadequate provisions for bad debt losses. Lack of transparency in project design.
Line of credit supporting PFI's overall activities	PFI	PFI financial performance and financial condition	Standard analysis of a credit institution (e.g., CAMEL suitably modified)	Data inaccessability. Poor data quality. Inadequate provisions for bad debt losses, which overstates portfolio value, earnings, and capital.

does not necessarily indicate that a project or intermediary promotes development. Analysis of Issue 2 to determine project impact or intermediary profitability should be supplemented by an examination of the context in which a profit was earned. For example, if a project's value to an intermediary is positive or an intermediary is profitable because of a monopoly position guaranteed by government charter, from subsidies, or from nonmarket activities (directly unproductive behavior) to protect a franchise, performance is not necessarily developmental because it is not based on market operations and is probably not efficient. In contrast, profit earned from innovation or from superior performance in a competitive or contestable market is more likely to contribute to development because it reflects success in reducing costs.

The developmental implications of an intermediary's profit arising from project activities can be inferred from the impact of project activities on financial market development. Profits promoting financial market development are more desirable than those constraining it because efficient financial markets assist social and economic development.

The majority of credit projects backed by development assistance agencies through the mid-1990s may well have negative NPVs and RNWs, and many of the institutions involved are in fact unprofitable when their bad debt losses are properly accounted for. Here, too, the relation of project activities to financial market development is important. It would be reassuring to find that such losses represent no more than creative failure or start-up costs of activities that produce tremendous benefits while imposing few long-run social and economic costs. This possibility can be at least partially tested by examining the impact of loss-making projects and intermediaries on financial market development.[9]

Project Credit Delivery Occurs Through Financial Instruments

The contribution of projects to financial development consists of financial innovations and improvement of procedures and practices. These lengthen term structures, reduce transaction costs, and refine valuation

9. An excellent review that successfully combines subborrower activity, lender performance and financial development issues is H.A.J. Moll's *Farmers and Finance: Experience with Institutional Savings and Credit in West Java* (Wageningen, The Netherlands: Pudoc, 1989). This work and that of Mahabub Hossain cited earlier on Grameen Bank set a new standard in credit project review.

processes as explained in chapter 1. Projects should increase the volume of intermediation and create financially stronger intermediaries, and possibly realize economies of scope and scale.

Examination of this contribution begins with review of the performance of the financial instruments that structure intermediaries' transactions with their clients. Instruments are defined for this purpose as in chapter 5 to encompass financial services such as checking accounts, savings accounts and direct deposit arrangements for wages and crop deliveries, and specific types of loans, as well as the financial infrastructure supporting these services, including methods used to evaluate the eligibility of loan applicants. Appropriateness of a project or a project component's financial instruments is demonstrated by their sustainability. Transaction costs, pricing and incentives determine sustainability, and these should be explored in review. In part, this analysis can be built upon the institutional analysis generated in the study of the second issue, the impact of a project on the financial intermediary implementing it, which should be conducted prior to financial development impact analysis.

ARE PROJECT INSTRUMENTS INNOVATIVE? Examination of instruments should determine whether the project was innovative, or whether it simply expanded the coverage of an existing way of doing business. Once the analyst has ascertained the status of the project instrument or instruments, the next step is to determine the significance of the project instrument by reviewing the innovativeness of the rest of the financial market segment in which the project operates.

For example, an innovative small scale industry credit project should be compared with other lending to small scale industrial firms, while a small scale savings mobilization campaign should be compared with the performance of other small scale savings services. In most cases at the frontier this comparison should include informal financial intermediaries and instruments as a point of departure. This overall inventory of innovations should review changes in formal and informal finance and identify innovations that have been successful and sustainable and those that failed. Was the project instrument a bold entrepreneurial leap in a sleepy market, one attempt at innovation among many in a dynamic market, or destined for failure because it was designed without reference to conditions in the financial market?

DID PROJECT INSTRUMENTS PROMOTE COMPETITION IN FINANCE? Examination of instruments and trends in their development permits evaluation of the degree of competition in financial markets. Competitive markets are characterized by innovation in the form of new instruments. Competitiveness also reduces transaction costs and changes their distribution as intermediaries seek to reduce the costs of savers, borrowers and their own operations. Where competition is absent, intermediaries' costs are high, and the transaction costs of users of financial services are also high, consisting in part of those passed on to them by intermediaries.

Review should examine transaction costs to ascertain whether the project was consistent with or in opposition to market trends, and how transaction costs associated with the project compare to those in other parts of the financial market similar to or in competition with the project's niche. The analyst should use hard data whenever feasible. Where data are not available and the costs of obtaining them are high, proxies may offer qualitative indicators of competition. Proxies include queuing time, increased accessibility through longer opening hours and voluntary expansion of branch networks, simplifications in loan documentation, and reductions in minimum balance requirements, loan sizes and money transfer fees. Review should indicate the extent to which the project contributed to a competitive market, and whether this contribution was catalytic, novel, or trivial.

Financial Market Structure

What is the relationship of the project to the structure of the financial market and changes in its structure? How did PFIs fare relative to other institutions? Have they retained, lost or gained market share, and is the overall market share of the PFIs' subsector or peer group growing or shrinking within the formal financial market? Have project interventions influenced nonPFIs and the pricing of credit and saving instruments? What information exists about financial market flows and of the extent to which financial instruments have competed with nonfinancial forms of savings and credit?

Many projects attempt to lengthen the term structure of financial markets initially in the hope that DFIs could implement a refinement in valuation that would generate a demonstration effect that would stimulate competition and the spontaneous development of term markets. This dimension deserves considerable analytical attention in review whenever a shortage of term funds is cited as a rationale for a project: the following discussion of term transformation responds to donors' emphasis on term lending.

The variety of instruments offered is another dimension of financial market structure. Greater variety demonstrates refinement of valuation processes and offers more flexibility to issuers of instruments and to their buyers. Flexibility provides more approaches to risk management, which in turn helps to lengthen term structures. This is achieved in two ways. First, greater confidence attracts longer-term funds, and intermediaries can match longer-term loans with longer-term deposits. This is a useful, low-risk but somewhat plodding way to lengthen term structure.

Second, flexibility permits intermediaries to lengthen term structures by borrowing short and lending long, a process known as term transformation or as gapping. Term transformation may enable an intermediary to increase profits because long-term lending rates are generally higher than short-term rates. Because of this, gapping is a more exciting and risky way of lengthening term structure. Risk operates in two directions. One is the liquidity risk of losing deposits in the short run while loans remain on the books for the long run, and the second is the pricing risk of having to raise deposits rates to retain deposits while not being able to raise lending rates fixed in loan contracts. Liquidity risk and pricing risk are related, because liquidity can be purchased by offering higher prices for deposits or other sources of funds.

TERM TRANSFORMATION AND LIQUIDITY. The extent of term transformation and one aspect of the risk it produces can be shown by comparing the term structure of intermediaries' liabilities and the term structure of their assets. This can be done crudely by using the usual balance sheet classifications of short-term and long-term assets and liabilities and comparing the net short- and long-term balances, or in detail by identifying the mismatch or gaps between the maturities of a lender's assets and liabilities, which shows the extent of borrowing short and lending long or vice-versa.

Table 14.9 shows the maturity mismatches between the two sides of a hypothetical balance sheet for time periods of up to and beyond 36 months. Borrowing short and lending long occurs when the intermediary's

Table 14.9 Schedule of Assets and Liabilities by Maturity December 31, 19XX
(US$ millions)

	Months to Maturity						
	0-1	2-3	4-6	7-12	13-36	36+	Total
Assets							
Marketable securities	37.1	10.7	7.4	14.0	9.4	.1	78.7
Loans: floating rate							
overdrafts	188.6						188.6
project lines of credit	82.7						82.7
machinery & equipment	.2	.4	.8	1.5	6.2	3.7	12.8
mortgages	.1	.2	.3	1.2	5.0	23.5	30.3
Loans: fixed rate							
bills discounted	18.4	26.9	10.3				55.6
consumer	2.5	5.1	7.8	14.0	10.3		39.7
vehicles	4.0	7.9	11.7	22.0	30.6		76.2
machinery & equipment	.4	.9	1.4	2.6	9.6	2.0	16.9
mortgages	.3	.6	1.1	2.2	8.0	3.1	15.3
Total earning assets	*334.3*	*52.7*	*40.8*	*57.5*	*79.1*	*32.4*	*596.8*
Cash & due from banks	31.4						31.4
Premises & equipment, net						13.2	13.2
Other assets						43.9	43.9
less: Loan loss reserve						(17.9)	(17.9)
Total assets	*365.7*	*52.7*	*40.8*	*57.5*	*79.1*	*71.6*	*667.4*

		Months to Maturity					
	0-1	2-3	4-6	7-12	13-36	36+	Total
Liabilities & Net Worth							
Interest-bearing deposits:							
floating rate	5.2	10.6	16.0	35.8	45.5	12.1	125.2
fixed rate	192.9	58.9	23.1	3.0	.2		278.1
Development project loans:							
floating rate	.2	.4	.6	2.8	12.5	31.8	48.3
fixed rate	.1	.2	.3	1.3	5.5	36.6	44.0
Total Interest-bearing liabilities	*198.4*	*70.1*	*40.0*	*42.9*	*63.7*	*80.5*	*495.6*
Demand deposits	99.7						99.7
Other liabilities	30.5	9.0					39.5
Net Worth						32.6	32.6
Total Liabilities & Net Worth	*328.6*	*79.1*	*40.0*	*42.9*	*63.7*	*113.1*	*667.4*
Maturity Mismatch							
Current	37.1	(26.4)	.8	14.6	15.4	(41.5)	
Cumulative	37.1	10.7	11.5	26.1	41.5	-0-	

liabilities (primarily deposits) falling due within a time period are smaller than the assets (primarily loans) maturing during that period. This is a positive mismatch, which is indicated in the table by the differences between total assets maturing in each period and total liabilities and net worth maturing in each period.

(Net worth has no meaningful maturity for a corporation as a going concern. It is included here conceptually because it provides a cushion against mismatching and mechanically so that total footings equal those in the balance sheet. Lumping net worth and noninterest–bearing liabilities and nonearning assets into the final period, 36+ months in this case, also balances the cumulative mismatch from previous periods.)

In the situation portrayed in Table 14.9 the intermediary has a positive mismatch in all periods except two-to-three months out and the final period, and a cumulative positive mismatch up to the final period. This intermediary engages moderately in term transformation, with a cumulative mismatch of $41.5 million in the most distant bounded period, 12-36 months, equal to slightly more than 6 percent of total assets.

TERM TRANSFORMATION AND EARNINGS. Gap analysis shows the rate at which assets and liabilities can be repriced. Table 14.10 shows the same data spread by repricing intervals. An asset reprices when it matures, as it is recycled into another loan or cash or some other asset. An asset may also reprice before maturity if it is prepaid or if specific provision is made in the loan contract for a change in the interest rate. Gap analysis provides a static view of the risk to earnings arising from borrowing at one set of repricing intervals and lending at another. This analysis permits intermediaries to determine their crude sensitivity to changes in interest rates. (Gap analysis is discussed here as a measure of term transformation. It is not a sufficient basis for asset/liability management, which is designed to relate earnings and portfolio structure strategies in response to risk.)[10]

A positive gap exists when assets reprice more rapidly than liabilities and net worth, which means that a rise in interest rates will tend to increase intermediary profitability because assets will command higher prices faster

10. One article exploring this distinction is John R. Segerstrom and Greg D. Meadows, "Why Gap Doesn't Work: Using Traditional Gap to Measure Interest Rate Risk Is Like Tallying Up the Money in Your Vault by Simply Counting the Bills—Whether They're $1s or $100s," *ABA Banking Journal*. lxxxii, 10, October 1990. pp. 44 ff.

than liabilities. Intermediaries with negative gaps stand to gain from interest rates declines. They suffer when rising interest rates puts upward pressure on the cost of funds that cannot be immediately passed on to all borrowers.

Table 14.10 portrays an aggressively gapped bank. Its cumulative positive repricing gap for all items repricing in 36 months or less amounts to $132.6 million, as shown at the bottom of the table. The cumulative gap equals almost 20 percent of total assets, making the institution highly rate sensitive.

Concerns about risks to liquidity and earnings lead back to consideration of data quality. If the numbers in financial statements are not worth much, neither are their analyses. A fundamental question is whether loan maturities are a realistic indicator of repayment expectations. The loan loss reserve amounting to more than 3 percent of interest-earning assets in Tables 14.9 and 14.10 would be high for a commercial bank and low for a development finance institution. Are loans being charged off against this provision so that balance sheet assets are a reasonable approximation of their realizable value? To the extent that delinquency separates maturity from collectability, liquidity analysis has to be refined to include the probable effect of arrears.

Neither gap analysis nor liquidity analysis tells the entire story of term transformation. Different items on the balance sheet have different degrees of "stickiness." For example, demand deposits would be unlikely to be withdrawn all at once except in liquidation; nor would the savings deposits among the fixed rate interest-bearing deposit liabilities, even though these are generally payable on demand. This stickiness illustrates the importance of the intermediary's capital, its range of services to clients, and its management, which provide confidence to clients. Capital is thin in this case, however, amounting to less than 5 percent of total assets.

Likewise, overdrafts and project lines of credit are made against demand notes that may be called for repayment at any time but are only theoretically realizable immediately. Not all borrowers could repay immediately because of the time required to rearrange their financial affairs or liquidate their business in the event of a call. Strict classifications based on scheduled maturities and contractual interest rates reveal but also conceal.

Table 14.10 Schedule of Assets and Liabilities—Subject to Repricing by Time Period December 31, 19XX
(US$ millions)

| | Months to Repricing | | | | | | |
	0-1	2-3	4-6	7-12	13-36	36+	Total
Assets							
Marketable securities	37.1	10.7	7.4	14.0	9.4	.1	78.7
Loans: floating rate							
overdrafts	188.6						188.6
project lines of credit	82.7						82.7
machinery & equipment	4.0	7.8	1.0				12.8
mortgages	7.5	15.2	7.6				30.3
Loans: fixed rate							
bills discounted	18.4	26.9	10.3				55.6
consumer	2.5	5.1	7.8	14.0	10.3		39.7
vehicles	4.0	7.9	11.7	22.0	30.6		76.2
machinery & equipment	.4	.9	1.4	2.6	9.6	2.0	16.9
mortgages	.3	.6	1.1	2.2	8.0	3.1	15.3
Total earning assets	*345.5*	*75.1*	*48.3*	*54.8*	*67.9*	*5.2*	*596.8*
Cash & due from banks						31.4	31.4
Premises & equipment, net						13.2	13.2
Other assets						43.9	43.9
less: Loan loss reserve						(17.9)	(17.9)
Total assets	*345.5*	*75.1*	*48.9*	*54.8*	*67.9*	*75.8*	*667.4*

| | Months to Repricing | | | | | | |
	0-1	2-3	4-6	7-12	13-36	36+	Total
Liabilities & Net Worth							
Interest-bearing deposits:							
floating rate	125.2						125.2
fixed rate	192.9	58.9	23.1	3.0	.2		278.1
Development project loans:							
floating rate	4.4	8.6	11.2	24.1			48.3
fixed rate	.1	.2	.3	1.3	5.5	36.6	44.0
Total Interest-bearing liabilities	*322.6*	*67.7*	*34.6*	*28.4*	*5.7*	*36.6*	*495.6*
Demand deposits						99.7	99.7
Other liabilities						39.5	39.5
Net Worth						32.6	32.6
Total Liabilities & Net Worth	*322.6*	*67.7*	*34.6*	*28.4*	*5.7*	*36.6*	*667.4*
Repricing Gap							
Current	22.9	7.4	13.7	26.4	62.2	(132.6)	
Cumulative	22.9	30.3	44.0	70.4	132.6	-0-	

The impact of rate sensitivity depends upon how quickly clients respond to interest rate changes. If no client withdrew funds or prepaid loans in response to unattractive rates, the institution would clearly be less sensitive than one taking and issuing smart money or "hot money" that moves around quickly in search of better rates.

As financial markets develop, the concentration of assets and liabilities in the shortest period, up to one month in the example in Tables 14.9 and 14.10, decreases. The distribution becomes more spread out. The final period used in gap analysis can be made more distant so that it contains few earning assets and interest-bearing liabilities. As this occurs, intermediaries have more alternatives for creating and managing their gaps. This of course also provides more choices to their depositors and borrowers. These refinements are beneficial for development because the role of finance can be performed more efficiently, reducing interest rates, spreads and transaction costs.

Is Liquidity a Binding Constraint?

Review should also attempt to identify environmental factors, exogenous to project design, that contribute to a project's impact on financial market development. A hypothesis to be tested is whether this dimension of project impact is related to the liquidity of the financial market. Do projects injecting liquidity into tight markets have greater direct impact on the development of these markets than projects that provide additional funds in financial markets already awash with liquidity? In highly liquid markets do structural factors inhibit the flow of domestic liquidity to activities supported by the project? For this purpose, a review of the liquidity of the overall market is required, including the matching that helps ensure liquidity as maturity structures lengthen.

Resource Mobilization and the Banking Habit

The contribution of the financial system to development is enhanced when banking relationships are developed that extend over long periods, and when these relationships grow to encompass an expanding variety of services. Review should determine whether projects tend to generate durable relationships and expanded use of financial services. Durability is reflected in repeated borrowing and in continuous use of deposit services, provided at prices that cover costs.

Issue 4: Macroeconomic and Macrofinancial Impacts

The content and methodology of macroeconomic and macrofinancial impact analysis cannot be so tightly defined as in the analysis of subproject level and institutional impacts because the impact of credit projects is indirect and because of their small size within the economy. Also, credit projects frequently have few or no macro objectives, although policies usually do. Macro dimensions are best explored last, so that results from the micro analyses may help guide macro review.

General areas for examination include market links associated with project credit; subsidies provided through or in association with project credit; any significant fiscal, monetary, trade and external debt questions associated with the project; relationships between the project or credit component and relevant national policies such as those governing interest rates and credit distribution; and relationships between aggregate reported credit issued or outstanding to a sector and value added in that sector.

Market Links

Links between markets are a rapidly evolving area of development research.[11] Financial markets are linked with many other markets by creditors and others who seek economies by providing financial services in conjunction with the acquisition of goods, use of assets or other services. Issues include the extent to which credit projects use links, as in the case where a project agency supplying fertilizer does so on credit, whether links contained in projects have proved commercially and economically sustainable, and whether links have created economies. Does failure to provide links make project activities unsustainable due to system failure or to competition from linked services outside the project? Other markets that may be examined include those for labor, land, raw materials for industry, wholesale supplies for retailers, farm inputs and farm produce, and markets for other goods and services produced by subborrowers.

Another perspective on market links is more traditional, focusing on forward and backward links and on spillover effects. Forward and

---

11. For an overview of theoretical issues and an extensive bibliography, see Avishay Braverman and Luis Guasch, "Rural Credit Markets and Institutions in Developing Countries: Lessons for Policy Analysis from Modern Theory and Practice." *World Development.* 14, 10/11, November 1986.

backward links concern the effects of innovation and investment on suppliers and on purchasers. Was a project associated with the development of new sources of raw materials or semifinished goods, with new channels of supply or distribution, and with employment creation or destruction? Spillover effects include the adoption of the project financial instrument by intermediaries outside the project and the impact of the project on other parts of the financial market. For example, was the project associated with any changes in informal finance, such as declining interest rates or the demise of traditional sources?

Market links are a useful area for consideration that will probably command more and more attention in the 1990s. This is likely to occur as the poor results of conventional credit projects become more widely documented, their implications understood, and the rationale for their continuation more openly debated. In the search for alternative means of providing credit to farmers, for example, it will be discovered that much of the credit used in agriculture in less developed as well as in developed countries is trade credit. It will be realized that this funding is working capital finance, which is said by many industrialists, traders, and farm operators to be in short supply.

Some project designers may feel unease over funding commercial activities rather than primary production, and over the loss of control inherent in putting funds in at the top of a system of market links in an effort to help those at the bottom. But, they will be able to claim credit for strengthening links all along the supply and marketing chain, and for assisting private and cooperative enterprises that compose it, some of which are relatively small scale and, in certain countries, operated by women.

Subsidies

Credit projects and components typically offer intended subborrowers interest rates below those they could obtain in commercial markets. Other vehicles of subsidy include preferred access to controlled goods financed by credit, supplemental grants to target group borrowers, special tax credits in the case of credit for "priority" industrial facilities or exports, for example, and transfers through lenders' failure to recover loans. Evaluation and sector work should classify the avenues of subsidy through or associated with projects and credit components, and quantify in the aggregate and for typical subborrowers each significant type of subsidy associated with the project.

Subsidies prompt rent-seeking by those controlling credit allocation and those petitioning for loans. This behavior would be expected to produce concentrations of credit favoring those with the ability or potential ability to pay for access, to exert political pressure, or to provide other rewards for those controlling credit access. Evaluation and sector work should document evidence of such behavior and of credit concentrations, especially where these are disproportionate among groups other than intended beneficiaries. The distribution of agricultural credit may be compared with the distribution of agricultural land, assets and income where such measures are available or easily calculated. Where this has been done, the distribution of credit usually has been found to be more skewed or concentrated than those of agricultural land, assets and income.[12]

Concern for subsidy will also be heightened by accumulation of data showing the poor financial performance of conventional credit projects. Losses incurred by financial intermediaries from undertaking the agendas of governments and donors as reflected in credit projects constitute a subsidy for borrowers under these projects. These subsidies have all the deleterious effects discussed in chapter 6 with respect to interest rates and in chapter 5 with respect to targeted credit. The arguments against targeted credit apply because defaults that result in bad debt losses for lenders are often a privilege that is politically distributed. Both of these dimensions of loss-making credit projects can hardly be considered developmental except within the extremely small margin of creative failure.

The Project-Policy Nexus

Credit projects and components are conceived and operate within a policy environment. Exploration of this dimension should identify the types of policies reinforced or challenged by credit projects and components. Affected policies should be examined with regard to their economic efficiency, the interest groups they protect and those they tax or otherwise disadvantage. Changes in policies related to project activities

---

12. See, for example, Robert C. Vogel, "The Effect of Subsidized Agricultural Credit on Income Distribution in Costa Rica," in Dale W Adams, Douglas H. Graham and J.D. Von Pischke, eds., *op. cit.* pp. 133-145.

should be reviewed to identify impacts that can be associated with the project, related sector work, or sponsorship by a development assistance agency.

Fiscal, Monetary, Trade, and External Debt Impacts

Fiscal dimensions of credit project impact include subsidies, contributions to tax revenues by project activities, and the recurring costs of government operations initiated or funded by the project. Monetary issues may arise if credit projects contribute to inflationary pressures, either generally or for those goods and services for which subloans are provided. Trade and external debt aspects may be significant when production supported by project finance is exported or substitutes for imports, and when credit projects are funded by external loans.

Projects funded by external loans make a direct contribution to foreign debt. The local currency equivalent of the debt burden frequently increases over time as the domestic currency depreciates against the foreign currency or currencies in which the project obligation is denominated. Appreciation of the foreign currency in which debt owed to the donor is denominated may even surpass and cancel any grant element arising from concessional funding of the assistance. In evaluation and sector work the local currency equivalent of the external obligation should be calculated and the costs of credit funded by external borrowing compared with the cost of domestic resource mobilization through the local financial system.

Agricultural Credit and Agricultural Value Added

Many governments accept the view that agriculture has unduly limited access to credit and that special measures are in order to direct credit to the sector. This motivation underlies many credit projects and components and is also reflected in requirements that commercial banks lend a specified portion of their portfolio to "agriculture." Because this perspective animates much intervention in frontier finance, analysis of macro issues usefully includes examination of the hypothesis that providing additional credit to agriculture increases agricultural output. Strangely, or predictably, depending on the reader's conclusions about the subject matter and point of view presented in this book, this hypothesis is rarely tested.

Data problems associated with classifying credit by loan purpose discredit this examination, but some insights should be available by comparing credit outstanding and credit issued during a period with agricultural value added during the period or with a lag during subsequent periods. A more sensitive measure compares changes in credit outstanding or issued with changes in agricultural value added. Where credit is targeted by end use, evaluation and sector work should attempt to obtain the data required to make these comparisons for the targeted sector and, if possible, for specific subsectors.

Annex A

THE REPAYMENT INDEX

The Repayment Index ranks loans or loan portfolios on a numerical scale of repayment performance. The Index compares actual arrears with the worst case alternative, which is a total absence of repayment. This permits it simultaneously to capture both timeliness of repayment and adequacy of repayment, making it unique among repayment performance measures. Compared to other single measures, the Repayment Index offers a more comprehensive quantification of repayment behavior. While widely-used indicators of loan repayment, such as the aging of arrears, collection ratios and the portion of a portfolio in arrears or infected by arrears basically seek to measure the value of an outstanding loan or of a portfolio, the Index's main application is in research, including strategy formulation within credit institutions.

The Mathematics of the Repayment Index

The Index is calculated by comparing the cumulative total of balances in arrears over the life of a loan with the cumulative total of balances in arrears that would have accumulated if no repayments were made. This is illustrated by a comparison of amounts due and amounts collected in Table 1 which shows a loan due in five equal annual installments of 100 each and repayments of 50 for each of the five periods.

Table 2 uses data from Table 1 to calculate the Repayment Index denominator, which portrays the situation in which no repayments are received. Each installment is composed of principal and interest at 10 percent. Interest at 10 percent is also compounded on amounts in arrears: each amount in column 2 is the sum of columns 4 and 5 for the previous period.

Table 1. Illustrative Loan Repayment Assumptions

Start of Period	Installment Schedule	Amount Received by Lender
1	100	50
2	100	50
3	100	50
4	100	50
5	100	50

Table 2. Calculation of the Repayment Index Denominator: Amounts Due if no Repayments Received

Period (1)	Arrears Brought Forward (2)	Amount Falling Due at Start of Period (3)	Arrears for the Period (4) = (3) + (2)	Compound Interest at 10% (5) = (4) x .10
1	0	100	100.00	10.00
2	110.00	100	210.00	21.00
3	231.00	100	331.00	33.10
4	364.10	100	464.10	46.41
5	510.51	100	610.51	61.05
Totals (for use as denominator)			*1715.61*	*171.56*

The numerator is calculated in Table, 3 which shows actual amounts due based on the data in Table 1.

The Repayment Index number is found by dividing the sum of amounts actually due by the sum of the amounts that would have been due if no repayments were received, or the sum of column 5 in Table 3 divided by the sum of column 4 in Table 2, and subtracting the result from 1.

Table 3. Calculation of the Repayment Index Numerator: Amounts Actually Paid

Period (1)	Arrears Brought Forward (2) = (5) + (6)	Amount Falling Due at Start of Period (3)	Received by Lender on Due Date (4)	Arrears for the Period (5) = (2) + (3) - (4)	Compound Interest at 10% (6) = (5) x .10
1	0	100	50	50.00	5.00
2	55.00	100	50	105.00	10.50
3	115.50	100	50	165.50	16.55
4	182.50	100	50	232.05	32.20
5	255.25	100	50	305.25	30.53
Totals (for use as numerator)				857.80	85.78

An Index number of 0.00 indicates zero repayment, while 1.00 shows repayment in full exactly on time or overall performance mathematically consistent with timely repayment behavior, with prepayment at certain times offsetting arrears at others. Data from Tables 2 and 3 yield a Repayment Index value (R) of .50. The derivation is

$$R = 1 - (857.80/1715.61)$$
$$= 1 - .50$$
$$= .50$$

An alternative that produces the same result but with less effort in practice is found by dividing the interest charged on actual arrears by the interest that would be charged on arrears if no repayments were made, as shown by the sums of the final columns of Tables 2 and 3. This derivation, from columns (5) and (6) in Tables 2 and 3, respectively, is

$$R = 1 - (85.78/171.56)$$
$$= 1 - .50$$
$$= .50$$

In these simple examples the Index number, 0.50, is intuitively obvious because payments by the borrower are uniformly half of amounts falling due and are received on due dates.

Repayment Index values can often be generated easily without extensive data manipulation by the researcher. For example, interest charges on amounts in arrears are routinely calculated by accounting systems. Computing the cumulative totals over the life of an installment schedule imposes only a small added burden on such systems.

An algebraic development of the Index is found in Annex B. The algebraic statement may be helpful to researchers working from scratch where accounting records are not maintained, where they are poorly maintained or where they do not contain separate calculations of interest on arrears. The Index is applicable to single and to serial maturity (installment) loans.

Applications of the Repayment Index

Evaluation of repayment performance is important when delinquency is a significant problem. Consumer finance portfolios are often considered risky, and lenders attempt to reduce costs and risk by encouraging good payers to make greater and more frequent use of installment credit. The Repayment Index could help credit managers identify those customers with whom it could be most worthwhile to develop more extensive relationships. Agricultural credit portfolios and small scale business loans are often characterized by high rates of delinquency. Many credit schemes in developing countries seek to provide institutional credit to people who have not previously had access to it. The objective is to encourage new borrowers to purchase farm inputs and capital goods embodying improved technologies which will enhance their productivity. In the design and evaluation of these projects it is helpful to know how repayment performance is correlated with farm, firm, borrower, and loan characteristics.

The Repayment Index provides a research tool for this purpose because it quantifies repayment performance on a uniform, comparative basis. This aspect of borrowers' behavior can be compared with quantifiable variables related to their economic, social, technical and personal characteristics or situations. Cross tabulation, correlation and regression analyses and more complex statistical techniques using Repayment Index values enable researchers to study repayment performance with more precision then otherwise could be achieved.

The Index also permits economies in credit decision making. For example, clients with historic repayment performance yielding an Index value exceeding 0.95 who have fully repaid their loans might be accorded new credit equal to not more than 125 percent of the principal amount of their previous loan with greatly simplified application procedures. Those with Index numbers below 0.70 could automatically be excluded from further access to credit. Those in the 0.70-0.95 range but with no arrears outstanding could be interviewed prior to being issued loans up to 80 percent of the principal amount of their last loan, and so on. Index numbers showing low levels of repayment performance on past loans provide a basis for follow-up or supervision of repeat borrowers. These initiatives could be oriented narrowly toward timely loan collection or more broadly toward ensuring that borrower productivity is increased to a point where cash flow is adequate for debt servicing.

Applied to portfolio performance evaluation, the Index can show the record for different classes of loans within a portfolio; for portfolios under different managers; for groups of loans stratified by region, by borrower occupation, income or education and other relevant variables in an effort to identify strengths and weaknesses in the portfolio, in credit administration, or in the design of credit programs. This use of the Index in development finance could be directed toward removing constraints associated with particular categories of poor payers. For any portfolio it could be a basis for rewarding outstanding performance by borrowers or lending officers.

Limitations of the Repayment Index

The Repayment Index is not a universal measure of repayment performance. In fact, it is not possible to construct a universal measure because of the diverse decisions which are based on repayment data. The decision to foreclose on a defaulted loan, for example, may depend, among other factors, on the extent of arrears at the time the decision is being made. The decision to negotiate a revised installment schedule may rest on the borrower's willingness to work down arrears by making regular, if insufficient, payments under the existing schedule. The decision to issue a new loan to a present or old borrower may depend largely on repayment history. The amounts involved and the point in the life of an installment loan where repayment difficulty is experienced will also determine lender reactions to delinquency. No single measure of repayment performance can portray all aspects of repayment behavior. Hence, several caveats should be observed by users of repayment performance measures.[1] Those that apply to the Repayment Index are that (a) it is a ratio showing performance in relative rather than in absolute terms, (b) its usefulness has a time dimension, and (c) it portrays the average repayment performance of a loan.

a) *Repayment Index numbers are relative.* As a ratio, the Repayment Index does not show the absolute amount, or value, or deviations from perfect repayment performance. A lender would obviously be concerned about the absolute amount of arrears as well as about the extent of arrears relative to amounts which have fallen due. Complementary use of an indicator of the absolute size of arrears, such as the average balance in arrears over a relevant period, could assist in providing a more complete picture of repayment performance than given by the Index alone.

b) *Usefulness of the Repayment Index over time: Setting a cut-off date.* The Repayment Index is most useful when repayment is scheduled to occur over several compounding periods. In the cases of very short spans, such as one or two weeks, differences in repayment performance may be immaterial and not justify the analytical effort involved in Index computation. In these cases an aging of arrears or collection rate may be sufficient to portray the repayment situation for purposes of portfolio analysis and research.

The validity of the Repayment Index as a comparative measure for serial maturity loans deteriorates following the period *opening* on the date of the final installment. After the close of that period the absence of further installments falling due alters the relationship between (a) the incremental changes in the values of the numerator and denominator of the Index formula, and (b) the cumulative Index value derived from repayment performance up to that date. If, for example, the analyst is studying the behavior of a sample of three-year loans issued over a five-year period, consistent application of the formula would require cutting off the

---

1. See J.D. Von Pischke, Robert C. Vogel, Peter Flath and Maurice C. Mould, "Measurement of Loan Repayment Performance." Course Note 030/086. Economic Development Institute of the World Bank, Washington, DC, April 1988.

calculation for each loan at the earlier of the close of the study period or the close of the period that is defined as opening on the date the final installment of the loan fell due.

c) *The Repayment Index is an average.* As a cumulative average it does not show which borrowers are current or delinquent at any particular time. Variations in repayment performance over a succession of amortization periods could yield a Repayment Index of 1.00 over the life of a loan during which the effect of arrears is offset by interest credits on prepayments. A lender would presumably not be indifferent between (a) a cumulative Repayment Index of 1.00 over the life of a loan reflecting an unbroken series of Index numbers of 1.00 for individual periods, and (b) a cumulative Index of 1.00 resulting from an erratic series. The cost of administering a loan, including collection expenses and portfolio and liquidity management, tends to rise as payments become increasingly erratic. The complementary use of some measure of variation between periods could compensate for this shortcoming. Possible alternatives include the range of observations from each period, the sum of the absolute value of Repayment Index deviations from 1.00 and the sum of the absolute value of deviations divided by the number of periods under review.

d) *Other limitations.* Nonperfoming loans may be placed on a nonaccrual basis, which means that no interest income is recognized on their outstanding balances, except when a payment is received. Nonperforming loans may also be written down, which means that part of the outstanding balance is charged off as a bad debt loss to reflect diminished prospects of recovery. In each of these cases, adjustments are required for Repayment Index calculations.

Loans in nonaccrual status normally require simulated continuation of interest calaculations if these are not being routinely made. If accrued interest calculations are being made in the accounting records, the interest accrued is transferred to a suspense account rather than to income. These amounts may be used for Repayment Index calculation if they are calculated in the same way that interest is accrued on good loans. If written-down loans are to be compared with continuously performing loans for periods than include the date of a write down, the Repayment Index calculation should assume that writing down never occurred. This ensures consistency in measurement. If written down loans are renegotiated, repayment performance may be monitored on the renegotiated balance according to the renegotiated loan contract as for any other loan, disregarding earlier unfortunate performance.

The Repayment Index is vulnerable to the same types of data problems that compromise other measures of repayment performance. These include inconsistency of accounting treatment of repayment behavior and incomplete specification of the basis for presentations of information. For example, the Repayment Index offers the reseacher no protection against the impact of clandestine rescheduling of arrears or of changes in the manner in which arrears are charged off. This limitation constitutes a greater obstacle to portfolio analysis than to the monitoring of individual loans. The study of individual loans requires data collection from the primary source, which is the account ledger. All entries for the account are given in the ledger, which permits testing for consistency and reconstruction of accounts on a consistent basis as required.

In common with other measures, the Index does not embrace wider issues of portfolio quality. For example, the Index formula in itself does not distinguish unsecured from fully secured loan arrears, or reflect the nature of any security taken or the borrower's previous repayment behavior on other loans. However, the Index can be applied to portfolio segments, classified according to criteria such as type of security and borrower credit rating to analyze differences in performance.

Likewise, the Index does not explain the impact on collection performance from changes in the terms upon which credit is issued. Change may be direct, when conditions specified by the lender are altered, or indirect, when the general level of interest rates or credit availability changes in relation to the terms specified on loans outstanding. Debtors with access to more than one source of credit may adjust their performance with respect to each source as its relative attractiveness changes.

Some credit institutions use hand or mechanical bookkeeping systems which calculate interest on arrears only on balances beyond some threshold level determined by the costs of making the accounting entry. The range of error resulting from ignoring small arrears when calculating interest on arrears may be quantified as plus or minus so many Index points, depending upon installment size, the threshold level and the number of periods for which the loan is outstanding.

Annex B

ALGEBRAIC TREATMENT OF THE REPAYMENT INDEX

The Index's *general notation* is

$$R_n = 1 - \frac{\sum\limits_{t=1}^{n} i A_t}{\sum\limits_{t=1}^{n} i A_t^{max}} \qquad (1)$$

where R is the Repayment Index number representing repayment performance at the end of period n, A_t is the balance in arrears at the close of period t, $\sum i A_t$ is the cumulative total of interest calculated on balances in arrears (net of any prepaid balances) over the life of the loan or portfolio study horizon t extending from period 1 to period n, and $\sum i A^{max}$ is the cumulative total of interest calculated on balances in arrears which would have accumulated if no loan repayments were made.

The following presentation assumes loans falling due in installments over several periods. The cumulative total of interest charged on balances in arrears, $\sum i A_t$, is simply the sum of the amount of interest calculated on arrears for each period, from 1 through n.

$$\sum\limits_{t=1}^{n} i A_t = i A_1 + \ldots + i A_t + i A_{t+1} + \ldots + i A_n \qquad (2)$$

A period is defined as having an installment falling due at its start (in practice, at the close of the preceding business day) and having interest on arrears calculated and debited at its close. For illustration, assume that no

391

repayment is received in the first period a repayment is due, which begins on the first day the loan is due and hence in arrears. The calculation of the numerator of the general formula (1) is then simply

$$\sum_{t=1}^{1} iA_1 = iD_1 \tag{3}$$

where iD_1 is the interest calculated on the amount due at the start of period 1. Since no repayment was received, this notation also gives the denominator for the general formula (1), and the Repayment Index number would be 0.00, indicating total default:

$$R_1 = 1 - \frac{iA_1}{iA_1^{max}} \tag{4}$$

$$= 1 - 1/1$$
$$= 0$$

To accommodate the case of partial payment, M is used to signify payments received. Assuming a payment is received at the start of the first period, the numerator describing the situation at the close of that period becomes

$$R_1 = 1 - \frac{iD_1 - iM_1}{iD_1} \tag{5}$$

The exposition may be expanded to include the calculation of iA for the second or subsequent periods for serial maturity loans. The amount due at the opening of the first period is simply the amount of one installment. Assuming no repayment, the amount due at the opening of the second period (signified by the subscript of A_2) is equal to two installments plus interest on the arrears, consisting of the first installment, which remained unpaid throughout the first period. Thus

$$A_{2_0} = (D_1 - M_1) + i(D_1 - M_1) + (D_2 - M_2) \tag{6}$$

$$= (D_1 - M_1)(1 + i) + (D_2 - M_2)$$

and $\quad A_2 = \left(D_1 - M_1\right)\left(1 + i\right)^2 + \left(D_2 - M_2\right)\left(1 + i\right) \quad (7)$

at the close of the second period with M_1 and M_2 both equal to zero in this limiting case. D is the amount of each installment, with D_1 falling due on the opening of period 1 and D_2 falling due at the start of period 2. The calculation of interest on arrears, $i(D_1 - M_1)$ in (5), is assumed to occur at the close of each period. This amount is compounded and treated as an amount in arrears in all subsequent periods until adequate payment is received to clear arrears. Extending the notation to cover periods through j in which installments fall due,

(8)

$$R_j = 1 - \frac{(D_1 - M_1)(1 + i)^j + \cdots + (D_t - M_t)(1 + i)^{j-t+1} + \cdots + (D_j - M_j)(1 + i)}{D_1(1 + i)^j + \cdots + D_t(1 + i)^{j-t+1} + \cdots + D_j(1 + i)^{j-(t-1)}}$$

The exponent for the final or jth period is j-j+1 which equals 1. Compounding does not occur on the final contractual installment, as the calculation concludes with the close of the jth period.

A change in the rate of interest charged on amounts in arrears during the life of a loan changes the rate at which arrears compound. However, any change other than to zero requires no change in calculation of the Repayment Index because the Index is based on the relationship between actual arrears and the maximum possible level of arrears. A change in interest rates alters both of these variables.

The assumption that payment is received only on the opening day of a period must be discarded. *Payments are generally accepted on any business day*. Dealing with a payment received within a period rather than at its opening is accommodated by adjusting the numerator of the Repayment Index formula to reflect the different levels of arrears during the period, dividing the period into subperiods.

$$iA_t = i\left(1 - \frac{p}{t}\right)A_{t-p} + i\frac{p}{t}A_p \qquad 0 < p < 1 \qquad (9)$$

iA_t is a weighted average of A_{t-p}, A_p; the weight p is the portion of time not yet elapsed when payment M was received. iA_{t-p} denotes interest charged on the balance in arrears during the portion t-p, while iA_p signifies interest on the balance in arrears during the portion of period t that follows receipt of payment M.

If more than one payment is received during a period, the period may be further subdivided into a number of parts equal to 1 plus the number of days on which payments were received. Separate iA's must be calculated for each part and summed. A variation of this method would be to use average (mean) daily balances in arrears over the period. A in the numerator of the Repayment Index formula (1) would be the actual average daily balance in arrears, and accordingly A in the denominator could be the average daily balance in arrears assuming no repayments. This alternative may be the easiest to use in practice where accounting systems routinely compute average daily balances.

REFERENCES

"A Lender that Gets Repaid," *The Economist,* October 18, 1986. p. 26.

Dale W Adams, "Agricultural Credit in Latin America: A Critical Review of External Funding Policy," *American Journal of Agricultural Economics,* 53, 2, May 1971. pp. 163-172.

Dale W Adams, "Are the Arguments for Cheap Agricultural Credit Sound?" in Dale W Adams, Douglas H. Graham and J.D. Von Pischke, eds., *Undermining Rural Development with Cheap Credit.* Boulder, Colorado: Westview Press, 1984. pp. 65-77.

Dale W Adams, "Do Rural Financial Savings Matter?" in Dennis Kessler and Pierre-Antoine Ullmo, eds., *Savings and Development.* Paris: Economica, 1985. pp. 9-15.

D. W Adams and G.I. Nehman, "Borrowing Costs and the Demand for Rural Credit," *Journal of Development Studies,* 15, 2, January 1979. pp. 165-176.

Dale W Adams, Claudio González Vega and J.D. Von Pischke, eds., *Crédito Agrícola y Desarrollo Rural: La Nueva Visión.* Columbus, Ohio: Ohio State University, 1987.

Dale W Adams, Douglas H. Graham and J.D. Von Pischke, eds., *Undermining Rural Development with Cheap Credit.* Boulder, Colorado, and London: Westview Press, 1984.

Dale W Adams and Robert C. Vogel, "Rural Financial Markets in Low Income Countries: Recent Controversies and Lessons," *World Development,* 14, 4, April 1986.

Agricultural Credit. Washington, DC: World Bank, 1975.

Agricultural Credit in Latin America. Report of the Seminar on Agricultural Credit for Small Farmers in Latin America, Quito, Ecuador, 25-30 November 1974. Rome: FAO, 1975.

Agricultural Finance in East Pakistan. Dacca: Asiatic Press, 1968.

Raisuddin Ahmed and Mahabub Hossain, "Developmental Impact of Rural Infrastructure in Bangladesh." Research Report 83. Washington, DC: International Food Policy Research Institute, October 1990, in collaboration with the Bangladesh Institute of Development Studies, Dhaka.

Zia U. Ahmed, "Effective Cost of Rural Loans in Bangladesh," *World Development,* 17, 3, 1989. pp. 357-363.

William Allan, *The African Husbandman.* Edinburgh and London: Oliver & Boyd; New York: Barnes & Noble, 1967.

Louis L. Allen, *Starting and Succeeding in Your Own Small Business.* New York: Grosset and Dunlap, 1968.

Gunther Aschoff and Eckart Henningsen, *The German Cooperative System: Its History, Structure and Strength.* Frankfurt-am-Main: Fritz Knapp Verlag, 1986.

Asian Reinsurance Corporation, "Crop Insurance." Bangkok: 1984.

Warren C. Baum, "The Project Cycle," *Finance and Development,* January 1978.

Warren C. Baum, "The Project Cycle." Washington, DC: World Bank, 1982.

Guy Bédard, "People's Banks in Rwanda: A Case Study," in Guy Bédard, Gerd Günter Klöwer and Martin Harder, eds., *The Importance of Savings for Fighting Against Poverty by Self-Help.* Vol. II. Berlin: Deutsche Stiftung für internationale Entwicklung (DSE-German Foundation for International Development), 1987. pp. 61-79.

Michael Behr, "The Savings Development Movement in Zimbabwe," in Guy Bédard, Gerd Günter Klöwer and Martin Harder, eds., *The Importance of Savings for Fighting Against Poverty by Self-Help.* Vol. II. Berlin: Deutsche Stiftung für internationale

Entwicklung (DSE-German Foundation for International Development), 1987. pp. 91-112.

Amit Bhaduri, "On the Formation of Usurious Interest Rates in Backward Agriculture," *Cambridge Journal of Economics*, 1, 1977.

V.V. Bhatt, "Financial Innovation and Development," in J.D. Von Pischke, Dale W Adams and Gordon Donald, eds., *Rural Financial Markets in Developing Countries: Their Use and Abuse.* Baltimore and London: The Johns Hopkins University Press, 1983. pp. 43-49.

Harry W. Blair, "Agricultural Credit, Political Economy, and Patronage," in Dale W Adams, Douglas H. Graham and J.D. Von Pischke, eds., *Undermining Rural Development with Cheap Credit.* Boulder, Colorado, and London: Westview Press, 1984. pp. 183-193.

Board of Governors of the Federal Reserve System, *Commercial Bank Examination Manual.* Washington, DC. (looseleaf)

Romulo Borlaza, "Moneyshops: The Story of One Bank's Social Commitment," *PCI Unibank World.* Manila, January 1984. pp. 4-6.

Anthony Bottomley, "Interest Rate Determination in Underdeveloped Rural Areas," *American Journal of Agrticultural Economics,* 57, 2, 1975; also in J.D. Von Pischke, Dale W Adams and Gordon Donald, eds., *Rural Financial Markets in Developing Countries: Their Use and Abuse.* Baltimore and London: The Johns Hopkins University Press, 1983. pp. 243-250.

Kenneth E. Boulding and Thomas Frederick Wilson, eds., *Redistribution through the Financial System: The Grants Economics of Money and Credit.* New York: Praeger Publishers, 1978.

F.J.A. Bouman, "Indigenous Savings and Credit Societies in the Third World: A Message," *Savings and Development,* 1, 4, 1977; excerpted as "Indigenous Savings and Credit Societies in the Developing World," in J.D. Von Pischke, Dale W Adams and Gordon Donald, eds., *Rural Financial Markets in Developing Countries: Their Use and Abuse.* Baltimore and London: The Johns Hopkins University Press, 1983. pp. 262-268.

F.J.A. Bouman, "Informal Savings and Credit Arrangements in Developing Countries: Observations from Sri Lanka," in Dale W Adams, Douglas H. Graham and J.D. Von Pischke, eds., *Undermining Rural Development with Cheap Credit.* Boulder, Colorado, and London: Westview Press, 1984. pp. 232-247.

F.J.A. Bouman, *Small, Short and Unsecured: Informal Rural Finance in India.* Delhi: Oxford University Press, 1989.

Avishay Braverman and Luis Guasch, "Rural Credit Markets and Institutions in Developing Countries: Lessons for Policy Analysis from Modern Theory and Practice," *World Development,* 14, 10/11, November 1986.

Maxwell Brown, *Farm Budgets: From Farm Income Analysis to Agricultural Project Analysis.* Baltimore and London: The Johns Hopkins University Press, 1979.

Steven J. Brown and Mark P. Kritzman, eds., *Quantitative Methods for Financial Analysis.* Homewood, Illinois: Dow Jones-Irwin, 1981.

Nicholas A. Bruck, ed., *Capital Markets Under Inflation.* Buenos Aires: Stock Exchange of Buenos Aires, 1982, assisted by the Inter-American Development Bank.

Jaime Carvajal, "Microenterprise and Urban Development." Speech delivered at the Pan American Economic Leadership Conference, Indianapolis, June 1987. [Bogota]: The Carvajal Foundation.

Dennis J. Casley and Krishna Kumar, *Project Monitoring and Evaluation in Agriculture.* Baltimore and London: The Johns Hopkins University Press, 1987.

Jean Causse, "Necessity of and Constraints on the Use of Savings in the Community in which they are Collected," in Denis Kessler and Pierre-Antoine Ullmo, eds., *Savings and Development.* Paris: Economica, 1985. pp. 153-181.

David C. Cole and Yung Chul Park, *Financial Development in Korea, 1945-1978.* Cambridge: Council on East Asian Studies, Harvard University, 1983.

Paul R. Crawford, *Crop Insurance in Developing Countries.* Unpublished masters dissertation, University of Wisconsin-Madison, 1977.

Carlos E. Cuevas, "Costs of Financial Intermediation under Regulations: Commercial Banks and Development Banks." Economics and Sociology Occasional Paper No. 1127, Agricultural Finance Program, Ohio State University, Columbus, September 1984.

Carlos E. Cuevas and Douglas H. Graham, "Agricultural Lending Costs in Honduras," in Dale W Adams, Douglas H. Graham and J.D. Von Pischke, eds., *Undermining Rural Development with Cheap Credit.* Boulder, Colorado, and London: Westview Press, 1984. pp. 96-103; translated as "Costos de Prestamos Agrícolas en Honduras," in Dale W. Adams, Claudio González Vega y J.D. Von Pischke, eds., *Crédito Agrícola y Desarrollo Rural: La Nueva Visión.* Columbus, Ohio: Ohio State University, 1987. pp. 192-205.

V.M. Dandekar, "Crop Insurance in India," *Economic and Political Weekly,* June 1976. Review of Agriculture.

C.D. Datey, "The Financial Cost of Agricultural Credit: A Case Study of Indian Experience." Staff Working Paper No. 296. Washington, DC: World Bank, 1978.

Auguste Daubrey, "Mobilization of Savings for Rural Development in Africa," in Denis Kessler and Pierre-Antoine Ullmo, eds., *Savings and Development.* Paris: Economica, 1985. pp. 231-237.

Cristina C. David and Richard L. Meyer, "Measuring the Farm Level Impact of Agricultural Loans," in J.D. Von Pischke and Dale W Adams, Gordon Donald, eds. *Rural Financial Markets in Developing Countries: Their Use and Abuse.* Baltimore and London: The Johns Hopkins University Press, 1983. p. 84-95.

Paulo F.C. de Araujo y Richard L. Meyer, "Dos Décadas de Crédito Agrícola Subsidiado en Brasil," in Dale W Adams, Claudio González Vega y J.D. Von Pischke, eds., *Crédito Agrícola y Desarrollo Rural: La Nueva Visión.* Columbus, Ohio: Ohio State University, 1987. pp. 192-205.

Hernando de Soto, *The Other Path: The Invisible Revolution in the Third World.* New York: Harper & Row, 1989.

"Endless Dealing: US Treasury Debt is Increasingly Traded Globally and Nonstop," *The Wall Street Journal,* September 10, 1986. p. 1.

Gordon Donald, *Credit for Small Farmers in Developing Countries.* Boulder, Colorado: Westview Press, 1976.

Gordon Donaldson, "New Framework for Corporate Debt Capacity," *Harvard Business Review,* September-October 1978. pp. 149-164.

"The Economic Impact of Trust and Confidence," The 5th Column, *Far Eastern Economic Review,* 30 May 1985. pp. 78-79.

"Farmers Play Uncle Sam for Uncle Sap: Taxpayers are the Big Losers in the Federal Crop-Insurance Plan that is Badly Conceived, Badly Run and Made Moot by Free Bailouts," *U.S. New & World Report,* August 8, 1988. pp. 27-28.

Milton Friedman, *Money and Economic Development.* The Horowitz Lectures of 1972. New York: Praeger Publishers, 1973.

Milton Friedman and Anna Jacobson Schwartz, *A Monetary History of the United States, 1867-1960.* Princeton, New Jersey: Princeton University Press, 1968.

Maxwell J. Fry, *Money, Interest and Banking in Economic Development.* Baltimore and London: The Johns Hopkins University Press, 1988.

Andreas Fugelsang and Dale Chandler, *Participation as Process--What We Can Learn from Grameen Bank, Bangladesh.* Oslo: Norwegian Ministry of Development Cooperation-NORAD, 1986.

Bruce L. Gardner and Randall A Kramer, "Experience with Crop Insurance Programs in the United States," in Peter Hazell, Carlos Pomareda and Alberto Valdés, eds., *Crop Insurance for Agricultural Development: Issues and Experience.* Baltimore and London: The Johns Hopkins University Press, 1986. pp. 195-222.

J. Price Gittinger, *Economic Analysis of Agricultural Projects*. 2nd ed. Baltimore and London: The Johns Hopkins University Press, 1982.

Claudio Gonzalez-Vega, "Credit-Rationing Behavior of Agricultural Lenders: The Iron Law of Interest Rate Restrictions," in Dale W Adams, Douglas H. Graham and J.D. Von Pischke, eds., *Undermining Rural Development with Cheap Credit*. Boulder, Colorado, and London: Westview Press, 1984. pp. 78-95.

Grameen Bank, *Annual Report 1987*. Dhaka, [1989].

Grameen Bank, "Training System of Grameen Bank," in Guy Bédard, ed., *Savings and Credit as Instruments of Self-reliant Development of the Poor*. Proceedings of an international workshop held in Feldafing, January 25-28, 1988. Feldafing, Federal Republic of Germany: Deutsche Stiftung für internationale Entwicklung (DSE-German Foundation for International Development), 1988. pp. 79-100.

William M. Gudger and Luis Avalos, "Planning for the Efficient Operation of Crop Credit Insurance Schemes," in Peter Hazell, Carlos Pomareda and Alberto Valdés, eds., *Crop Insurance for Agricultural Development: Issues and Experience*. Baltimore and London: The Johns Hopkins University Press, 1986. pp. 263-280.

Jonathon R. Hakim, ed., "Equipment Leasing." IFC Occasional Papers, Capital Market Series. Washington, DC: International Finance Corporation and the World Bank, 1985.

Paul Halstead and John O'Shea, eds., *Bad Year Economics: Cultural Responses to Risk and Uncertainty*. Cambridge: Cambridge University Press, 1989.

Barbara Harriss, "Money and Commodities: Their Interaction in a Rural Indian Setting," in J.D. Von Pischke, Dale W Adams and Gordon Donald, eds., *Rural Financial Markets in Developing Countries: Their Use and Abuse*. Baltimore and London: The Johns Hopkins University Press, 1983. pp. 233-241; extracted from a paper in John Howell, ed., *Borrowers & Lenders: Rural*

Financial Market Institutions in Developing Countries. London: Overseas Development Institute, 1980.

Peter Hazell, Carlos Pomareda and Alberto Valdés, eds., *Crop Insurance for Agricultural Development: Issues and Experience.* Baltimore and London: The Johns Hopkins University Press, 1986.

Robert L. Heilbroner, *Behind the Veil of Economics: Essays in the Worldy Philosophy.* New York and London: W.W. Norton & Company, 1988.

Jürgen U. Holst, "The Role of Informal Financial Institutions in the Mobilization of Savings," in Denis Kessler and Pierre-Antoine Ullmo, eds., *Savings and Development.* Paris: Economica, 1985. pp. 121-152.

John A. Hopkin, Peter J. Barry and C.B. Baker, *Financial Management in Agriculture.* Danville, Illinois: Interstate Printers and Publishers, Inc., 1973.

Mahabub Hossain, "Credit for Alleviation of Rural Poverty: The Grameen Bank in Bangladesh." Research Report 65. Washington, DC: International Food Policy Research Institute, February 1988, in collaboration with the Bangladesh Institute of Development Studies, Dhaka.

C.J. Howse, "Agricultural Development without Credit," in J.D. Von Pischke, Dale W Adams and Gordon Donald, eds., *Rural Financial Markets in Developing Countries: Their Use and Abuse.* Baltimore and London: The Johns Hopkins University Press, 1983. pp. 134-137.

John Howell, ed., *Borrowers & Lenders: Rural Financial Market Institutions in Developing Countries.* London: Overseas Development Institute, 1980.

"Industrial Firms Are Using Receivables to Back Commercial Paper, Preferred," *The Wall Street Journal,* October 7, 1987. p. 41.

"Informal Capitalism Grows in Cameroon: Grass-Roots Credit System," *The New York Times,* November 30, 1987. p. D8.

International Fund for Agricultural Development (IFAD), *The Role of Rural Credit Projects in Reaching the Poor: IFAD's Experience.* Oxford: Tycoolly Publishing, 1985.

Inter-American Development Bank, "Summary of the Evaluation of Global Agricultural Credit Programs." GN-1493. Washington, DC: February 1984.

"Investing in Equity Markets," *Hermes* (alumni publication of the Columbia University Graduate School of Business, New York), Summer 1985.

Reed J. Irvine and Robert F. Emory, "Interest Rates as an Anti-Inflationary Instrument in Taiwan," in J.D. Von Pischke, Dale W Adams and Gordon Donald, eds., *Rural Financial Markets in Developing Countries: Their Use and Abuse.* Baltimore and London: The Johns Hopkins University Press, 1983. pp. 393-397.

Omotunde E.G. Johnson, "Credit Controls as Instruments of Development Policy in the Light of Economic Theory," in J.D. Von Pischke, Dale W Adams and Gordon Donald, eds., *Rural Financial Markets in Developing Countries: Their Use and Abuse.* Baltimore and London: The Johns Hopkins University Press, 1983. pp. 323-329.

Edward J. Kane, "Good Intentions and Unintended Evil," in J.D. Von Pischke, Dale W Adams and Gordon Donald, eds., *Rural Financial Markets in Developing Countries: Their Use and Abuse.* Baltimore and London: The Johns Hopkins University Press, 1983. pp. 316-322.

Edward J. Kane, "Political Economy of Subsidizing Agricultural Credit in Developing Countries," in Dale W Adams, Douglas H. Graham and J.D. Von Pischke, eds., *Undermining Rural Development with Cheap Credit.* Boulder, Colorado, and London: Westview Press, 1984. pp.166-182.

Peter Kilby and David D'Zmura, "Searching for Benefits." AID Special Study No. 28. Washington, DC: US Agency for International Development, June 1983.

Peter Kilby, Carl E. Liedholm and Richard L. Meyer, "Working Capital and Nonfarm Rural Enterprises," in Dale W Adams, Douglas H. Graham and J.D. Von Pischke, eds., *Undermining Rural Development with Cheap Credit*. Boulder, Colorado, and London: Westview Press, 1984. pp. 266-283.

Charles P. Kindleberger, *Manias, Panics and Crashes: A History of Financial Crises*. New York: Basic Books, 1978.

Paul H. Kratoska, "The Chettiar and the Yeoman." Occasional Paper No. 32. Singapore: The Institute of Southeast Asian Studies, June 1975.

Herman E. Kroos and Martin R. Blyn, *A History of Financial Intermediaries*. New York: Random House, 1971.

"La confiance ne paie pas," *Le Monde*, 13 juillet 1979. p. 29.

Jerry R. Ladman, "Loan-Transactions Costs, Credit Rationing and Market Structure: The Case of Bolivia," in Dale W Adams, Douglas H. Graham and J.D. Von Pischke, eds., *Undermining Rural Development with Cheap Credit*. Boulder, Colorado: Westview Press, 1984. pp. 104-119.

"Le rapport de la Cour des comptes sur l'indemnisation des calamités agricoles met en évidence de nombreux abus," *Le Monde*, 13 Juillet 1979. p. 29.

"Loan Melas--for Whose Benefit?" Bangalore: Karnataka State Janata Party, n.d. (1987?)

J. Peter Marion, "Building Successful Financial Systems: The Role of Credit Unions in Financial Sector Development." Madison, Wisconsin: World Council of Credit Unions, September 1987.

Arnaldo Mauri, "A Policy to Mobilize Rural Savings in Less Developed Countries," *Savings and Development*, 1, 1, 1977. pp. 1-26.

Arnaldo Mauri, "Le crédit agricole aux petits exploitants dans les pays en voie de développement," *Finafrica Bulletin*, 2, 1, 1975. pp. 119-126.

Arnaldo Mauri, "The Potential for Savings and Financial Innovation in Africa," *Savings and Development*, 7, 4, 1983. pp. 319-337.

J. Alister McGregor, "Credit and the Rural Poor: The Changing Policy Environment in Bangladesh," *Public Administration and Development,* 8, 4, October-December 1988. pp. 467-482.

Richard L. Meyer and Adelaida P. Alicbusan, "Farm-Household Heterogeneity and Rural Financial Markets: Insights from Thailand," in Dale W Adams, Douglas H. Graham and J.D. Von Pischke, eds., *Undermining Rural Development with Cheap Credit.* Boulder, Colorado, and London: Westview Press, 1984. pp. 22-35.

Richard L. Meyer and Aruna Srinivasan, "Policy Implications of Financial Intermediation Costs in Bangladesh." Paper presented at the Seminar on Bank Accounting Issues in Bangladesh, Dhaka, October 18, 1987. Economics and Sociology Occasional Paper No. 1389, Agricultural Finance Program, Ohio State University, Columbus, October 1987.

Hans Mittendorf, "Savings Mobilization for Agricultural and Rural Development in Africa," in Denis Kessler and Pierre-Antoine Ullmo, eds., *Savings and Development.* Paris: Economica, 1985. pp. 217-229.

Roberto Mizrahi, "Credit and Financial Intermediation for the Informal Sector." Washington, DC: Sectoral Policies Division, Plans and Programs Department, Inter-American Development Bank. Working Paper No. 4. August 1988.

H.A.J. Moll, *Farmers and Finance: Experience with Institutional Savings and Credit in West Java.* Wageningen, The Netherlands: Pudoc, 1989.

J. Carroll Moody and Gilbert C. Fite, *The Credit Union Movement: Origins and Development, 1850-1970.* Dubuque, Iowa: Kendall/Hunt Publishing Co., 1984.

Maurice Mould, "Financial Information for Management of a Development Finance Institution: Some Guidelines." World Bank Technical Paper Number 63, Industry and Finance Series. Washington, DC: World Bank, 1987.

J.O. Müller, "Early Savings and Credit Cooperatives on the Basis of Self-Help to Combat Poverty and Dependence in Germany," in Guy Bédard, Gerd Günter Klöwer and Martin Harder, eds., *The Importance of Savings for Fighting Against Poverty by Self-Help.* Vol. II. Berlin: Deutsche Stiftung für internationale Entwicklung (DSE-German Foundation for International Development), 1987. pp. 43-60.

Mohammad Rashrash Mustafa, "Agricultural Credit Fund Activities in Tihama: April 75-October 77, Final Report." Yemen Arab Republic, Tihama Development Project, November 1977.

National Credit Union Administration, *NCUA Letter No. 111*, September 29, 1989. Washington, DC.

C.P.S. Nayar, *Chit Finance.* Bombay: Vora & Co., 1973.

Benjamin Nelson, *The Idea of Usury: From Tribal Brotherhood to Universal Otherhood.* 2nd ed. Chicago: University of Chicago Press, 1969.

A. Jamil Nishtar, "The Mobile Supervised Agricultural Credit System for Small Farmers." Karachi: National Bank of Pakistan, August 1982.

Syed Nuruzzaman, "Grameen Bank in Bangladesh: A Preliminary Assessment." RSI-86-10. Honolulu, Hawaii: Resource Systems Institute, East-West Center, September 1986.

Ohene Owusu Nyanin, "Lending Costs, Institutional Viability and Agricultural Credit Strategies in Jamaica," *Social and Economic Studies,* 32, 1, 1983. pp. 103-133.

Organization for Economic Cooperation and Development, *Capital and Finance in Agriculture.* Vol. I, *General Report.* Paris: OECD, 1970.

Hugh T. Patrick, "Financial Development and Economic Growth in Underdeveloped Countries," *Economic Development and Cultural Change,* 14, 2, January 1966; excerpted in J.D. Von Pischke, Dale W Adams and Gordon Donald, eds., *Rural Financial Markets in Developing Countries: Their Use and*

Abuse. Baltimore and London: The Johns Hopkins University Press, 1983. pp. 50-57.

Henry Petroski, *To Engineer is Human: The Role of Failure in Successful Design.* New York: St. Martin's Press, 1982. ·

PCAC/TBAC (Presidential Committee on Agricultural Credit/Technical Board for Agricultural Credit), *The First Five Years: 1976-1980.* Manila: Presidential Committee on Agricultural Credit, n.d.

Presidential Committee on Agricultural Credit, *A Study on the Informal Rural Financial Markets in Three Selected Provinces of the Philippines.* Manila: 1981.

V.S. Raghavan, "Some Issues Relating to Financial Policies of Development Banks," in William Diamond and V.S. Raghavan, eds., *Aspects of Development Bank Management.* Baltimore and London: The Johns Hopkins University Press, 1982.

F.W. Raiffeisen, *The Credit Unions.* 8th ed. (1966), Konrad Engelmann, trans. Neuwied on the Rhine, Federal Republic of Germany: The Raiffeisen Printing and Publishing Company, 1970 [1866].

P.K. Ray, *Agricultural Insurance: Theory and Practice and Application to Developing Countries.* 2nd ed. Oxford: Pergamon Press, 1981.

P.K. Ray, "The Role of Crop Insurance in the Agricultural Economy of the Developing Countries," *Monthly Bulletin of Agricultural Economics and Statistics,* May 1975.

Reserve Bank of India, *All-India Rural Credit Survey,* Vol. 1, *The Survey Report, Part 1 (Rural Families).* Bombay, 1956.

Reserve Bank of India, *All-India Rural Credit Survey,* Vol. 1, *The Survey Report, Part 2 (Credit Agencies).* Bombay, 1957.·

Reserve Bank of India, *Report of the Expert Group on State Enactments Having a Bearing on Commercial Banks Lending to Agriculture.* (The Talwar Report). Bombay, 1971.

E.B. Rice, *History of AID Programs in Agricultural Credit.* Vol. XVII, AID Spring Review of Small Farmer Credit. Washington, DC: Agency for International Development, Department of State, June 1973. pp. 12-20.

Jose Ripoll, "Contribution of Agricultural Insurance toward Economic Development." Paper delivered at the UNCTAD/UNDP Seminar on Agricultural Insurance, Colombo, Sri Lanka, 1-5 September 1979. Geneva: UNCTAD/INS/33 GE.79-54061.

Dwight S. Ritter, *Cross-Selling Financial Services*. New York: John Wiley & Sons, 1988.

Bruce L. Robert, Jr., "Agricultural Credit Cooperatives, Rural Development and Agrarian Politics in Madras, 1893-1937," in J.D. Von Pischke, Dale W Adams and Gordon Donald, eds., *Rural Financial Markets in Developing Countries: Their Use and Abuse*. Baltimore and London: The Johns Hopkins University Press, 1983. pp. 354-362.

R.A.J. Roberts, W.M. Gudger and D. Gilboa, *AGS Bulletin on Crop Insurance*. Rome: FAO, 1987. (draft)

Joan Robinson, *Economic Philosophy*. Chicago: Aldine Publishing Company, 1962.

Jerry M. Rosenberg, *The Investor's Dictionary*. New York: John Wiley & Sons, 1986.

Aloys Rukebesha, "People's Banks in Rwanda," in Guy Bédard, Gerd Günter Klöwer and Martin Harder, eds., *The Importance of Savings for Fighting Against Poverty by Self-Help*. Vol. II. Berlin: Deutsche Stiftung für internationale Entwicklung (DSE-German Foundation for International Development), 1987. pp. 163-177.

S.K.D., "Nattukottai Chettiars in Malaya," *The Malaysian Law Journal*, February 1958.

Orlando J. Sacay, Meliza H. Agabin and Chita Irene E. Tanchoco, *Small Farmer Credit Dilemma*. Manila: Technical Board for Agricultural Credit, 1985.

Katrine Anderson Saito and Delano P. Villanueva, "Transaction Costs of Credit to the Small-Scale Sector in the Philippines," *Economic Development and Cultural Change*, 29, 3, April 1981.

João Sayad, "The Impact of Rural Credit on Production and Income Distribution in Brazil," in J.D. Von Pischke, Dale W Adams and

Gordon Donald, eds., *Rural Financial Markets in Developing Countries: Their Use and Abuse.* Baltimore and London: The Johns Hopkins University Press, 1983. pp. 379-386.

João Sayad, "Rural Credit and Positive Real Rates of Interest: Brazil's Experience with Rapid Inflation," in Dale W Adams, Douglas H. Graham and J.D. Von Pischke, eds., *Undermining Rural Development with Cheap Credit.* Boulder, Colorado, and London: Westview Press, 1984. pp.146-160.

Walter Schaefer-Kehnert, "Methodology of Farm Investment Analysis." Course Note 030/031. Rev. Dec. 1981. Washington, DC: Economic Development Institute of the World Bank.

Walter Schaefer-Kehnert, "Success with Group Lending in Malawi," in J.D. Von Pischke, Dale W Adams and Gordon Donald, eds., *Rural Financial Markets in Developing Countries: Their Use and Abuse.* Baltimore and London: The Johns Hopkins University Press, 1983. pp. 278-283.

Walter Schaefer-Kehnert, "Time Adjusted Cash Flow Projections in Farm Investment Analysis," *Zeitschrift für Ausländische Landwirtschaft (Quarterly Journal of International Agriculture),* 3, 1978.

Sayre P. Schatz, *Economics, Politics and Administration in Government Lending: The Regional Loans Boards of Nigeria.* Ibadan: Oxford University Press, 1970.

Sayre P. Schatz, "Government Lending to African Businessmen: Inept Incentive," *Journal of Modern African Studies,* 6, 4, December 1968. pp. 519-529.

R.H. Schmidt and Erhard Kropp, eds., *Rural Finance: Guiding Principles.* Eschborn: Bundesministerium für wirtschaftliche Zusammenarbeit (Federal Ministry for Economic Cooperation), Deutsche Gesellschaft für Technische Zusammenarbeit (GTZ-German Agency for Technical Cooperation), Deutsche Stiftung für internationale Entwicklung (DSE-German Foundation for International Development), 1987.

Joseph A. Schumpeter, *The Theory of Economic Development: An Enquiry into Profits, Capital, Credit, Interest and the Business Cycle.* Cambridge: Harvard University Press, 1934.

Peter Schwed, *God Bless Pawnbrokers.* New York: Dodd, Mead & Co., 1975.

John R. Segerstom and Greg D. Meadows, "Why Gap Doesn't Work: Using Traditional Gap to Measure Interest Rate Risk Is Like Tallying Up the Money in Your Vault by Simply Counting the Bills—Whether They're $1s or $100s." *ABA Banking Journal,* 1xxxii, 10, October 1990.

Hans Dieter Seibel and Bishnu P. Shrestha, "Dhikuti: The Small Businessman's Informal Self-Help Bank in Nepal," *Savings and Development,* xii, 2, 1988. pp. 183-200.

Edward S. Shaw, *Financial Deepening in Economic Development.* New York: Oxford University Press, 1973.

Parker Shipton, "How Gambians Save--and What Their Strategies Imply for International Aid." Policy, Research, and External Affairs Working Papers: Agricultural Policies. WPS 395. Washington, DC: World Bank, April 1990.

Parker Shipton, "Time and Money in the Western Sahel: A Clash of Culture in Gambian Local Rural Finance," in Michael Roemer and Christine Jones, eds., *Markets in Developing Countries.* San Francisco: Institute for Contemporary Studies Press, for the International Center for Economic Growth, 1990.

Karam Singh, "Structure of Interest Rates on Consumption Loans in an Indian Village," *Asian Economic Review,* 10, 4, 1968; excerpted in J.D. Von Pischke, Dale W Adams and Gordon Donald, eds., *Rural Financial Markets in Developing Countries: Their Use and Abuse.* Baltimore and London: The Johns Hopkins University Press, 1983. pp. 251-254.

Supriya Singh, *Bank Negara Malaysia--The First 25 Years, 1959-1984.* Kuala Lumpur: Bank Negara Malaysia, 1984.

Aruna Srinivasan, *A Multiproduct Cost Study of Rural Bank Branches in Bangladesh.* Unpublished PhD dissertation, The Ohio State University, 1988.

Joseph E. Stiglitz and Andrew Weiss, "Credit Rationing in Markets with Imperfect Information," *American Economic Review,* lxxi, June 1981. pp. 393-410.

Marcia Stigum, *Money Market Calculations: Yields, Break-Evens and Arbitrage.* Homewood, Illinois: Dow Jones-Irwin, 1981.

Louis Tardy, *Report on Systems of Agricultural Credit and Insurance.* Geneva: League of Nations, 1938.

Daniel and Alice Thorner, *Land and Labour in India.* New York: Asia Publishing House, 1962.

Thomas A. Timburg and C.V. Aiyer, "Informal Credit Markets in India," *Economic Development and Cultural Change,* 33, 1, October 1984. pp. 43-59; "Informal Credit Markets in India." Domestic Finance Studies 62. Washington, DC: World Bank, 1980.

Christopher Udry, "Credit Markets in Northern Nigeria: Credit as Insurance in a Rural Economy," *The World Bank Economic Review,* 4, 3, September 1990. pp. 251-269.

United Nations Conference on Trade and Development, "Invisibles: Insurance-Crop insurance for developing countries." Study by the UNCTAD secretariat for the Trade and Development Board, Committee on Invisibles and Financing related to Trade, Ninth session, second part, Geneva, 29 September 1980, Item 7 on the provisional agenda. TD/B/C.3/163, 5 May 1980.

United Nations Conference on Trade and Development, "Third world insurance at the end of the 1970s." TD/B/C.3/169/Add.1/Rev.1. New York: United Nations, 1981.

United States Department of Agriculture, *Agricultural Statistics 1986.* Washington, DC: United States Government Printing Office, 1986.

United States Department of Agriculture, Economic Research Service, *Agricultural Finance Outlook and Situation.* (periodic)

Antoine W. van Agtmael, *Emerging Securities Markets.* London: Euromoney Publications, 1984.

James C. Van Horne, *Function and Analysis of Capital Market Rates.* Englewood Cliffs, New Jersey: Prentice-Hall, Inc., 1970.

Carlos G. Velez-Ibanez, *Bonds of Mutual Trust: The Cultural Systems of Rotating Credit Associations Among Urban Mexicans and Chicanos.* New Brunswick, New Jersey: Rutgers University Press, 1983.

Frank Veneroso, "New Patterns of Financial Instability." Washington, DC: World Bank Industry Department, February 1986 (processed).

Frank Veneroso, "Systems of Indexation and their Impact on Capital Markets," in Nicholas A. Bruck, ed., *Capital Markets Under Inflation.* Buenos Aires: Stock Exchange of Buenos Aires, 1982, assisted by the Inter-American Development Bank. pp. 191-205.

Robert P. Vichas, *Handbook of Financial Mathematics, Formulas and Tables.* Englewood Cliffs, New Jersey: Prentice-Hall, Inc., 1979.

Robert C. Vogel, "The Effect of Subsidized Agricultural Credit on Income Distribution in Costa Rica," in Dale W Adams, Douglas H. Graham and J.D. Von Pischke, eds., *Undermining Rural Development with Cheap Credit.* Boulder, Colorado, and London: Westview Press, 1984. pp. 133-145.

Robert C. Vogel, "Savings Mobilization: The Forgotten Half of Rural Finance," in Dale W Adams, Douglas H. Graham and J.D. Von Pischke, eds., *Undermining Rural Development with Cheap Credit.* Boulder, Colorado, and London: Westview Press, 1984. pp. 248-265.

J.D. Von Pischke, "A Penny Saved: Kenya's Cooperative Savings Scheme," in J.D. Von Pischke, Dale W Adams and Gordon Donald, eds., *Rural Financial Markets in Developing Countries: Their Use and Abuse.* Baltimore and London: The Johns Hopkins University Press, 1983. pp. 302-307.

J.D. Von Pischke, "Farm Credit in Kenya: The Poor Farmer Paradox." Nairobi: Institute for Development Studies, University of Nairobi, 1973. (processed).

J.D. Von Pischke, "Malawi--Lilongwe Land Development Project; Smallholder Credit Arrangements and Proposals for the Development of Smallholder Credit." Memo to T.C. Creyke, December 7, 1973.

J.D. Von Pischke, "The Pitfalls of Specialized Farm Credit Institutions in Low-income Countries," in J.D. Von Pischke, Dale W Adams and Gordon Donald, eds., *Rural Financial Markets in Developing Countries: Their Use and Abuse.* Baltimore and London: The Johns Hopkins University Press, 1983. pp. 175-182.

J.D. Von Pischke, "Toward an Operational Approach to Savings for Rural Developers," in J.D. Von Pischke, Dale W Adams and Gordon Donald, eds., *Rural Financial Markets in Developing Countries: Their Use and Abuse.* Baltimore and London: The Johns Hopkins University Press, 1983. pp. 414-420.

J.D. Von Pischke and Dale W Adams, "Fungibility and the Design and Evaluation of Agricultural Credit Projects," *American Journal of Agricultural Economics,* 62, 4, November 1980; also in J.D. Von Pischke, Dale W Adams and Gordon Donald, eds., *Rural Financial Markets in Developing Countries: Their Use and Abuse.* Baltimore and London: The Johns Hopkins University Press, 1983. pp. 74-83.

J.D. Von Pischke, Dale W Adams and Gordon Donald, eds., *Rural Financial Markets in Developing Countries: Their Use and Abuse.* Baltimore and London: The Johns Hopkins University Press, 1983.

J.D. Von Pischke, Peter J. Heffernan and Dale W Adams, "The Political Economy of Specialized Farm Credit Institutions in Low Income Countries." Staff Working Paper No. 446. Washington, DC: World Bank, 1981.

J.D. Von Pischke and John Rouse, "Selected Successful Experiences with Agricultural Credit and Rural Finance in Africa," *Savings and Development,* vii, 1, 1983. pp. 21-44.

J.D. Von Pischke, Robert C. Vogel, Peter Flath and Maurice C. Mould, "Measurement of Loan Repayment Performance." Course Note 030/086. Washington, DC, Economic Development Institute of the World Bank, April 1988.

U Tun Wai, "Interest Rates Outside the Organized Money Markets of Underdeveloped Countries," *IMF Staff Papers*, VI, 1957-58.

Doreen Warriner, *Economics of Peasant Farming*. 2nd ed. London: Frank Cass & Co. 1964.

Leila Webster, "World Bank Lending for Small and Medium Enterprises: Fifteen Years of Experience." Industry and Energy Department Working Paper, Industry Series Paper No. 20. Washington, DC: World Bank, 1989.

R.J.G. Wells, "An Input Credit Program for Small Farmers in West Malaysia," *Journal of Administration Overseas*, 17, 1, 1978; excerpted in J.D. Von Pischke, Dale W Adams and Gordon Donald, eds., *Rural Financial Markets in Developing Countries: Their Use and Abuse*. Baltimore and London: The Johns Hopkins University Press, 1983. pp. 218-224.

R.J.G. Wells, "The Informal Rural Credit Market in Malaysia." Working Paper No. 1. Faculty of Economics and Administration, University of Malaya, Kuala Lumpur, October 1980.

"Where the Right Policies Get No Credit," *The Economist*, October 18, 1986. p. 24.

Martin C. Wilmington, "Aspects of Moneylending in Northern Sudan," *Middle East Journal*, 9, 1955; excerpted in J.D. Von Pischke, Dale W Adams and Gordon Donald, eds., *Rural Financial Markets in Developing Countries: Their Use and Abuse*. Baltimore and London: The Johns Hopkins University Press, 1983. pp. 255-261.

The World Bank Annual Report 1989. Washington, DC: 1989.

World Bank, *Compounding and Discounting Tables for Project Evaluation*. Washington, DC: 1973.

World Bank, *World Development Report 1985*. New York: Oxford University Press, 1985.

World Bank, *World Development Report 1987*. New York: Oxford University Press, 1987.

World Council of Credit Unions, *1988 Statistical Report and Directory*. Madison, Wisconsin: 1989.

Walter Wriston, "A New Kind of Free Speech," *Forbes*, December 14, 1987. p. 264.

Walter Wriston, "In Search of a Money Standard: We Have One: It Comes in a Tube," *The Wall Street Journal*, November 12, 1985. p. 28.

B.J. Youngjohns, "Agricultural Cooperatives and Credit," in John Howell, ed., *Borrowers & Lenders: Rural Financial Market Institutions in Developing Countries*. London: Overseas Development Institute, 1980. pp. 179-198.

INDEX

(Page numbers in italics indicate material in figures or tables.)

Financial constraints, development and, 83-84

Financial crises, 46-49

Financial decisionmaking, discounting to determine value in, 6-8

Financial deepening, 199

Financial development: contributions of projects to, 366-68; formal and informal finance and, 220-24; sustainability and, 247. *See also* Development

Financial development processes, 202-08

Financial frontier. *See* Frontier

Financial information systems that facilitate credit judgments in an asset-based credit environment, 260. *See also* Information

Financial innnovation as key to creating value at the frontier, 171. *See also* Innovation

Financial institution(s): destroyed by defaulters, 109; failure to charge positive real interest rates, 274; failure to solve problems of a, 113; of the poor at the frontier, 13; in poor vs. in richer countries, 163. *See also* Banks; Institutions; Rotating savings and loan associations (RoSCAs)

Financial institutions, information for well-run, 327-31

Financial instruments: emphasis on, 112; innovative developmental, 112; prices of, 59

Financial markets, 5-9; attempts to change access to, 59; innovations in, 143, 201; lengthening the term structure of, 308-09; market niche approach to development of, 172; problems in, 153; risk assumption in, 36-37; risk management and, 319-20; risks managed in, 28-31. *See also* Credit markets; Equity markets; Informal financial markets; Markets

Financial performance, 313-14

Financial project review activities, *324*

Financial rate of return (FRR), 328

Financial relationships: establishing, 12; role of confidence in, 55; trusted client, 208

Financial services: access to, 11, 123-24; factors that create more users of conventional, 200; primary type needed at the frontier, 204; users of, 210-11

Financial statements, investment cost tables vs. traditional, 81

Financial strength, economic rate of return and, 145-46

Financing gaps, filling, 90-91

Food and Agriculture Organization (FAO): agricultural insurance and, 136; reports on agricultural credit, 131

Foreclosure on debtor's property, 256. *See also* Bad debt losses; Bad loans

Foreign exchange rates, 59

Foreign exchange risk, 36

Ford Foundation, 239

Forfaiting, 36-37

France, 139

Fraud, 48-49

Frontier, 1-2; cheap credit and the, 119, 123-24; defined, 317; development and, 3-4; expanded by innovation-based market niches, 225; as fault line along which movement occurs in response to innovation, 202; finance beyond, 2-3; financial innovation at the, 171; financial instituions of the poor at, 13; financial services needed at, 204; flaws in channeling credit to, 93-94, 94-99, 99-106, 106-08, 108-10, 110-15; flaws in traditional strategies to force the, 93-94. *See also* Strategic flaws in channeling credit to the frontier

Frontier financing data, scarcity of, 128

Frontier institutions, financial

Provident Perpetual Sixes, 37-39

Prussia, 43

Puerto Rico, agricultural insurance in, 139

Quantitative controls over credit market: efficient alternatives to, 105-06; externally imposed targets and quotas as, 100; shortcomings of, 100-05

Raiffeisen, F. W., 43, 187-88, 191-92, 304

Rate of return, 266-68; internal (as decision criterion for projects), 301

Rediscounting, 104, 109

Redistribution of income and wealth, quantitative control failure in, 104

Reforms, financial adjustment loans and, 322

Rent seeking, 227, 379

Repayment, exploring with defaulters causes of poor, 331

Repayment capacity: importance for the lender of borrower's unutilized, 286; responses to low, 302-10; senior claims and, 295-96

Repayment cycle of farmers, 284-85, 287-91

Repayment Index, 330, 391; algebraic treatment of the, 391-94; mathematics of the, 383-90

Repayment schedule tailored to variations in project's expected cash flow, 291

Reporting requirements, irrelevant, 166

Residual net worth (RNW), 313-14, 352-54, 357, 360-61

Resource allocation, savings mobilization to improve, 96

Resource gaps. *See* Financing gaps

Returns, relationship between risk and, 35

Risk, 3; credit, 30-31; expectation of (in African slash-and-burn

agriculture), 26; finance and, 41; financial analysis and, 28; foreign exchange, 36-37; how financial markets manage, 31-39; inseparable from finance, 25-28; of non-simultaneous flows (finance to harmonize), 26-27; organizational transaction costs to manage, 17; relationship between returns and, 35; rural lenders' evaluation of, 289; value and confidence and, 41-42. *See also* Credit risk; Interest rate (or pricing) risk; Maturity risk; Pricing risk; Debt capacity calculation

Risk assumption in financial markets, 36-37

Risk management: division of financing into debt and equity as a device for, 34; through innovation, 163; through insurance, 137; as quantitative function of financial markets, 319-20; vehicles for, 37

Risk pooling, 32-34

Rotating savings and credit associations (RoSCAs), 50, 306; basic value-creating feature of, 15-16; "borrowers" and "savers" in, 16; chit funds (chitties) in, 217; the classic, 14-16; hospitality for friends at meetings of, 17; and incentives to reduce risk, 16-17; to reduce transaction costs and create value, 13-17

Rural credit cooperatives: in Germany, 191-92; in India, 191, 192-93; in Malaysia, 193-96

Rural credit unions, confidence creation through, 43-46

Rural Finance: Guiding Principles (Schmidt and Kropp), 307

Rural households not receiving offical credit, 71

Rural poverty, credit as means of attacking, 98

Savings: linking credit with, 95-97; low interest rates discourage, 124; mobilization of, 213

www.ingramcontent.com/pod-product-compliance
Lightning Source LLC
Chambersburg PA
CBHW071827270326
41929CB00013B/1922